This book is dedicated to the loving memory of
Edmund Doerflein and Mary O'Donohue

LN 4145

Ros £ 14.99

0 28351

MANAGEMENT AND ADMINISTRATION SKILLS FOR THE MENTAL HEALTH PROFESSIONAL

MANAGEMENT AND ADMINISTRATION SKILLS FOR THE MENTAL HEALTH PROFESSIONAL

Edited by

William O'Donohue
Department of Psychology
University of Nevada
Reno, Nevada 89557

Jane E. Fisher
Department of Psychology
University of Nevada
Reno, Nevada 89557

ACADEMIC PRESS

San Diego   London   Boston   New York   Sydney   Tokyo   Toronto

This book is printed on acid-free paper.

Academic Press
a division of Harcourt Brace & Company
525 B Street, Suite 1900, San Diego, California 92101-4495, USA
http://www.apnet.com

Academic Press
24-28 Oval Road, London NW1 7DX, UK
http://www.hbuk.co.uk/ap/

Library of Congress Catalog Card Number: 99-06593

International Standard Book Number: 0-12-524195-X

PRINTED IN THE UNITED STATES OF AMERICA
99 00 01 02 03 04 QW 9 8 7 6 5 4 3 2 1

CONTENTS

3

Management of a Mental Health Clinic

DAVID J. DRUM

4 University Hospital Administration

RONALD B. MARGOLIS AND C. ALEC POLLARD

5 Managing a Managed Care Organization

NICHOLAS A. CUMMINGS

6 Managing Quality Improvement and Clinical Outcomes in Behavioral Health Settings: A New Role for Psychologists

ELIZABETH C. MCDONEL, L. DIANE ASHLEY, MICHAEL A. ASHLEY, GRACE LONG, GORDON GIBSON, ARMEN SARKISSIAN, SHARON KRAUS, AND KIRK WHEELER

II HIGHER EDUCATION ADMINISTRATION AND MANAGEMENT

7 Higher University Administration

CHARLES A. KIESLER

8 Directing a Clinical Training Program: A Task Analysis

ADELE S. RABIN AND SHARON L. FOSTER

9 Academic Entrepreneurship

LINDA J. HAYES, RAMONA HOUMANFAR, MONICA M. GARLOCK,
PATRICK M. GHEZZI, W. LAWRENCE WILLIAMS, AND JAMES E. CARR

III GOVERNMENTAL ADMINISTRATION

10 Public Policy Administration and the Psychologist

ROBERT L. DYER

IV OTHER ADMINISTRATIVE DUTIES

11 Managing a Professional Association

RAYMOND D. FOWLER

12

Managing a Psychology Internship Program

ANTONETTE M. ZEISS

13 Information Management in Behavioral Healthcare

RICHARD KELLEY FREEMAN

CONTRIBUTORS

Numbers in parentheses indicate the pages on which the authors' contributions begin.

Nicholas P. Armenti (15) Psychological Consultants Group, P.C., Randolph, New Jersey 07869

L. Diane Ashley (153) Grant Blackford Mental Health, Inc., Marion, Indiana 46952

Michael A. Ashley (153) Grant Blackford Mental Health, Inc., Marion, Indiana 46952

James E. Carr (225) Department of Psychology, University of Nevada, Reno, Nevada 89557

Nicholas A. Cummings (133) Foundation for Behavioral Health, Scottsdale, Arizona 85251

David J. Drum (93) Counseling and Mental Health Center, The University of Texas at Austin, Austin, Texas 78712

Robert L. Dyer (261) Criterion Health, Inc., Bellevue, Washington 98008

Jane E. Fisher (1) Department of Psychology, University of Nevada, Reno, Nevada 89557

Sharon L. Foster (201) California School of Professional Psychology, San Diego, California 92121

Raymond D. Fowler (275) American Psychological Association, Washington, DC 20002

Richard Kelley Freeman (313) Wilford Hall Medical Center, San Antonio, Texas 78229

Monica M. Garlock (225) Department of Psychology, University of Nevada, Reno, Nevada 89557

Patrick M. Ghezzi (225) Department of Psychology, University of Nevada, Reno, Nevada 89557

Gordon Gibson (153) Center for Behavioral Health, Inc., Bloomington, Indiana 47401

Linda J. Hayes (225) Department of Psychology, University of Nevada, Reno, Nevada 89557

Ramona Houmanfar (225) Department of Psychology, University of Nevada, Reno, Nevada 89557

Charles A. Kiesler (185) University of Missouri, Columbia, Missouri 65211

Sharon Kraus (153) Tri-City Mental Health, East Chicago, Indiana 46312

Grace Long (153) Quinco Behavioral Health Systems, Inc., Columbus, Indiana 47202

Ronald B. Margolis (119) Saint Louis University of Medicine and Saint Louis Behavioral Medicine Institute, Saint Louis, Missouri 63110

Elizabeth C. McDonel (153) Grant Blackford Mental Health, Inc., Marion, Indiana 46952

William O'Donohue (1) Department of Psychology, University of Nevada, Reno, Nevada 89557

C. Alec Pollard (119) Saint Louis University School of Medicine and Saint Louis Behavioral Medicine Institute, Saint Louis, Missouri 63110

Adele S. Rabin (201) California School of Professional Psychology, San Diego, California 92121

Armen Sarkissian (153) Center for Behavioral Health, Inc., Bloomington, Indiana 47401

Kirk Wheeler (153) Adult & Child Mental Health, Indianapolis, Indiana 46227

W. Lawrence Williams (225) Department of Psychology, University of Nevada, Reno, Nevada 89557

Antonette M. Zeiss (293) VA Palo Alto Health Care System, Psychology Service, Palo Alto, California 94304

PREFACE

This book originated from four interrelated considerations: (1) Many, if not most, psychologists at some point in their careers encounter significant managerial, administrative, or business problems and responsibilities. Some contemporary shifts in the market for psychologists, particularly the industrialization of healthcare (Cummings, Ch. 5, this volume), suggest that psychologists will be assuming more of these responsibilities in the future. (2) However, psychologists typically receive little or no formal training in how to handle these issues and responsibilities (and informal training largely consists of unsystematic exposure to good and poor models). (3) The quality with which a psychologist discharges these managerial, administrative, and business responsibilities and problems can have an enormous impact on the welfare of many people—clients, students, supervisees, co-workers, employees, employers, and, of course, the psychologist himself or herself. (4) To a significant degree these issues concern human behavior—the exact purview of psychologists.

However, little has been written on the psychologist's role as an administrator/manager/businessperson. What has been written is scattered throughout many places and thus fails to provide a sustained examination of this role. In this book, we have attempted to correct these deficiencies by enlisting a set of accomplished psychologists with a wide variety of managerial concerns (e.g., director of clinical training, chief executive officer of a health maintenance organization) who have excelled in these roles. What follows are their analyses and recommendations regarding the best practices in these areas.

Although the chapter authors have a superlative list of accomplishments, the reader should still be somewhat skeptical of the claims contained in this book. None of these claims was produced by research. The "evidence" for the truth of these claims rests largely on the authors' successful reliance on these (essentially their) case studies, their coherence with other seemingly reasonable claims, and at times reliance on fairly traditional practices and principles (such as law of supply and demand or the foundational quality of a business plan). Their claims are necessarily the result of idiosyncratic experiences (and attributions) and have not been tested to ascertain their resistance to falsificatory attempts or to their generality. Psychologists are typically trained to trust claims that are produced by well-designed research. For a variety of reasons that we will discuss at greater length in Chapter 1, there is still no managerial science relevant to the psychologist's role as manager/administrator/businessperson. Currently, we believe that this book offers the best that we have—the analysis of smart, successful psychologists who have excelled in these roles.

We thank first and foremost our superlative chapter authors for taking time from their productive, busy careers to write these chapters. They provided the substance of this project. We thank Nick Cummings for submitting his chapter on time. We also thank our children, Katie and Anna, for their forbearance while their parents worked on various aspects of this project. Finally, we thank our editor at Academic Press for the support and stewardship she has extended to us during this project.

I

INTRODUCTION

WILLIAM O'DONOHUE AND JANE E. FISHER

Department of Psychology, University of Nevada, Reno, Nevada 89557

MANAGEMENT AND ADMINISTRATIVE SKILLS
EPISTEMIC PROBLEMS
REFERENCES
BIOGRAPHIES

MANAGEMENT AND ADMINISTRATIVE SKILLS

If there is a prototypical script for the practice of the mental health professional it is one that is relatively simple organizationally. The script may be as follows: the mental health professional sees clients in his or her office and needs a secretary/receptionist as well as a billing and client record system. Beyond this, there are few management or organization problems that the mental health professional faces. Thus, according to this stereotype, an ignorance of management skills on the part of the mental health professional is fairly benign. Furthermore, this ignorance can be allowed to continue indefinitely. Graduate programs need not include management skills in their curricula, practicing psychologists need not learn these, and consumers and co-workers need not be concerned about whether the professionals they deal with have acquired these skills.

However, we believe that this stereotype of the work setting of the mental health professional is incorrect when applied to the current practice of the mental health professional. Most importantly, we also believe that it will become increasingly more inaccurate in the future. This stereotype is incorrect for several reasons:

1. Many mental health professionals are not in solo practice, but instead work in large organizations: hospitals, clinics, universities, research institutes, schools, prisons, large group practices, various consulting and business settings, and, increasingly, managed care organizations.

2. Even in solo practice, administration skills can be critical: marketing is a key issue, as can be constructing a sound business plan.

3. Because of economies of scale the solo practice will soon become a rarity. Psychologists will increasingly see themselves as parts of larger organizations.

4. The mental health professional in any organization is rarely asked to occupy the lowest rung in the organization. Rather, the mental health professional usually, even at the beginning of his or her career, is situated at a level where he or she has managerial responsibilities; for example, even an assistant professor has graduate students to manage. As careers advance, the management and administration tasks usually increase in scope and complexity.

5. Some data have been interpreted to suggest that masters level mental health professionals can have the same therapeutic outcomes as doctorate level therapists. Some managed care organizations see this as pointing to a way of reducing costs: hire cheaper masters level graduates to do front-line psychotherapy. But what then is the doctorate level professional to do? One answer to this question is that the doctorate level professionals' skills are best used in management and quasi-management activities, such as supervision, outcomes assessment, and program development.

There is an argument that the mental health professional is so well trained, and so generally trained, in people skills and problem-solving skills that this generic training is sufficient to provide the mental health professional with the knowledge and skills necessary to solve management problems. Although we think that this view has some merit, it is ultimately naive and incorrect. These skills may be useful to address some of the management problems that a psychologist faces but they are not sufficient for optimally addressing all of these problems. These generic skills must be augmented by more specific skills relevant to the diverse management tasks the psychologist will face.

Moreover, it must be pointed out that psychotherapy skills may, in fact, interfere with effective management. Management is not psychotherapy. One cannot run a management team as one runs group psychotherapy. One of the authors had a manager who tried to do exactly this. This example is of a social worker who managed an inpatient unit at a community mental health center. It was the policy of the unit that inpatients would be seen at least three times a week in individual therapy. A week after referring an acutely distressed outpatient to the unit, the author received an angry call from one of the patient's relatives stating that the patient left the unit because she was never seen even once by an individual therapist. The author apologized and phoned the manager of the unit to see what the problem was. He said that the unit was busy and that a number of therapists were on vacation so many inpatients were not seen in individual therapy. I told him this was unacceptable for a number of reasons, including the low-quality treatment that was being provided in the inpatient unit, but also because he was placing referring outpatient therapists in the position of making false promises to their clients which would undermine the therapeutic relationship. He promised this would never happen again. It did happen when the next patient was referred a few months later. In the author's phone call to discuss this problem, the manager noted "anger" in the conversation and wanted to have a meeting where he could get at the "root" of the anger. During this meeting he tried to see whether this problem was related to problems with the author's father in childhood and thus problems with "authority figures." The manager was encouraged to try this experiment: Attempt to keep his promises and attempt to provide high-quality inpatient treatment and *then* see if there are any residual emotional problems to deal with in his relationships with outpatient referral sources.

Thus, one type of management mistake that mental health professionals fall prey to is to manage as a psychotherapist. Generally, managers using this style tend to leave co-workers alone until meetings (group therapy) or until an individual "presents" with a problem. Then, this type of manager attempts to figure out what personal psychological problems the individual has (usually emanating from their childhood). Once these are identified, and interpreted by the manager, the situation is predicted to improve. One more story on this type of manager (there could be more than a few of these stories because the incidence of this type is significant): Once when working as an outpatient therapist in an organization, the social worker/supervisor thought that the first author was "obsessed" with research results in that he would suggest therapies based on outcome research and testing based on evidence of reliability and validity. She thought the first author needed to "grow beyond" this. She suggested the following: with the next client that presented to the organization, the author should do the "opposite" of what the research literature suggested. She thought this would cure his "fixation" on research and be a valuable personal growth experience. His reactions were as follows: *1*) We are here to help clients. They are not here to "help" us. Her recommendation was unethical. How would she feel if the next time she had a medical problem, her physician's supervisor suggested that the physician do the "opposite" of what the research literature suggested? *2*) The notion of "opposite" of what the research literature suggests is confused. What, for example, is the "opposite" of Beck's cognitive therapy for depression?

We have observed other problematic management styles and strategies. These managers may not know how else to function given their educational limitations in the areas relevant to management. We will describe some of the major types below.

The Enmeshed, Personally Needy Manager.   This manager does not want to deliver therapy as a manager. Instead, this type of manager wants to receive therapy from co-workers and subordinates. He or she is quick to disclose what many co-workers would regard as rather private, personal matters, often interjecting personal problems into meetings and management decisions. There is often a lot of emotion—anxiety, dysphoria, or anger displayed in professional contexts. Alignments with co-workers can change quickly and dramatically based on how these people are seen to be meeting the manager's personal needs. The organization starts to assume the quality of a soap opera as these highly emotional personal issues become too salient in the organization. All issues become more complex than they need to be because the manager adds a complex, personal dimension to them.

The Impaired Manager.   This is a manager who is suffering from actual pathology and this interferes with his or her functioning. Substance abuse is one of the most frequent reasons why these individuals are impaired. At social functions they can embarrass themselves and alienate others. They can miss key events and meetings because of their problem. Co-workers may try to cope with this problem by avoidance. However, these managers can also have tremendous strengths— when sober and not suffering from side effects. Nonetheless, the organization is clearly damaged by the impairment.

The Unassertive Oiler.   This manager functions according to the principle that the squeaky wheel gets the oil. People who complain (often the "silver backs") get attention and generally what they want. Quiet competence gets ignored or punished. The manager seems to assume that when no one is complaining, all is well. A common result is that the competent workers find this to be an aversive, nonsensical environment and leave (or worse, become squeaky themselves).

The Obsessive Compulsive.   This manager works by command and attention to detail. He or she knows how many copies of Form 1782-Q need to be in which office by when, and is shocked and angered if any co-worker does not know this. We had one department chair who managed by obsessive attention to rather trivial detail. For example, he spent a lot of his time taking inventory. He knew the placement of every filing cabinet in the department. When a faculty member wanted to use an overhead projector to teach, he or she had to be walked down to the first floor by a department secretary who had a key to the room where the overheads were kept. She then completed a form which the faculty member had to sign. The entire process then was reversed an hour later after class. The advantage of this of course is that the chair knew at all times the location of the $150 overheads. Another downside of this management style is that there is no vision of the forest. This manager had no plan for the department (beyond cataloging new equipment purchases), no assessment of changes in the environment that were affecting the department, university, or field, and thus the department was adrift in a sea of memos regarding minutia. (One particularly revealing memo informed the faculty that resources within the department would be allocated according to the following prioritization: *1*) bureaucratic needs, *2*) teaching needs and *3*) research needs.) This management approach results in an organization that is ill prepared for challenges, misses opportunities, is actually disorganized with respect to large issues, and is enjoyed only by fellow obsessives.

The Jerk.   This person manages by being aversive. (They can also be susceptible to all of the other kinds of management style errors.) Insults are given easily and liberally. Negative emotions are quickly and frequently displaced. Snide or angry comments (often poorly stated) occur when expectations are not met. These managers seem perennially annoyed, grumpy, and angry. Tasks that should be construed as a normal part of their job, such as responding to problems that fall within their job description, seem particularly to provoke their negative emotions. Co-workers tend to be fairly unhappy and to avoid contact with this type of manager (the latter action may actually negatively reinforce this person's "jerkiness").

The Feather Bedder.   These managers use their position of authority largely to maximize their personal benefit, often in the gray area of permissibility. Organizational decisions seem to be made on the principle of what maximally benefits them. Perks seem to be created that mainly aid them, and money seems to flow in their direction. There is often a general aura of scandal and secrecy. Trust is problematic. Careers and the organization are often impacted by some sort of small- or large-scale scandal. Secrets and scandals in an organization can create a poor reputation inside and outside the organization.

The Dilettante.   This person may like the perks associated with the management position (e.g., the title, the pay) and thus takes the job solely for them. He or she may have been forced into the role. However, what is clear about this management style is that these managers don't or won't do their job. Their management principle is to minimize effort. They avoid their duties, and often by default others are placed in the position of doing their job. This results in poor morale and poor quality of task completion.

The Pigpen.   These managers are trying to do their job but the job does not get done because of their own poor organization. This is in many ways the opposite of the Obsessive Compulsive. Matters are constantly in disarray, despite apparently putting in a fair amount of time. Deadlines are missed, things are lost, meetings are missed, and so on. A sign that this might be the case is that these people usually have desks that have about two feet of papers on them. Co-workers are often quite frustrated and pessimistic.

The Philosopher.   These managers see the forest but do not see the trees. They spend a huge amount of time on the big picture, without attending to any other level. They also tend to be quite impressed with dictums such as "we have to remain competitive" or "quality is key." They miss the point that these sorts of pronouncements need not take the majority of their time and that "God is in the detail" regarding many of these grand visions.

The Preservationist.   These managers place emphasis on preserving the status quo and minimizing risk. Maintaining practices and policies based on institutional memory is emphasized at the cost of substantive issues associated with the quality of the service or product the organization exists to provide. Creativity and innovation are stifled because they deviate from the standard of "how we've done it in the past."

We believe that these problematic management styles emerge for a variety of reasons. One obvious reason is that mental health professionals assume management roles without any formal education in these matters and with little on-the-job training. Another is that there is little knowledge in the management field to convey to these managers. We turn now to a discussion of the relationship between knowledge and management in the mental health field.

EPISTEMIC PROBLEMS

We as a species have learned over our history how to learn more efficiently. We would argue that the rise of science has contributed greatly to the speed at which we learn. Although philosophers of science differ greatly in their analyses of what is special about science that accounts for its extraordinary growth of knowledge, one analysis that we think has considerable merit is the notion that science relies on criticism (Bartley, 1984; Popper, 1963). What is the substance of behaving scientifically? And why is it a good thing to behave in this manner? The Popperians have suggested that science begins with *fallibilism*. That is, the notion that our current beliefs, despite the fact that they are "ours" and despite all the attractions that they hold for us, may still be wrong. (Fallibilism also applies to the previously stated belief, see Bartley, 1984, for his comprehensive critical rationalism.)

That our set of beliefs may not have optimal verisimilitude can be quickly discerned from a few considerations. First, we frequently encounter refutations of our beliefs in our daily life. Teams that we are sure to win, lose. People who we are sure will behave in one way, don't. The hot stock tip, isn't. Another way we can see that we may be wrong is when people disagree with us. The logical principle of noncontradiction entails that when we assert A and someone else asserts not-A, one side is wrong.

Science is concerned with error and ways of eliminating error. A vigorous scientific attitude involves a desire to detect error in one's beliefs and to attempt to replace these beliefs with ones of greater accuracy. Science involves belief change—that is, learning. (It is ironic that those committed to a thorough scientific approach are often called "dogmatic" inasmuch as they are dedicated to the very process of belief change. It is those outside the purview of science that are in the most important sense dogmatic—they experience far less frequently the corrective potential of science.)

An assumption of psychometrics, for example, is that all measurement contains error. Statistical inference is concerned with errors or falsely rejecting the null hypothesis. Experimentation is concerned with valid (not invalid) causal inference. And so on. This is as it should be: we need to be worried that our confirmation biases and other heuristic errors may be influencing us to believe something we ought not.

When we are managing, we can make the following kinds of errors:

1. False descriptive statements. We can claim, for example, that a consumer wants x, when in fact they do not want x.

2. False causal statements. We can believe that our marketing strategy will function to causally increase consumer's knowledge of our products, when it does not.

3. False ontic statements. We can believe that things exist when in fact they do not. We may believe that there is some organizational climate problem, when there is not.

4. False relational claims. We can believe that therapy x produces more change than therapy y, when this is not the case.

5. False predictions. We can believe that quality assurance strategy x will result in the greatest quality improvement, when it does not.

6. False professional ethical claims. We can believe that it is ethically permissible to engage in a certain type of practice, when it is actually ethically impermissible.

Next, one must realize that *all professional behavior is based on knowledge claims.* That is, when a manager recommends that the organization implement a certain strategy to achieve a certain end, this act is based on a knowledge claim, to wit, that in this situation this strategy is the best (perhaps most reliable, cost-efficient, etc.) for this end to be achieved. Furthermore, this act is based on the knowledge claim, "that I know that it is a good thing and a priority for the organization to achieve this end."

Next, one must realize that *all knowledge claims need to be evaluated with respect to the quality of the epistemic procedures used to form them.* If I claim that I know that tomorrow you will experience a serious stressor because I have read your horoscope, then one must evaluate horoscopes as a means of reliably attaining such knowledge.

Importantly, the decision regarding what epistemic methods we should use has been made for us. Most mental health professionals, through their training models and through their ethical codes have explicitly stated that the way we seek to gain knowledge is through science. This is a wise decision because the application of science to problems has caused a historically unprecedented growth of knowledge. The problem is not that these professions are committed to a problematic epistemology. The problem is that the commitment of many mental health professionals to this epistemology has been too superficial, sporadic, and rhetorical.

Finally, one must realize that *epistemic errors in management can cause serious harm.* When we make a descriptive claim about an administrative situation that is not true, for example, we can miss something that actually requires a certain action to be taken and thus cause harm to our organization. On the other hand, we can overreact and hold false ontic and causal beliefs that result in unnecessary actions being taken. We can implement courses of action that we erroneously believe cause certain changes, when they do not, resulting in a waste of resources. Economists state that all activities have opportunity costs: engaging in activity has the cost of forcing the actor to forgo engaging in another. All ineffective practices have opportunity costs in that they displace the opportunity to engage in other more productive options.

Let us not mince words here. Our epistemic mistakes can cause a lot of harm. Our financial mistakes can bankrupt an organization. Our hiring mistakes can result in malpractice. Our strategic planning mistakes can cause us to lose key opportunities. Our administrative mistakes can cause personnel to experience un-necessary stress, job loss, and a poor organizational climate. Mistakes in the men-tal health profession can result in poor service to our clients and this poor service can result in suicides, abuse, and prolonged suffering. As administrators and man-agers, psychologists can and do meddle with situations in which the stakes are very high.

To behave scientifically is to behave in an explicitly critical manner, particu-larly in a self-critical manner. That is, one acknowledges that one's beliefs may be in error and therefore one seeks to criticize rigorously one's beliefs to see whether they are in error and thus in need of revision. Why is this a good thing? Because we are often wrong and because criticism allows error to be eliminated and knowl-edge to grow. The problem with the bad management styles given here is not that they started out bad, it is that they do not promote learning or improvement. The same errors are committed repeatedly.

Before we discuss this characterization of science in more detail, we want to acknowledge that this answer might be somewhat surprising. Some might think that science involves the inductive building of generalities from observations of particulars. However, this is not the case, because of the problems in establishing a sound logic of induction and because it is actually a special case of the more gen-eral property of science: criticism. That is, if one is trying to criticize the belief that all swans are white, it is reasonable to examine a large sample of swans. Howev-er, what one is actually doing is attempting to criticize the universal claim by see-ing if one can uncover a nonwhite swan. Others may claim that science is the un-covering of a puzzle-solving paradigm which then becomes an exemplar for future problem solving (following Kuhn). However, Kuhn's methodology for coming to this generalization is quite problematic as he studied only a few instances in the history of science and then extrapolated to all sciences (see O'Donohue, 1993, for a critique of Kuhn's meta-scientific claims). Moreover, there is still an important role for criticism, as Kuhnian scientific revolutions occur when a new paradigm exceeds the problem-solving ability of the older paradigm by producing fewer anomalies.

The characterization of science that we are giving here is neo-Popperian. In this view science is simply an epistemology—a way of knowing—that is, we all start out with a "web of belief." For example, a manager may hold beliefs such as "If we bring product x to market, then we will be profitable", "Hiring person x will be good for this organization"; and "This quality assurance measure will accu-rately track quality problems." Science begins when one realizes that one's cur-rent beliefs—no matter how commonsensical, no matter how well they seem to cohere with other beliefs, no matter how much they are generally accepted by oth-ers, and no matter how many times they have appeared to be confirmed by one's experience—may still be false. Science begins with the epistemologically humble attitude of: I may be wrong.

The next step is exposing beliefs to criticism to see how well they hold up. This step involves designing tests of beliefs to see how they stand up to these tests.

Sometimes testing beliefs is easy. If one believes that one's spouse is on the phone, one simply needs to pick up the extension. If one hears a dial tone then the belief is falsified. In another example, if one believes that all depressives make internal, stable global attributions, then a reasonable form of criticism is to gather a decent sample of depressives and accurately measure their attributions to see whether this experience contradicts the prior belief. If one believes some proposition that is expressed more tentatively, such as "People who are depressed make more global stable attributions than people who are not depressed," one essentially does the same thing. One just needs to get a little more mathematically sophisticated to look at correlations and conditional probabilities.

The distinction we want to make is between the details of criticism and the general commitment to criticism. The details (research design) can get complicated as one attempts to investigate subtle or complicated criticisms. However, the general process remains the same: one is testing some claim by allowing it to be exposed to criticism; one is not being critical for the sake of being critical. Rather, criticism is the means to detect error, and is thus a way of experiencing a growth of knowledge and a way of basing one's professional acts on less error.

Note that this general characterization nicely captures what is learned in research methodology. Research methodology essentially is a codification of some standard criticisms. Why do we seek a representative sample to begin our research? So that we are not vulnerable to the criticism that our sample was biased and therefore the results are skewed. Why do we seek random assignment to groups? Because we do not want to be vulnerable to the criticism that observed differences at the end of the experiment were due to initial differences. Why do we worry about manipulating one variable at a time? Because if we want to say that differences were due to one variable, and to avoid the criticism that some other variable also changed, we need to make sure we only manipulate one variable at a time. Why do we make sure our conclusions are worded so that they cover only the domains that we studied? Because we do not want to be vulnerable to the criticism that we are generalizing to facets not directly studied.

Now let us describe how this plays out in the day-to-day activities of managers. First, managers, in order to make decisions, must commit to some descriptive claims. That is, their actions are based on beliefs that predicate something about their organization, personnel, market, or clients. The manager must commit to claims such as: "Our gross proceeds are declining," "there is no market for this product," "interns are coming to us with excellent knowledge of psychometrics," and so on.

Now, both fallibilism and the criticism principle come into play. The manager may be wrong in any of these claims. The manager may think the organization is accurately measuring client satisfaction, when it is not. This is why we worry about the psychometrics of our measurement instruments. When a measurement instrument has not been shown to be reliable and valid, we do not know how much error and "signal" it gives us. We have little reason to believe the readings from it because it has not been shown to be accurate. Because we know that all of our tests contain error, we develop strategies such as the late Donald Campbell's independent measurement approach. In this approach there are reasons to believe that measurements that differ in a number of important regards will each contain different kinds of error. (In our terms, they are criticizable as having a certain degree of inaccuracy but we exploit the likelihood that they have different kinds of inaccuracies.) However, when multiple independent measurements all yield a similar result, this result is less criticizable because of the convergence of the independent measures.

The typical manager or administrator seeks and accepts the status of expert. This expert status is associated with the privileges that we accept as managers, for example, high earnings, special titles, and a fairly respected social role. However, with the status of "expert" come responsibilities. A central responsibility is that we are supposed to have special knowledge. It is this special knowledge that we suggest is key to allowing managers to enjoy special privileges. "Customers" come to professionals because they believe they are purchasing extraordinary knowledge. This is how the professions work. Ordinary knowledge of what might be causing a dog to limp soon becomes exhausted. The owner may look to see if it has a thorn in its paw, or to see if its ankle is swollen. When these "lay" tests are exhausted, the owner can seek the expertise of a veterinarian. The owner is willing to pay a high fee (many times minimum wage) because the owner expects that the veterinarian will have specialized knowledge that the owner does not have. The owner believes that this specialized knowledge will result in a more efficient cure to this problem than his or her own efforts (see O'Donohue & Henderson, in press, for a more detailed treatment of epistemic duties).

We argue that professionals are experts because of their specialized knowledge. Lawyers know how to write wills that will stand legal tests, physicians how to best combat various medical problems, and psychologists how best to measure and change psychological conditions.

Thus, we argue that *a supreme duty that we hold as professionals is an epistemic duty.* Respect for the truth can be seen as an intellectual duty in much the same way as respect for human life can be seen as a moral duty. In short, scientific mental health professionals not only pursue truth as the ultimate goal, they also see it as the goal that everyone in the profession should recognize and pursue ardently and competently.

However, "managerial science" is currently more rhetorical than substantive. There are few studies that are properly designed to allow valid causal inference. Even those that do exist may not be generalizable to the particular situation facing the manager. Thus, managers often have to make educated guesses regarding what has caused certain effects and what will cause other effects in the future. This is a problematic epistemic situation. Certain variables must be ignored as they are mere noise in the causal nexus. Others are key. But how is the manager to *know* which fall into which category? Moreover, how does the manager measure phenomena such as organizational climate, quality, and trends in competition. There are often few validated measures that are relevant to management dimensions. In addition, it is often the case that measurement tasks are expensive for the manager. However, with the advent of computers, some management information systems are quite remarkable in their power and efficiency. Kelley Freeman's chapter in this book is a good illustration of this. However, in sum, managing is in some ways more difficult than front-line psychotherapy, because of the relative paucity of basic knowledge regarding management issues.

Thus there is much underdetermination for a manager's decisions. That is, managers must still use their judgment in extrapolating what they know to a particular situation. Good judgment is key here. The philosopher of science Harold Brown (1987) has argued that good judgment may be an irreducible trait of the good scientist. Judgment and certainly what we regard as good judgment need to be studied more. However, this goes a long way toward describing the epistemic dilemma of the manager: How can I gain knowledge about what I need to know? If I can't know in any epistemically secure sense, how am I to make reasoned guesses? (And more deeply: How do I know what I need to know?)

But these educated guesses need to come from a sound knowledge base: Basic economics, health economics, basic business skills (e.g., creating a good business plan; see Cummings, this volume), accounting (reading a financial statement, understanding tax implications), business law (what is permissible? what is wise?), and basic medicine (how do we reasonably incorporate the biological side of the field). And then there is all of the knowledge and skills for which mental health professionals have been traditionally trained: measurement, research design, clinical protocols, and so on. It is from this kind of knowledge base that higher quality educated guesses can be formed.

The fads that periodically sweep through the business and management fields are partly the result of this difficult epistemic situation. Because much rides on their decisions, and because these decisions ride on knowledge claims, managers desperately want knowledge and jump toward management gurus. Part of the rationale for this book was to provide an alternative to the latest fads and gurus.

We have chosen excellent managers and administrators as chapter authors to present case studies of their experiences. In doing so we have asked them to present what they believe are the object lessons that they have learned along the way. We hope this will allow others to profit from the authors' experience and have a steeper learning curve.

REFERENCES

Bartley, W. W. (1984). *The retreat to commitment.* La Salle, IL: Open Court.

Brown, H. I. (1987). *Observation and objectivity.* Chicago: University of Chicago Press.

O'Donohue, W. T. (1993). The spell of Kuhn on psychology: An exegetical elixir. *Philosophical Psychology, 6,* 267–287.

Popper, K. R. (1963). *Conjectures and refutations.* New York: Harper & Row.

BIOGRAPHIES

Jane E. Fisher   Jane E. Fisher is an associate professor and Director of Clinical Training in the Department of Psychology at the University of Nevada, Reno. She received a doctorate in clinical psychology from Indiana University, Bloomington.

William O'Donohue   William O'Donohue is an associate professor and associate chair in the Department of Psychology at the University of Nevada, Reno. He received a doctorate in clinical psychology from the State University of New York at Stony Brook and a Masters' in philosophy from Indiana University. He has participated in over 100 publications.

PART I

MENTAL HEALTH DELIVERY MANAGEMENT

2

MANAGING A BEHAVIORAL HEALTHCARE PRIVATE PRACTICE

NICHOLAS P. ARMENTI

Psychological Consultants Group, P.C., Randolph, New Jersey 07869

INTRODUCTION

What makes managing a private practice in the behavioral healthcare marketplace a complex and creative challenge is the nature of the problems presented for solutions. Professionals who assume the responsibility for managing service delivery in any area of healthcare face many sensitive decisions. They must command the skills to regulate the delicate balance between the moral concerns related to patient care and the practical issues that affect resource consumption in the business of healthcare. As Strosahl (1994) points out, "Therapy is never practiced in an economic void," and he alludes to the "ethical quandary" facing providers of care (pp. 18–19). I would add that the ethical quandary is perhaps even more acute for those who manage the behavior of those providers and other staff in the private practice setting.

The management team of a private behavioral healthcare practice must combine the best procedures from the domain of the clinician with those from the world of the business professional. This is the exacting task confronting those who conduct the management and administration of a private practice in the behavioral healthcare marketplace.

A manager is defined by one basic source (Encyclopedia Britannica, 1965) as, "One who manages, especially, one who has the control of a business or a business establishment" (p. 773). The same source defines the verb *to manage* as "to direct or conduct the affairs or interests of: to manage a business" (p. 773).

Very few behavioral healthcare professionals have been formally trained in the business skills required to execute the role definitions suggested above. However, healthcare is and will continue to be a business enterprise (Currey, 1992). The overwhelming majority of behavioral healthcare practitioners, that is, social workers, psychologists, psychiatrists, and others, I believe, are in the category of the non-business trained. In an interesting presentation, Sobell (1996) calls attention to the consequential fact that, to date, behavioral scientist/researchers also are included among the ranks of the non-business oriented. This reality, as it exists in the current marketplace, cannot continue if healthcare professionals are to service customers effectively. Those who are responsible for managing a behavioral healthcare private practice in the competitive healthcare marketplace must acquire the management skills demanded by the current and evolving business environment of healthcare.

I do not presume to impart such business skills in this chapter. I do not present the material in the traditional manner of laying out a series of narratives describing the management skills required of private practice managers. In addition, the coverage of the subject matter is not intended to be exhaustive. In Section I of this chapter, I try to increase the reader's knowledge base, a *prerequisite* to the acquisition of the management skills under consideration. My emphasis is on the fundamental prerequisite information that managers need to know to be effective in the competitive marketplace. This is followed in Section II by a discussion of several selected core management skill areas and their associated procedures. The management skills, themselves, will be the outcome of the manager's ability to assimilate a fund of appropriate and, perhaps, new information. For some it may be necessary to complete a cognitive restructuring of beliefs and assumptions about the business of behavioral healthcare. This is often a difficult process involving the unlearning of previously learned, unproductive beliefs and behaviors and replacing them by a repeated trial and error experience in the "real time" marketplace; a process not dissimilar in some ways to what has come to be called "psychotherapy."

My rationale for selecting this presentation format is based on experience consulting with colleagues regarding the management of behavioral private practices. I have found that many behavioral professionals have not mastered the necessary knowledge base that would give them a sound justification for implementing, fully, those management procedures consistent with the demands of the current marketplace. I am familiar with much of the literature that gives managers in behavioral healthcare a set of management procedures and I have found the recommendations made to be both instructive and very sound. Yet, however valuable those recommendations have been, I believe that the intended audience of managers will continue to balk in committing to those recommendations until an appropriate and *persuasive* fund of information is assimilated by them. Only then will managers have the cognitive foundation to implement fully and in adequate detail those management procedures that have a high probability of success in private practice. As the saying goes, "the devil is in the details," although a few rare souls may find God there. Managers will have much difficulty implementing the necessary procedural details unless they are convinced that the effort is worth it. I hope that this presentation will be an effective "exercise in persuasion" (Sobell, 1996, p. 306) and as such move some readers to an effective execution of their management procedures and skills.

Several valuable sources of information are available in the healthcare literature that are germaine to the topic here. This chapter presents a critical selection of this literature. In addition, the author's own experience will be shared as it is deemed relevant to the issues presented.

An effort is made to introduce information not frequently found in the behavioral literature per se. A handful of visionary leaders in behavioral healthcare have been responsible for the dissemination of the bulk of the meaningful information to the behavioral community. I have taken much from them and their works are cited throughout this presentation. In addition, I found much that is helpful regarding management in this marketplace in the general medical literature on the managed care system. For me, this literature has been enlightening and has helped to clarify the position that behavioral healthcare occupies in the much larger healthcare marketplace. The behavioral healthcare literature often lags behind developments in the larger healthcare marketplace. I recommend that the reader at least sample the journals in general medicine and in managed care (e.g., *Group Practice Journal, Family Practice Management, Business and Health, Modern Healthcare, Medical Interface,* etc.) for sources of current and meaningful business-oriented information to enhance skill acquisition.

THE AUTHOR'S EXPERIENCE IN THE MARKETPLACE

My clinical training was fortunately a combination of an initial experience with psychodynamic approaches to treatment followed by an end-stage exposure to behavioral approaches to care delivery. Having had the opportunity to compare over time the two orientations, I strongly committed my resources to a behavior therapy–cognitive behavioral approach to the delivery of services. The explanation for this decision is simple: behavior therapy–cognitive behavioral procedures work best for me at helping patients improve.

I offer a brief description of my market-based business experience. After employment as a staff psychologist in three different community mental health centers (CMHC) from 1970 through 1975, I was appointed the executive director and chief psychologist of a CMHC. I maintained a small solo private practice during these early years. In 1979, a health management organization (HMO) asked for consultation in the design of their mental health program, which I supplied only to have my model (community based and multidisciplinary) rejected in favor of an all psychiatry-based plan; this was an important lesson in marketplace competition. In 1980, the State of New Jersey Division of Mental Health Hospitals introduced a new set of procedures in publicly funded CMHCs that were managed care quality assurance and accountability procedures, that is, utilization review and case management procedures. As I experienced this initiative, the intent was to implement a set of procedures designed to address the long waiting lists for outpatient care and the unnecessarily long lengths of treatment provided to the *non*-deinstitutionalized consumers. From the perspective of the government funding sources, this situation represented an ineffective use of resources in tax-funded facilities and thus required correction. This effort was introduced and eventually implemented by two knowledgeable and assertive leaders, Tom Blatner and Geraldine Botwinick, both graduates of the Woodrow Wilson School of Public and International Affairs at Princeton University. The program was immediately resisted and actively opposed by most of the CMHC directors and staff who we primarily trained in psychodynamic, long-term approaches and who had waiting lists too long to justify tax dollar spending. I was one of a small minority of directors who supported the new direction. After much debate and frenzy the state ended the controversy in 1983 by unilaterally making the new procedures required for CMHCs. So much for cooperation with managed care procedures in 1983.

In 1981, I left the CMHC as executive director but stayed on as chief psychologist until 1983, at which time I began to develop my own group practice and a behavioral preferred provider organization (PPO) in New Jersey. A PPO is essentially a network of providers who have agreed to discount their fees for service and to cooperate with utilization and quality management procedures in exchange for an increase of referrals from third-party payers. I introduced the PPO idea initially to my colleagues in the state psychological association in 1984. The idea was, at first, congenially stonewalled and soon after rejected by my colleagues. I decided to develop my own PPO and eventually my own managed behavioral care organization (MBHO) in 1986. I remain its chief executive officer as of this writing. An MBHO is a managed care organization (MCO) specializing in the management of mental health and substance abuse services. The MBHO usually manages behavioral healthcare on a carveout basis, that is, separately from other components of a benefit plan. It establishes networks of providers and manages the utilization, quality, and cost of services provided through a variety of accountability mechanisms.

In 1995, a subsidiary of the MBHO was developed, that is, a management service organization (MSO), to provide administrative services to developing and operating group practices and specialty independent provider associations (IPAs).

In addition, I have been on the Board of Directors of General Psychological Services, Inc., the only known national PPO of psychologists in the United States, since 1988. This PPO was founded by Dr. Al Wellner and Dr. Carl Zimet. My MBHO took over administration of the PPO in October 1992, with co-director Dr.

Bob Ericksen, in an attempt to maintain it as a viable business venture. This has not materialized as of this writing for a variety of reasons that will not be covered here.

The group practice has grown over the past 16 years. As of this writing, we maintain a small staff model group employing behavioral clinicians. This group is supported by an affiliated network of several group practices and many solo providers. The MSO addresses the nonclinical business activities of the group and its wraparound network of providers. In addition, the managers of our group attempted unsuccessfully to merge eight groups including its own over a period of two years. This effort was a difficult and complex process that did not result in the proposed merger. The reasons for the unsuccessful venture are as follows: two groups were not ready to merge, one group developed a competing business opportunity, two groups determined that their clinical and business approaches were incompatible with the managed care direction being taken, one group determined that its psychiatrists' income would decrease as a result of the merger, and one group lost its motivation to merge as a result of the above. I have learned much over the past several years and unfortunately have lost a few friends in the process of managing the entities described briefly above. It is with this background that I present the contents of this chapter.

SECTION 1: CORE PREMISES FOR MANAGEMENT AND ADMINISTRATIVE SKILLS REQUIRED IN PRIVATE PRACTICE

Several core premises (six in this presentation) emerge from the recent healthcare literature. Each premise is presented here with a selection of supporting references chosen to establish the substance and the consensus basis for the position taken. In this presentation I have attempted to remain consistent with the scientist–practitioner model to which I am committed.

The core premises are presented in some detail with the view that they will establish a foundation upon which appropriate management and administrative procedures can be implemented. The discussion of the premises offers a fund of information and data which are intended to serve as a decision-support information base for those who will manage behavioral healthcare entities. My position here is that the skills a manager acquires are only as good as the information base upon which the skills are supported. The discussions summarize the market trends and market dynamics as presented by many currently recognized marketplace analysts.

Premise 1: Behavioral Healthcare Is a Business Like All Areas of Healthcare in America

It is well established that healthcare is today and will be in the future a business enterprise driven by the marketplace dynamics that influence the conduct of all commercial activities. This reality is comprehensively presented in a volume by Richard Currey (1992) entitled, *Medicine for Sale—Commercialism vs. Profes-*

sionalism. The short (69 pages) but well written book analyzes the Federal Trade Commission's (FTC) 1975 case against the American Medical Association (AMA) for what the FTC held as the AMA's curtailing of "any sort of competitive business behavior among doctors" (Currey, 1992, p. 2). As Currey observes, "Medicine-as-a-business received the formal imprimatur of the Supreme Court in 1982 when the Court found in favor of the FTC" (p. 2). He goes on, "The AMA was ordered to cease and desist. Physicians were, in effect, given permission to sell their skills in any legitimate manner they saw fit. It was the gateway to a new kind of medicine—the medicine of franchises, telemarketing, direct mail and celebrity doctors. The medicine of the 21st century" (p. 3).

By extension all areas of healthcare including behavioral healthcare were affected by the court decision. In the March 1988 edition of the American Psychological Association's (APA) *Monitor,* an article was published entitled, "FTC demands an end to ad, fee-splitting restriction" (Bales, 1988, p. 19). Following this article, the APA sent a letter to its membership regarding the FTC decisions (Wiggins, 1993). The APA reported that it "has signed a consent agreement with the Federal Trade Commission under which the Commission has entered a cease and desist order that became final on December 27, 1992." The order covers an array of issues that essentially make behavioral healthcare, as practiced by psychologists, a business enterprise as it is for all other behavioral healthcare professionals.

Currey (1992) presents a very balanced analysis of the consequences and potential consequences of this momentous event in healthcare, both positive and negative, to consumers and healthcare providers. He found that many physicians he spoke to were unprepared and "mystified by the issues of commercialism in healthcare" (p. 67). He adds that

> Such reactions stem from ignorance and the persistent, hidebound image of the physician as a professional who is beyond the influence of commerce . . . Nothing is further from the truth and doctors can ill afford to pretend otherwise. Commercialism is a reality; physicians who do not control it will be controlled by it. Simply put, medicine must find a way to retain its status as a profession while reaping the benefits of commercialism. (p. 67)

This is the dilemma that all healthcare professionals face in this healthcare marketplace.

Competition in Healthcare

At the center of the business of healthcare is the sensitive and challenging reality of *competition.* After citing the sections of the 1981 Ethical Principles of Psychologists with which the FTC expressed concerns, Bales (1988) states that

> These sections of the principles, the FTC contends, illegally restrain *competition* among psychologists to the detriment of consumers. Further, the commission says, the principles hinder *competition* in the delivery of services and sale of products and publications based on price, service and quality. Clients are also deprived of *competition* in referral services and institutional arrangements and are deprived of truthful information about the availability of services and products, according to the proposed order. (p. 19) (Italics mine)

One of the most vocal anti-managed care spokesman and former director of the APA's Practice Directorate, Bryant Welsh, expressed his disagreement with the approach taken by a group of behavioral healthcare providers in their suit against several MBHOs. In this regard, he acknowledged that the reality of competition alone does not constitute a restraint of trade (Seaman, 1996b).

Competition in healthcare is characterized as, "rivalry between healthcare plans and providers for customers, through reducing prices and/or improving quality of care" (Blumenthal, 1996, pp. 171–172). In his examination of the business components of healthcare, Blumenthal (1996) points out that providers who, "decry commodification and the consequent threats to professionalism" present themselves at times as "either antiquated or self serving" (p. 179). In his discussion of healthcare services as a commodity, Blumenthal observes that, "It is possible for cutthroat competition to breed successful adaptations that are humane and progressive and, indeed, embody some attributes that professionalism has sought to instill" (p. 179). Also, he points out the potential negative consequences of such a dynamic. He comments on the possible decline in provider altruism, in particular a reluctance to provide free care to the uninsured and the poor, the most vulnerable populations, and an erosion of trust in providers as a result of changing financial arrangements and incentives (p. 180).

Perhaps our best efforts to provide quality care in this competitive arena will be the procedures encompassed within the framework of the developing "managed competition" approach to healthcare delivery. Etzioni (1988) states in his discussion of competition that, "Economists long have recognized that the prerequisites of perfect competition may never be satisfied and most important—that whenever one of them is missing, the benefits of perfect competition may not be available" (p. 200). His argument is relevant to competition in healthcare and the challenge confronting providers as he states that

> If competition is left on its own, it will escalate into a destructive, all out conflict. Hence those who see virtue in competition must recognize that it is nothing but *contained* conflict, that it can be sustained only within a moral, societal and governmental context which ensures that conflicts remain confined within prescribed limits. True, the same contextual elements may also unduly restrict the scope of competition. The question therefore, is how to provide a context that is strong enough to contain competition but not so powerful to undermine it, rather than disregard the role and dynamic of the moral, societal, governmental contextuating factors. (p. 182)

It appears to me that Etzioni's point is most relevant to the economic environment of the healthcare market generally and to behavioral healthcare in particular. It is prudent to keep in mind that competition between group practices continues to increase (Montague, 1994b); and being alert to the reality that group practices, including behavioral group practices, must be prepared to compete is both prudent and market wise. Managers have an interesting and exciting challenge ahead of them in conducting the business of behavioral healthcare, that is, to be competitive in the marketplace and to remain advocates for what is best for the patient in the clinical setting.

Premise 2: Essential Features of the Managed Care Approach Will Provide the Framework for the Business of Behavioral Healthcare

Managed care in contrast to unmanaged care is and will remain the predominate operating system for behavioral healthcare from this time forward. This is a position expressed before (N. P. Armenti, 1991) and one that has been reported by many other active participants in behavioral healthcare. "Managed care is no longer the model *proposed* for the American health care system. It *is* the American healthcare system" (Belkins, 1996, p. 68). What alternative forms managed care will take is the critical question. Those providers who expend their resources to oppose the managed care movement have often emerged as self-serving and struggling to defend and preserve provider-induced demand for services, called supply-induced demand (see Giles, 1993a, p. 21; B. H. Gray, 1991, pp. 245–246; Keisler & Morton, 1988, pp. 997–998). Those providers who elect to participate as managers in the competitive marketplace will do well to understand the full meaning of managed care on an operational level. The practice they will manage, that is, a local integrated group practice, a regional group, an IPA, a group without walls, and so on, will, of necessity, operate as a managed care entity, or MBHO, in its delivery of care.

Defining the term "managed care" is not a simple matter when approached operationally. When managed care is used here it refers to a multicomponent system of delivering healthcare services. The term subsumes a range of procedures designed to control costs and simultaneously to ensure the quality of care provided to the consumer. This chapter is not the forum for presenting a comprehensive examination of managed care and the many procedures incorporated in the system of managed care. However, two critical characteristics of managed care will be briefly discussed because an understanding of them is essential for those responsible for managing a private practice in the current and future marketplace of behavioral healthcare. The two critical characteristics that distinguish managed care from its competing alternative, unmanaged care, are *organized systems of care* and *accountability.*

Organized Systems of Care

The characterization of a system as "organized" is often used synonymously with the descriptive modifier "integrated" in the managed care literature. Although there are, at times, some meaningful differences, for example, *integrated* delivery system (IDS) often refers to a system incorporating various levels of care besides being organized. True integrated managed care entities are effectively defined by Sullivan and Kunkle (1993) as follows:

> The integration of the healthcare delivery system relates to its capacity to provide a full range of services along a continuum of care with the interactive communication and coordination among providers. Integrated systems work in harmony because it is easy to determine at any point along the continuum where a patient is and why. It moves away from the fragmentation of a fee-for-service world where providers operate autonomously to one in which collaboration and management of patient care are routine. Integrated delivery sys-

tems centralize operations, minimize administrative complexity, computerize records, and are conducive for meeting the needs of patients for prompt care and comfort. (p. 49)

In a similar vein, Trabin (1994) states that, "the industrialization of behavioral healthcare has shifted delivery systems from disconnected private practice offices and treatment facilities to organized systems of care" (p. 2). Edley (1996, p. 179) expresses a similar message regarding IDSs. Others support this message (Dowell, 1995; Greene, 1995; McCue, 1996; Ramay, 1996; Unger, Findlay, & Vail, 1994). Success as a manager of a provider system requires a keen awareness that, ideally, purchasers of care want to buy services from an efficient, well organized, integrated, and one-stop-shopping entity. The closer a private practice can come to that organized system of care the more competitive and successful that practice will be in the marketplace.

Accountability

The second critical characteristic, accountability, is contingent on the first characteristic. Managed care is essentially synonymous with accountable care. However, without the organized system defined above the coordinated collection and evaluation of information and data required for the accountability of providers, consumers, purchasers of care, and MBHOs will be impossible.

> It has been made quite clear by more than one healthcare marketplace observer that: More than any time in the past healthcare buyers today are questioning the value healthcare providers deliver. These buyers are giving providers, healthplans and insurers the same scrutiny that they have long applied to other vendors. (Stepnick, Rybowski, & Burns, 1997, p. 20)

The unorganized fee-for-service world of behavioral healthcare is and has been lacking any effective mechanisms of accountability. The procedures that have been available (meeting graduate degree requirements, state licensing, supervision) hardly address, in any effective way, the requirements for a truly accountable system of care within the context of a competitive market. In a fee-for-service community, monitoring by state licensing boards is not designed for provider accountability on a day-to-day basis. Boards of Examiners provide some monitoring and oversight in the service of consumer protection but on a *macromanagement* level. Clinical supervision is a form of accountability and one traditionally provided in the fee-for-service environment for managing care (N. P. Armenti, 1990). However, neither of these procedures provides the daily mechanism of accountability required for effective oversight in the marketplace.

What is required in any accountable healthcare delivery system is a set of procedures that closely monitors the behavior of the participants in the healthcare marketplace, that is, consumers, providers, purchasers, and the MBHOs. The mechanisms of accountability must effectively achieve what has been labeled a *sentinel effect*. The sentinel effect may be defined as:

> An increase in likelihood that a person will behave with closer compliance with standards of performance because they know they are being watched as opposed to when they know

they are not being watched and it is understood that those who are watching them will reward and/or punish them for clearly specified behavior. (N. P. Armenti & Ericksen, 1995, p. 26)

The need to implement the sentinel effect is the basis for the mechanisms of accountability within the managed care movement as we have come to know them, for example, utilization review, provider profiling, outcomes research, practice guidelines compliance, and so on. This sentinel effect is a core dynamic in accountable healthcare systems, one that any manager of a private practice must come to know and to implement in the practice's daily operations.

There are several valuable works that present the origins of the managed care movement. For a brief but insightful presentation Giles (1993a, pp. 14–22) is recommended. His treatment of "Cost Escalators" is helpful in understanding some of the stimuli that elicited the managed care response from third-party payers. An in depth and perhaps most comprehensive treatment of the origins of managed care is found in B. H. Gray's (1991) volume, *The Profit Motive and Patient Care: The Changing Accountability of Doctors and Hospitals*. As the title suggests, accountability is a key issue in healthcare. Gray presents arguments throughout the work that strongly support the need for effective accountability in the rendering of healthcare services. The need to eliminate unnecessary and inappropriate services which waste resources and do not effectively help the patient is at the heart of the accountability issue. As healthcare becomes more commercial and competitive providers are becoming, as Gray states, "increasingly accountable to organizations that have their own agendas and economic interests and to which the physician's income is tied. This has the potential to correct significant shortcomings in the traditional solo, fee-for-service system" (B. H. Gray, 1991, pp. 4–5). He goes on to say that

Accountability . . . refers to the mechanisms by which individuals and organizations are held responsible for their behavior. Used thus, the term refers to a relationship of power and authority and can be defined empirically: organizations or individuals are accountable to the parties that control the access to the resources they seek. (p. 10)

Before the arrival of managed care both consumers and third party payers relied on their sense of trust in providers' professionalism, competence and integrity. There were no formal mechanisms of accountability. However, the growing concerns over escalating costs and questionable provider behavior eroded customer confidence and trust in providers. Kovacs (1987) presents an interesting discussion of fraudulent billing procedures by providers that is germaine to this phenomenon. Gray concludes that, "In implementing methods that require authorization before the provision of services, third-party purchases of medical care have made it clear that *trust will no longer substitute for accountability*" (p. 320) (italics mine).

For those who manage a private practice this observation presents one important challenge. Managers will need to behave in ways that will maintain the trust of their customers, that is, patients, purchasers of care, and MBHOs. For at least 20 years, behavioral healthcare providers have been discussing the issue of accountability (Strupp & Hadley, 1977, p. 188). The time has arrived for the behavioral healthcare professional to respond effectively to this mandate. The reality of the establishment of The Foundation for Accountability (FACCT) and others like it attest to the growing commitment to accountability in healthcare. "FACCT would become the *Consumer Reports* of health plans, providing data that consumers could use to make quality comparison" (Belkins, 1996, p. 106).

Competition in the marketplace is good for the consumer. The competitive dynamic is consistent with human nature and creates the system of rewards and punishments that elicit from providers their best practices. The mechanisms of accountability, which include methods for comparisons between competitors, are the key ingredients to a successful healthcare system. Competition requires comparisons against benchmarks; for without comparisons between competitors there is no way to determine who provides quality care. Behavioral care groups need to prepare for this kind of process. They are likely to be included in such a competitive enterprise.

Managers of a private practice in behavioral healthcare are required to establish organized and accountable systems of care. If they are to be viable players in the competitive business arena of healthcare today and in the future they must respond to this mandate.

Critics of Managed Care

Managed care is hardly without critics. The space allotted to me here will only allow scratching the surface of the large and growing literature in this area. A recent and well-publicized critique by Anders (1996) is worth commenting on here. Anders' primary focus is on those who have financially profited most within the HMO and managed care industry. He points an accusing finger at those executives and medical professionals who have supported and directed, in particular, the HMO sector of the managed care movement. I do not disagree with Anders with the fact that there are abuses in corporate healthcare. This reality is similar to the abuses of compensation in corporate business, generally, and Anders acknowledges its presence in the healthcare provider community as well (cf. Snow, 1997, p. 3). However, Mr. Anders perpetuates a misunderstanding about the definition of managed care. He uses the terms HMO and managed care interchangeably throughout his book. The system of HMOs in the marketplace is only one segment of the managed-care delivery system. HMOs are only one form of managed care. Anders does acknowledge, on occasion, that there are several other types of managed-care organizations (e.g., PPOs). However, in my judgment, he does not make this fact clear enough to the reader. Anders states that, "there is a dark side to managed care" (p. 13). Yet much more to the point, managed care is an approach to and a system of care delivery and as such is not the culprit. A parallel may be made to other systems available in the marketplace. I refer here to other marketplace systems such as the banking system, the political system, the manufacturing system, the wall street securities system, and so on, which are also subject to abuse in the wrong hands. The flaw lies not in the system per se but in the way in which the persons and organizations using these systems behave. Managed care is a *system* of care delivery. The challenge before us is determining who the *right persons* are to administer this system and which are the *right entities* through which to provide healthcare. This is still evolving. It appears that the current situation regarding managed care is a case of deciding how to "do the right thing right." We have not yet come to that determination.

The fact that there is so much profit to be siphoned off by the "Fat Cats" in the healthcare system suggests that there is still much fat to be eliminated. We need to lower costs to consumers and not encourage excess profits to business men as Anders suggests. The 10 steps that he recommends for improving the managed care approach are essentially reasonable and sound (pp. 244–262). For example, Anders recommends that

1. *Consumers need to make managed-care systems work for their own interests.* Without doubt, a well-educated consumer is the best customer, as the saying goes.

2. *Doctors need to accept the principles of cost-effective medicine but be able to challenge specific managed-care rules without fear.* Providers of care must have input into both the design and management of managed care entities and must remain primary advocates for their patients if the system is to work effectively for the consumer.

3. *Doctors, employers, regulators, and HMOs need to combine forces to develop treatment guidelines that people can trust.* Treatment must be founded on empirical evidence and outcomes data if it is to be effective. Providers must remain close to the scientist-practitioner model if they are to achieve their clinical goals. I do not agree at all with Anders' statement that, "As the managed-care industry becomes dominated by publicly traded for-profit companies, objective research within the industry is becoming rarer" (Anders, 1996, p. 250). He does not cite the source for this troubling observation.

4. *Regulators need to control the ways that HMOs pay doctors.* I would agree that capitation and other "at-risk" payment arrangements to providers need monitoring and perhaps regulation. However, in my opinion, regulation that would not allow the managed care marketplace to mature through market-driven solutions will not serve consumers in the most effective way.

Anders' remaining six recommendations are important for the managed care industry, especially the ninth, which addresses the profit motive in healthcare, that is, "Regulators need to keep the profit motive in check" (p. 257). The healthcare system, including the managed care approach, does need correction and refinement. This is the mission of continuous quality improvement, a daily activity within the managed care system in contrast to the unmanaged fee-for-service environment.

In this regard, recalling what Ellwood observes about managed care is interesting:

The greatest threat to managed care is its success. It's cutting costs, it is threatening to doctors in terms of their income, it is a concern to some groups who are used to limitless care on demand and it is vulnerable to unjustified attacks. We are working with anecdote here when we should be working with epidemiological evidence. (Belkins, 1996, p. 70)

This reference is in no way intended to minimize the abuses and the cases of denial of necessary care which Anders presents in both the general medical and behavioral areas of healthcare. However, I submit that Anders can record and analyze such events *because of* the managed care system. The fact that it is both organized and accountable permits the capturing and reporting of such information. This is a process that was impossible to conduct in any effective way in the unmanaged healthcare environment.

Premise 3: Group Practice Is the Preferred Provider Entity in the Current and Future Marketplace

This premise was initially presented to the attendees of a seminar at the American Psychological Association Convention in Boston in 1990 (N. P. Armenti, 1991, p. 124) within the context of advocating for a managed care approach. The message was met with much resistance. The presenter and the other panel members were accused of being "true believers." This label has lost its pejorative sting for me since then.

A group practice has been defined by the AMA as, "three or more physicians working together and agreeing to distribute their income according to some prearranged formula" (MacLeod, 1989, p. 9). Another source offers a different definition of a group practice. Dr. Alan Daniels, executive director of a 50-professional, 11-year-old behavioral group practice, is quoted by Schachner (1994), "It's five or more clinicians with different specialities that provide 24-hour coverage, have quality assurances and have computer linkage with payers" (p. 36). This definition approaches the ideal behavioral group structure in terms of its multispeciality (and perhaps multidisciplinary) accountability mechanisms and computerization components.

Progressive MBHOs have been contracting with group practices for several years (Schachner, 1994). In addition, they have gone beyond contracting with groups by actively encouraging solo practitioners to form groups. This has been especially the case in areas of high consumer population density and where provider density is high, that is, oversupplied. Even in areas of low-density population the networking activity of MBHOs has created a de facto system of networked solo practitioners. As a result the system is "organized" by virtue of membership in the MBHO's network system. In this way the managed care approach applies both organization and accountability to its provider system in spite of the absence of bona fide group practices. Dr. Nick Cummings has long been known for his accurate forecasting of developments in the behavioral healthcare marketplace. He takes a very strong position on the value and advantages of group practices and urges providers to organize as soon as possible into group practices

(Cummings, Pallak, & Cummings, 1996). Throughout the volume, which is appropriately titled, *Surviving the Demise of Solo Practice,* Cummings and several other contributors present their observations regarding the advantages of a group practice approach in contrast to a solo practice. The work is strongly recommended for those who assume the management responsibilities of a group practice. The number of behavioral healthcare group practices has increased dramatically over the past few years (Schachner, 1994). This development follows the trend in medicine that began after World War II (MacLeod, 1989). "The 2.6% of physicians who engaged in group practice in 1946 increased exponentially over the next four decades, so that by today approximately one third of all physicians are practicing in groups" (MacLeod, 1989, p. 4). The AMA reports that, "Between 1965 and 1995, the number of groups increased by 361 percent and the number of group physicians increased by 643 percent" (Havlicek, 1996, p. 43). In addition, single-speciality medical groups are reported to have increased approximately 45% between 1980 and 1991 (Jaklevic, 1994, p. 71).

The behavioral healthcare sector of the industry may be following this trend. This direction is spurred on by a marketplace that demands systems of care that are organized and accountable, that is, within the managed-care framework.

The structures that the group may take are several:

- A group practice [professional corporation (PC) or limited liability company (LLC)]
- An independent provider association (IPA)
- Group practice without walls (GPWW)
- Integrated group practice (IGP)

These systems have yet to mature in the healthcare marketplace (see Zucker, 1995, pp. 12–14). The definitions of these structures have not been standardized across all geographic areas and, as such, are not always clear-cut (D. E. Goldstein, 1995a, p. 132). An interesting example in behavioral healthcare is a professional affiliation group (PAG), defined as, "a small group of four to eight fully licensed independent practicing mental health professionals from different disciplines" (Pomerantz, Liptzin, Carter, & Pearlman, 1995, p. 505). The PAG is described as, "not a corporation or other legal entity, nor even an independent organization" (p. 509). The term "virtual" is used to characterize this group practice.

Another example is an entity called a provider-sponsored organization (PSO). It is described as, "an evolving entity which should bring greater equilibrium between HMO's and insurance intermediaries and between physicians and other providers" (Pomerantz et al., 1995). "PSOs are generally local level healthcare delivery systems created through the formal affiliation of providers" (Cain, 1996, p. 57).

These entities are organized and integrated systems of care. How they will affect behavioral healthcare entities is yet to be established. However, these entities are organized and accountable service delivery systems, that is, managed care. In deciding the appropriate structure for a delivery system, legal consultation is required within the state where managers intend to incorporate. Astute legal advice will be required to deal with issues such as the level of integration of the group practice (IPA, group practice without walls, totally integrated group practice, etc.), the legal entity (PC, LLC) antitrust considerations, and so on. For an informative discussion of group practices in transition and the legal issues related to this evolving component, see the review of articles in *Group Practice Journal* introduced by Bouey et al. (1996).

With respect to the size of a behavioral group practice, simply stated, they can be small to very large. The definition of size will depend on more than the number of staff in the group. The number of office locations and their distribution throughout a geographic area is also a factor in determining the size of a group (from coverage of a local town, small county, several counties, a state, or several states).

Cummings (1996a, pp. 15–16) distinguishes between what he labels, "prime or retained provider groups" and "regional provider groups" (RPG). He describes both groups as taking capitation arrangements. Capitation and subcapitation are defined in the next premise and aspects of these, "at risk arrangements" are discussed there in some detail. The types of groups that Cummings presents are groups operating in mature managed care markets. These are the types of groups that managers and those who aspire to be managers will want to establish ultimately. However, some group practice leaders may want to start more modestly. For most, waiting to have a completely organized group practice with state-of-the-art mechanisms of accountability and computerization in place will not be realistic as a beginning. Getting started by building affiliations with other providers, with a few locations, and building economies of scale is often a more realistic beginning.

Most groups can begin to contract with MBHOs (even without capitation or case rate arrangements) short of complete organization, utilization management, and fully developed accountability mechanisms in place. Many MBHOs are willing to help groups in their development in specified geographic areas. Also, even small group practices can be attractive to small or moderately sized "self-insured" employers who have structured their benefit plans under the Employee Retirement Income Security Act (ERISA plans) and labor–union welfare funds on a direct contracting basis for mental health, substance abuse, and employee assistance program (EAP) services (Ansel & Berte, 1996). With regard to ERISA plans, it should be noted that employers who structure their health benefits under this federal regulation are essentially preempted from state laws regulating health plans. This has been a controversial issue. Employers have used ERISA to move aggressively to implement managed-care approaches in providing health benefits to their plan participants; whereas opponents of managed care have attempted and still are attempting to eliminate the preemption of state regulation under ERISA. This issue will be tested in the near future in the courts.

In all aspects of its operations in the marketplace, the group practice will take on the features and functions of an MBHO; that is, the group in reality becomes the managed care entity. "As small groups grow into multispeciality providers, they frequently take on more capitation and subcapitation which causes them to become more like managed care companies and less like private practices" (Morrison, 1996, p. 242).

The group practice format, small or large scale, is becoming the preferred provider entity in behavior healthcare. Those who wish to participate successfully in the healthcare marketplace will do well to begin group development if they have not yet done so.

Premise 4: At-Risk Payment Arrangements to Provider-Driven Service Delivery Systems Will Be the Preferred and Predominant Funding Mechanism in the Behavioral Healthcare Marketplace

Provider groups in the behavioral healthcare market are sharing and will continue to share in the financial risk of providing services to populations of consumers in defined geographic areas. At-risk arrangements take the form of capitation, case rates and other related forms of healthcare services funding. Capitation appears to emerge as the currently predominate funding mechanism, and probably for the future as well.

A simple explanation of capitaltion is presented here. A capitation arrangement is a method that third-party payers use to fund providers of care for the delivery of services within which payment to the provider is made *prior* to service delivery. This prepayment is made on the basis of predicted utilization of services by the population of benefit plan participants who reside in a given geographic area for a specified period of time, usually a 12-month period. The prepayment is usually expressed in a per member per month (pm pm) amount. For example, the provider who is responsible for the delivery of care, for example, outpatient and/ or other levels of care to 1000 plan participants, may be paid a pm pm of $0.90 per participant or $900 a month. As such, the capitated provider is "at risk" for the necessary services required by the 1000 members each month for the prepaid $900. Depending on the provider's cost to deliver care, the provider will either realize a profit or lose money through underutilization or overutilization of services by the population of members covered in the provider's contracted area.

In a *subcapitation* arrangement, the provider group, which is directly capitated by a third-party payer, subcontracts with another provider to deliver care to a segment of the specified population (the group of 1000) for a fixed portion of the original pm pm (the $900 amount). The capitated and subcapitated providers share the risk for service delivery in these arrangements because they must do the job within the agreed upon pm pm.

After reviewing many definitions of capitation, the following composite definition attempts to capture the essential features of this financing mechanism:

Capitation is a third-party payer initiative for funding a provider-managed health service system in which the provider group is prepaid an agreed upon fixed amount of money per benefit plan member based on the predicted costs of both administrative and clinical services required to provide specified services to a defined population of consumers in a defined geographic area for a defined time period. The amount paid to the provider entity is expressed traditionally as a per member per month (pm pm) figure.

This payment system is not a simple mechanism and it requires complex management to implement and control. This premise is a position taken not without experience, critical reflection, and a critical review of the literature. My own caution about capitation arrangements has been expressed previously (N. P. Armenti, 1991, p. 125) at a time when capitated arrangements with behavioral healthcare providers were not well understood and the mechanisms for managing capitation were not well developed. The marketplace has matured much since then. Capitation as a funding mechanism requires management in the same manner as clinical services require management. We are now in an era of more effective *managed capitation* as opposed to unmanaged capitation. Others have expressed a similar concern about the possible ethical, legal, and, most important, quality of care issues related to at-risk arrangements (Fitzpatrick, 1994; Giles, 1993c, pp. 120–127; Kelley, 1996; Reich, 1995, 1996). Yet, each of these healthcare market analysts conclude that capitation is, in fact, the most effective form of healthcare service financing.

As for behavioral healthcare services, per se, there is substantial support for accepting capitation as the most effective form of funding (Bell, 1995, p. 61; Kongstvedt, 1989, p. 94). Cummings (1996b) goes so far as to suggest that, "prospective reimbursement (capitation) will be the only method of payment" (p. 37) in behavioral healthcare. My suspicions are that this characterization of capitation is much too broad in scope (i.e., "the only method") and that other payment systems, besides capitation, will continue for the future although at-risk arrangements will predominate very soon.

Capitation funding has been called the "glue that binds together integrated delivery systems" (Cerne, 1994, p. 28). I would add that it is the glue for those managers who operate group practices as well. Capitation arrangements more effectively mesh the provider's incentives to render high quality care with the patient's and the third-party payer's incentives to control costs (Fitzpatrick, 1994, p. 50).

Within the capitated system of care all of the participants stand to benefit (Hladky & Johnson, 1996, p. 49). Charles Inlander, president of People's Medical Society, a consumer advocacy group of some 80,000 members, comments on what is best for *consumers*. Inlander states that, "capitation is a much better system in the long run than traditional indemnity insurance because the latter paid doctors for anything they did or ordered . . . Capitating a doctor takes away the incentive to do more" (Appleby, 1996a, p. 30).

From a *provider* perspective, Daniel Friend, executive vice president of the National Association of Managed Care Physicians, reports that those physicians with most of their practices (40%) in capitated arrangements, "are making well in excess of what they made under fee-for-service. That is because they became good at it. They have become efficient, mean, lean delivery machines" (Stevens, 1995, pp. S1–S19). Friend makes it clear that the providers have become good at controlling unnecessary utilization. Also, providers under capitation are freer to control their own practices and to make their own treatment decisions, unencumbered by excessive external monitoring and administrative procedure (Appleby, 1996a, p. 32; Fitzpatrick, 1994, p. 50).

Third-party payers in capitation arrangements have a much more effective way to control costs and quality of care. By joining providers on the basis of sharing financial risk, third-party payers and providers are combining their resources in an organized and cooperative way to ensure quality care at reasonable prices to their members. It is only through funding by stable and predictable levels of financing that this partnership will be successful. Behavioral healthcare managers will benefit from understanding capitation and other risk-sharing funding and must acquire the management skills required to implement and control these essential funding arrangements.

Premise 5: Clinical Procedures That Are Outcomes Based and Supported by Empirical Evidence Are the Foundation for Accountable Healthcare Services to the Consumer

This core premise is the most salient tenet in this presentation in terms of clinical services. The presentation of it which follows is comprehensive in scope.

An empirically validated procedure (EVP) is a clinical procedure that has achieved an acceptable level of empirical certainty in a healthcare specialty. Empirical certainty is established along the continuum of validation from low to high. The degree of empirical certainty that is established for an EVP is based on the amount and type of evidence that supports it. This evidence may range from meeting well-defined, agreed upon research criteria to merely the consensus of some experts in a specified clinical area. The position taken in this discussion is that, whenever possible, the clinical procedures used to treat a patient should be those having achieved some established degree of empirical certainty.

Eddy (1990) presents what I refer to as three levels of certainty in his discussion of the development of what he calls, "practice policies." Eddy specifies the three levels of certainty using the terms *Standards, Guidelines,* and *Options.* He describes each as follows:

> Standards are intended to be applied rigidly. They *must* be followed in virtually all cases. . . . Guidelines are intended to be more flexible. They *should* be followed in most cases. . . . Options are neutral with respect to use of an intervention . . . Options leave practitioners free to choose any course. (p. 3077)

Eddy (1990) specifies his criteria for each of these levels of empirical certainty:

> **Standard**—to write a standard for or against the use of an intervention, the main health and economic consequences of the intervention *must* be known sufficiently well to permit decisions and there must be virtual unanimity among the patients about the overall desirability (or undesirability) of the outcomes . . . at least 95%, perhaps 99%, of the people who are candidates for the intervention should agree on the desirability of the outcomes. . . .

Guideline—to write a guideline, at least some of the important outcomes of the intervention must be known, and what is known about the outcomes must be preferred (or not preferred) by an *appreciable but not unanimous* majority of people. Such a majority might be said to exist if 60% to 95% of people agree on the overall desirability (or undesirability) of outcomes. . . .
Option—everything else is an option. . . . (p. 3081)

Eddy presents four types of options: Option, With Outcome Unknown; Option, With Preferences Unknown; Option, With Preferences Indifferent; and Option, With Preferences Split. Eddy states that each option has "different implications for the responsibilities of practitioners when applying an option to individual patients, as well as for quality of care and for research" (p. 3081).

Eddy does offer a number of cautions to providers in their use of options. In healthcare, generally, and in behavioral healthcare as well, standards are likely to be rare, guidelines will be frequent, and options will, I suspect, abound for some time.

In the behavioral healthcare area, Chambless (1993) presents the consensus report of the APA's Division 12 Task Force on Promotion and Dissemination of Psychological Procedures. In that report, three categories of treatment efficacy are proposed: 1. Well-established treatments, 2. Probably efficacious treatments, and 3. Experimental treatments. The first two categories are defined by research criteria presented in Tables 1 and 2 of the report (p. 10). However, I will present the more recent Table 1 from Chambless et al. (1996, p. 16).

Table I presents the criteria that the task force recommends to establish levels of empirical validation or certainty, that is, well established and probably efficacious. The third category, which does not appear in Table 1, places treatments that "have not been established as probably efficacious" in the "experimental" category and is found in Chambless (1993, p. 1).

It appears from the report and from Table 1 that the Division 12 Task Force is being true to its scientist–practitioner approach in establishing levels of empirical certainty for clinical procedures. The criteria presented in Table 1 are more specific in their requirements for scientific evidence than those specified by Eddy (1990) to establish empirical validity of clinical procedures. The task force's first two categories emerge as two levels of what Eddy calls guidelines, and category 3 seems to correspond to Eddy's options. In either case both parties attempt to specify some criteria, based on outcomes, to establish a level of empirical validity for procedures. There is at least a beginning to the process of establishing the scientific basis for the clinical procedures in use. I can only hope that behavioral health professionals, especially in psychology, do not bog down this effort with needless debate around theoretical and turf issues. Consumers deserve more from us.

EVPs and Practice Guidelines

Empirically validated and outcomes-based clinical procedures, or EVPs, are not exactly synonymous with what the healthcare literature has customarily called practice guidelines. EVPs are the evidenced-based clinical interventions and methods (parent training, desensitization, cognitive restructuring, relapse prevention training, etc.) used by providers during their face-to-face interactions with patients

TABLE I   Criteria for Empirically Validated Treatments

Well-established treatments

I.   At least two good between-group design experiments demonstrating efficacy in one or more of the following ways:
    A.   Superior to pill or psychological placebo or to another treatment
    B.   Equivalent to an already established treatment in experiments with adequate statistical power (about 30 per group)

OR

II.   A large series of single case design experiments ($n > 9$) demonstrating efficacy. These experiments must have:
    A.   Used good experimental designs and
    B.   Compared the intervention to another treatment as in I, A

Further criteria for both I and II:

III.   Experiments must be conducted with treatment manuals

IV.   Characteristics of the client samples must be clearly specified

V.   Effects must have been demonstrated by at least two different investigators or investigatory teams

---

Probably efficacious treatments

I.   Two experiments showing the treatment is more effective than a waiting-list control group

OR

II.   One or more experiments meeting the well-established treatment criteria I, III, and IV, but not V

OR

III.   A small series of single case design experiments ($n > 3$) otherwise meeting well-established treatment criteria II, III, and IV

---

to achieve their clinical goals. As such, EVPs are the cornerstone components of practice guidelines development. Because EVPs and practice guidelines are inevitably woven together, I will discuss them as equivalents. Practice guidelines and EVPs are also known by a variety of other labels: practice protocols, practice policies, clinical algorithms, clinical standards, clinical criteria, clinical indicators, critical pathways, physician-directed diagnostic and therapeutic plan, empirically validated treatments, and so on. They are emerging as the cornerstone components of both clinical services and service monitoring and review mechanisms in the competitive business of healthcare. Professionals with intentions of continuing or initiating managing a behavioral group practice will do very well to acquire the knowledge to use EVPs in their practice. For the sake of a uniform presentation I refer to the clinical procedures and practice guidelines under discussion as empirically validated procedures or EVPs. I have selected this terminology to remain consistent with the industry's standard procedural terminology, that is, the Physicians' Current Procedural Terminology or CPT 1997 codes (American Medical Association [AMA], 1996).

A definition of a practice guideline (EVP in this presentation) has been offered by the Agency for Health Care Policy and Research (AHCPR). AHCPR uses the Institute for Medicine's definition, "systematically developed statements to help practitioner and patient decisions about appropriate healthcare for specific clinical circumstances" (AHCPR, 1993, p. ii). Clifford Gaus (1994), AHCPR Administrator, states that, "AHCPR supported practice guidelines are designed to help practitioners and patients in decision making about healthcare" (p. 64). Gaus goes on to explain that practice guidelines are used for medical review criteria, in utilization review activities, for performance measures, to evaluate provider practice patterns, and for standards of quality in provider performance (p. 64). This is a critical range of applications for EVPs. It is a resource that managers of a private practice should not ignore but rather embrace in their skills acquisition efforts.

The managed-care movement and the development and implementation of practice guidelines are inextricably intertwined (Sandrick, 1993). Managed care with its emphasis on organized systems of care and especially on its demand for accountable systems of care dovetails naturally with the EVP movement (Pincus, 1994; Smith & Hamilton, 1994; Trabin, 1994). Wilson (1996) addresses the issue of EVPs in clinical practice very persuasively and places clinical practice squarely on the basic principles of EVPs in a presentation which is recommended to managers. Gosfield (1994) offers a thought-provoking perspective on the place of EVPs in the healthcare system when she observes that

> In the last analysis, guidelines are a technique to assist payors, providers, and patients to make critical decisions as to what and how care will be delivered. Analysis and evaluation of the data, whether in guideline form or otherwise, will continue to be required. Guidelines are a means to an end, but in that regard they merit considerable attention from attorneys and others struggling with the fundamental values at issue for the healthcare delivery system today and into the next century. (p. 99)

EVPs Permeate the Healthcare Marketplace

EVPs are now embedded in many critical areas of the healthcare system. They have been established firmly as part of the daily operations of most MBHOs, utilization review companies, research entities, quality assurance and accreditation bodies, and the legal and health insurance industries. This is a movement that is not going to fade away.

EVPs and MBHOs

Large MBHOs, such as Greenspring, Human Affairs International, Value Behavioral Healthcare (VBH), and MCC-Cigna, have been using EVPs for years in their utilization review (UR) activities and in their training of network providers. For example, MCC first published its *Preferred Practices—Guide,* "a group of outpatient practice guidelines" for training its own staff in 1989 (Bartlett, 1992, p. vii). Their second printing in 1992 extended its mission to include the training of network providers, and to conduct care management and clinical outcomes. This process predates most current efforts by behavioral healthcare professionals outside managed behavioral healthcare. EVPs are used by MBHOs to determine the most appropriate services for a patient, giving serious consideration to the complexity of each case. Both MBHO staff and providers knowledgeable about managed care work as a team during the treatment planning process on behalf of the patient.

EVPs and Utilization Review

Companies that provide UR services as a stand-alone product or as part of their complete managed-care system rely heavily on EVPs. The development and use of EVPs are fundamental in providing decision support for UR staff regarding both level of care placement and appropriateness of care determinations. Decisions related to the appropriateness of care made by UR staff during precertification, concurrent review, retrospective review, and during reviews of any services proposed for or rendered to a patient are founded on EVPs (Beavert & Mogaffin, 1993).

EVPs and Research Entities

Research related to the development of EVPs has been initiated by many entities. In 1993, one source reports that, "30 different commissions . . . and at least 80 professional societies are working on more than 1400 sets of guidelines" (Sandrick, 1993, p. 30). In 1989, Congress showed its commitment to this effort, "to enhance the quality, appropriateness, and effectiveness of healthcare services" by establishing the AHCPR (Beavert & Mogaffin, 1993, p. 53). The AHCPR is no longer developing guidelines but it is collecting, analyzing, and synthesizing scientific data for use by private and public entities that are developing EVPs (De-Pinho, 1996b, p. 24). Within behavioral healthcare, considerable research has been completed by many university-based researchers, especially those who are members of the Association for Advancement of Behavior Therapy (AABT). The work of these researchers has been the foundation for many current EVPs that have been used in the managed behavioral healthcare system (N. P. Armenti, 1995). Their work is also represented in the findings of the APA Division 12 report on empirically validated treatments (Task Force, 1995). I believe their contributions will continue to be the major component of EVP development (N. P. Armenti, 1993, p. 15).

EVPs and Accreditation Bodies

Organizations that *accredit* MBHOs have incorporated EVPs in their accreditation procedures. The Joint Commission on Accreditation of Healthcare Organizations (JCAHO) has been committed to the value of EVP development and implementation for a number of years as presented in the *Journal of Quality Assurance* (O'Leary, 1993; Owens & Wease, 1993). The National Committee for Quality Assurance (NCQA; 1997) has incorporated in its Standards for Accreditation of Managed Behavioral Healthcare Organizations requirements for MBHOs to adopt and disseminate "clinical practice guidelines" as part of the Quality Management and Improvement component of the MBHO's program (QI 5, p. 47). The use of empirically validated clinical procedures will play a major role in the health-care accreditation process. Group practices will want to be familiar with this process.

EVPs and the Law

The legal implications of the EVPs present a serious and very consequential issue for providers and for those who have responsibility for managing providers. Gosfield (1992) points out that compliance with guidelines affords protection for providers in the Medicare program and that this law has been on the books since 1972 (p. 46). She also reports that Maine's 1990 law covered and allowed a limited number of medical specialty physicians to use compliance with guidelines as a defense shield. However, the law does not allow plaintiffs to cite them in filing a complaint (see also Wallen, 1995, p. 22). Maine, Minnesota, Vermont, and Florida have some form of legislation addressing the use of EVPs in malpractice cases (DePinho, 1996c, p. 34). The potential use of EVPs in cases involving behavioral healthcare providers is addressed briefly by Applebaum (1992) but no cases are cited in that article. Hyams, Shapiro, and Brennan (1996, p. 6) in their report on practice guidelines and the law cite four cases in which plaintiffs successfully sued psychiatrists. The plaintiffs' attorneys used standards issued by the American Psychiatric Association guiding provider behavior toward their patients. One case involved Tarasoff, that is, "failure to warn," and three other cases involved the standard prohibiting sexual misconduct by a psychiatrist. Although these are not the EVP-type practice guidelines being discussed here, they do demonstrate the importance of standards of care in guiding provider behavior and the possible legal consequences for provider noncompliance. For an in-depth analysis of the legal issues related to EVPs, Gosfield (1994) and the publication by National Health Lawyers Association (1995) are recommended.

EVPs and Malpractice Insurance Costs

The malpractice industry has considered the role of EVPs in coverage costs. Malpractice insurers have offered premium discounts to providers "who participate in risk management seminars or follow practice guidelines" (Szabo, 1995, p. 18). This trend is likely to continue as a risk-management incentive.

It appears that EVPs have made their way into the critical areas of healthcare. I believe EVPs will be a significant influence in service delivery and in the management of clinical services.

Procedure-Based Service Is Fundamental to Appropriate Patient Care

Years ago as a graduate student, I was very positively influenced by a brief article by Lazarus (1967) that encouraged providers to use empirically supported techniques or procedures in treating their patients. Lazarus' "technical eclecticism" eventually was presented some years later as *Multimodal Behavior Therapy* (1976). In addition, Phillips and Wiener (1966) present what I believe is one of the most cogent works lending strong support to the need for a procedure-based psychotherapy. Their volume, which reviews the early studies comparing brief and long-term therapy, provides substantial support for a structured procedural and short-term approach to the treatment of behavioral disorders. This is a work I strongly recommend to the reader.

The work of Dr. Bernard Guerney (1969) is germaine to a procedure-based approach to behavioral care delivery. He recommends the use of nonprofessional "psychotherapeutic agents" trained to apply appropriate clinical procedures both to prevent and to "treat" behavioral disorders in children and adults. Guerney emphasizes the use of "significant others," parents, teachers, and others, to bring about the desired behavioral change outcomes. Training and supervision is provided by behavioral healthcare professionals to ensure that the procedures are applied appropriately. Guerney's method is clearly consistent with managed care's focus on cost-effective care inherent in the managed-care approach. It addresses the need to control the cost of labor in the healthcare system. Over the years, I have found Guerney's approach very helpful to those I have treated and recommend that his approach be revisited by others. In addition, as a staff psychologist in an inner-city, medical school-based CMHC in 1973, I was equally influenced by an approach called *Structured Learning Therapy: Toward a Psychotherapy for the Poor* (A. Goldstein, 1973). I was fortunate to have taken a workshop with Dr. Goldstein in 1973 at the APA convention in New Orleans. My experience with this approach convinces me that his set of procedures is, in fact, one of the earliest and finest of what is now called "manualized" treatment. These approaches were, in my opinion, the forerunners of the practice guidelines and empirically validated treatments (EVTs) movements, or what I prefer to call the empirically validated procedures (EVPs) movement.

A problem for behavioral healthcare providers and those who manage them is what I have alluded to previously as follows: "One of the most frequent difficulties is that providers do not make (a) distinction between modalities of service and service interventions or procedures" (N. P. Armenti & Ericksen, 1995, p. 27).

Providers and managers of group practices are accustomed to thinking along the lines of the Physician's Current Procedural Terminology (CPT) codes (AMA, 1996, pp. 343–345) for which they are reimbursed. These codes, with a few exceptions, specify *modalities* of service, for example, individual (90844), family (90847), and group (90853) psychotherapy with duration of time spent indicated. In only a minority of CPT codes are true procedures specified, for example, pharmacological management (90862); electroconvulsive therapy (90870); individual psychophysiological therapy" (90875); biofeedback training by any modality (90901); and biofeedback training, anorectal, including electromyography and/or manometry (90811). Our analysis of these codes and the message they convey discourages providers from thinking in terms of true procedures and encourages a mind-set in terms of only time spent with the patient. I will not continue this topic here as I have examined this issue elsewhere in more detail (S. Armenti and Armenti, in press).

My recommendation is that providers abandon the "time spent" mind-set and become adept at treatment planning *for what they will do during* that time spent, that is, what procedures they will use. More to the point, providers must decide to use established and appropriate EVPs during their sessions to improve patient functioning and quality of life. That is the critical clinical issue. Procedures for change must be the foundation for psychotherapy in the new and accountable marketplace. Wilson (1996) presents a strong and valuable presentation supporting this position and his chapter is well worth reading. The term *procedure* is consistent with the current industry terminology. Curiously, the APA's Division 12, Task Force on Promotion and Dissemination of Psychological Procedures elected to use the term *empirically validated treatments* (EVTs) rather than *procedures* as their name suggests. I see this as an unnecessary inconsistency and I would suggest the use of *procedures* as opposed to *treatments*. Unfortunately, organized psychology is at war with itself, and the "arrant" nonsensical tribal warfare within the APA appears destined to stultify the discipline while the behavioral healthcare marketplace speeds on.

The Practice Guideline Controversy

The role of practice guidelines, procedures, and EVPs in healthcare is not without controversy (see DePinho, 1996b; Munoz, Hollon, McGrath, Rehm, & VandenBos, 1994; Vibbert, 1993). This issue is succinctly characterized by Gosfield (1994) as, "Every attempt to standardize care in the history of policy development to date has been met by cries of potential rigidity and, 'cookbook medicine'" (p. 79). Also, EVPs are not without opposition in behavioral healthcare (see Kovacs, 1995; Levant, 1995; E. W. L. Smith, 1995). There are those who have addressed this opposing stance elsewhere and, as such, lend support for the position expressed in this presentation regarding the value of clinical procedures (see Barlow, 1994; Chambless et al., 1996; Giles, 1993b; Giles, Neims, & Prinal, 1993; Hayes, 1995; Persons, 1996; Sanderson, 1995, 1997; Wilson, 1996).

Providers of behavioral healthcare know the value of the provider–patient relationship and do not want to minimize it. The requirement that providers communicate effectively with their patients and establish the necessary "therapeutic alliance" is well established especially in behavioral healthcare. The need to communicate to patients that they are understood and respected is the foundation on which compliance with recommended procedures and motivation to improve is, in fact, established in both general medicine (Appleby, 1996b; Paist, 1994, p. 16; Scherger, 1994, p. 17) and especially in behavioral care (E. W. L. Smith, 1995). Still, this provider–patient relationship alone is not enough to achieve desired change in most clinical cases (Wilson, 1996, p. 168). There are providers who are, perhaps, excellent technically and procedurally but who lack the interactive skills to "connect" with their patients and as a result this contributes to premature termination of care. Likewise, those who do establish the positive therapeutic alliance may fail to achieve a positive clinical outcome. Also, those providers who do achieve positive outcomes may unnecessarily extend treatment too long for lack of providing appropriate clinical procedures for changes in care. I suspect this latter scenario may account for the finding in the *Consumer Reports* (1995) article on psychotherapy outcomes. In that study, it is not really known whether treatment length would have been shortened for those who had good outcomes with long-term treatment if their treatment included EVPS; this cannot be determined from the report.

Seligman (1995) provides us with a comprehensive and very interesting analysis of the CR survey study of psychotherapy. Seligman served as a consultant to the CR staff during the survey project. He also had input from several respected behavioral professionals regarding the data set produced by the 26-item survey questionnaire (p. 965). The many issues raised by Seligman's analysis and evaluation of the CR survey are comprehensively addressed by Jacobsen and Christensen (1996). However, I will offer some thoughts about the analysis as it relates to the premise under discussion here.

The essential observation I wish to offer about the Seligman (1995) analysis is that I am unable to discern from my reading of it any discussion about clinical *procedures* used by the mental health professionals and/or medical doctors whom the survey respondents saw for treatment. Even after a careful reading of both Seligman's article and the CR report article I am left with the question as to what active, therapeutic elements account for the positive outcomes reported for long-term psychotherapy in the CR survey study. What is left unanswered by the CR project's effectiveness method of inquiry, which Seligman vigorously defends, is what really worked to produce the changes reported by the respondents in the CR study. The CR project and Seligman's defense of it appear to this reader only to perpetuate the scientifically unsubstantiated claims about the benefits of long-term therapy. I am left with the message from both sources that the amount of time spent talking to mental health professionals is the significant and active ingredient in the formula for therapeutic change, i.e., the "dose response" effect that Seligman highlights (p. 968). This is in my judgment an unfortunate and unproductive conclusion. Rather, what is needed in the behavioral healthcare field is research, i.e., efficacy studies, which elucidate the active, causal procedures used by clinicians during the time they spend with their patients and which account for the positive behavioral changes achieved. CR refers to efficacy studies as those studies that "have shown which techniques can help which problems (see "What Works Best?," p. 737), but they aren't a realistic reflection of most patients' experiences" (p. 734). In fact this is true about efficacy studies. Efficacy studies are not designed to "realistically reflect most patients' experience." They are scientific inquiries to determine what accounts for the behavioral changes achieved within the relationship between the patient and the provider, i.e., "to establish the existence of an effect" (Jacobsen and Christensen, 1996, p. 1031) or to make "inferences about causality" (p. 1036). That is the role of science and not the role of surveys. The CR article goes on to say that their survey looked at what happens in real life and "where some therapists try one technique after another until something works" (p. 734). Yet I am unable to find in either CR or Seligman's analysis of it any clear discussion of the techniques tried by the therapists who saw the survey respondents. I submit that this is a serious shortcoming in the survey project.

In analyzing and evaluating the CR results, Seligman states that "No specific modality of psychotherapy did any better than any other for any problem. These results confirm the 'dodo bird' hypothesis, that all forms of psychotherapies do about equally well. . . . They come as a rude shock to efficacy researchers, since the main theme of efficacy studies has been the demonstration of the usefulness of specific techniques for specific disorders" (p. 969). I don't believe any "efficacy researchers" will be shocked by the CR results as the survey completely misses the point about the value of specific techniques or procedures that I strongly suggest ultimately account for cost-effective care to the consumer. In addition, I believe that Seligman's use of the term "modality" confuses the issue at hand, i.e., the benefits of using specific techniques or procedures for specific clinical disorders. In the previous quote, his use of the term "modality" and in his use of that term on page 967 of his article, i.e., "Modality (psychodynamic, behavioral, cognitive, feminist)" more correctly refers to the "theoretical approach" (see CR, under "The Types of Therapies and Therapists," 1995, p. 739) or theoretical orientation that a therapist uses. The term modality is traditionally reserved for the designation of individual, group, family, and/or couples therapy. I present this issue because there is an implication in Seligman (1995) that no difference was found in long-term therapy outcomes as a function of the orientation used by the therapist. As such, according to Seligman, the 'dodo bird' hypothesis is confirmed. However, how are we to know which theoretical orientation was employed by the therapist who saw the survey respondents? Seligman explains that the respondents actively chose their therapists as "active shoppers" (p. 969). But in his discussion of "active shoppers" there is no presentation of the criteria used by the respondents to determine which orientation their therapists used. How did a patient know which orientation was being used in their treatment? I do not believe this question is answered in Seligman (1995) or in CR. Also, it appears that respondents were not asked to identify what procedures their therapists used and/or which procedures were most helpful to them. This inquiry of the respondents could have shed significant light on what really worked in the therapy that was provided to them aside from the duration of treatment.

Seligman attempts to address this issue by stating that, "It is also relevant that patients attributed their improvement to treatment and not time (determined by responses to 'How much do you feel that *treatment* helped you in the following areas?' (italics mine), and I conclude that the benefits of treatment are very unlikely to be caused by their mere passage of time" (p. 972). Just exactly what the treatment is that Seligman refers to here is very unclear. In defining treatment in these two articles we are left only with a *time spent in therapy* definition. Treatment is nowhere defined in terms of procedures or techniques used. Perhaps the next survey will define the treatment rendered in more definitive and operational terms. Unfortunately, as the saying goes, CR and Seligman's analysis of it raises more questions than they answer, in this reader's view.

I believe that EVPs, practice guidelines, or evidence-based procedures by any other name are the foundation for appropriate care to patients.

Providers Are Slow to Adopt EVPs

Managers of provider systems will be required to have a significant working knowledge of EVP procedures to manage successfully. In this regard, those who manage a private practice will benefit from a reading of Persons' (1996) presentation of the causes that she has uncovered for why psychologists are slow to adopt empirically validated procedures. I list the causes she presents as they relate to all mental health and substance abuse providers:

1. Providers receive little training in methods supported by empirical evidence of efficacy.
2. Providers often receive extensive training in methods that are not supported by empirical evidence of efficacy.
3. Many providers do not read the outcome literature.
4. Research findings are difficult for providers to use.
5. Many providers believe that all psychotherapies are equivalent.
6. Consumers are uninformed.

Persons goes on to offer sensible solutions on eliminating these barriers and on adoption and use of EVPs in clinical practice. In a related development, the resistance of family physicians to expanding their office medical procedures is covered in a very interesting article by Zuber and Pfenninger (1994). They discuss twelve "common reasons for resistance to office procedures" in their presentation, which, in a number of ways, are germaine to the problems confronting behavioral healthcare providers. Managers of clinical staff must be prepared to deal with this predictable resistance, especially from those staff who are neither well trained nor committed to a behavior therapy and cognitive behavior therapy approach to care.

EVPs and the Consumer Community

It is noteworthy that Persons (1996) begins and ends her analysis of the barriers to the adoption of EVPs by providers with a discussion of consumer-related issues (pp. 141 and 152–154). Among the several customers for behavioral healthcare service products the consumer–patient is our single most important one. Persons points out in her presentation of the uninformed consumer that, "they are accustomed to following the doctors' orders" (p. 152). Consequently, when "doctors" are unaware of or resistant to adopting EVPs then they (providers) are not sources of information for consumers about evidence-based care. Each cause analyzed by Persons contributes to the ignorance of consumers on this important issue. However, I would add two additional causal fators which exacerbate this consumer information gap. The first is the conflictual debate within behavioral disciplines, for example, organized psychology in particular and the turf rivalries between disciplines which impede the efforts to mount an effective consumer education strategy on a large scale. The second obstruction in the path of a better-informed consumer community is the often encountered preoccupation of the behavioral healthcare community with establishing unquestionable certainty about the reliability and validity of research findings to be disclosed to the public. This pursuit of certainty is laudable but often presents an unnecessary delay in disseminating information to a needy and deserving consumer population. Eddy (1990) presents standards, guidelines, and options, and addresses patient education, especially, regarding options. He states that even with options, "there is still value in conducting the analyses and issuing those policies. It is honest, it alerts physicians to the lack of information, it helps keep patients' expectations more realistic, it decreases the threat of malpractice and it stimulates research" (p. 3084).

The comments of Wilson (1996) emerge as relevant in this regard in which he raises the issue of "what to do in areas where there is little or no scientific research, no treatment manuals and no empirically validated techniques" (p. 187). His recommendation to providers is sound and consistent with other expert opinion. The consensus recommends using procedures that are guided by "principles of behavior change that are consistent with (at least not in violation of) what is known . . . More prosaically, clinicians should be guided also by the best available standards of care" (Wilson, 1996, p. 187). Wilson's admonition is quite relevant to what Eddy (1990) calls options and others (Applebaum, 1992) discuss as treatments at least supported by the consensus of experts in a given area of healthcare.

I strongly recommend that those who manage behavioral private practices be prepared to address the consumer's "right to know" what level of certainty our industry's behavioral procedures have achieved. In his discussion of empirically validated treatments as the basis of clinical practice, Wilson (1996, pp. 163–164) cites Klerman's (1990) analysis of the *Osheroff vs. Chestnut Lodge* case and Klerman's recommendation that "the patient has the right to be informed as to the alternative treatments available, the relative efficacy and safety, and the likely outcomes of these treatments" (pp. 416–417). I strongly suspect that in clinical practice this duty to inform will become the norm especially as eager attorneys hunt down unprepared providers in cases of malpractice. In a very accurate portrayal of the marketplace situation, Persons (1996) alludes to the "marketplace pressure" on providers from educated consumers and third-party payers for the delivery of evidence-based procedures "in order to stay in business" (p. 153). I strongly agree that the power of the consumer as the primary market force will, in fact, change provider behavior. The efforts to address the consumer education issue regarding EVPs on the part of the disciplines within behavioral healthcare, so far, has been a dismal failure. In the competitive marketplace, "the silence of the guilds" on this matter will result only in obstructing the dissemination of valuable quality information to both providers and consumers and ultimately to the eventual self-destruction of those guilds.

Ellwood supports the position that public disclosure of quality information is an enabling dynamic for improving the quality of care, as he states in Schiff and Service's (1996) article that, "Reform depends on the power and ability of consumers to make choices based on quality" (p. 35). Ellwood goes so far as to say that, "My contention is that the premature release of quality information [i.e., before risk adjustors are fully developed] is what will be required to perfect the systems that gather and disseminate information to the public" (p. 39)

In behavioral healthcare, providers and managers of provider systems must avoid repeating what Giles (1993b) reports when he concludes that several professional surveys "Indicate that only a minority of psychotherapists use empirical results to guide their practices . . . A disturbing implication of these findings is that therapies with greatest proven efficacy are not implemented by the majority, or perhaps even a significant minority, of practitioners" (p. 482). In sum, Vibbert (1993) is perhaps correct in his examination of this subject in his volume, *What Works* when he remarks as follows:

> The question is a simple one: What works? Hardly anyone will disagree that finding an answer to that question would be good for you, me, and the world at large. In the end, whether or not the guidelines and outcomes movements succeed or fail will depend not only on the soundness of research, but on political factors as well. Who more than the physician could want the best of these initiatives to succeed? Surely the alternative—more utilization review, no consensus on the best practices, and an antagonistic relationship between physicians and payers—won't work at all. (p. 75)

I interpret Vibbert's reference to "physicians" to include all providers of healthcare including providers of behavioral services.

Premise 6: Preventive Behavioral Healthcare Services Are Critical to Assisting Consumers to Live Healthy Lifestyles and to Conserve Healthcare Resources

Prevention has been included in the definition of a practice guideline by one organization that develops guidelines as a private group. The Institute for Clinical Systems Integration (ICSI), according to DePinho (1996b), defines a guideline as, "a process specification for prevention or treatment of a given condition" (p. 26). This definition of a guideline is a welcome one as it encourages movement toward preventive services development along the lines of procedures, EVPs, and manualized approaches to care. Most providers of healthcare services would agree in theory that prevention of health problems is a significant goal to achieve. Yet, putting this belief into practice has been difficult to date and I suspect it will remain the most challenging of the healthcare initiatives to implement in the current and future healthcare marketplace. The inclusion of preventive healthcare services under insurance coverage and in the service delivery systems of MBHOs has been called the "third generation of managed care" (D. R. Smith, Wong, & Eichert, 1996). However, this is a generation only in the making, as "Currently managed care companies and payers have little incentive to invest dollars saved through short-term interventions on long-term preventive medicine programs" (D. R. Smith et al., 1996, p. 821). This includes MBHOs as well.

In their presentation, D. R. Smith et al. (1996) examine the barriers to implementing preventive services and recommend solutions to the problems discussed. They express the need to shift the emphasis in the marketplace "from medical care to healthcare . . . and reinvest the short-term savings realized through utilization management into a long-range strategy that promotes health, lessens disability, reduces morbidity and mortality and ultimately achieves long-term savings" (pp. 823–824).

The absence of incentives for payers to move ahead with preventive services in behavioral healthcare is related to an interesting healthcare phenomenon generally and in the mental health and substance abuse field as well. It is a dynamic associated with the reality of *supply-induced demand* or provider-initiated utilization alluded to earlier. B. H. Gray (1991) cites the example of what is called "Roemer's law: that a hospital bed built is a hospital bed filled" (p. 245). He goes on to explain a related perception on the part of third-party payers which is associated with outpatient care, "that a service that will be paid for is a service that someone will provide" (pp. 245–246). This message is reported elsewhere by Hudson (1996) in her examination of the *Dartmouth Atlas of Health Care in the United States* (Wennberg & Cooper, 1996). She states that the research shows that "supply generates demand putting traditional economic theory on its head" (p. 26) and "the more providers in a region the more services and resources used there" (p. 30). When one considers this finding with what is reported by marketplace analysts as an oversupply of providers, especially specialists (Coleman, 1996, p. 36; Epstein, 1995; News and Trends, 1996; Solovy, 1997, pp. 28–29), and behavioral healthcare providers are indeed included (Cummings, 1996a, p. 25; 1996b, p. 37; Gorman, 1996, p. 45; Keisler & Morton, 1988, pp. 997–998), one might readily understand third-party payers, *managed care response* with its various utilization management mechanisms and watchdog techniques.

In a related and very interesting development Eaton (1997) describes "A unique pilot project underway in New York State may ultimately provide the solution to the nation's oversupply of physicians. In a plan that is reminiscent of farm subsidies, 41 New York hospitals will be paid by the Health Care Financing Administration *not* to train residents" (p. 3). I suspect that behavioral healthcare providers in all disciplines will not escape procedures for reducing their supply in the near future.

The perception, based on the experience of third-party payers, was and still is that the abundance of providers in the unmanaged fee-for-service environment were compelled to fill all of their billable hours. Third-party payers in the fee-for-service environment were essentially passive check writers acquiescing to every provider invoice sent to them. This had to stop. Traditionally in fee-for-service markets, providers of behavioral healthcare have used what is considered preventive services (stress management workshops, parenting training lectures and workshops, smoking cessation, weight reduction seminars, assertiveness training groups, communication training for couples, alcohol and drug abuse education, etc.) for marketing and new case finding. This approach was designed to increase caseloads, utilization, and income. In the managed care approach to service delivery and especially in capitated systems this supply-induced demand is unacceptable and self-destructive to providers and to those who manage them and ultimately to patients.

Employee Assistance Program (EAP) services, when offered to employers, often raise their concerns. Concern is aroused because an aim of EAP services is to identify troubled employees and their dependents early and to intervene early, and as a result this initially has the potential to increase utilization of behavioral services. Any possible initial increase in utilization due to EAP case finding is often daunting to some employers and requires explanation and persuasion. What must be emphasized is that this preventive approach will payoff in the long haul with offset medical costs (Mastrich & Beidel, 1985; McDonnell Douglas Corporation & Alexander Consulting Group, 1989). The message to employers is that they will save healthcare dollars eventually by using the EAP as a gatekeeper mechanism within their health benefit plan. At times this is a hard sell.

Population-Based Care

The costs of "lifestyle disease" (LaPuma, 1996, p. 57) such as smoking, excessive weight gain, not using seatbelts and helmets, alcohol and drug abuse, lack of exercise, violence, unsafe behavior resulting in accidents, sexually transmitted disease, and so on, are high and yet preventable to a significant degree (see AMA, 1993; LaPuma, 1996).

These lifestyle problems need to be addressed from the perspective of a *population-based* delivery system. This population-based view of healthcare takes into consideration the limited resources available and attempts to address the delivery of care from a broad economic picture. In this approach, providers need to keep in mind that what services and resources they provide for any one individual influences the resources available for all members of the benefit plan (N. P. Armenti, 1991, pp. 125–126). This approach is especially important in capitated funding systems where the provider group is responsible for the care of a defined population (Eddy, 1995a; Strosahl, 1996, p. 53). It will pay to keep the population in that system healthy, that is, living healthy lifestyles, to lower utilization of services. This is not without a concern for the individual (Appleby, 1996, p. 32). Yet, this population-based approach must balance the needs of any one individual against the needs of the larger community of consumers. This will not be an easy road to travel for managers of a private practice who are funded by capitation and other at-risk arrangements.

Demand Management

There is another market dynamic pushing preventive behavioral healthcare along. Health promotion and wellness programs developed by corporations for their workers and by hospitals for their communities (Cerrato, 1995; Chapman, 1990; Coile, 1995; Elias, 1995; Kerr, 1996) have led to a new approach called *demand management* (Barnett, 1995; Fries, 1994; Gramblin, 1995; Mihlbauer, 1992, Powell, 1996; Sawyer, 1995). This approach attempts to manage utilization and reduce unnecessary care by encouraging consumers to take responsibility for their own healthcare behavior. This approach is expected to reduce inappropriate consumer-initiated utilization and consumption of healthcare resources. The initial impetus for this approach is cost control. "Controlling demand is how many major volume purchasers are going to demand control of costs" (Mihlbauer, 1992, p. 20). However, if healthcare professionals are genuinely concerned about improving the quality of life in their communities, then their commitment to provide preventive care will be guided by a moral imperative to pursue quality in healthcare. "Optimal outcomes are to be achieved not only through the provision of competent medical services but by attending to those individuals not yet sick and not yet requiring care" (Fries, 1994, p. 57). Healthcare providers will need to reach out actively to promote the consumer's personal responsibility for self-care behavior.

Disease State Management

A related development in the healthcare marketplace is *disease state management* (Blackwell, Szeinback, Barnes, & Garner, 1996; Marro, 1995; Spalding, 1996) addressing disorders such as obesity (Wyeth-Ayerst Laboratories, 1996), diabetes (Drapin, 1995), asthma (Braly, 1995), and depression (Ross, 1996). Each of these areas of healthcare has clear behavioral components that are appropriate for behavioral procedures, especially preventive services.

A current marketplace example in this area is a recent invitation our group received from an MBHO for whom we are network providers. The letter to us said that the MBHO was looking for "contracted providers who have documented experience/expertise in the behavioral health treatment of patients suffering from the following medical conditions: 1. Chronic fatigue, 2. Asthma, 3. Fibromyalgia, 4. Cancer, 5. Irritable bowel syndrome, 6. Other chronic illnesses." It is apparent that the managed care system is moving toward the closer integration of behavioral and medical services and that preventive approaches will be a major component of that integration.

Accreditation and Preventive Services

MBHOs that intend to pursue accreditation by the National Committee for Quality Assurance (NCQA) will be required to have preventive behavioral healthcare services as a clearly defined and well-implemented component of their offering to the enrollees (NCQA, 1997, pp. 97–101). This requirement will be an enabling boost to a long needed approach to improving the health status of our communities, that is, through prevention.

Managers of private practices will benefit significantly from developing preventive services in the new marketplace. Services promoting healthy lifestyles in children, as described by Peterson, Chaney, and Harbeck (1989), and an array of preventive behavioral services addressing hypertension (Dubbert, 1992), weight control (Kirschenbaum, Fitzgibbon, Conviser, Shrifter, & Langdon, 1992), smoking cessation (Shipley, 1992), and alcohol screening (Schmidt & Cooney, 1992) are some preventive behavioral care services which may be offered in a private practice setting. This is an area that will, in the long run, bring great dividends to all participants in healthcare—consumers, payers, and providers.

SECTION II: A SELECTION OF MANAGEMENT SKILL AREAS AND THEIR ASSOCIATED PROCEDURES IN THE BEHAVIORAL PRIVATE PRACTICE SETTING

Introductory Remarks

What emerges from each of the six core premises presented above is a mandate to adopt appropriate management procedures that will operationalize the marketplace requirements, both clinical and administrative, for successful management of a private practice. This presentation covers several selected areas of management skills in the private practice setting and the related management procedures found to be relevant through experience and within the practice management literature.

It is a given that successful management is a blend of both technical and nontechnical elements. Those who manage successfully in behavioral healthcare will need to bring to the enterprise a set of appropriate "personality" characteristics which operationally define good leadership and management ability. Covey (1992) presents a contrasting description between the different and, at times, dichotomous roles of a leader and a manager when he states that

> The basic role of the leader is to foster mutual respect and build a complementary team where each strength is made productive and each weakness made irrelevant. The essential role of a manager is to use leverage and to multiply the work and the role of the producer. A producer roles up his sleeves and does what is necessary to solve problems and get results. (p. 246)

The nontechnical components of management and leadership will not be covered comprehensively in this presentation. However, by virtue of the causal relationship they have to effective management skills they will be alluded to throughout this section. I believe that with a few rare exceptions, both experience and history confirm the reality of the Darwinian dynamic in *selecting out* of the competitive business marketplace those participants who do not bring with them the appropriate leadership and managerial behaviors, both technical and nontechnical.

Sources of Management Information

The healthcare literature provides several sources of information which managers and aspiring managers will find valuable while refining their skills. Most recently the volume by Cummings et al. (1996) is replete with information relevant to the topic under discussion. In particular the chapter by Browning (1996) entitled, "Practical survival strategies: Business basics for effective marketing to managed care," and the one by Edley (1996) addressing the topic of "The practitioner as owner," are particularly valuable to managers of behavioral private practices. Both chapters cover an important range of management procedures and Browning's chapter includes sample forms to use within some of those procedures. Browning's chapter is an abbreviated rendition of Browning and Browning (1996) and both are valuable to managers especially for staff training and marketing strategies. Both also address the attitudinal changes and cognitive restructuring required of most providers and managers in order to achieve success in the current and future marketplace. In addition, Giles (1993b) offers a comprehensive treatment of the behavioral marketplace with important historical perspectives, case illustrations, and practical advice for providers and managers of care.

I could go on to recommend several other sources of relevant information addressing the acquisition of management skills for behavioral healthcare managers. However, at this point I refer the reader to the reference section of this chapter which cites several books and journals providing relevant information regarding both clinical and administrative skills acquisition. The remainder of this presentation covers a number of procedures helpful in managing a private practice. Many of these procedures are presented in the literature. Other procedures are an amalgam of the wisdom of others and my own experience along with my colleagues' over several years of private practice management in the managed and unmanaged behavioral marketplace.

Selected Management Skills Areas and Procedures

In the delineation of the first core premise, that is, that behavioral healthcare is a competitive business, I emphasize the competitive nature of the behavioral practice enterprise. To fulfill the requirements of a competitive business, managers of a private behavioral healthcare practice need to adopt some basic business procedures that all viable commercial entities use in offering their services and products to their customers. Admittedly, approaching the behavioral marketplace with a competitive, business frame of reference is not familiar to most of us in the "helping professions." Yet, those managers who accept the message and the mandates in the first core premise, must commit themselves seriously to the execution of some basic business procedures designed to position their practices as identifiable competitors in the marketplace (Browning, 1996).

As a competitive marketplace participant, the management team of the private practice must think and plan along the lines of implementing a range of basic business procedures. The procedures that management adopts and the skills managers eventually acquire need to address several areas of administration. One source recommends that the management team of a private practice master some 25 management skill areas (Molinari, Lee, Williams, Riddle, & Zuber, 1993). The curriculum the authors designed teaches practice managers these skill areas in 25, three-hour didactic sessions. They do not present in their article the contents of that curriculum. Another source briefly outlines a set of seven broad areas subsumed under the description of a "practice administrator's skills" (Ellis, Johnson, & Bagley, 1996, p. 57). These skill areas are presented as follows:

- Leadership
- Management of human resources

- Management of communication
- Management of finances
- Management of time
- Management of offices
- Management of nonclinical crises

Each skill area has a set of responsibilities with associated procedures for getting the job done. This list includes neither the skills required to manage the practice's clinical services nor the clinicians who provide them. The areas of clinical management include at least the following:

- Clinical staff recruiting
- Clinical staff credentialing
- Clinical staff training
- Clinical staff supervision
- Clinical staff profiling
- Utilization management
- Clinical quality improvement

When both the nonclinical and clinical management functions are assumed by staff who are trained primarily as clinicians and who still function as clinicians, the task of combining the two areas is complex and is best handled by a management team. This is recommended especially in larger groups with many staff and several office locations.

Additionally, the procedures for expanding an existing group practice require astute attention to several areas of organizational detail and contribute to the complexity of operating the existing group. Establishing or expanding a behavioral business entity requires procedural attention in the areas of law, accounting, regulations, literature research, management information systems (MIS), and other areas of business. The entire range of procedures and skills required to achieve the outcomes for viable business ventures are too numerous to cover comprehensively in this chapter-length presentation. Instead, I will cover a selection of skill areas and procedures that are valuable in conducting the business of a behavioral practice. The skills and procedures presented are "flexible" and change frequently as new information is presented or encountered, compelling management to modify and improve its approach. In all circumstances, management must be mindful of the admonition by Currey (1992, p. 67) that healthcare professionals must be skilled at balancing the clinical needs of patients with the business requirements of managing a commercial enterprise.

The clinical and nonclinical (those skills *not* requiring a clinical license) management skill areas and procedures covered here have been helpful to managers of private practices in the managed healthcare marketplace. These are

- Product development
- Staff management
- Marketing

- Utilization management
- Financial management
- Nonclinical administrative activities within a behavioral group practice
- Quality improvement and outcomes management

These management and procedural areas are discussed briefly with an emphasis on placing management skills firmly on a foundation of effective management procedures both clinical and nonclinical.

Product Development

Defining clearly the service and/or product offered for sale to the customer is a fundamental procedural issue in any successful commercial undertaking. In behavioral healthcare, this activity has not been addressed in a way that has presented services or products to customers with any clarity. Behavioral healthcare has essentially been "generic" in its offerings to the customer community. Psychotherapy has been the service-product offered. The term has been modified, perhaps, by the various modalities called "individual," "family," "group," or "couples." Providers of care have yet to accept, and become at ease with, the reality that behavioral healthcare services are products and commodities (N. P. Armenti, 1991, p. 126; Blumenthal, 1996, p. 179).

Although we have hardly approached the brand-name stage which would allow consumer "market basket analysis" (Ericksen, 1996), the behavioral healthcare industry would benefit greatly from movement in the direction of product development activity. The *Consumer Reports* (1996) article is interesting in this regard. On page 737 of that article under the heading of "What Works Best?—The Right Treatment for Your Troubles" is a presentation of a number of treatments that approximates an advertisement for a number of service-products: cognitive therapy, interpersonal therapy, drug therapy, electroconvulsive therapy, meditation, relaxation, cognitive-behavioral therapy, systematic desensitization, and flooding. Although not exactly a brand-name presentation (except for two drugs), this rendition of "best" treatments is service-product oriented in its layout. I recognize that this approach will not meet the approval of all professionals in the mental health and substance abuse field (see E. W. L. Smith, 1995, pp. 38–40).

Nevertheless, in managing a private behavioral healthcare practice managers need to be well informed about the "top-of-the-line" service-products that are available in their business. It is important to know which service-products (EVPs) offered the consumer are well established empirically, and what level of empirical certainty—that is, standards, guidelines, or options (Eddy, 1990), or empirically validated, probably efficacious, or experimental (Chambless, 1993) a clinical procedure has attained. Procedurally, we need to read the literature, attend conferences, and communicate with our colleagues to keep abreast of developments in this area. There are several insightful sources of suggestions for addressing this area (Persons, 1996; Sobell, 1996; Wilson, 1996).

Four service–products are recommended to managers of private practice for inclusion in their service-product line.

- Clinical procedures (EVPs)
- Preventive services
- Other services
- Employee Assistance Program (EAP) services

Clinical Procedures (EVPs)

This service-product includes all procedures used to provide direct treatment to patients. I will cut to the chase and without hesitation recommend that managers of clinical staff require that their staff become well trained to provide behavior therapy (BT) and cognitive behavior therapy (CBT) procedures within their treatment approaches. There is ample support in the literature to strongly recommend these behavioral treatments and their associated procedures. I recommend a careful reading of the article by Sanderson and Woody (1995) in which the manuals for EVPs addressing thirteen clinical disorders are listed along with the phone numbers, references sources, and in some areas where training is available. The articles by Chambless et al. (1996) and Sanderson (1997) will be helpful. Handbooks by Giles (1993a) and Barlow (1993) are valuable sources of evidenced-based procedures as well.

I would also urge managers to encourage their staff to join the Association for Advancement of Behavior Therapy (AABT) (212-647-1890) to keep current with the latest in EVP developments. Without top-of-the-line service-products, especially in the direct clinical services area, a private practice will not be positioned to compete effectively in current and future markets. This is especially the case in a market in which capitated funding arrangements exist or are developing. EVPs are the key to quality care and to achieving effective and profitable behavioral healthcare practices.

Preventive Services

Progressive group practices will develop an array of preventive services to address the approaches to care that incorporate population-based care, demand management strategies, and disease state management. Again, these services when designed appropriately will provide to consumers a level of care that is attractive to them in terms of preventing both physical and behavioral health problems. In addition, the practice communicates to consumers through preventive approaches a genuine concern for their well-being and for the well-being of their family. This is a critical message to communicate to consumers and to their employers. There are several preventive services that a practice will want to consider offering in its product line as a stand-alone service or as a component of its EAP services.

Besides the preventive services already presented under *Premise 6,* those who manage a practice may want to include in their product line the following preventive services:

- Alcohol and drug education for parents and child care personnel
- Assertiveness training

- Child management training
- Communications training for couples
- Premarital marriage readiness evaluation and education
- Stress management

I would strongly recommend, in particular to managers of a private behavioral practice, smoking cessation services. As a result of our own group's interests in promoting this service, we conducted a brief comparative analysis of programs identified as offering smoking cessation services. We settled on using the Quit-Smart program (Shipley, 1992). I took the training program conducted by Dr. R. H. Shipley and I am now a QuitSmart certified facilitator. The appeal of this approach is that it is "manualized," uses a kit for the consumer, incorporates procedures for behavioral change that are outcomes based, and gives the QuitSmart facilitator effective marketing tools and procedures.

There is a very large market for this service in terms of providing real quality of life enhancement (DiFranza & Lew, 1995) and in terms of cost savings. As one source observes, "Despite the risks, an estimated 50 million Americans continue to smoke, costing the nation an estimated $68 billion annually in healthcare and lost productivity" (Legorreta, Kashian, & Franklin, 1996, p. 831). The medical and business-related cost offsets resulting from this service are enormous.

Other Services

Additional service-products may be included to provide a comprehensive range of services to the customer community. These may include:

- Critical incident stress debriefing
- Divorce mediation
- Eating disorders services
- Forensic evaluations
- An intensive outpatient program (IOP) for substance abusers
- Neuropsychological evaluation and cognitive rehab services
- Pain management services
- Organization consultation to businesses

Many of the services in the preventive services and other services categories may and even should be delivered in the group modality. In most situations the group format will be didactic in its delivery. In the current marketplace psychoeducational groups are very much in demand. The traditional "psychodynamic group therapy" is clearly not the direction to take for most populations today.

EAP Services

These services have been neglected by many private practitioners. Yet, this is a service-product that is very attractive to employers. Employers are important customers who are amenable to direct contracting with provider groups, especially in the small to moderate size self-insured (ERISA) marketplace. I strongly suggest that managers explore for themselves and for their staffs attaining the credential of Certified Employee Assistance Professional (CEAP) by calling the EAP Association for information (1-703-522-6272). This is a certification more valuable than most would believe when bidding for EAP contracts.

There are several other service-products a manager may wish to include in his or her practice's offerings to customers. These include utilization review and case management services. I have put the focus here on outpatient services. However, as a group practice moves from an integrated group to an integrated delivery system (IDS) it will pursue affiliation with partial hospital (PH), detox, rehab, and mental health inpatient facilities. Discounted per diems can be negotiated with these service entities. The IDS will, in fact, be the preferred system providing the comprehensive product line necessary in a capitated funding environment. With this complete product line in place, the service delivery system has a distinct competitive advantage in marketing to third-party payers.

The central issue here is that the service-products health care practices offer to the public should be procedures that have attained, through outcomes research or through a consensus of experts, an acceptable level of empirical certainty supporting their efficacy. The service-product line is the foundation for the ability to compete in the healthcare marketplace. It will benefit managers both clinically and commercially to present that produce line with clarity to their customers.

Staff Management

The management of staff in a private practice setting is a process fraught with complexities. Those who manage a behavioral practice are confronted almost daily with a host of ambiguities and uncertainties. I recall a professor saying in my early graduate school days that mental health professionals are, in fact, specialists in dealing with uncertainty and ambiguity. I would certainly agree that we should be specialists in handling the ambiguity and uncertainty that emanates from the nature of the clinical issues presented for resolution in the practice. At the same time, many events and conditions emerging from the expectations and behavior of staff and from the regulatory environment are frequent challenges and are, at times, anxiety provoking for management.

There are three levels of core staff that are the focus of this discussion along with administrative issues germaine to these levels. My emphasis, however, is on the managerial issues related to clinical staff. The three levels of core staff are management staff, clinical staff, and support staff.

Management Staff

The effective management of the staff of a private practice is contingent on the reality that those who manage must first manage themselves effectively. Although this statement may appear somewhat simplistic, in my experience, it is a profound consequential fact in private practice. The management team must present itself to the organization's subordinate staff as just that, a team. The message and image of management unity should be communicated to staff. To ensure that this happens, management must be characterized by "shared vision, strong leadership and common objectives" and to have in place "solid governance and administrative structure" (Benedict, 1996, pp. 44–45). Especially in the rapidly changing healthcare environment, management must share a common knowledge base and belief system to ensure its effectiveness. The core premises covered in Section I of this chapter are presented to provide a common knowledge base for the members of a private practice management team to share. Steps to ensure that every member of the management team is "reading off the same page" is essential to administrative efficiency, to do otherwise is to court disaster for the group practice. A central issue in effective management and administration is to keep *uncertainty* among staff to a minimum. Although uncertainty cannot be eliminated, especially in the evolving healthcare marketplace, "clarity" in the presentation of roles, procedures, and purpose is critical to team building among all levels of staff.

One management approach, which is recommended here, is what may be called "the uncertainty reduction model" (Sethi, Caro, & Schuler, 1987). This management model is described in terms of managing "technostress," that is, "a perceived and dynamic state of uncertainty in the face of technological change that occurs at individual, organizational and societal levels. 'Technostress' refers to uncertainty experienced by the person in different contexts in adapting to the new technological environment" (Sethi et al., 1987, p. 8). Although this model was originally presented to address the management of stress uncertainty, resulting from the rapid introduction of electronic information systems into business organizations, its applicability to the current and rapidly changing behavioral healthcare marketplaces is superb.

One example of the variables this management model addresses are what Schuler, Jackson, and Sethi (1987) describe as "Major environmental sources of uncertainty operating at the organizational level of analysis are suppliers, customers, competitors, creditors, government agencies and unions. These represent the immediate sources of uncertainty experienced by an organization" (p. 75). This does not cover all of the relevant sources of uncertainty besieging private practice managers and their staffs in the accelerated healthcare marketplace. Yet, I believe it gives a reasonably accurate portrayal of the factors management needs to address in controlling its business, including staff.

Clinical Staff

Training and Supervision. Clinical staff are critical to the direct delivery of the service-product to the consumer of clinical services. From a clinical perspective, managers must be diligent in their efforts to assess the competency of clinical staff. It has been suggested that the skill level of the clinician is a key factor in the delivery of sophisticated treatments "such as interpersonal therapy" (Barlow, 1994, p. 114). This may be obvious but it is also a very practical staff management issue in a private practice and must be addressed through proper recruitment, supervision, and training. Regarding supervision and training, managers should commit to adopting, where possible, EVPs as their primary treatment procedures. Staff will require training to understand the concept of cost-effective care criteria (Garson, 1996). *Profiling* staff so that compliance with current EVPs is monitored, and so that comparisons between clinical peers within the group can be made, are critical management procedures (Montague, 1994b). This profiling procedure should be conducted in a collegial and cooperative way designed to help clinical staff improve their skills to achieve positive clinical outcomes. It has been recommended, on the basis of research addressing treatment patterns of providers in general medicine (Cave & Geehr, 1994), that efforts to change provider treatment patterns might effectively be achieved by providing feedback to practitioners in the following procedural steps:

- On an individual basis, face to face, by an "influential" clinician leader
- On a monthly or quarterly basis
- Provide cost information relevant to the clinician's pattern of care, especially in a capitated practice environment

These recommendations appear quite appropriate for the behavior healthcare setting. Managers must strive to reduce uncertainty in this provider feedback procedure so that clinical staff willingly adopt available EVPs in treating their patients. The supervision and direction of staff is, in fact, "managing care" (N. P. Armenti, 1990). For a helpful discussion of the role of a supervisor in the current and future marketplace, see Kalous' (1996) chapter on this subject. It is important for the management team to provide an appropriate level of supervision and oversight to ensure that a *sentinel effect* remains operative throughout the practice, especially in patient and customer contacts. The areas of staff profiling, feedback to staff, and comparisons of staff treatment patterns are critical to cost-effective management and to the quality of care provided.

Staff Selection and Recruitment

Managing staff requires management to address the goal of a group practice "in obtaining the right people for the right job at the right time" (Schuler et al., 1987, p. 83). With appropriate recruitment and selection procedures, managers will build an organization of staff who share a set of values that are consistent with those of the management team. This staffing outcome must be achieved to increase the probability of achieving the group practice's mission. Successful managers of private practices have recruitment criteria available to them as decision support tools when deciding on the right professional to include in their practice (Parshall & Huber, 1993). A few suggestions are offered here based on experience and on the literature addressing this issue.

The most pressing issue regarding clinical staff selection is to address both the business and clinical decision process in a cost-effective manner. The marketplace requires managers to control their costs. Managers must be committed to hiring staff who are both affordable and clinically competent. Masters level psychologists (Seaman, 1996a), social workers, and professional counselors have emerged as competent practitioners who have achieved licensing status in most of the 50 states (Cummings, 1996a, p. 22). This is a reality that enlightened management will embrace as a distinct advantage in their staffing decisions. Masters level clinicians will be the predominant practitioners in the future, with doctorate level professionals taking on other training, supervisory, and administrative responsibilities (Cummings, 1996b, pp. 31, 33; Hayes, 1996, p. 184). Managers of a private practice will need to respond to this reality thoughtfully and skillfully.

A word here about part-time clinical staff. Managing staff who are not committed to a substantial block of hours in a private practice has been difficult. "Hobbyists" who want to work a few hours a week create a staff management problem and, at times, a provider credentialing conflict. In the managed care system, preference is for staff who are available to put in at least 15 hours weekly to see patients. We know that many staff have been reluctant to leave their "day jobs" for full-time private practice. They fear that, in the managed care marketplace, they may eventually be forced to learn the expression, "would you like a large coke and fries with that, sir" as my colleague, Dr. Bob Ericksen has often pointed out (personal communication, November 1996). Until we can assure clinical staff a secure and predictable level of compensation and until we have in place a faster MBHO network credentialing process, managers are locked into this unfortunate clinical staffing straightjacket. MBHOs, as of this writing, have neither streamlined nor standardized across the industry the credentialing of network providers. I believe that MBHOs can be more helpful to group managers in the processes of both group development and group staffing procedures. Managers should approach MBHOs to seek out their assistance. MBHOs executives who express indifference to this initiative are shortsighted and reveal a contradiction in their, often, expressed interest to moving to group contracting within their networks. It is of mutual benefit to both managers of group practices and MBHO professionals to work cooperatively in pursuit of this managed care objective.

Compensation of Clinical Staff

Designing a compensation arrangement for clinical staff is a task that requires considerable management skills. With the unquestionable requirement to control costs in operating any business, the high cost of labor becomes a prime focus for administrative cost control (Cummings, 1996b, p. 31). Managers of a commercial private practice come to know very fast that their most costly and complex budget line items are those specifying staff salaries, payroll taxes, and benefits—all labor-related costs. Issues of professional autonomy, participation in group decision making, and other nonfinancial factors are clearly important in staff management. Yet, no one issue is more significant in influencing staff behavior than the pocketbook issue of compensation. Creative skills are required to craft a compensation arrangement that promotes both satisfaction and productivity among clinical staff (Carlson, 1996; Epstein, 1996). Managers need to create a work environment in which the compensation arrangement provides incentives to encourage staff clinicians "to be highly productive without wasting costly resources" (Denning, 1996).

The compensation landscape is crisscrossed with a variety of paths of uncertain access and terrain. Superior legal and accounting advice are required to ensure compliance with federal and state employment regulations. It is important for managers to show flexibility in dealing with staff who are "traditional" employees as opposed to others who wish to participate as equity owners. In this regard, Cummings (1996b) advises that "Participant ownership requires strong management, with strict limitations on the provider's ability to meddle in administration" (p. 37). This may sound like a rather stern admonition but I can attest to both its wisdom and its challenge. Many, if not most clinicians today were trained and expected to be "independent providers" and are, at times, not very willing team players.

Until funding to group practices comes in the form of "hard dollars," that is, predictable, fixed revenue provided by the third-party payer community, controlling staff compensation and other costs will be difficult for managers. Capitation and other fixed income will be required to operate a private practice in the most effective business manner. The marketplace is not there yet in most areas of the country.

In at-risk capitated funding systems the central procedural issue in arranging compensation for clinical staff is to provide base salary and bonus incentives that are *not* contingent on the level of patient utilization of service. In the current managed-care marketplace most groups are stuck with a situation in which staff compensation is still tied to the number of patients seen on referral to the group by an MBHO, HMO, or another third-party payer.

An important core issue here is the following: *The group in which the individual clinicians are employed must be paid directly through capitation. The individual clinician employed by the group should not be compensated on a capitation basis.* Both Arnold Relman, editor emeritus of the *New England Journal of Medicine,* and John LaPuma, a well-known healthcare ethicist, agree that the group employing the clinician should be the recipient of capitated funding and not the individual provider (Kelly, 1996). According to critics of capitation, the individual staff clinician, in fact, should be kept blind to which patients in his or her caseload are in a capitated system and which are not. This condition will significantly decrease any temptation to underserve patients. The financial incentive to underserve must be removed from the treating provider. However, attempts to keep clinical staff "blind" to how the group is funded and to which patients are and are not in at-risk payment arrangements are vulnerable to being counter productive. Efforts to keep staff uninformed will require maneuvers to disguise and hide the realities of how and from where the group's money is earned. Rather, I advocate for clearly informing clinical staff about how the group is funded just as employees of other businesses know how their company earns its money. Clinicians need to know the funding mechanisms so that they will be motivated to cooperate with management to implement the practice patterns required to achieve the group's mission, i.e., to provide the consumer with cost-effective care. Keeping clinical staff well aware that the group is spending its own financial resources when it delivers services under capitation or case rates as opposed to spending "other people's money" (third-party payers) under fee for service arrangements is an important distinction for clinicians to understand. This operating dynamic has the potential to transform the ideas of cost-effectiveness, resource conservation, practice guidelines, procedure-based care, necessity for and appropriateness of care, continuous quality improvement, etc., from theoretical concepts to guiding principles of clinical practice. Within the at-risk payment environment, the psychology and motivation of clinicians providing care changes significantly. As clinicians move from a fee-for-service mindset of increasing the volume of visits and to "filling all billable hours" to an at-risk cost-effectiveness frame of reference the group's management will need to educate and train staff to adopt and to implement a new approach to service delivery. Yet in spite of such efforts, in the real private practice world of healthcare there will be some clinicians who are not above the temptation to under serve in a capitated or case-rated environment. In like manner, there will be those clinicians who will be tempted and seduced to over serve in the non-at-risk fee for service compensation arrangement. The group's management must address these financially driven provider behaviors and assure that services to the consumer are never compromised. This is that challenge facing managers of any group practice in healthcare.

Of course, those who fund the groups—third-party payers—must be ready to pursue this at-risk payment mechanism. This development is still evolving in behavioral healthcare. A staff compensation arrangement that is consistent with the funding of the group and addresses the expensive issues of payroll taxes and other payroll expenses will be an added challenge for management to implement. The most workable compensation approach in a private practice setting is a combination of base salary and production-based pay for specified contributions to the group's effectiveness and profitability. These staff contributions to the group will need to be clearly specified and made a part of the compensation agreement. In most situations a compensation committee made up of members of the management team and, at times, a representative of the clinical staff is the most effective group for handling this important issue. This is not a simple undertaking. Our own group continues to refine its compensation package along these lines. It is my belief that until capitation and other predictable funding arrangements are in place for group practices, compensation will remain uncertain for managers to some degree. The uncertainty in this critical area needs to be reduced to achieve a more effective approach to clinical staff management.

Support Staff

Support staff refers to those personnel traditionally called office staff, clerical staff, and/or customer service staff. Their roles today are more complex than before as a result of increases in accountability procedures, computerization, and other technological advances in business operations. Managers of a private practice must oversee with diligence their support staff's interaction with customers at all levels (consumers, third-party payers, EAP vendors, utilization review (UR) companies). These customer contacts can directly and indirectly affect a practice's reputation and ultimately the revenues of the practice. One primary role for support staff is to process calls from plan participants of MBHOs, other third-party payers, capitated enrollees, and from direct-pay consumers. These are sensitive calls to handle. Support staff will require instruction and training in both registering referrals for care, asking questions appropriately, and answering questions accurately. They also need to know when to seek assistance from a supervisor when the occasion arises. In addition, support staff needs to know when to transfer the telephone calls directly to clinicians for handling callers with sensitive clinical problems and/or those in need of crisis intervention.

Support staff is, almost invariably, the first line of contact with the practice's various customers or potential customers. Procedurally, support staff will require training for communication skills and ongoing supervision which will allow the sentinel effect to operate without being overbearing. Support staff must be well informed about the identity of key persons in the third-party payer customer base. Staff must have a clear description of procedural issues related to each customer so that uncertainty is kept at a minimum. This is a key issue to the group's success.

Staff Policies and Procedures

Central to the functioning of staff at all levels of a group practice is the mechanism that specifies the lines of authority and each staff member's responsibilities. The policies and procedures by which staff members are required to fulfill their respective roles need to be communicated to the staff in several ways. Written communications in the form of timely memoranda and notices keep staff alert and informed about recent modifications in the group's operation. Staff meetings and supervisory sessions clarifying job functions, lines of authority, and administrative procedures are essential. Management's best approach to reducing uncertainty about policies and procedures is "ensuring that members of groups are certain about what is expected in light of new technology and that leaders are matched with the needs and characteristics of the group" (Schuler et al., 1987, p. 94).

Regarding written manuals or documents explaining personnel policies and procedures, it is recommended that legal consultation be obtained. Managers will find that there are some issues in this area that should be clearly listed, whereas others are better left undefined. This is a situation that emerges from the nature of business and its participants.

Team Building

Coordinating each staff component to establish an organized system of care is the key to an efficient behavioral private practice. Achieving the proverbial "well-oiled machine" requires that the management team exhibit both inspiring leadership and effective management procedures.

Developing a sense of belonging to a team or as is often said a "family" within the group practice will raise the probability of effectiveness in staff performance. Experiencing a sense of "social support" within the group practice "mitigates against the effects of role ambiguity, role conflict, future ambiguity and role overload" according to research findings (Schuler et al., 1987, p. 95).

On an individual basis, management procedures that detect early on both underload and overload for staff are important for controlling staff problems and maintaining teamwork. Both underload and overload are risk factors in the group, as "there appears to be several needs not satisfied by either underload or overload conditions, particularly challenge, meaningfulness and self control" (Schuler et al., 1987, p. 96). Effective administrative efforts designed to address these conditions will serve the individual staff members and the organizational team very well.

Final Note on Staff Management

Managers who operate a group practice know the challenge of trying to change an industry culture that has for so long encouraged a solo, independent, and non-teamwork practice environment. The challenge in managing private practice staff today is nicely captured in the following statement: "managers who are sensitive to and can manipulate the values, rituals and heroes of the culture will have the best chance of coping (with) technostress" (Sethi et al., 1987, p. 206). I believe that this comment is quite fitting to the challenge of managing staff in the current behavioral healthcare marketplace.

Marketing Strategies

With a service-product line in place and a staff prepared to deliver those commodities to the customer community, managers can move to marketing strategies. Getting the group's product line to the customers is contingent on several procedural activities.

Marketing for Payers Not Patients

In today's marketplace the emphasis in marketing behavioral healthcare service-products must be on increasing the number of third-party customers rather than increasing one's patient caseload (Edley, 1996, p. 187). Although there is still some benefit in pursuing consumer-patients as sources of direct revenue this population is surely decreasing. The recently introduced, "medical savings account" experiment will be interesting in this regard (News and Trends, 1997, p. 13). Yet, patients remain our most important customers in terms of service delivery, clinical outcomes, and satisfaction.

Knowing Your Customers

There are a number of customers who directly or indirectly affect a practice's revenues. Among them are patients, third-party payers including MBHOs, HMOs, PPOs, self-insured employers and labor unions, some EAPs, and utilization review (UR) vendors (Strosahl, 1994, pp. 13–14). These and others are potential sources of increases and/or decreases in the income levels of the practice.

Becoming knowledgeable about what each customer needs is the key marketing issue. For example, consumer-related research reveals that consumers want briefer treatment than clinicians expect, for example, from 5 to 15 sessions (Pekarik, 1993, p. 417). Also, this research shows that patients "expect a high level of direct advice, concrete problem definition, problem solving and therapist activity" (Pekarik, 1993, p. 416). With this information in mind, marketing material needs to reflect clearly an offering of service-products that address brief, solution-focused care. That is what the consumer is asking for in most outpatient situations.

The MBHO, HMO, and PPO markets are the most visible and obvious to managers of group practices. To maintain a competitive position with these entities, groups will need to present themselves as organized, accountable, and, if possible, integrated, as an IDS. The practice must demonstrate 24-hour, 7 days a week coverage and an ability to respond quickly to referrals and especially to crises and emergencies. A quality assurance (QA) plan is often required by most third-party payer entities. Browning (1996) and Browning and Browning (1996) have presented several helpful recommendations, including sample letters and dialogue, which are helpful to managers in their marketing approaches to these third-party payers.

Another important emerging market is the small to moderate size self-insured employer and labor union welfare fund. It is my observation that this is the most fruitful market for group practice managers to pursue. The larger employers (the Fortune 1000 plus) will be more easily serviced for the foreseeable future by the larger MBHOs, HMOs, and PPOs which can address large geographic areas and multistate accounts. This may change in the future. For now, I recommend that group practices market their service-products to the self-insureds in more local areas. Many of these employers and union welfare funds are better prepared now than they were a few years ago to negotiate direct contracting arrangements with provider-driven systems. In the past, and in some situations even now, the small third-party payers are skeptical about contracting directly with provider-owned systems of care, seeing them as "the fox watching the hen house." I am better received when introduced without the "Dr." before my name in marketing to these smaller third-party payers. There are times when using a nonclinician marketer *up front* is the most advantageous approach.

Cost Offset

That the provision of appropriate behavioral services (mental health, substance abuse, and EAP) has the power to lower medical and labor-related costs is well established (Burns, 1996; Cummings, 1996b, p. 23; Glazer, 1993; Jones & Vischi, 1979; Mastrich & Beidel, 1985; McDonell Douglas Corporation & Alexander Consulting Group, 1989; Sipkoff, 1995). This fact should be a core message in the marketing materials and in the approach used by managers of a practice. However, this message is not as convincingly conveyed as one might expect. Being persuasive by using the medical–labor cost offset reality has not been easy in my experience. The explanation for this apparent marketing paradox is "overdetermined" with at least two factors: 1) behavioral healthcare's current place and lack of political power vis-à-vis the larger healthcare marketplace (Barlow, 1994;

Sobell, 1996), and 2) most self-insured employers' concern about immediate results and the current pricing of services. Still, the cost offset phenomenon is the
behavioral manager's single most important marketing message. Today, third-party payers and employers are more receptive than before to this message: They
should be presented at some point in the marketing effort with cost offset data to
show long-term savings. A corollary is that managers, as marketers, should negotiate when possible a long-term contract of at least 3 to 5 years to monitor cost offset outcomes on the medical–surgical side of the benefit plan claims experience.
This will be an interesting challenge in healthcare.

There certainly are other important marketing issues such as preparation of
marketing materials which must be considered by management. I will, however,
leave that topic to others for the moment and I will move onto the next management skills area.

Utilization Management

Managers of a private behavioral healthcare practice know the "hassle factor"
inherent in externally conducted utilization review (UR) procedures. This UR
process is the most widely used and best known of the utilization management
(UM) procedures. These UR procedures and other UM procedures are mechanisms
for resource conservation that managers of a practice must understand and eventually assume when their practice takes on at-risk funding, for example, capitation.

Brief Overview of UM

There is no area of the managed healthcare system that elevates the arousal
level of clinicians more than the area of UM (see Brown, 1994). The procedures
that constitute UM impact directly and indirectly the behavior and the income of
providers of care. Utilization management in its several forms is usually the target
of the criticism most often expressed about unreasonable denials of coverage for
care. It is the term that encompasses the array of procedures that attempts to control utilization of services and healthcare resources in general, from both sides of
the service delivery equation—the provider (supply) side and the consumer (demand) side.

Broadly defined, UM includes procedures such as benefit plan designing,
which specifies consumer deductible and out-of-pocket co-pays, provider network
development, gatekeeping, capitation funding, case management, discharge planning, prevention, demand management services, disease management, and UR
functions. These procedural practices are designed to accomplish one complex
mission—to ensure that cost-effective care is provided to persons in need of care
and that *unnecessary* and *inappropriate* care is eliminated or, at least, kept to a
minimum.

Most providers of care are familiar with UM in its most well-known form, that
is, UR procedures. Utilization review procedures are used by entities that operate
according to the managed care approach to determine the *necessity* for treatment
and the *appropriateness* of the care recommended or already rendered by a clini-

cian. These procedures influence the clinical decisions of providers. The expectations of reviewers who conduct UR is that a sentinel effect will prevail and influence providers to render only necessary care and to provide only appropriate procedures, that is, EVPs, at some level of empirical certainty.

The following procedures are used by UR staff.

- Types of Reviews:
  - —Precertification review (certification of care determined before service delivery)
  - —Concurrent certification review (certification determined during the episode of care)
  - —Retrospective certification review (certification determined after services are rendered)
- Resolving Denials of Certification
  - —Appeals procedure
  - —Grievance procedure
- Recertification Procedures

The literature in this area sometimes refers to *authorization for services,* which is often used synonymously with *certification.* I prefer and recommend the term certification when applied to the outcome of a review process. Certification establishes a level of *certainty* regarding the necessity for and appropriateness of care. Authorization may follow, but the process is one of establishing a level of certainty, and as such I recommend the use of certification.

Those who conduct UR have a set of criteria which is used as "decision support" information for making their certifications of necessity and appropriateness. Decision support is usually in the form of diagnostic criteria, level of care criteria, or existing practice guidelines or EVPs. These clinical criteria are used to evaluate the necessity for care, the appropriateness of levels of care, and the appropriateness of the procedures planned for the disorder presented.

It is important for managers of a private practice to be aware of what is being certified and/or authorized. Professionals in UR believe that what is being certified is the necessity for care, that is, that necessity for care has been established according to some criteria. Similarly, a UR determination of appropriateness of the care which is planned or already delivered is certified according to accepted criteria. There is still some uncertainty in the field about whether these procedures constitute or are synonymous with authorization or denial of *payment* for services. The courts have addressed this issue in a few cases and case law has yet to resolve this debate. As capitation funding increases in scope and providers assume the UR functions internally to manage utilization, the issue of outcome, that is, to certify or deny certification of care or to authorize or deny payment for care, becomes the direct responsibility of the provider system and its staff, not some external UR vendor. This is revolutionary. Managers of a private practice will need to understand what it takes to determine what is necessary and appropriate in order to conserve resources and yet provide quality care to the patient.

Necessity for and Appropriateness of Treatment Determinations—A Brief Procedural Overview

Determination of the necessity for treatment and of the appropriateness of treatment are essential procedural activities for those responsible for overseeing the consumption of healthcare resources. Although third-party payers may conduct these determinations directly, they often delegate this UR activity to others who specialize in this area. Managers of a private practice that is funded by at-risk financial arrangements (capitation, etc.) will be included in the ranks of the third-party payer community. As such, they will assume this UR activity themselves and take responsibility for necessity for treatment and appropriateness of treatment determinations with their own staffs and networks.

To clarify the procedures used to make these determinations, I outline the essential ingredients of the necessity and appropriateness processes in Table 2 (necessity) and Table 3 (appropriateness). First, these two processes of determination are complex (G. V. Gray & Glazer, 1995). Those who are not familiar with the UR process as conducted by MBHOs often assume that these treatment certification decisions are made without much reflection and/or clinical acumen. This is certainly not true in the overwhelming number of MBHOs, as their decisions are made by clinically experienced staff. This is, and certainly should be, the case for provider-driven, capitated groups as well. An examination of the tables reveals the complexity of the decision process.

Table 2 presents the evaluation steps required to determine the necessity for treatment. One or more diagnoses are established, impairment of the person's functioning and quality of life is determined, and a level of severity of illness (SI) or disorder is assigned. The key issue is to determine the level of impairment and the level of distress experienced by the person in need of treatment.

There is an infinite number of scenarios that require a determination of ne-

---

TABLE 2 Necessity-for-Treatment Determination Process in Behavioral Healthcare[a]

Objective: Evaluation of information presented established that the clinical condition presented meets all three of the criteria below:

1. **Diagnostic criteria** of the current DSM or ICD are present

2. **Impairment** of functioning and/or quality of life are observable and measurable
   Severity of illness (SI) determination, or the degree of functioning impairment and/or dangerousness

3. **Clinical treatment** is required to achieve desired change as opposed to nonclinical intervention according to the known scientific literature

   Outcome
   A. Necessity supported (certification made)
   B. Necessity not supported (certification denied)

---

[a]Source: Lifecare Management Systems, Inc., Hope, New Jersey, 1996.

cessity for care. In my experience, a small but not insignificant number of them do not meet the necessity for treatment requirements. Again, at the risk of oversimplification, I allude to cases which require interventions other than clinical interventions (e.g., judicial, legal, educational, general medical, financial, etc.). Making the critical distinction between presenting problems that require clinical treatment and those that do not (as opposed to other, nonclinical interventions) is often a very thorny process. The outcome of the necessity determination will specify that clinical treatment is required or that necessity for treatment is not supported. Providers of clinical treatment may appeal denials and so may plan participants. Having established necessity, appropriateness of treatment must be determined.

Table 3 presents the steps required to establish the appropriateness of the treatment planned or already rendered (subject to retrospective review). The complex decision process must complete all seven of the evaluation steps and answer these questions:

> What level of care (1), for how long (2), employing which modalities (3), for what periods of time (4), with what frequency (5), using which clinical procedures will yield an intensity of service (IS) which matches the patient's severity of illness (SI) so that there is a reasonable probability of achieving the desired clinical outcome?

I doubt that most providers of care in private practice ever ask these questions or answer them in the manner in which most MBHO UR staffs do on a daily basis. However, when *providers* assume the UR function they will, in fact, routinely ask and answer these questions.

Each step in the process evaluates a component of the treatment plan which contributes to IS determination. *Intensity of Service* is an expression of resource consumption resulting from the delivery of healthcare services. This is an important definition to understand. The assessment and determination of IS is directly related to the management of both staff and financial resources dedicated to the delivery of care and must be conducted astutely.

The UR staff conducting step 1 - level of care determinations use decision support tools called level of care criteria or guidelines. These criteria are often established by the organization itself on the basis of existing research (e.g., comparing the relative efficacy of outpatient vs. inpatient care for suicidal patients or substance abusers). The "Patient Placement Criteria" used to determine the appropriate level of care for patients presenting with substance abuse were developed by members of the American Society of Addiction Medicine (Hoffman, Halikas, Mee-Lee, & Weedman, 1991). This is standard procedure among MBHOs. Managers whose behavioral private practice conducts such determinations should take advantage of such resources. All of the MBHOs with which I am familiar have developed and used level-of-care placement criteria for level of care determinations in mental health and substance abuse cases. Some MBHOs may have their criteria for sale, and others provide them to network providers.

TABLE 3 Appropriateness-of-Treatment Determination Process in Behavioral Healthcare[a]

Objective: Evaluation of the clinical treatment plan establishes reasonable probability that the treatment provided will *benefit* the patient, i.e., will result in the change required to *improve* functioning and quality of life.

The components of the treatment plan below are evaluated for appropriateness:

1. **Level of care:** What is the treatment setting or combination of settings?
   a. Inpatient or rehabilitation facility
   b. Partial hospitalization
   c. Intensive outpatient
   d. Outpatient
   e. Home care
Refer to internal level of care criteria/guidelines or other criteria/guidelines.

2. **Length of stay (LOS):** Treatment (specify)
   a. Number of days for a, b, c, above
   b. Number of weeks or months for d, above

3. **Duration of treatment unit** (billable episode, i.e., inpatient day, CPT code, etc.)
   a. 24 hours (per diem)
   b. Full day, 6–8 hours
   c. Half day, 3–4 hours
   d. 1.5–2 hours
   e. 1 hour
   f. 0.5 hour
   g. Other

4. **Frequency of treatment** (specify)
   a. 1–7 times per week
   b. 1–31 times per month
   c. Number of times per year
   d. Other

5. **Modalities of treatment:** Specify modality or combination of modalities
   a. Individual
   b. Couples
   c. Family
   d. Group
   e. Other

6. **Clinical Procedures:** Specify empirically validated and/or consensus-based procedures used during modalities of treatment for the patient. Refer to internal practice guidelines and/or research literature for other available clinical guidelines.

7. **Intensity of Service (IS) Determination** (IS, the selected combination of numbers 1 through 6 above)

Outcome
   a. Appropriateness certified
   b. Appropriateness certification denied

[a]Source: Lifecare Management Systems, Inc., Hope, New Jersey, 1996.

Step 6 addresses practice guidelines and EVPs and requires access to the latest developments in outcomes research data in behavioral healthcare. Keeping up with recent developments in outcomes research is essential in this UM area.

The basic model that most MBHOs follow and which managers of a private practice will want to assimilate is the Severity of Illness (SI) Intensity of Service (IS) paradigm borrowed from physical medicine (see Jacobs & Lamprey, 1991). The outcome of establishing the necessity for treatment and the appropriateness of treatment is a determination of the necessity for treatment expressed as the SI and a determination of the appropriateness of the treatment plan expressed as IS. The final step in the determination process is expressed as SI matches IS.

I know of no reports on the quantification of this procedure. Our own company initiated a scaling procedure some time ago but we did not have the time or capital resources to pursue the effort to completion. This is another area ripe for research. There are data and information collection forms, usually called treatment review forms or outpatient treatment review (OTR) forms, that are used to conduct UR determinations. Managers need to develop these information-capturing instruments for their own internal UR activities.

Figures 1 and 2 are sample forms addressing the collection of necessity-for-treatment data (Fig. 1) and the collection of appropriateness data (Fig. 2). Figure 1 guides the capturing of data required in Table 2 to establish necessity for treatment. Similarly, Figure 2 guides data collection to meet the criteria presented in Table 3 to establish the appropriateness of the treatment plan proposed. The process is an exercise of making a fit between the clinical condition of the patient as presented by the clinician and the treatment plan as proposed by the clinician. The ideal treatment review procedure involves a cooperative and collegial process in which the clinician and UR staff work as a team on behalf of the patient to provide the best care possible. In my experience, this is the usual scenario. However, there are many occasions when the process is not so ideal. From a management perspective, ensuring that staff is well versed in conducting reviews is indispensable. Staff must be familiar with the following: using the diagnostic and statistical manual (DSM) five axes correctly, evaluating functional impairment, writing clear treatment goals, and keeping up with current research related to treatment outcomes and EVPs. The forms presented in Figures 1 and 2 will be helpful in this staff training activity.

The UR process also includes criteria to determine *continuation of treatment, termination of treatment,* and *discharge from treatment.* I will not describe these procedures here. I end by suggesting that the entire UM domain is a management skill area that all private practice managers should master, especially when they are recipients of at-risk funding arrangements.

Financial Management

A Team Approach

The management of a practice's income and expenses is a skill area that is challenging, often unfamiliar, and occasionally anxiety provoking. The complex-

Necessity Determination Form

Date_____Date of 1st Visit or Admission_____Total # Visits or Days To Date_____
Provider_____Phone (____)
Patient _____Gender_____Age _____
SS# _____Payer _____

I.   Diagnoses: BE SURE TO EVALUATE PRESENCE OF SUBSTANCE ABUSE
Axis I: 1.   DSM#_____ Disorder _____
                2.   DSM#_____ Disorder _____
                3.   DSM#_____ Disorder _____

Axis II: 1.   DSM#_____ Disorder _____
                2.   DSM#_____ Disorder _____

Axis III: (PHYSICAL DISORDERS including risk of seizures, DT's etc. requiring intervention)
                1.   Disorder_____   2. _____

Axis IV: SEVERITY OF PSYCHOSOCIAL STRESSORS (0 TO 6)   Axis V: GAF (1 - 100)
                1. Acute _____ 2. Enduring _____ Specify Stressors= _____1. Current _____ 2. Past_____

II.   CHECK OFF PRESENCE OF MENTAL STATUS SYMPTOMS CURRENTLY MANIFESTED BY THIS
        PATIENT. IF NONE APPLY CHECK HERE _____
        ☐   Danger to Self   ☐   Perceptual Disorder   ☐   Disorientation (X3)
        ☐   Danger to Others   ☐   Inappropriate Affect   ☐   Impaired Memory
        ☐   Thought Disorder   ☐   Impaired Judgement
        Comment:_____

III.   BRIEFLY DESCRIBE IMPAIRMENT OF FUNCTION IN BEHAVIOR AND RELATIONSHIPS BELOW:
        Family_____

        Work_____

        School_____

        Community_____

IV.   DESCRIBE MOTIVATION FOR TREATMENT. NOTE IMPROVEMENT OR NONIMPROVEMENT IN
        FUNCTIONING DUE TO TREATMENT.
        _____
        _____
        _____

FIGURE I   Necessity Determination Form (source: Lifecare Management Systems, Inc., Hope, New Jersey, 1996).

ity of the procedures and skills required to exercise control effectively over the financial matters of a practice increases with the size and complexity of the practice itself. Yet, this complexity is shrouded in the simplicity of the mission statement for financial management "maximize income and minimize costs." In my experience, a fundamental procedural requirement is to establish an excellent working relationship with a superior accountant. Although this may seem obvious, serious errors in judgment in this area result in significant consequences for managers. The opportunity to discuss financial *management,* and not just "the numbers," with an accountant is an important financial management procedure that I strongly recommend.

In a group practice setting it is wise to involve more than one person to oversee the financial matters. A committee or team approach to budgeting and spend-

Appropriateness Determination Data Form

A.   SERVICE GOALS: (State specific behavioral goals. e.g. Improve Assertiveness, Achieve Sobriety-Abstinence, Achieve Impulse Control, Reduce Anxiety Attacks, Reduce Depression, Improve Marital Communication, Improve Child Management, Etc.)

1. _____
2. _____
3. _____
4. _____
5. _____

B.   MODALITY AND PROCEDURES: (Specify all modalites and procedures proposed including medication. Modality - circle and specify frequency (IP, IOP, individ., family, group) - Freq =
_____

Procedures (e.g. Assertive Training, Cognitive Restructuring, Parenting Training, Detox, Relapse Prevention, Self Help Group, Communication Training, Values Clarification, Positive Self-Talk, Impulse Control, Desensitization, Etc.)

1.   medication:_____   dose:_____ freq:_____
2.   medication:_____   dose:_____ freq:_____

Other procedures: 1. _____
                           2. _____
                           3. _____
                           4. _____
                           5. _____

C.   TO THE PATIENT: Your signing this statement indicates that you agree with the above goals and plan for achieving those goals.

Provider Signs_____   Patient Signs_____
                                                                                      (patient - age 14 and over)

Print Name _____   Signature_____
              (parent or guardian if minor)

SUBMIT COMPLETED FORM BEFORE CERT. ENDS TO: SERVICE REVIEW DEPT, IGP, LLC

Reviewer Comments_____

Reviewer_____ Signs_____ Date _____
            (print name)

FIGURE 2   Appropriateness Determination Data Form (source: Lifecare Management Systems, Inc., Hope, New Jersey, 1996).

ing decisions brings a set of checks and balances to this critical area, ensuring that a "risk management" process is in place.

Managing Income and Expenses

Three areas of financial management are briefly discussed in this section in terms of the procedural skills required in any business setting, but also with an emphasis on skills that are germane to behavioral healthcare. These areas are income management, expense management, and balancing income and expenses. I begin by discussing the fundamental financial issue of predictability.

Predictability of Income and Expense Streams

A key factor in financial management is the "character" of each income stream coming into the practice's financial pool and of those expense or cost streams flowing out of a practice's dollar pool. Reducing uncertainty in these cash flow streams is a significant objective to achieve in any business enterprise. Increasing predictability of incoming and outgoing dollar streams is critical to effective financial management. This is true even for companies with substantial operating reserves, because long-term viability is always vulnerable to cash-flow problems.

Predictability applies to two important variables of cash flow streams: volume and scheduling. These two variables can be described as follows:

1. **Volume:** refers to the amount of dollars flowing in and out of the practice's financial pool. The objective with regard to volume is to stabilize fluctuations in the amount of dollars flowing in and out of the financial pool so that variability in volume is reduced from month to month or even from week to week.

2. **Scheduling:** refers to the timing of the arrival of income and the timing of the outflow of expense payments. Ideally, managers exercise some control over the timing of receipts to the group and the timing of payment of expenses by the group. In this way financial planning is conducted with some sense of certainty.

The more predictable the incoming and outgoing streams are, the more financially viable the group will be. In negotiating payment arrangements with third-party payers, it becomes obvious from this brief discussion that capitation is the direction in which a group practice should move. The more sources of income and the more expense items characterized by a high degree of predictability, the more *certain* the practice's financial management will be, and thus fewer anxieties for the managers.

What is critical here is to remove the *variability* and *uncertainty* from the income and cost streams as much as possible. This essentially means removing as much income as possible from dependency on uncertain service utilization (i.e., patient visits and other direct service) and contingency arrangements and placing income and cost items in more predictable and fixed streams. I suspect that aside from greed, some of the psychology behind fraudulent billing practices, nicely presented by Kovacs (1987), is explained by the variability and uncertainty of income and cost streams with which providers have had to struggle. I believe that increasing certainty in financial management through arrangements such as capitation reduces the probability of such fraudulent activities.

Income Management

Diversification of Income Streams. The maximization of income to the group is the central objective in the management of income. One of the first procedural issues to address is *diversification of income streams* into the group. "Putting all your eggs in one basket" is very risky regarding sources of income. The objective is to multiply the practice's sources of revenue so that it is not dependent on any one major source of income which could dry up "over night" and threaten the practice's viability. It does happen. Allow me to give an elementary illustration. Assume that a practice has an annual income of $300,000. There is more security in having that income supplied by more than one income source, for example, a combination of five or more income sources, than by one source. Rather than depend on any one source for either all income or for a significant percentage of a practice's income it is safer to have the following income breakdown: $100,000 from Source I, $40,000 from Source II, $80,000 from Source III, $50,000 from Source IV, and $30,00 from Source V. As elementary as this depiction may appear I know of two real business situations where diversification of income was not achieved and serious damage resulted from the rapid loss of revenue to the practices. Marketing strategies designed to ensure that this diversification is established are essential. Recall the advice of Edley (1996, p. 187): increase payers not patients by your marketing efforts.

Categories of Income.   Table 4 presents a line-item layout of income sources which I believe managers will find helpful. I call attention to the listing of income sources in Table 4 according to the categories: A. Fixed and B. Variable. Given this breakdown, the strategy for management to pursue is to arrange for as many income streams to be placed in the Fixed category as possible. The fewer the sources of income in the Variable category, the more certainty there is during financial management of income. There is no better way to establish this condition of high financial certainty, concerning income, then to nail down as many capitated funding arrangements as possible. That is the strategy to pursue when negotiating with payers. Remember, many payers may not be ready to negotiate fully at risk funding arrangements. As a result, negotiations should secure as certain a funding arrangement as possible so that budgeting can be achieved with some level of efficiency.

Types of Income Funding Arrangements to Negotiate.   Table 5 presents several types of funding arrangements that are available from third-party payers and that managers of a group practice may wish to pursue and negotiate. The eight categories of funding arrangements may not be exhaustive but they cover most classes of payment arrangements from payers in return for the delivery of service-products in behavioral healthcare.

TABLE 4   Line Item Budget: Income Sources and Categories for IGP, LLC

			From:_____	To:_____
Categories: Fixed and Variable				
Fixed Income Sources:	Monthly Amt	%	Yearly Amt	%
1.				
2.				
3.				
4.				
5.				
Total Fixed Income				
Variable Income Sources	Monthly Amt	%	Yearly Amt	%
1.				
2.				
3.				
4.				
5.				
Total Variable Income				
TOTAL INCOME				

TABLE 5   Funding Arrangements in the Managed Healthcare System

1. Capitation—full risk
2. Subcapitation—risk sharing
3. Administrative fee pm pm (ASO)
4. Case rate
5. Fee for service
6. Administrative add-on—cost plus
7. Percent of savings
8. Combinations of the above

Categories 1 through 3 are funding arrangements with income streams that have the highest probability of meeting the characteristics of high stability, predictability, and reliability—making budget management a much more certain process than the other categories. Category 3 (administrative add-on and cost plus) is interesting in that it is a kind of borderline arrangement concerning variability. Payment to the vendor may be highly certain when paid as a fixed pmpm (per member per month) fee or it may be a percentage of activity (i.e., number of claims processed and paid, etc.). It may also be a combination of these payment mechanisms. The administrative fees paid to a group or in more cases to MBHOs or to third-party administrators (TPAs) are usually for services called ASO (administrative service only). This is a lower risk-bearing arrangement in which the pmpm is paid for administrative services but the provider of them is not at risk for clinical services payment. There is no direct tie between clinical services used or not used and the amount paid by the payers to the vendor of the ASO product. In ASO arrangements the vendor is not at risk for paying for care.

The income arrangements from categories 4 through 8 are quite variable and in most situations they are tied to the level of utilization of care. That means income depends on referrals to the group practice and the volume of sessions rendered. Taken to the extreme, this means no referrals no income. Clearly, as managers move their income streams and funding arrangements to the top of the list they are better able to manage their practice's finances. I hope this abbreviated version of income management gives some idea of the issues managers face in executing their financial management skills regarding income to their practice.

Expense Management—Reducing Uncertainty in Cost Management

Table 6 presents a typical expense line-item budget or chart of accounts. This, and the income line items, should be arranged with the consultation of the group's accountant or financial advisor if it has one. The central procedural issue in managing expenses is to stabilize and ultimately reduce costs to a minimum. This is the financial reality whether or not a practice is capitated. Certainly in a capitated environment this is indispensable. As Cummings (1996b) states, "without the ability to predict costs there can be no determination of the capitation rate for which

TABLE 6   Operating Expenses for IGP, LLC

Expense	Category	Monthly Amt %	Yearly Amt %
1. Accounting	F[a]		
2. Advertising	F		
3. Auto expense	V		
4. Bank charges	F		
5. Board of directors	F		
6. Cleaning service	F		
7. Computer hardware	V		
8. Computer software	V		
9. Conferences/meetings	V		
10. Consultants	F		
11. Delivery service	V		
12. Depreciation	F		
13. Dues for memberships	F		
14. Entertainment	V		
15. Insurance			
a. Business owners	F		
b. Workers compensation	F		
c. Health insurance	F		
d. LTD	F		
e. Income protection	F		
16. Leasing: Office equipment			
a. Computers	F		
b. Photocopier	F		
17. Legal	V		
18. Loan payment	F		
19. Maintenance: Equipment	V		
20. Marketing	F		
21. Network development	V		
22. Office equipment	V		
23. Office supplies	V		
24. Payroll	FV		
25. Payroll taxes (FICA, UD, SS)	F		
26. Postage	V		
27. Printing	V		
28. Quality improvement	F		
29. Rent			
a. Office 1	F		
b. Office 2	F		
c. Office 3	V		
30. Repairs	V		
31. Retirement plan	F		
32. Staff credentialing	V		
33. Staff training	V		
34. Subscriptions	F		

(continues)

TABLE 6 *(continued)*

Expense	Category	Monthly Amt %	Yearly Amt %
35. Telephone			
a. 800 number	V		
b. AT&T	V		
c. Equipment and installation	V		
36. Travel	V		
37. Utilities			
a. Gas & electric	V		
b. Heat	V		
Total expenses			

*^a*Categories: F, fixed expenses; V, Variable expenses.

the practitioner will assume the risk to perform all of the services" (p. 25). Yet, even in noncapitated funding arrangements cost control is just as important, primarily because income and expenses are so variable and, at times, volatile. Again, expense lines that are fixed and meet the characteristics of high stability, predictability, and reliability are managed with more certainty than ones that are highly variable.

Table 6 presents two categories of expenses: A. Fixed and B. Variable. One of the strategies to follow for cost control and reduction is to move as many expense line items into the Fixed category. This improves planning and projection of financial activity by removing much uncertainty from the financial management process. I have indicated next to each line item an F for fixed expenses and a V for variable ones. The selection for line items is purely for illustration purposes; I am sure the line items and their designations as fixed or variable will vary with each practice's unique circumstances. The critical issue is to be able to monitor expense activity on, at least, a month-to-month basis and to adjust spending as needs dictate. The line-item budget approach as presented here is one method to achieve both monitoring and management of costs in a direct and relatively simple manner.

Balancing Income and Expenses

The bottom line objective in financial management is to ensure that income matches expenses as a minimum, and preferably that income exceeds expenses— a "no brainer" in theory. One approach to achieving this mission is to determine the practice's "hour of operation" (HO) related to both income and costs. Again, I will oversimplify the procedures in the example given here. Accept that the HO is defined as each hour that is available to provide the customer-base components of the service-product line of the practice. Now this definition of the HO can be approached from the income or from the cost side. From the income analysis side,

HO reflects the income generated when the HO is paid for on a fee-for-service basis, when income is tied to the direct delivery of a service to a paying customer. When the HO is approached from the cost analysis side, it reflects the costs incurred by the organization when it provides a service. In the real marketplace most practices experience the HO as a combination of income producing and cost incurring. As more income is subsumed under at-risk, capitation arrangements, the HO takes on a predominately cost-related dynamic within the capitated group practice—the practice incurs an expense when it delivers a service.

A little simple arithmetic presented in Table 7 may clarify this approach. Table 7 presents six steps to address the match between income and costs in a capitated or noncapitated practice. After total yearly and monthly income and expenses are calculated, the number of HOs available within the practice during a given period of operation, for example, a month, are determined (step 3). By following each step, the matching of income to cost is achieved for the period under consideration. The objective is to determine whether income exceeds, matches, or is less than total costs for the period. Of course, I have arranged the example to yield a positive cash flow, that is, income exceeds expenses. The power of positive thinking can be comforting—but it is never quite enough in the real business world.

This simplified analysis illustrates the value of knowing clearly the practice's income and costs per HO per month. Recall, also, that the number of staff in the table represents all staff: management, clinical, and support staff as well. Labor costs will be the largest expense line items in the practice; a fact that must be handled astute-

TABLE 7   Matching Income to Cost in a Group Practice for One Month of Operation Using Hour of Operation (HO) Analysis

Steps

1. Calculate monthly income					
Total annual income (all sources)	=	$360,000	÷	12 mo =	$30,000/mo
2. Calculate monthly expenses					
Total annual expenses (all line items) =		$345,000	÷	12 mo =	$28,750/mo
3. Calculate income amount per HO					
per month					
a. Full-time equivalent (FTE) HO/mo					
10 staff × 30 hrs staff	=	300 hrs/wk	×	4 wks =	1200 HO/mo
b. $30,000 ÷ 1200	=	$25/HO/mo			
4. Calculate cost per HO per month					
a. FTE HO/mo	=	1200/mo and costs		=	$28,750/mo
b. $28,750 ÷ 1200	=	$23.958/HO/mo			
5. Calculate difference between					
income HO and cost HO	=	$25.00 − $23.958		=	$1.042/HO/mo
6. Difference between income					
HO − cost HO	=	$1.042 × 1200		=	+$1250.4/mo[a]

[a]Decimal rounding correction.

ly. The obvious strategy is to reduce costs in every line item. However, staff costs seem an obvious cost item to reduce to stem the flow of dollars from the practice's financial pool. Labor costs are the largest items and the ones most amenable to trimming in terms of the numbers of staff and/or the amounts of compensation.

This brief coverage only scratches the surface of this subject. Understanding and negotiating capitated and the other funding arrangements will require more space then is allocated here. I hope the presentation in this section gives at least a snapshot of the management activities and responsibilities that are under the rubric of financial management.

Nonclinical Administrative Activities within a Behavioral Group Practice

There is a wide range of administrative activities that are considered to be "nonclinical" because they do not require a clinical license to perform. The activities covered in this section have not yet been presented, therefore. I will briefly cover some core issues related to three areas of nonclinical administrative skills: a) nonclinical management of the episode of care, b) other nonclinical administrative responsibilities, and c) development of a management service organization (MSO) for the group practice.

Nonclinical Management of the Episode of Care

There are many steps to be completed in addressing the nonclinical management of the episode of care. The process begins with the provider group's contractual relationship with third-party payers and their requirements for the delivery of care. A practice's competitive edge depends on its ability to respond to each request for service in a coordinated, accountable, and timely manner. Figure 3 presents the series of nonclinical steps that are involved in the process of providing care to a customer. It lays out 28 essential, nonclinical steps. The managed-care approach has introduced a number of steps not required in the less organized and much less accountable fee-for-service environment. An examination of the steps in Figure 3 reveals the need to work as a team player with the managed care organization (MCO) or payer responsible for managing each case and with the consumer in gathering the information needed to deliver services effectively. The entire process requires training of staff regarding appropriate procedures, a coordination of procedures designed to ensure a seamless continuity of care, and a continuous quality improvement (CQI) approach throughout. A support staff well trained to take a strong *customer service approach* is indispensable. Implementing and maintaining this flow of activity in an effective manner many times a day is a challenge for managers and staff. The steps presented in Figure 3 indicate the need to work closely with the MCO–payer. In a capitated arrangement the MCO–payer will be, in fact, the practice itself when treating many if not most of its consumer–patients. As such, the UR functions (certification, etc.) are conducted internally in most capitation arrangements. The practice is then the MBHO.

If Figure 3 is taken as a guideline or protocol for the nonclinical management of each episode of care, one gets a sense for the team work and the coordination

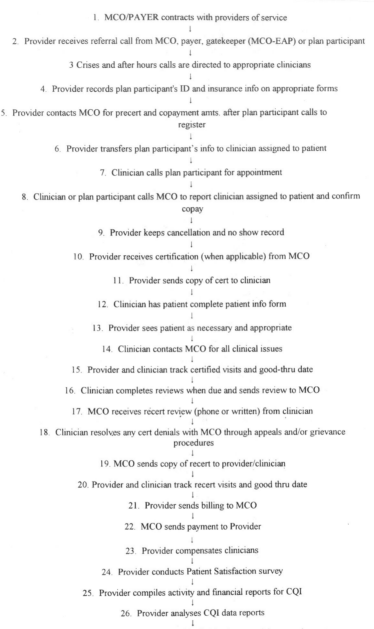

1. MCO/PAYER contracts with providers of service
↓
2. Provider receives referral call from MCO, payer, gatekeeper (MCO-EAP) or plan participant
↓
3 Crises and after hours calls are directed to appropriate clinicians
↓
4. Provider records plan participant's ID and insurance info on appropriate forms
↓
5. Provider contacts MCO for precert and copayment amts. after plan participant calls to register
↓
6. Provider transfers plan participant's info to clinician assigned to patient
↓
7. Clinician calls plan participant for appointment
↓
8. Clinician or plan participant calls MCO to report clinician assigned to patient and confirm copay
↓
9. Provider keeps cancellation and no show record
↓
10. Provider receives certification (when applicable) from MCO
↓
11. Provider sends copy of cert to clinician
↓
12. Clinician has patient complete patient info form
↓
13. Provider sees patient as necessary and appropriate
↓
14. Clinician contacts MCO for all clinical issues
↓
15. Provider and clinician track certified visits and good-thru date
↓
16. Clinician completes reviews when due and sends review to MCO
↓
17. MCO receives recert review (phone or written) from clinician
↓
18. Clinician resolves any cert denials with MCO through appeals and/or grievance procedures
↓
19. MCO sends copy of recert to provider/clinician
↓
20. Provider and clinician track recert visits and good thru date
↓
21. Provider sends billing to MCO
↓
22. MCO sends payment to Provider
↓
23. Provider compensates clinicians
↓
24. Provider conducts Patient Satisfaction survey
↓
25. Provider compiles activity and financial reports for CQI
↓
26. Provider analyses CQI data reports
↓
27. Provider shares CQI findings with clinician in supervision, meetings, etc.
↓
28. Provider implements system improvement changes based on CQI findings

FIGURE 3   Administrative steps in managing an episode of care within a provider group (source: Metrix MSO, Inc., Hope, New Jersey, 1996).

inherent in the managed-care approach to service delivery. Picture for a moment that the group practice maintains offices at several geographic sites, with several clinicians at each site. The volume of information sent to and received from the sites will require coordinated data-capturing mechanisms and a computerized management information system (MIS) (see Freeman, this volume) capable of handling the volume of administrative information and data. This operation is not for the fainthearted. It is my belief that managers who have assimilated the broad knowledge base of the core premises presented earlier will execute this protocol more effectively with that background. Without such a "cognitive set," elements of the protocol will be experienced as unnecessary and/or superfluous. Managers must be positioned to explain these procedures to their staff persuasively. The information presented in the six core premises provides a knowledge base for such a staff training approach and for supervision of staff.

Other Nonclinical Administrative Activities

There is an array of administrative activities that the management team of a behavioral practice must execute to accomplish its business goals. Although the range of activities covered here may not be exhaustive, it does encompass most business-related activities in most practices. This list of other "nonclinical" activ ities requires a variety of managerial and organizational skills.

- Contract negotiation and management
- Billing to payers—claims submission
- Collection and distribution of payments from customers
- Training of staff for administrative procedures
- Development of data capturing forms and procedures
- Report generation (activity and financial) and analysis
- Accounting and bookkeeping
- Purchasing of supplies and equipment
- Lease management
- Payroll services
- Recruiting and personnel management
- Group development
- Mergers
- Regulatory compliance

This list gives a picture of the broad areas of administrative skills managers must be familiar with, at a minimum. Someone on the management team must be in command of each of these areas. As a group moves from a small local operation to a regional one, and perhaps to a megagroup, business professionals with MBA talent will be an asset and should be considered. Much of this nonclinical activity can be outsourced to vendors. However, the group may be able to assume most of this activity internally or may consider developing its own administrative entity to provide the services to the group practice.

Developing an MSO

The nonclinical activities outlined above are such that they may be provided to a group practice by what has come to be called a management service organization (MSO). I recommend that managers consider this alternative. For a short description of the MSO see Waxman (1994a, 1994b) and Eskin (1995). For more comprehensive coverage see Goldstein (1995a, 1995b). In addition to the administrative services listed above, the MSO may assume responsibilities for the UR, marketing, and quality assurance activities of behavioral healthcare practices. All business activities that do not require a clinical license are eligible for assumption by the MSO.

The advantage in developing an MSO is that the administrative services that the MSO provides for the group are also available as a product line for sale to other providers both solo and in groups. The MSO is set up as a general business corporation which sells its services to the group practice and to other providers as a profit-driven entity. Figures 4 and 5 present the relationship between the integrated group practice (IGP) and the MSO. Figure 4 presents the proposed governance relationship between the IGP and the MSO. Figure 5 illustrates the possible ownership and financial issues between the provider–owners of the IGP and the provider–owners of the MSO. The MSO presents to the provider–owners an opportunity to participate in passive income generated through the sale of its service-product line to the IGP and to other customers. The realities of raising capital and inviting outside capital investors to participate in the MSO are topics that cannot be covered here. I refer the readers to Goldstein (1995a, 1995b) for comprehensive coverage of these issues. Also, legal consultation is advised especially around fraud and abuse and antireferral laws (Waxman, 1994a, p. 11). The business aspects of behavioral healthcare are clearly highlighted in the area of the nonclinical administrative activities of the practice. The MSO is one entity that managers of a practice might explore in this regard.

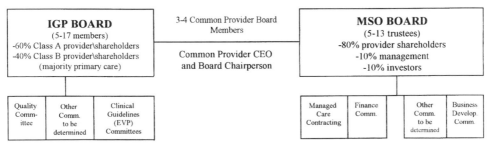

FIGURE 4   Provider equity alliance: IGP and MSO governance (adapted from Goldstein, 1995b; source: Medical Alliances, Inc., 1995).

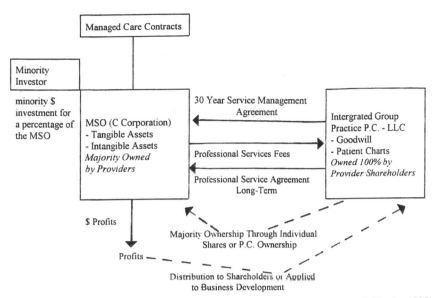

FIGURE 5 Provider equity alliance ownership and flow of funds (adapted from Goldstein, 1995b; source. Medical Alliances, Inc., 1995).

Quality Improvement Management and Outcomes Management

Quality improvement (QI) is an outgrowth of the managed-care approach that is characterized by organization and accountability. There are a number of ways to label the QI process: continuous quality improvement (CQI), quality assurance (QA), and total quality management (TQM). I am not sure there are differences between these labels but they all carry with them a similar message, that is, improving procedures, processes, and outcomes is a continuous exercise for those in healthcare intending to remain competitive.

I have placed QI and outcome management (OM) under the same topical heading because I believe that QI and OM are intertwined. As one observer states, "the goal of QI is to create an improved product or, in medicine, an improved outcome" (Silko, 1996, p. 60). Interestingly, Silko offers a warning that improving a process in healthcare delivery does not guarantee an improved outcome; a wise counsel. Nevertheless, QI and OM are tied together and should be coordinated efforts.

Managers of a practice who intend to remain competitive participants in the current and future marketplace must address QI and OM in a planned and well-co-ordinated manner. Involvement of all staff in the practice is essential. Again, a constant customer-service attitude is strongly recommended in this regard. As Bagley (1994) suggests, "The only requirement for perpetual improvement is an understanding of the customers' expectations and what it takes to exceed them" (p. 64). However, the primary motivation driving QI and OM activities should not be financial. Rather, improved patient care should be the driving force behind all QI efforts (Henrey, 1996, p. 57). Profits will follow as a by-product.

Quality improvement and OM are activities that address the need for a risk-management approach to practice management. Magnuson and Glader (1996) discuss the concept of "corporate compliance" in this regard. They state that, "One way to understand corporate compliance is to think of it as mini-government within a company. This jurisdiction spells out its own statutes and makes sure that its employees are trained to observe them and that any violations are detected and corrected" (p. 21). This strategy is a significant QI procedural issue.

Behavioral QI

Behavioral healthcare has recently responded in an organized way to the QI and OM movement to address the demand for quality measures by customers (Edlin, 1996; Theis, Geraty, Panzarino, & Bartlett, 1995; Trabin, 1994). Several initiatives have been undertaken and they are described by Theis et al. (1995) and Edlin (1996). Dr. Tom Trabin, director of the Research Division, Institute for Behavioral Healthcare, describes well the QI movement in behavioral care:

> Because behavioral healthcare has become organized and industrialized with sophisticated information tracking, it is now possible to determine important information about consumer access, quality of care delivered and outcomes. The potential is for systems to use the data to improve services and enhance patient care and for consumer/purchasers to make more informed choices on the basis of quality. (Edlin, 1996, p. 46)

This perspective is the most advantageous one for managers of a practice to adopt. The skills and procedures required to mount the QI systems to actualize improved quality in behavioral healthcare are still being refined. Yet, managers need to make a commitment to keep pace with if not stay ahead of the learning curve in this QI area. Theis et al. (1995) present an initiative to develop "report cards" for behavioral healthcare provider groups and MBHOs. These report card systems would require provider groups to monitor, evaluate, and report their standings on several "performance indicators." Domains, such as access to care, satisfaction with care, quality of care, and the outcomes of services rendered are QI focus areas.

In the current competitive business-oriented healthcare marketplace it is wise to keep in mind that "When selecting a group for capitation and the development of integrated healthcare networks these 'report cards' may have a major influence on the overall healthcare marketplace" (Theis et al., 1995, p. 80).

The National Committee on Quality Assurance (NCQA), based in Washington, D.C., has recently rolled out its accreditation standards for behavioral healthcare organizations (1997). These standards are expected to be "a Good Housekeeping seal of approval" (Edlin, 1996, p. 41) for groups and organizations in the behavioral healthcare competitive marketplace. There are eight sections reported in the NCQA 1997 *Standards for Accreditation of Managed Behavioral Healthcare Organizations* volume:

- Quality Management and Improvement (contains subsections on practice guidelines, QI 5, pp. 47–48)
- Accessibility, Availability, Referral, and Triage
- Utilization Management
- Credentialing and Recredentialing
- Member Rights and Responsibilities
- Preventive Behavioral Healthcare Services
- Clinical Evaluation and Treatment Records

These sections may change somewhat in the final version but their essential substance probably will not. I recommend that managers who intend to stay abreast of developments in the QI area and in other management areas obtain a copy of the standards from NCQA (1-800-839-6487).

Outcome Management

Outcomes management is, like QI, just coming into its own in behavioral healthcare. In a comprehensive review of OM systems Migdail et al. (Migdail, Youngs, & Bengen-Seltzer, 1995) point out that

Despite recent gains in outcomes measures, continuing tensions exist in trying to balance user friendliness with timeliness, manpower needs, and affordability of on-line outcomes systems. Most current systems rely on paper-and-pencil questionnaires which must typically be completed by both patients and clinicians at varying intervals before, during, and after the treatment process. The process creates significant ongoing manpower costs to collect, enter, and analyze data, reduces the timeliness of findings, and creates administratively unwieldy systems. (pp. 3–4)

This is not exactly what managers of a private practice want to buy into. Provider group practices need an OM approach much more congenial to the realities of daily practice. In their discussions of OM as it relates to organized psychology, Weins, Brazil, Fuller, and Solomon (1995) point out that although psychology "has done much work to identify competent practitioners and their specialties" through a variety of oversight procedures and entities it has not done enough to "document effectiveness" of the treatment rendered by those practitioners (p. 46). This reality is also applicable to other behavioral disciplines as well. Weins et al. (1995) present an interesting and, what I believe, is a useable outcomes monitoring system compatible with the daily experience of clinicians and managers in private practice. The *caveat* here is that any outcomes measuring system that is conducted internally by the practitioners designed to measure its own effectiveness is usually suspect. Customers often view the reported results as self-serving when they are positive (Are negative findings ever self-reported in the competitive marketplace?) This OM system is fine for internal QI purposes. However, I would recommend that outcomes be evaluated and reported by an external entity to protect a practice's integrity.

Managers of a private practice need to go cautiously in this OM area. There is much to consider here and my sense is that we have not yet matured in this important area yet—at least not for the smaller group private practice environment. However, in the competitive and soon-to-be predominately capitated marketplace managers must have the skills and procedures to monitor and evaluate the outcomes of their clinical procedures.

EPILOGUE

There are a number of management and administrative areas that have not been covered in this chapter. I have attempted to support the material presented here by as much consensual validation or empirical certainty as possible. The level of empirical certainty that has been established in this presentation is based primarily on a consensus of experts in the healthcare field. The area of management and administration is a natural area of focus for behavioral researchers.

I close with a few cautionary notes to the reader. I recommend strongly that managers should be very selective about where they spend their hard-earned dollars. I suggest that managers and their staffs exercise caution when deciding which organizations and causes to support financially and otherwise. Professional associations that seek our support often maintain a psychology, politics, and approaches that are incompatible with and, at times, antagonistic to the dynamics and objectives of the competitive marketplace. We must be astute enough when making our spending decisions to avoid the self-defeating act of funding our executioners. Those who deserve our support are those who promote our best interests—not a very novel suggestion, I admit.

Additionally, I caution managers of a behavioral practice to avoid wasting valuable resources by supporting so called anti-managed-care and "patient protection" legislation. These efforts are more frequently self-serving while being touted as methods to protect patients' confidentiality and their right to choice of provider. My analysis of these provider-driven activities is that they are usually attempts to hide behind the camouflage of confidentiality and to protect guild issues. I strongly recommend that managers reject support for what has been aptly labeled "legislation-by-anecdote" (Sprague, 1996, pp. 6–7). Rather than resort to desperate legislative solutions to the threat to survival in the marketplace I appeal to managers to pursue market-driven solutions in the competitive world of healthcare business. This is the road to better care for patients.

ACKNOWLEDGMENTS

My wife, Marie, deserves my genuine thanks for her personal sacrifice while she typed this chapter and guided me through this writing episode. Bob Ericksen, Ph.D. and Dan Fishman, Ph.D. provided helpful suggestions and Bob provided insightful proofreading. I thank them for their support.

REFERENCES

Agency for Health Care Policy and Research (AHCPR). (1993). *Depression in primary care: Vol. 2. Treatment of major depression.* Rockville, MD: U.S. Department of Human Services, Public Health Service.

American Medical Association (AMA). (1993). *Factors contributing to the healthcare cost problem.* Chicago: Author.

American Medical Association (AMA). (1996). *Physicians' current procedural terminology* (pp. 343–345). Chicago: Author.

Anders, G. (1996). *Health against health: HMOs and the breakdown of medical trust.* Boston: Houghton Mifflin.

Ansel, D. E., & Berte, E. R. (1996). Direct contracting between employees and behavioral health care providers. *Behavioral Health Care Tomorrow, 3*(6), 36–39.

Applebaum, P. S. (1992). Practice guidelines in psychiatry and their implications for malpractice. *Hospital and Community Psychiatry, 43*(4), 341–342.

Appleby, C. (1996a). Will states ban capitation? *Managed Care, 5*(11), 26–32.

Appleby, C. (1996b). Getting doctors to listen to patients. *Managed Care, 5*(12), 23–29.

Armenti, N. P. (1990). Clinical supervision—managing care. *Register Report, 16*(3), 12–14.

Armenti, N. P. (1991). The provider network in managed care. *Behavior Therapist, 14*(5), 123–128.

Armenti, N. P. (1993). Managed health care and the behaviorally trained professional. *Behavior Therapist, 16*(1), 13–15.

Armenti, N. P. (1995). *AABT—a sponsor of an institute for behavioral interventions and outcomes research and development.* Paper presented at the Association for Advancement of Behavior Therapy Convention, Washington, DC.

Armenti, N. P., & Ericksen, R. A. (1995). A managed care perspective for ADHD. *New Jersey Psychologist, 45*(1), 25–29.

Armenti, S., & Armenti, N. P. (in press). Modalities, procedures and service coding in behavioral healthcare.

Bagley, B. (1994). Making TQM work in a group practice. *Family Practice Management, 1*(5), 59–64.

Bales, J. (1998). FTC demands end to ad, fee-splitting restrictions. *American Psychological Association Monitor, March,* 19.

Barlow, D. H. (Ed). (1993). *Clinical handbook of psychological disorders* (2nd ed.). New York: Guilford Press.

Barlow, D. H. (1994). Psychological interventions in the era of managed care. *Clinical Psychology: Science and Practice, 1*(2), 109–122.

Barnett, A. A. (1995). Is knowledge really power for patients? *Business and Health, 13*(5), 29–36.

Bartlett, J. (1992). *MCC preferred practices.* Eden Prairie, MN: MCC Behavioral Health.

Beavert, C. S., & Mogaffin, C. J. (1993). Medical review criteria: A tool for quality management. *Group Practice Journal, 42*(4), 53–57.

Belkins, L. A. (1996, December 8). But what about quality? *New York Times Magazine,* pp. 68–71, 101, 106.

Bell, N. (1995). The trend toward capitation: Pros and cons. *Medical Interface, 8*(1), 57–61.

Benedict, G. S. (1996). What creates medical group success. *Group Practice Journal, 45*(4), 44–46, 48.

Berg, A. O. (1996). Clinical practice policies—believe only some of what you read. *Family Practice Management, 3*(4), 58–69.

Blackwell, S. A., Szeinback, S. L., Barnes, J. H., & Garner, D. D. (1996). A systems-based disease management model: Achieving optimal health care outcomes. *Medical Interface, 8*(12), 82–85.

Blumenthal, D. (1996). Effects of market reforms on doctors and their patients. *Health Affairs, 15*(2), 170–184.

Bouey, P. S., Grant, P. N., Groner, C., Hirsch, R. W., Ross, D., & Woods, L. (1996). Medical group practice in transition—legal issues facing medical groups in the 21st century. *Group Practice Journal, 45*(2), 10–11.

Braly, D. (1995, September). National Jewish Center launching disease—management message. *Health Management Technology,* pp. 20–21, 24.

Brown, J. (1994). Practice guidelines should simplify behavioral healthcare decision making correct? Think again. *Behavioral Health Management, 14*(5), 7–9.

Browning, C. H. (1996). Practical survival strategies: Business basics for effective marketing to managed care. In N. A. Cummings, M. S. Palack, and J. L. Cummings (Eds.), *Surviving the demise of solo practice: Mental health practitioners prosper in the era of managed care* (pp. 145–174). Madison, CT: Psychosocial Press.

Browning, C. H., & Browning, B. J. (1996). *How to partner with managed care.* New York: Wiley.

Burns, J. (1996). Risk sharing should include mental health. *Managed Healthcare, 6*(11), 64.

Cain, D. M. (1996). Provider sponsored organizations: Potential benefits and risks to physicians. *Group Practice Journal, 45*(1), 59–61.

Carlson, R. P. (1996). How salary trends are affecting family practice. *Family Practice Management, 3*(7), 22–29.

Cave, D. G. (1994). Capitation adjustments for physician risks. *Medical Interface, 7*(1), 134–137.

Cave, D. G., & Geehr, E. C. (1994). Analyzing patterns-of-treatment data to provide feedback to physicians. *Medical Interface, 7*(7), 117–128.

Cerne, F. (1994). Dollars and sense—creating incentives to effectively manage change. *Hospitals and Health Networks, 68*(7), 28–30.

Cerrato, P. L. (1995). Employee health: Not just a fringe benefit. *Business and Health, 13*(11), 21–26.

Chambless, D. L. (1993). *TaskForce on promotion and dissemination of psychological procedures—A report adopted by the Division 12 Board of the American Psychological Association.* APA, Clinical Psychology. Oklahoma City, OK.

Chambless, D. L., Sanderson, W. C., Shoham, V., Bennett Johnson, Pope, K. S., Crits-Christoph, Baker, M., Johnson, B., Woody, S. R., Sue, S., Beutler, L., Williams, D. A., & McCurry, S. (1996). An update on empirically validated therapies. *Clinical Psychologist, 49,* 2.

Chapman, L. (1990, May). Be a part of the winning hand—wellness can enhance corporate competitiveness. *Health Action Managers.*

Coile, R. C. (1995). Healthy communities: Reducing need (and costs!) by promoting health. *Inside preventative care.* Gaithersburg, MD: Aspen Publishers.

Coleman, D. L. (1996). Four ways to avoid being deselected. *Managed Care, 5*(11), 36–38.

Consumer Reports. (1995, November). Mental health, does therapy help? *Consumer Reports,* pp. 734–739.

Covey, S. R. (1992). *Principle—Centered leadership.* New York: Simon & Schuster.

Cummings, N. A. (1996a). The impact of managed care on employment and professional training: A primer for survival. In N. A. Cummings, M. S. Pallak, & J. L. Cummings (Eds.), *Surviving the demise of solo practice: Mental health practitioners prosper in the era of managed care* (pp. 11–26). Madison, CT: Psychosocial Press.

Cumminigs, N. a. (1996b). Behavior health after managed care: The next golden opportunity for mental health practitioners. In N. A. Cummings, M. S. Pallak, & J. L. Cummings (Eds.), *Surviving the demise of solo practice: Mental health practitioners Madison*, CT: Psychosocieal Press.

Cummings, N. A., Pallak, M. S., & Cummings, J. L. (Eds.). (1996). *Surviving the demise of solo prac-*

tice: Mental health practitioners prosper in the era of managed care. Madison, CT: Psychosocial Press.

Currey, R. (1992). *Medicine for sale.* Knoxville, TN: Grand Rounds Press, Whittle Books.

Denning, J. J. (1996). Has productivity become a bad thing? *Managed Care, 5*(12), 30.

DePinho, D. A. (1996a). I like cookies but I wouldn't want to be one . . . *Healthcare Business Digest, 1*(3), 2.

DePinho, D. A. (1996b). Clinical practice guidelines—the controversy continues. *Healthcare Business Digest, 1*(3), 26–36.

DePinho, D. A. (1996c). Guidelines: A legal club or a legal umbrella. *Healthcare Business Digest, 1*(3), 34–35.

DiFranza, J. R., & Lew, R. A. (1995). Effect of maternal smoking on pregnancy complications and sudden death syndrome. *Journal of Family Practice, 40*(4), 385–394.

Dowell, M. A. (1995). Legal issues affecting integrated delivery systems—a primer. *Group Practice Journal, 44*(3), 47–54.

Drapin, L. (1995, October). I/s component crucial to diabetes management program. *Health Management Technology,* pp. 30–32.

Dubbert, P. M. (1992). Implementing behavioral treatment for hypertension: Considerations for health psychologists. *Behavior Therapist, 15*(8), 182–185.

Eaton, J. A. (1997). N. Y. hospitals to cut residencies in effort to stanch physician glut. *Physician Financial News, 15*(5), 3–4.

Eddy, D. M. (1990). Clinical decision making: From theory to practice—designing a practice policy—standards, guideline, options. *JAMA, Journal of the American Medical Association, 263*(22), 3077, 3081.

Eddy, D. M. (1995a). From individual care to population care—making the transition. *Group Practice Journal, 44*(1), 32–33.

Eddy, D. M. (1995b). Health plans make case form rational, responsible, rationing. *Modern Healthcare, 25*(6), 84.

Edley, R. S. (1996). The practitioner as owner. In N. A. Cummings, M. S. Pallak, & J. L. Cummings (Eds.), *Surviving the demise of solo practice: Mental health practitioners prospering in the era of managed care* (pp. 175–190). Madison, CT: Psychosocial Press.

Edlin, M. (1996). Behavioral healthcare—new guidelines for your new market. *Managed Healthcare, 6*(11), 41, 45–46.

Elias, W. S. (1995). Demand-side management calls out for attention. *Employee Benefit News, 9*(2), 50.

Ellis, S., Johnson, L. W., & Bagley, B. (1996). Do you need a practice administrator? *Family Practice Management, 3*(10), 54–59.

Encyclopedia Britannica Inc. (1965). *Britannica World Language Edition of Funk and Wagnalls Standard Dictionary.* Chicago: Author.

Epstein, D. (1995). What the future holds for physician supply. *Managed Care, 4*(11), 25–32.

Epstein, D. (1996). Keeping salaried physicians satisfied and productive. *Managed Care, 5*(3), 26–36.

Ericksen, G. (1996). . . . And the basket counts! *Consumer Goods Manufacturer, 5*(5), 16–19.

Eskin, E. (1995). The ABC's of management service organizations. *Journal of Outcomes Management, 2*(4), 5–10.

Etzioni, A. (1988). *The moral dimension—Toward a new economics.* New York: Free Press. Macmillan.

Fitzpatrick, W. F. (1994). Capitation 101: A primer for family physicians. *Family Practice Management, 1*(3), 47–52.

Fries, J. F. (1994). Healthcare demand management. *Medical Interface, 7*(3), 55–58.

Gammel, J. D. (1996). How to evaluate the value of production-based compensation programs. *Group Practice Journal, 45*(5), 22–26.

Garson, A. (1996). Teaching tomorrows doctors to choose cost-effective care. *Managed Care, 5*(3), 47–48.

Gaus, C. R. (1994). Clinical practice guidelines: Paths to quality care. *Group Practice Journal, 43*(3), 60–65.

Giles, T. R. (Ed.). (1993a). *Handbook of effective psychotherapy.* New York: Plenum.

Giles, T. R. (1993b). Consumer advocacy and effective psychotherapy. In T. R. Giles (Ed.), *Handbook of effective psychotherapy* (pp. 481–488). New York: Plenum.

Giles, T. R. (1993c). *Managed mental health care: A guide for practitioners, employers and hospital administrators.* Boston: Allyn & Bacon.

Giles, T. R., Neims, D. M., & Prinal, E. M. (1993). The relative efficiency of prescriptive techniques. In T. R. Giles (Ed.), *Handbook of effective psychotherapy* (pp. 21–39). New York: Plenum.

Glazer, W. M. (1993). Approaching hidden psychiatric illness in PPOs: The 'medical offset' effect. *AAPPO Journal, 3*(3), 15–20.

Goldstein, A. (1973). *Structured learning therapy: Toward a psychotherapy for the poor.* New York: Academic Press.

Goldstein, D. E. (Ed.). (1995a). *Alliances: Strategies for building integrated delivery systems.* Gaithersburg, MD: Aspen Publishers.

Goldstein, D. E. (1995b). Organizing physician equity alliances for aggressive growth and capitation. *Group Practice Journal, 44*(3), 12–22.

Gorman, B. (1996). Behavioral/practice: Notes and observations from a managed behavioral health executive. In N. A. Cummings, M. S. Pallak, & J. L. Cummings (Eds.), *Surviving the demise of solo practice: Mental health practitioners prosper in the era of managed care* (pp. 41–51). Madison, CT: Psychosocial Press.

Gosfield, A. G. (1992). The developing law around practice guidelines. *Case Manager, 3*(1), 44–47.

Gosfield, A. G. (1994). Clinical practice guidelines and the law: applications and implications. In *Health law handbook* (pp. 65–99). New York: Thompson Legal Publishing.

Grambling, A. (1995). So what's new about demand management? *Managed Care, 4*(4), 33–37.

Gray, B. H. (1991). *The profit motive and patient care: The changing accountability of doctors and hospitals.* Cambridge, MA: Harvard University Press.

Gray, G. V., & Glazer, W. M. (1995). Defining medical necessity in mental health. *Behavioral Health Management, 15*(1), 38–30.

Greene, J. (1995). Clinical integration increases profitability, efficiency study. *Modern Healthcare, 25*(6), 39.

Guerney, B. G. (Ed.). (1969). *Psychotherapeutic agents: New roles for nonprofessionals, parents and teachers.* New York: Holt, Rinehart & Winston.

Harris, S. O. (1996). The practitioner as clinician: The business of practice. In N. A. Cummings, M. S. Pallak, & J. L. Cummings (Eds.), *Surviving the demise of solo practice: Mental health practitioners prospering in the era of managed care* (pp. 267–278). Madison, CT: Psychosocial Press.

Havlicek, P. L. (1996). *Medical groups in the U.S.: A survey of practice characteristics.* Chicago: AMA.

Hayes, S. C. (1995). What do we want from scientific standards of psychological practice? In S. C. Hayes, V. M. Follette, R. M. Dawes, & K. E. Grady (Eds.), *Issues and recommendations* (pp. 49–66). Reno, NV: Context Press.

Hayes, S. C. (1996). Working with managed care: Lessons from the acceptance and commitment therapy training project. *Behavior Therapist, 18*(10), 184–186.

Henrey, G. A. (1996). Why you should be collecting your own performance data. *Family Practice Management, 3*(5), 52–59.

Hladky, R., & Johnson, C. (1996). Take a long hard look before you leap into risk assumption. *Managed Healthcare, 6*(10), 48–49.

Hoffman, N. G., Halikas, J. A., Mee-Lee, D., & Weedman, R. D. (1991). *Patient placement criteria for the treatment of psychoactive substance use disorders.* Washington, DC: American Society of Addiction Medicine.

Holland, S. K. (1995). Clinical standards, critical pathways, and managed care [Special issue], *Journal of Outcomes Management, 2,* 10–11.

Hudson, T. (1996). Mirror, mirror. *Hospitals and Health Networks, 70*(7), 24–30.

Hyams, A. L., Shapiro, D. W., & Brennan, T. A. (1996). Law liability and defensive medicine—practice guidelines in malpractice litigation: An early retrospective. *Journal of Health Politics and Policy Law.*

Jacobs, M. C., & Lamprey, J. (1991). *The ISD: A review system with adult ISD criteria.* Westborough, MA: Inter Qual.

Jacobson, N. S., and Christensen, A. (1996). Studying the effectiveness of psychotherapy: How well can clinical trials do the job? *American Psychologist, 51*(10), 1031–1039.

Jaklevic, M. C. (1994). Staying single. *Modern Healthcare, 24*(20), 71–80.

Jones, O. F., & Vischi, T. (1979). Impact of alcohol, drug abuse, and mental health treatment on medical care utilization: A review of the literature. *Medical Care Supplement, 17.*

Kalous, T. D. (1996). Conducting psychotherapy supervision in the era of managed care. In N. A. Cummings, M. S. Pallak, & J. G. Cummings (Eds.), *Surviving the demise of solo practice: Mental health practitioners prospering in the era of managed care* (pp. 93–116). Madison, CT: Psychosocial Press.

Keisler, C. A., & Morton, T. L. (1988). Psychology and public policy in the health care revolution. *American Psychologist, 43,* 993–1003.

Kelly, T. (1996). Is paying physicians by capitation wrong? *Managed Care, 5*(11), 34–35.

Kerr, C. E. (1996). Patient self-management. *Managed Care Reporter, 1*(3).

Kirschenbaum, D. S., Fitzgibbon, M. C., Conviser, J. H., Shrifter, S. A., & Langdon, F. T. (1992). Nurturing healthy weight control programs. *Behavior Therapist, 5*(8), 185–188.

Klerman, G. L. (1990). The psychiatric patient's right to effective treatment: Implications of Osheroff vs. Chestnut Lodge. *American Journal of Psychiatry, 147,* 409–418.

Kongstvedt, P. R. (1989). *The managed healthcare handbook,* p. 94. Rockville, MD: Aspen Publishers.

Kovacs, A. C. (1987). Insurance billing: The growing risk of lawsuits against psychologists. *Independent Practitioner, 7*(2), 21–24.

Kovacs, A. C. (1995). We have met the enemy and he is us! *Independent Practitioner, 15*(3), 135–137.

Krohn, R. W. (1995). Eight essential rules of capitation contracting. *Group Practice Journal, 44*(4), 42–44.

LaPuma, J. (1996). Smoking, slimming and seatbelts: Is public health part of managed care? *Managed Care, 5*(5), 57–58.

Lazarus, A. A. (1967). In support of technical eclecticism. *Psychological Reports, 21,* 415–416.

Lazarus, A. A. (1976). *Multimodal behavior therapy.* New York: Springer.

Legoretta, A. P., Kashian, C., & Franklin, C. (1996). Results of a smoking cessation program in a managed care setting. *American Journal of Managed Care, 2*(7), 831–836.

Levant, R. F. (1995). Outcomes measurement and empirically validated treatments: What's all the fuss about? *Psychotherapy Bulletin, 30*(3), 20–22.

MacLeod, G. K. (1989). An overview of medical managed care. In P. R. Kongstvedt (Ed.), *The managed healthcare handbook* (pp. 3–9). Rockville, MD: Aspen Publishers.

Magnuson, R. J., & Glader, P. O. (1996). Corporate compliance—what every group practice leader needs to know. *Group Practice Journal, 45*(2), 20–24.

Marro, E. P. (1995). Is disease state management what customers really want? *Medical Interface, 8*(11), 144–146.

Mastrich, J., & Beidel, B. (1985). *The cost impact of employee assistance programs.* Trenton: New Jersey Department of Health, Division of Alcoholism, Occupational Section.

McCrady, B. J., & Eimer, M. J. (1996). Board briefs—managed care issues. *Behavior Therapist, 19*(9), 151.

McCue, M. (1996). Erase the seams and smooth the trail. *Managed Healthcare, 6*(10), 62–63.

McDonnell Douglas Corporation & Alexander Consulting Group. (1989). *McDonnell Douglas Employee Assistance Program Financial Offset Study, 1985-1989.* Westport, CT: Author.

Migdail, K. J., Youngs, M. T., & Bengen-Seltzer, B. (Eds.). (1995). *The 1995 behavioral outcomes and guidelines sourcebook.* New York: Faulkner & Gray.

Mihlbauer, M. E. (1992). Controlling consumer demand: The next generation of managed care. *Medical Interface, 5*(11), 20–22.

Molinari, C., Lee, J. M., Williams, C. L., Riddle, M. C., & Zuber, J. D. (1993). Educating physician leaders—Lexington Clinics strategy for the 1990's. *Group Practice Journal, 42*(5), 16–19.

Montague, J. (1994a). Precision maneuvers. *Hospitals and Health Networks, 68*(1), 26–36.

Montague, J. (1994b). Profiling in practice. *Hospitals and Health Networks, 68*(2), 50–51.

Morrison, D. P. (1996). The practitioner as informatics expert. In N. A. Cummings, M. S. Pallak, & J. L. Cummings (Eds.), *Surviving the demise of solo practice: Mental health practitioners prosper in the era of managed care* (pp. 239–263). Madison, CT: Psychosocial Press.

Munoz, R. F., Hollon, S. D., McGrath, E., Rehm, L. P., & Vandenbos, G. R. (1994). On the AHCPR depression in primary care guidelines. *American Psychologist, 49*(1), 42–61.

National Committee for Quality Assurance (NCQA). (1997). *Standards for accreditation of behavioral healthcare organizations.* Washington, DC: Author.

News and Trends. (1996). Where would all the doctors go? *Business and Health, 14*(12), 16.

News and Trends. (1997). An IRS guide to MSA kick-off. *Business and Health, 15*(1), 13.

National Health Lawyers Association (1995). *Colloquim report on legal issues related to clinical practice guidelines.* Washington, DC: National Lawyers Association.

O'Leary, D. S. (1993). Performance improvement in healthcare organizations. *Journal of Quality Improvement, 19*(7), 214–221.

Owens, D. K., & Wease, R. F. (1993). Development of outcome based practice guidelines. *Journal on Quality Improvement, 19*(7), 248–263.

Paist, S. S. (1994). Is family practice about procedures? *Family Practice Management, 1*(4), 15–16.

Parshall, M. J., & Huber, S. A. (1993). Recruiting the right associate for your group practice. *Group Practice Journal, 42*(4), 58–59.

Pekarik, G. (1993). Beyond effectiveness—uses of consumer-oriented criteria in defining treatment success. In T. R. Giles (Ed.), *Handbook of effective psychotherapy* (pp. 409–436). New York: Plenum.

Persons, J. B. (1996). Why practicing psychologists are slow to adopt empirically-validated treatments. In S. C. Hayes, V. M. Follette, R. M. Dawes, & K. E. Grady (Eds.), *Scientific standards for psychological practice: Issues and recommendations* (pp. 141–157). Reno, NV: Context Press.

Peterson, L., Chaney, J., & Harbeck, C. (1989). Programming for healthy lifestyles in children. *Behavior Therapist, 12*(7), 147–152.

Phillips, E. L., & Wiener, D. N. (1966). *Short-term psychotherapy and structured behavior change.* New York: McGraw-Hill.

Pincus, H. A. (1994). Dialogue: Are treatment guidelines at risk? Risks are outweighed by the benefits. *Behavioral Healthcare Tomorrow, 3*(3), 44–45.

Pomerantz, J. M., Liptzin, B., Carter, R., & Perlman, M. S. (1995). Development and management of a virtual group practice. *Psychiatric Annals, 25*(8), 504–508.

Powell, D. R. (1996). Demand-side management: Characteristics of a successful self-care program. *Healthcare Innovations, 6*(3), 22–28.

Ramay, J. (1996). Why integrate? A behavioral care perspective, *Behavioral Health Management, 16*(4), 20–21.

Reich, P. (1995). Medical management in a capitated world. *Medical Interface, 8*(5), 12.

Reich, P. (1996). Capitation and ethics. *Medical Interface, 9*(8), 14.

Ross, J. (1996, May/June). Still wanted: Comprehensive management of clinical depression. *Managed Care Pharmacy Practice*, pp. 27–29.

Sanderson, W. C. (1995). Can psychological interventions meet the new demands of healthcare? *American Journal of Managed Care, 1*(1), 93–98.

Sanderson, W. C. (1997). The importance of empirically supported treatments in the new healthcare environment. In L. Vande Creek (Ed.), *Innovations in clinical practice: A source book.* FL: Professional Resource Press.

Sanderson, W. C., & Woody, S. (1995). Manuals for empirically validated treatments—a project of the

Task Force on Psychological Interventions, Division of Clinical Psychology, APA. *Clinical Psychologist, 48*(4), 7–11.

Sandrick, K. (1993). Out in front—managed care helps push practice guidelines forward. *Hospitals, 67*(9), 30–31.

Sawyer, N. (1995). Management of health care from the demand side. *Case Manager, 6*(5), 96–102.

Schachner, M. (1994, January). Mental health group practices on rise. *Business Insurance, 10*(3), 36.

Scherger, J. F. (1994). A procedure bandwagon. *Family Practice Management, 1*(4), 17.

Schiff, L., & Service, R. (1996). Empowered patients buy more efficient care. *Business and Health, 14*(6), 35–42.

Schmidt, P. M., & Cooney, N. L. (1992). Implementing an alcohol screening program. *Behavior Therapist, 5*(8), 192–195.

Schuler, R. S., Jackson, S. E., & Sethi, A. S. (1987). 5 human resources strategies for technostress management. In A. S. Sethi, D. H. J. Care, & R. S. Schuler (Eds.), *Strategic management of technostress in an information society* (pp. 71–115). Lewiston, NY: C. J. Hogrefe.

Seaman, H. (1996a). Border war is heating up between masters and doctoral psychologists. *National Psychologist, 5*(5), 1, 4.

Seaman, H. (1996b). New York providers sue nine MCOs in class action suit. *National Psychologist, 5*(6), 10–11.

Sethi, A. S., Caro, D. H. J., & Schuler, R. S. (Eds.). (1987). *Strategic management of technostress in an information society.* Lewiston, NY: C. J. Hogrefe.

Shipley, R. H. (1992). Adding smoking-cessation services to your practice: Some practical considerations with an emphasis on recruitment issues. *Behavior Therapist, 5*(8), 188–191.

Silko, G. J. (1996). Simple tools for optimizing quality improvement in your practice. *Family Practice Management, 3*(6), 50–61.

Sipkoff, M. Z. (1995, August). Behavioral health treatment reduces medical costs. *Open Minds,* p. 12.

Smith, D. R., Wong, H. Y., & Eichart, J. H. (1996). The third generation of managed care. *American Journal of Managed Care, 2*(7), 821–828.

Smith, E. W. L. (1995). A passionate, rational response to the manualization of psychotherapy. *Psychotherapy Bulletin, 30*(2), 36–40.

Smith, G. R., and Hamilton, G. E. (1994). Dialogue: Are treatment guidelines a risk? Provider involvement is critical. *Behavioral Healthcare Tomorrow, 3*(3), 41–43.

Snow, C. (1997). A loss of confidence—AHA report: Public believes hospitals priorities have changed. *Modern Healthcare, 27,* 2–3.

Sobell, L. C. (1996). Bridging the gap between scientists and practitioners: The challenge before us. *Behavior Therapy, 27*(3), 297–320.

Solovy, A. (1997). Benchmaking guide-data rules. *Hospitals and Health Networks, 71*(3), 19–32.

Spalding, J. (1996). Taking the lead in disease state management. *Family Practice Management, 3*(4), 50–57.

Sperry, L., Brill, P. L., Howard, K. I., & Grissom, G. R. (1996). *Treatment outcomes in psychotherapy and psychiatric interventions.* New York: Brunner/Mazel.

Spraque, L. (1996). Managed health care after the 1996 presidential election. *Health Care Innovations, 6*(6), 5–7.

Stepnick, L., Rybowski, L. S., & Burns, J. (1997). How to define the gray issue of accountability. *Managed Healthcare, 7*(1), 20–23.

Stevens, S. (1995). Capitation seen no bar to profits and control. *Physicians Financial News, 13*(7), S1, S19.

Strosahl, K. (1994). Entering the new frontier of managed healthcare: Goldmines and landmines. *Cognitive and Behavioral Practice, 1,* 5–23.

Strosahl, K. (1996). There's 'goldmine-landmine' themes in generation 2 of healthcare reform. *Behavior Therapist, 19*(4), 52–54.

Strupp, H. H., & Hadley, W. H. (1977). A tripartite model of mental health and therapeutic outcomes. *American Psychologist, 32*(3), 187–196.

Sulger, R. J. F. (1996). A closer look at capitation. *American Journal of Managed Care, 2*(8), 1091–1096.

Sullivan, S., & Kunkle, C. S. (1993). Value-based health purchasing: The road to a healthy market. *Medical Interface, 7*(7), 47–49.

Szabo, J. (1995). Insurers offer discounts to doctors using electronic record systems. *Physician Financial News, 13*(5), 1, 18.

Task Force on Promotion and Dissemination of Psychological Procedures (1995). Training and dissemination of empirically validated psychological treatments. *Clinical Psychologist, 48*(1), 3–23.

Theis, G., Geraty, R., Panzarino, P. O., & Bartlett, J. (1995). Toward the behavioral health report card. *Medical Interface, 8*(3), 80–88, 122.

Trabin, T. (1994). Toward greater accountability for quality. More science, less art? *Behavioral Healthcare Tomorrow, 3*(1–2), 8.

Unger, W. J., & Findlay Vail, A. (1994). Integrated health care systems: Alliances for integration. *Group Practice Journal, 43*(3), 28–33, 55.

Vibbert, S. (1993). *What works—How outcomes research will change medical practice.* Knoxville, TN: Grand Rounds Press, Whittle Books.

Wallen, E. (1995). Clinical practice guidelines employed against doctors in malpractice suits. *Physician Financial News, 13*(1), 1, 22.

Waxman, J. M. (1994a). The MSO: The physician's IDS alternative. *AAPPO Journal, 4*(3), 9–12.

Waxman, J. M. (1994b). The MSO—group practice: A basic managed care building block. *Group Practice Journal, 43*(6), 32–35.

Weins, A. N., Brazil, P. J., Fuller, K. H., & Solomon, S. E. (1995). The practitioner's new weapon: Data. *Psychotherapy Bulletin, 30*(2), 46–53.

Wennberg, J. E., & Cooper, M. A. (1996). *Dartmouth Atlas of Health Care in the United States.* Chicago: American Hospital Publishing.

Wiggins, J. G. (1993). *Letter to APA members regarding APA consent agreement with Federal Trade Commission.* Washington, DC: American Psychological Association.

Wilson, G. T. (1996). Empirically validated treatments as a basis for clinical practice: Problems and prospects. In S. C. Hayes, V. M. Follette, R. M. Dawes, & K. E. Grady (Eds.), *Scientific standards for psychological practice: Issues and recommendations* (pp. 163–195). Reno, NV: Context Press.

Wyeth-Ayerst Laboratories Healthcare Systems. (1996). *Obesity management: Proceedings of Symposium.* Bronxville, NY: Medicom International.

Zuber, T. J., & Pfenninger, J. L. (1994). Family physical resistance to office procedures. *Family Practice Management, 1*(4), 48–52.

Zucker, M. (1995). The many faces of group practice. *Behavioral Health Management, 15*(2), 12–14.

BIOGRAPHY

Nicholas P. Armenti   Nicholas Armenti holds a Ph.D. from Rutgers University. He is owner and director of Psychological Consultants Group, PC, a group practice in Northern New Jersey that is very active in several managed behavioral healthcare organization networks. In addition, he is President and CEO of Metrix MSO, Inc., a provider-owned and -managed risk-bearing management service organization that manages capitated and noncapitated behavioral health carve out programs. He was Executive Director of Pequannock Valley Mental Health Center during the 1970s and early 1980s where he developed the center's peer review and utilization management programs. He worked at the Center for Alcohol Studies and at the Community Mental Health Centers during his career. He is a strong advocate for a managed care approach to the delivery of healthcare.

3

MANAGEMENT OF A MENTAL HEALTH CLINIC

DAVID J. DRUM

Counseling and Mental Health Center,
The University of Texas at Austin, Austin, Texas 78712

MANAGERIAL CHALLENGES

Today's Managerial Environment

The transition from psychologist to clinic manager—like that of the professional athlete to team manager, or faculty member to dean, or mechanical engineer to agency director—is one that transports a person from the world of the known and commonly experienced to one that is less familiar, even foreign. The transition to management across all of these examples has become more complex, demanding a greater degree of readiness and competence than ever before. Each year the tasks faced by the manager of a mental health clinic increase in complexity as standards of care rise, accreditation criteria expand, functions become more specialized, treatments are more differentiated, competition for resources intensifies, and the walls separating public and private sector care crumble, thereby changing the mixture of clientele agencies serve.

More than three decades ago, Emery and Trist (1965) described four types of organizational environments, one of which they labeled "turbulent fields." This type was characterized by uncertainty, complexity, and unexpected change. In today's world, mental health clinics face these environmental characteristics *on a routine basis.* The good news is that the manager of a mental health service sel-

Management and Administration Skills for the Mental Health Professional
Copyright © 1999 by Academic Press. All rights of reproduction in any form reserved.

dom lacks invigorating challenges, which if resolved successfully, can bring rewarding results. The bad news is that the manager must expect to cope with change, complexity, and turbulence on a day-to-day basis.

This chapter begins by laying the groundwork for understanding the environment today's mental health managers face, in particular the changing paradigm of the mental health field. At the heart of the clinic manager's task are ten core agency-wide processes that require constant attention and effective leadership. A description of these core processes and their challenges forms the second section of the chapter. The final section describes five challenging balancing acts successful managers of mental health clinics must be able to perform to keep their agencies vital.

Multiple Constituencies

Consumers and Potential Consumers

Managers of mental health clinics must serve many masters. These are the multiple constituents to whom they are accountable for the agency's performance. Foremost are the consumers and potential consumers who hold the manager responsible for administering an agency in a way that is responsive to their needs. This includes providing easy and timely access to services, satisfying customer expectations regarding friendliness and respect, adjudicating complaints and appeals fairly, offering high quality services that produce good outcomes, and providing a scope of care consistent with the agency's mission and consumer needs. Mental health clinics also operate in larger host organizations, such as hospitals or universities, or have governing bodies (boards of directors, community action groups) that are additional constituents with another set of expectations. These constituents hold the agency manager responsible for the quality of services, patient satisfaction with the care received, relevance of that care to the goals and mission of the host institution, and the efficient use of resources.

Staff

As if this weren't sufficient, mental health clinic managers have other important constituents to satisfy. The staff of the agency represents an internal constituency, which collectively expects the manager to create and maintain sound administrative systems that enable service to flow smoothly and equitably, distribute an agency's resources, maintain morale, resolve disputes, and provide security and leadership.

Accrediting Bodies

Added to this is a third set of "masters." The clinic manager is also accountable to the various accreditation bodies, state licensure boards, and professional organizations for compliance with ethics codes, standards of care and safety, training regulations, and other standards.

Changes in the Healthcare Marketplace

To further complicate matters, the rapidly changing nature of the healthcare marketplace has placed increased demands on the manager. Fundamental changes to the mental healthcare paradigm have resulted in new reimbursement systems, external care authorization systems, redefinition of medical necessity, an eroding of the sea wall separating public and private sector care, and greater public accountability for outcomes. How did this come about? During the 1990s, the healthcare system in which mental health care is provided changed at an unprecedented rate, dramatically altering the healthcare landscape and forcing clinic managers to re-examine the agency's values, mission, and services. Two major forces are shaping the healthcare marketplace: managed competition and managed care.

Managed Care and Managed Competition

Managed care is a system for managing access to treatment as well as the processes of treatment in order to achieve specific outcomes. Managed care seeks to achieve its goals by controlling access to treatment, treatment processes for cost containment and efficiency, and treatment outcomes for quality control.

Managed competition, however, is the more significant of the two forces, for its changes fuel changes in managed care. Managed competition in healthcare refers to the process of organizing the healthcare marketplace and aligning the incentives of the various stakeholders so that predictable and balanced marketplace dynamics operate to produce a more efficient and accountable system of healthcare. Managed competition came to light as a feature of President Bill Clinton's healthcare proposal. Its goals are to produce predictable and relatively stable healthcare costs, to eliminate waste, to produce cost-sensitive care, to increase consumer choice of health plans, to increase accountability to consumers and bulk purchasers of healthcare services (corporations and government agencies), and to align the incentives among the stakeholders in the healthcare enterprise in order to achieve these goals.

Who are the primary stakeholders in healthcare? They are healthcare insurers, managed care entities, consumers, corporate purchasers, providers and provider groups, facility owners and managers, and community and governmental entities.

Currently, the interests and needs of these stakeholders are not well aligned. Healthcare insurers, managed care entities, and to some extent corporate purchasers have enjoyed the most success in having their needs addressed. Voices of consumers, providers, and facility owners are just beginning to have an impact as they succeed in raising issues pertinent to them. Various governmental entities have begun to enact laws at the state and federal level aimed at patient protection, insurance portability, minimal hospital stay entitlements, fair appeal processes for providers and consumers, and other initiatives designed to help balance and align incentives among all stakeholders.

Unfortunately, following the demise of the Clinton healthcare plan, managed competition no longer has a command center where stakeholder issues can be addressed in a coordinated manner. Stakeholders' interests are left to the mercy of everyday marketplace forces. This has led to a highly unregulated playing field for insurance corporations and managed care entities. As a consequence, the managed care industry has had the most direct influence of all of the stakeholders so far. However, as the stakeholders in managed competition increasingly exert their individual influences they continued to complete the shift of the healthcare paradigm away from the traditional system toward the new system. The following describes some of the paradigm shifts in healthcare that have recently taken place.

Healthcare Paradigm Shift

What has occurred during the 1990s is no less than a major paradigm shift in the field of healthcare, one with profound implications for the mental health clinic manager. For a period of more than 20 years until the late 1980s the traditional paradigm for healthcare produced a relatively stable system for providing healthcare services. This paradigm created an expanding demand for mental health care. Public and private sector care were separate markets. Public sector care was typically provided through clinics funded by governmental entities or governmentally funded healthcare programs, such as Medicaid and Medicare. Publicly funded community mental health centers, community agencies, state hospitals, and veteran's administration clinics provided most of the care for patients whose healthcare was funded through the government. Private sector care was largely provided through a "cottage industry" model in which private practitioners, often in solo practices, provided care.

Now, however, because of the changes brought about through managed competition, private sector care is increasingly provided through group practices that function like mental health clinics. As privately owned and operated mental health clinics have become operational they have competed increasingly with publicly funded mental health clinics for the right to serve patients whose healthcare is funded by governmental entities. Managed competition supports this trend as it seeks to eliminate the public–private distinction, merging all prospective patients into one larger competitive market.

Comparing the traditional paradigm for healthcare with the new one reveals that the new model has changed the three key dimensions of healthcare: service delivery, finance, and care management. For example, it is clear that in the new service delivery system, instead of solo practitioners competing independently for new clients, the competition has shifted to large, integrated practice groups and clinics competing with each other for the right to be the exclusive provider for large populations of potential consumers. As these integrated delivery systems (composed of provider networks, hospitals, and mental health clinics) grow larger, bulk purchasers of healthcare services (such as national corporations and governmental entities) form healthcare purchasing consortia to influence control over costs, benefits, and quality.

Changes in the financing system for mental health care have had equally profound impact on the structure of healthcare. For example, in the traditional system the insurer and providers were distinct entities. In the new system, large practice clinics and integrated delivery systems take on financial risk in the form of capitated, performance-based, case rate, and other new payment-for-care systems. Although the traditional system reimbursed providers directly and per unit of care, the new systems direct payments through intermediary management organizations, such as managed-care organizations or physician–hospital organizations. As much as possible these systems avoid paying per unit of service and instead pay for aggregated care.

The care management system has been equally affected by the change away from the traditional system. The right of the insured person to initiate care and receive reimbursement has been greatly diminished. The right to choose from among all of the licensed providers in the insured's community has also become greatly restricted, as the new system requires preservice certification to see specific providers. Once care was initiated in the traditional system its management was the responsibility of the providers. In the new system mental health professionals have to seek authorization for the right to be reimbursed for care they provide. Thus, the new system introduces as intermediary the utilization or case manager, whose function it is to monitor and certify the care provided to patients.

Understanding the profound shifts in healthcare that have taken place is essential for grasping the enormous challenge that mental health clinic managers face today.

Management Theories

One bright spot in the horizon is the widely available variety of useful management theories, along with their assorted tools and techniques. A new manager can certainly benefit from some of these, not necessarily to become a disciple of any particular approach, but to understand the complexities of the managerial world and the ways some theorists suggest those complexities can be addressed. Some management theories are quite comprehensive and lend themselves to wholesale adoption. Others address specific managerial dilemmas or issues. Managers often draw on a combination of these to craft a coherent management system for their agency. With an effective management system in place, it is possible for an agency to manage core processes and resolve critical challenges central to its effectiveness and survival, including fulfilling constituents' expectations.

MANAGING CORE PROCESSES

At the heart of every organization there is a set of core processes that must be efficiently designed, managed, and reengineered as necessary. A process is considered to be a core process when it is essential to fulfilling the agency's mission, undergirds some critical function, or helps fulfill goals. For example, a core process supports the agency's goals of assuring appropriate access to services, promoting efficiency, fostering consumer satisfaction, and improving quality. Core processes are not tasks or goals that are completed at a particular time and then set aside. Rather, they are ongoing processes that require continuous management and refinement. If not given the requisite attention, core processes degrade and may have a negative impact on the agency's goals. The responsibility for keeping core processes in tune falls on the manager. A description of ten core processes central to the smooth functioning of a mental health clinic follow. They have been grouped into three categories: foundational processes, staff effectiveness processes, and process evaluation.

Foundational Processes

An agency's core values, its strategic planning process, the way it manages demand for services, and the way it makes policy are all fundamental processes that establish and structure the foundation of an agency. Without these firmly in place and operating harmoniously, an agency will lack a common center. It will be like a ship without an anchor, being moved around by the wind and tides, often in the wrong direction.

Core Values

An agency's values show its intent and desires. They are an important part of an agency's guidance system, directing it to attend to some issues and exclude others. Some values are explicitly stated, and others are implied in an agency's operations. The more explicitly stated and embraced an agency's basic values, the more these values can be effectively implemented and consciously revised to reflect changing organizational pressures or culture. Core values are reflected in a number of aspects. Among these are customer values, ethical standards, philosophy of treatment, and accountability.

Customer Values

All agencies have to understand their customers' values. For example, how much does the customer value *respect?* How about *easy and equal access?* What about *staff diversity* and desire to *serve a diverse population* of consumers? The way an agency responds to the values of its customers reflects the agency's own values.

Ethical Standards

Setting ethical standards in a multidisciplinary setting is another key aspect of core values. Today's typical mental health clinic boasts a multidisciplinary staff of psychiatrists, psychologists, social workers, marriage and family practitioners, addiction specialists, and professional counselors. Each of these disciplines has its own code of ethics and each has substantial differences from the others, making it difficult for an agency to embrace any single code of ethics. However, the various codes do represent a good starting point for staff discussion regarding establishment of an agency code of ethics.

Philosophy of Treatment

A third area where the values of an organization affect its practice is in its philosophy of treatment or caregiving. Agencies have a wide variety of mental health treatment approaches to choose from, ranging from passive–reactive to highly proactive. If an agency adopts values that place it toward the passive–reactive end, then it is likely to serve primarily help seekers who are motivated to initiate care, and it will have as its focus helping customers resolve the problem at hand or recover from an episode. However, if an agency were to implement values that placed it on the more proactive end of the continuum, then it is likely to have a more population-centered system of patient care, treating not only help seekers, but also engaging in disease management programs and other services that aid people who are episode free.

Accountability

Another important value for an organization to establish early is the degree to which it is going to hold itself accountable for its performance. Some agencies limit their accountability to client satisfaction, others to satisfaction and outcomes, and yet others set the threshold for accountability at the accreditation level where outcomes, standards compliance, and other factors are examined and evaluated.

Strategic Planning Process

Management theorists and the management systems they devise uniformly recognize the importance of devoting a portion of an agency's resources to strategic planning. Doing so is seen as fundamental to the success of the organization. Underlying the need for planning is the acknowledgment that changes affecting an organization are constantly occurring. Some changes can be adapted to without making fundamental shifts in either an organization's culture or its products or services. Other changes, however, may so profoundly affect an agency that it must shift its operating paradigm.

Changing an Operational Paradigm

Although changes resulting from strategic planning can often be carried out within an organization's existing paradigm, this is not always the case. The most difficult challenge an organization will face is when its strategic planning initiatives lead it to change paradigms. Shifts in paradigms affect core processes and often require agencies to make radical changes in the way they do business. Barker (1992) points out that paradigm shifts create both crises and opportunity. Specifically, he observes that an agency's current operational paradigm often interferes with its ability to see the validity and necessity of shifting to a new evolving paradigm. It is crucial for managers to be open to the need for changing an agency's paradigm.

Shifts in Service Paradigm of Mental Health

As explained in the first section, for the past several years the mental health field has been undergoing significant shifts within its service paradigm. For example, the movement toward managed care and away from indemnity insurance has completely changed the reimbursement system for providers of health care. The shift from treating episodes of dysfunction in favor of focusing on the well-being of all subscribers to an agency's health plan has resulted in more focus on early and preventive interventions. The movement away from independent practitioners functioning autonomously to large integrated delivery systems in which providers agree to operate according to set procedures has transformed the marketplace for mental healthcare. These and other changes occurring at an unprecedented pace in healthcare make strategic planning essential to the survival of an agency. Thus it is imperative that managers of mental health clinics understand how to lead their organizations through strategic planning processes.

Phases in Strategic Planning

Regardless of whether one uses Management by Objective (Odiorne, 1995), Situational Leadership (Hersey, 1984), Total Quality Management (Deming, 1986; Gitlow & Gitlow, 1982; Johnson, 1993), or some other common managerial approaches, strategic planning usually involves several phases: reconnaissance, brainstorming, analysis of ideas, problem solving, decision making, implementation, and evaluation. An attempt to understand the forces creating the need to change occurs first. This phase is similar to the scouting or reconnaissance functions of the military prior to action. From a thorough understanding of change forces, agencies typically then begin brainstorming about strengths, weaknesses, and opportunities. Brainstorming leads to an analysis of generated ideas to see which ideas are potentially high yield and feasible. The strategic planning process moves next to problem-solving issues raised during the analysis phase. At this point, the process moves into decision making, where the agency must face the reality of what it can and cannot accomplish within the constraints of its resources and mission. This leads to the final phase of implementation and evaluation.

Leading the Strategic Planning Process

Leading an agency's strategic planning process requires the manager to make important decisions based on the answers to several questions. How much time can the agency afford to invest in strategic planning? Who needs to be included in the planning process? How far into the future should strategic planning project the agency? How can a strategic plan be crafted that staff will embrace? And, what are the constraints on ideas or plans that must be considered during the planning process?

Agencies with effective strategic planning processes create their own future. Those that do not are often caught up responding to crises that could have been anticipated. As with paradigm shifts, change often creates both crises and opportunities. When an organization is deficient in strategic planning, change usually signals the beginning of a crisis.

Demand Management Process

The demand management process comprises the methods an agency uses to balance consumer need and demand for services with the way it prefers to deploy its resources. In some agencies demand management is informal and implicit, whereas in others it reflects a desire to manage explicitly and intentionally the care patients receive. A good demand management process is important to regulating patient access and to channeling patients to specific services. There are several key elements of a demand management system.

Treatment Modality

First, an agency must develop criteria for deciding what treatment modality will be offered to which patients. Increasingly, mental health agencies are developing lines of services and are becoming less dependent on individual treatment as the exclusive modality of care. Currently, it is not uncommon for a mental health agency to have available a variety of treatment options such as inpatient programs, partial hospitalization programs, intensive day treatment programs, specialized thematic groups for specific problems, parent education programs, and other options.

Chronic Care

A second key element of a demand management program is a plan for providing care to patients with chronic illnesses. No longer must agencies take a passive-reactive stance and merely treat episode after episode spawned by a chronic illness. With the advent of disease management programs, agencies have the opportunity to develop more proactive programs for helping consumers with chronic mental and physical health conditions. Effective disease management programs enable agencies to work with patients not only when they experience an episode or flare-up but on an ongoing basis to reduce disease burden more directly and in some cases slow the progression of the underlying disease process.

Level of Care

Another keystone of an agency's demand management process is the establishment of criteria to determine who has the authority to initiate care and at what intensity is care provided. In the era of indemnity insurance, the insured person had the right to initiate care and access the intensity of care desired as long as it was a covered benefit in the health plan. In the age of managed care, authorization or precertification to receive care is standard practice. Managed care organizations have developed criteria to determine medical necessity for care and the appropriate type of care to be offered. Mental health agencies, like managed care entities, if they are to make efficient use of their resources, must develop clear and fair processes for determining when and at what level care is to be offered.

Scheduling

A third key element of a demand management system is the appointment or service scheduling system. The scheduling system is often the most visible aspect of an agency, as most consumers access an agency through its scheduling process. If an agency does not have a good demand management process, then its scheduling system is likely to be inefficient. Scheduling systems reflect an agency's triage process for determining who gets what type of care and when care is received. In an age when the resources an agency has available to meet the needs of its consumers is often less than desired, a good scheduling system can make the difference between the agency being viewed as a marginally performing organization or a good, customer-friendly one.

Policymaking Process

An agency's policymaking process is related to its strategic planning and decision making, because each of these core processes charts a course into unknown dimensions. Policymaking, however, should be viewed in its own right. Strategic planning and decision making establish goals or outline desired changes, whereas policymaking interprets and codifies intent and moves decision from agreement in principle to actual practice.

Elements of a Policymaking Process

The policymaking process includes how an agency sets standards, informs and educates staff about those standards, establishes compliance goals, and revises policy based on feedback. As with other key organizational processes, the manager has to decide who should be involved in setting specific policies, how policy is recorded, how it is disseminated, how it is evaluated for effectiveness in supporting desired outcomes, and how the process for changing established policy and practices is initiated.

Policy and Procedures Manual

It is currently standard practice for mental health clinics to have a policy and procedures manual which serves as a comprehensive source for all policies affecting the operation of the agency. Such manuals are also critical to effective orientation of new staff.

Staff Effectiveness Processes

For the staff to work effectively, several core processes need to be well thought out: decision making, authority and empowerment, information flow, and staff development.

Decision-Making Process

Organizations are continuously confronted with issues and problems that require decisions. An organization's decisions can be classified into two types: 1) those made within already established policy or guidelines, 2) and those that set precedents, chart new directions, or change operating procedures. If an agency lacks a clear decision-making process for the latter, the manager may find that these decisions unnecessarily stimulate resistance, confuse practice, and otherwise disrupt the ongoing business of the clinic. There are several critical factors that the clinic manager must account for in a good decision-making process: delegation versus participation, staff involvement, and the problem-solving method.

Delegation versus Participation

The first critical decision-making element is determining when to delegate decisions and when to participate. Few managers can or should participate in all decisions. However, when delegating decision-making authority, the manager must communicate clearly to those empowered on his or her behalf the constraints that must be taken into consideration or the criteria the decision must fulfill. By doing so, the manager avoids the awkward situation of rejecting decisions by introducing criteria that could have been made a part of the process.

Staff Involvement

A second important factor is who to involve in making decisions. Management theorists stress the importance of including as much as possible those people who are directly affected by the decision. In general, the more staff are empowered to participate in decisions which affect them the more pride and ownership they feel and the less resistance there will be at implementation.

Problem-Solving Method

Finally, it is important that the manager have a method for ensuring good problem solving, one that can generate as many potentially useful solutions as is practical. As with management theories, there are many problem-solving approaches from which the manager can choose.

Authority and Empowerment

Comments like "my supervisor micromanages my work," or "does not know what's going on in the agency," or "cannot make the difficult decisions," or "plays favorites," or "cannot control so and so" are frequent occurrences in organizations in which the authority and empowerment process is not well regulated. Agencies are social systems in which both functional and dysfunctional interpersonal dynamics arise and need to be resolved. Dysfunctional interpersonal dynamics can be caused by an individual staff member's personality or may be a result of a poorly managed authority–empowerment process. What makes agencies particularly complex social systems is that they also are performance systems in which the nature and frequency of interpersonal involvement is determined by job duties.

Granting Appropriate Authority to Staff

Establishing and maintaining a healthy authority and empowerment process is one of the most difficult challenges a manager will face, and one that too many managers fail to handle properly. It is a fact of agency life that staff members will have different degrees of authority to make decisions, solve problems, resolve disputes, and supervise activities. However, for staff to discharge their responsibilities properly they must have the requisite authority to do so. The leader of a mental health agency must therefore have a process for ensuring that staff are accorded the necessary authority to conduct or direct activities according to their duties. The leader of an agency is also responsible for monitoring how sensitively and functionally staff utilize the authority that has been delegated. Poorly distributed authority or abuse of it undermines staff morale, as well as the efficiency and quality of services.

Maldistribution of Authority

It is easy to underestimate how carefully a manager must balance authority in an agency. Maldistribution of authority is one of the most common problems in agencies. There are two ways that it typically occurs. The first is when leaders hold on to too much authority and do not share enough of it with other managers, supervisors, and staff, compromising their ability to perform their duties. Typically, this type of leader is viewed as a micromanager or controlling boss. In this situation very few staff, regardless of duties, feel empowered. The second type of problem with distribution of authority is the mirror opposite of the first. Here the leader or manager fails to retain enough authority to effectively lead and manage the processes of the agency. Typical of this pattern is an agency in which the nonmanagerial staff members hold most of the authority but because they have little formal role authority for administering an agency, they cannot consistently exercise it for the agency's welfare. When this happens, morale declines, power struggles are everyday occurrences, and decisions become difficult to make.

Appropriate Distribution of Authority

Authority must be appropriately distributed so that the agency can meet its goals and the staff, in contributing to those goals, can feel appropriately empowered to do its job. The task of the manager is to determine how to distribute and manage a finite amount of authority. The manager must first determine how much of the authority to retain in order to maintain control over the agency; how much to vest in midlevel managers so they can carry out their duties; how much frontline supervisors need; and how much each staff member must have to make necessary decisions, implement policies, carry out responsibilities, and not be subjected to unnecessary control or negative interpersonal dynamics. Although authority will of necessity differ among employees of an agency, the sense of empowerment staff feel should be more uniform.

It is not enough for managers to see their role merely as distributing authority properly. The manager must monitor how well others in the agency exercise their authority. Where people abuse it, underutilize it, or in other ways mishandle it, the leader serves as a mentor, coach, or manager for those people to facilitate the authority–empowerment process. The benefit of a well-balanced authority system is that it empowers everyone with the requisite authority and autonomy to be able to do his or her job.

Information Flow Process

The administrator of a mental health clinic is going to devote a significant amount of energy in managing the information processes of the agency. It is critically important that mental health clinics develop and continuously strive to improve two types of information systems: management information systems and mental health information records systems.

Management Information Systems

A management information system is basically a method for capturing and displaying data vital to understanding the agency's customers, its effectiveness, and its efficiency on a variety of dimensions. At a minimum, a management information system should contain data on patient diagnoses or problems treated at the clinic, consumer satisfaction with care received at the agency, treatment outcomes, provider productivity and effectiveness, service costs for different lines of service, and account or billing data. Such information is essential to understanding an agency's performance on key elements of the care system.

Organizations can custom build their own management information systems or they can purchase a system from any of a number of vendors. In the last five years several comprehensive management information systems have been developed that not only capture essential management information but allow agencies to link to national databases for comparison purposes. However, the downside is that these systems are still relatively expensive and not entirely debugged.

Mental Health Information Systems

A mental health information system is basically a method for gathering relevant patient information, documenting it in reliable and standardized formats, making the information available to providers to facilitate care, storing confidential information safely, and determining appropriate conditions for its release or disclosure.

Generally speaking, the patient record is the key aspect of any mental health information system. Patient records often contain input from multiple providers, covering years of treatment received in more than one agency. In addition, they contain laboratory reports, results of psychological testing, authorization to receive treatment forms, requests for release of information, and other routinely utilized information and forms. These multiple sources of data, along with ongoing progress notes, need to be thoughtfully organized in a patient's record so that attention is drawn to treatment goals as well as to urgent treatment data such as suicidal or homicidal potential and drug allergies. It also needs to be organized effectively so that members of the quality improvement program can review and evaluate the care provided to patients as part of ongoing evaluation of care. Standards for recording information, adding or deleting comments, and signing and dating records need to be set and referenced in the agency's policy manual.

Standards relating to patient records can be found in the accreditation manuals of the Accreditation Association for Ambulatory Health Care (1993), National Committee for Quality Assurance (1997), and the Joint Commission on Accreditation of Healthcare Organizations (1995). Mental health agencies should consider reaching the standards for patient records of at least one of these three accreditation associations so they can reassure themselves and their consumers that they conform to records management standards.

Staff Development Process

Need for Staff Development

The mental health profession is a relatively young profession compared with medicine, law, and dentistry. As a result, it is generating new science every day, and that new science needs to make its way into practice. New areas of specialization and proficiency are emerging, codes of ethics are evolving and expanding to include more principles, experts are reaching consensus on treatment guidelines for some disorders, and new pharmacological interventions are being promoted. Collectively, these changes result in a continual rise in standards of care and in practice sophistication.

Organizations need a process to infuse new knowledge, incorporate changing professional values, advance practice techniques, and stay on the cutting edge of the profession. Typically, agencies accomplish these goals through a staff development program. In order for such a program to maintain or advance service quality, there must be a logical relationship between the goals of its activities and the mission, goals, and needs of the agency.

Role of the Manager

It is the role of the manager to determine an agency's staff development process. This is usually accomplished through feedback from the quality improvement process and consultation with staff. The effectiveness of staff development depends on an agency's ability to detect changes in standards in the larger profession, accurately assess its own standards of practice, and determine when formerly uniform high quality services have too much variation across providers for the good of the consumer.

The agency manager has several decisions to make in establishing and operating a staff development process. First, whom to involve in determining the needs and goals of the program. Second, where to obtain data to determine which of the potential staff development activities receives priority. Last, which staff development activities should be designed for the entire staff and which for subgroupings (administrative, clinical, clerical staff, etc.).

Process Evaluation

Quality Improvement Process

High quality and effective performance do not just happen. They are a result of intentional efforts directed at achieving those goals. It is only through a well-conceived and implemented quality improvement process that an agency can evaluate and ultimately improve its effectiveness in carrying out its mission. Constant attention to and adjustment of the processes described in this chapter is required.

Evolution of Quality Improvement

The approaches or techniques for improving an agency's quality of care have evolved over time. Initially, quality improvement activities were not systematic nor were they structured processes. Rather they were corrective actions taken after it was clear that existing processes had broken down, creating crises that needed to be addressed. Over time quality improvement efforts changed to become more systematic, becoming known as quality assurance programs. These performance improvement programs were modeled after the industrial quality inspection process. In this model, when deficient performance is noted, it signals the manager to promote better compliance with existing procedures designed to ensure greater uniformity of outcomes.

During the 1990s, the paradigm for performance improvement shifted from the inspection-based quality assurance process to quality improvement programs. The essential difference between these models is that quality improvement programs, instead of viewing their primary objective as high compliance with procedures that are essentially sound, look for ways to improve the processes themselves. Instead of viewing defective performances as the exclusive target of change, quality improvement programs find opportunities to improve the processes so that less variance in performance occurs.

Modern Quality Improvement Program

For most agencies, the engine that propels the performance improvement process is their quality improvement program. To improve an agency's performance to the maximum degree, these programs must be comprehensive and not limited to evaluating service processes. True performance improvement processes must focus on service, evaluate effectiveness of agency leadership, evaluate its environment of care (such as safety and privacy), and examine how the various core processes interact to produce an efficient, high-performance agency.

The modern quality improvement program is designed to facilitate an organization's ability to analyze and improve core processes continuously. Commonly, quality improvement programs have at least the following components: a system for gathering data; procedures for analyzing information; a method for breaking down larger processes into reviewable elements; and a feedback system that informs other core processes such as strategic planning, staff development, demand management, and information flow. Even though quality improvement programs can generate feedback about an individual staff member's performance, their true value is in identification of critical elements or junctures in an agency's core processes that could be improved.

Establishing a Quality Improvement Program

Ideally every mental health agency will have a formal quality improvement program. Unfortunately, many do not. Effective quality improvement programs are challenging to design and difficult to keep invigorated. They require a commitment to change, not to the status quo. Successful programs depend on broad participation of staff and the presence of formal processes that are reviewable. If a manager of a mental health agency has to develop a quality improvement program de novo, there are several actions that must be taken, beginning with the establishment of a quality improvement committee whose membership is drawn from all departments of the agency. That committee, broadly reflecting the agency, must establish goals and objectives. Then it must select those processes to be given priority for review. Once the priorities are determined, then baseline performance measures must be established to evaluate current performance. These data then can be used to set aspirations and to facilitate improved performance either with the same processes or with new or refined processes. Once a process has been reengineered it is subjected to the same quality review cycle to evaluate the impact of the changes.

Resource Allocation Process

A well-orchestrated resource allocation process supports a manager's ability to accomplish the goals of the agency, to promote efficiency, and to reward meritorious performance. The manager of a mental health clinic often has limited resources, both in personnel and in finances, which because they are finite must be deployed strategically to best serve the agency. The manager's task is to ensure that there is a rational process for gathering information about resource needs for programs, a method for analyzing the data, and a procedure for understanding funding priorities.

Prioritizing Needs

What makes resource allocation a particularly challenging process for mental health clinic managers is that the resources are seldom adequate to fund fully all agency needs. Obviously the manager will be held accountable for ensuring that the agency's key tasks and processes have appropriate human and material resources so that the services provided are of acceptable quality. Managers are often forced to examine programs and services closely to determine which are necessary and where they fit within the priorities of the agency. Managerial systems, such as Zero-base Budgeting (Austin, 1979) or Management by Objectives (Odiorne, 1995), have useful concepts for establishing necessity and determining priority for allocation of resources.

Rewarding Performance

Agency managers are also responsible for using resources to create performance incentive systems that reward meritorious performance. An important aspect of a manager's resource allocation process is a system for accurately distinguishing levels of contribution of staff to an agency's goals and then developing a fair system for rewarding that performance. In designing a performance incentive system, the manager must ask the following: Who should be included in its development? What should be rewarded? Productivity? Client satisfaction? Outcomes? Or some combination? How can the process be implemented so that it promotes good morale?

FIVE CHALLENGING BALANCING ACTS

Now that the ten core processes have been described, it is time to describe the five challenging balancing acts successful managers must be able to perform to create and maintain a harmonious and effective mental health care clinic. These balancing acts involve resolving conflicts among competing forces or processes. How the manager resolves these tensions determines how well the agency's balance is maintained.

Harmonizing Operating Values with Changing Healthcare Paradigm

Managing a mental health clinic requires constant attention to how the healthcare marketplace and healthcare paradigm is changing. Not doing so could compromise an agency's viability and allow it to drift out of the mainstream of healthcare practice. As managers of healthcare agencies endeavor to incorporate changes in services and goals stimulated by the marketplace, they must reexamine the agency's commitment to its core values, asking, for example, what are the customer values the agency wishes to uphold, what is its philosophy of treatment, and what level of accountability shall it strive for? Managers also need to look at the agency in the light of possible changes in the three key dimensions of healthcare: service delivery system, finance system, and care management system.

Managers of a mental health clinic need to lead their agencies through the crosscurrents of changes and the demands of the new service paradigm. Mental health clinics will seek to compete with other practice groups and will also face competition for their clients, and the competition will be intense. The merging of the public and private care systems means that mental health clinics will begin serving populations of patients who are quite different from their typical clientele. Mental health clinics will increasingly need to take on financial risk, requiring them to become extremely prudent managers of tight resources. Clinics and provider systems must become efficient to be successful competitors in the arenas of cost and quality. Finally, mental health agencies must become more proactive in their treatment schemes in order to be more focused on the health of the population they serve. This requires effective demand management systems and disease management programs, among other systems of care.

The changes these challenges bring undoubtedly will clash with some agency values. Resolving these conflicts requires adjusting values or limiting the amount of change undertaken in order to preserve values. For example, in many public sector mental health clinics, a high value is placed on training of future mental health practitioners. To make their training programs financially viable, clinics require trainees to provide services under the supervision of a licensed professional. Under the new finance systems, care provided by trainees may not be reimbursable, causing agencies to debate their ability to continue offering such programs.

Another factor that will have an impact on an agency's values is the pressure provider groups will feel to become linked contractually to larger integrated care systems. Such alignments often functionally merge organizations operating from different value systems. These systems will increasingly promote and may eventually require uniformity in the way the various units operate. Value clashes will put the leader of a mental health clinic in the middle, between the desires of the staff and the requirements of the megasystem.

The new healthcare system also requires the manager of a mental health clinic to take a careful look at the agency's values. Historically, mental health clinics have operated from a carve-out model of healthcare. In this model mental healthcare is managed separately from general healthcare and is provided by agencies that focus exclusively on mental health services. Such care is offered by mental health clinics operating independently of the remainder of a patient's healthcare providers. This created a discontinuity in the care system. Now, specialty mental health agencies are likely to be part of larger care systems that include all types of healthcare services an insured person might need. For example, in integrated delivery systems, the mental health clinic is likely to be part of a system that includes primary care services. Data on help seekers indicate that many people seek care for emotional problems from their primary care physician. Further, only a small fraction of those patients follow through on referrals to a specialty mental health clinic or practitioner. If an agency has as its core value, for instance, improving the mental health of the population it serves, then it may need to consider more active partnership with primary care physicians and seek to provide care more collaboratively.

The preceding situations are just a few of the reasons why leaders of a mental health clinic need to examine the agency's core values and adjust them as necessary to be consistent with everyday operational realities. Changes as profound as those occurring in the service delivery, finance, and care management systems will surely affect an agency's core values, sometimes beneficially and other times detrimentally. Regardless, change stimulated by factors outside the agency will provide challenges to the managers of mental health clinics.

Balancing Staff Member Desires with Funding Authority

A second critical balancing act centers on how an agency manager resolves the inevitable conflicts that arise between the desires of the agency staff and the needs of the host institution or funding source.

Funding Authority Expectations

Typically, mental health agencies have governing boards, host institutions, or other key constituents to whom they are accountable. These entities have expectations regarding how the agency functions, that is, how many people it serves, how much respect it affords its clientele, and how efficient the agency is with its resources. Sometimes the desires of the governing boards or host institutions are unrealistic, counterproductive, and if implemented would invite dysfunction. Other times there are legitimate concerns for greater efficiency, patient respect, improved access, broader scope of care, new service lines, and other needs of the consumer. It is a fact of agency life that from time to time pressure to change will originate from these groups. When it does, these key constituents expect the manager to accomplish their objectives.

Staff Expectations

The vast majority of a mental health clinic's budget goes toward paying staff salaries and this group also has a number of expectations. Staff members want managers to compensate them adequately and equitably and keep workload pressures in a manageable range to prevent burnout. They also need to feel in control of the cases they handle or tasks they perform. Providers of services also often have a vested interest in offering certain services, especially those they enjoy doing or in which they specialize. Providers are concerned about status as reflected in job titles or chances for promotion. They also want to work in systems that respect their judgment and professional codes of behavior. Regardless of efficiency, staff members often want to establish training programs in their agency. To further complicate the demands on the manager of a mental health agency, many staff who work in those agencies were trained in and identify with the traditional model of healthcare. In the traditional model of service, with its emphasis on passive-reactive care, there were few limits on length or intensity of treatment, and the providers enjoyed high autonomy. This gratified staff members' needs relatively well. Despite the pressure to shift to a new model of service and the desires of those with oversight of the agency, staff members expect the clinic manager to endorse and be an advocate for their needs even if it means conflict with the funding authority.

Role of Clinic Manager

The clinic manager is the interface among the multiple constituencies the agency must satisfy and is seen as being responsible for responding to the legitimate needs of all constituent groups. Obviously, there are places and points in time when the demands of one group conflict with the interests of another. Managers must be effective in handling or negotiating these competing demands. At times this means educating and negotiating with the funding authority about what is realistic, safe, legal, or ethical. Often key constituents have difficulty gauging the appropriateness of demands. One example of potential conflicting demand is when a governing board wants the agency to have only experienced staff providing service to consumers, which might mean the agency would have to shut down its training program. Another example is when a manager receives a request from a board member to keep the agency open 24 hours a day and staff it as inexpensively as possible. Staff members who would have to cover those hours may have concerns about safety and about the intrusion into family life, concerns that increase the cost of providing such care beyond what the initiator of the request considers reasonable. To these two examples could be added dealing with release of information about patients, conflict with ethical standards, and other concerns that need to be properly balanced in any decision.

Need for Efficiency and the Mandate for Quality

There are immense pressures on mental health care agencies to simultaneously improve both quality of care and efficiency. Although there is opportunity in many organizations to improve both quality and efficiency without sacrificing one for the other, fulfilling both mandates may, at times, place these goals in conflict with each other. The manager must succeed in meeting the demands to be a good, efficient steward of an organization's resources without surrendering quality of care.

Pressure for Efficiency

The pressure on all healthcare organizations to be as efficient as possible in the use of resources has clearly risen over the past decade, with competition spurred on by an increasingly organized healthcare marketplace. Local, regional, and even national provider groups are forming into integrated delivery systems. The boundary separating the public and private care sectors has blurred, and corporate purchasers of healthcare are forming purchasing consortia to leverage better deals from vendors of health plans. Managed competition has, indeed, contained or lowered healthcare costs, resulting in fewer dollars flowing to agencies and provider groups to provide the same amount or more service. Every mental health agency needs to thoroughly examine its efficiency and ultimately determine when further initiatives to improve efficiency conflict either with quality of care provided or the organization's core values.

Workload Distribution

Although how well a leader manages the core processes of the agency will determine to a large part that agency's efficiency, so will two other factors: the workload distribution system and the treatment modalities. Workload distribution systems establish expectations for the productivity level of each staff member, and facilitate fulfillment of those expectations through systems for scheduling care, managing utilization, and other means.

Treatment Modalities

Every agency has available a number of treatment modalities it can use to serve patients. These include inpatient services, intensive day treatment programs, individual psychotherapy, group treatments, seminars and workshops, and disease management programs. Efficient use of an agency's resources requires the manager to be able to determine definitively which treatment options the agency should offer and also to choose the method of determining which patients receive what treatment modality. Care must be taken to not sacrifice quality on the altar of efficiency. Essentially what an agency strives for is finding the most efficient care modality, that is, the treatment modality that gets equally good results compared to more time- and labor-intensive options.

Quality and Accountability Mandates

Although the pressure to be more efficient has been rising dramatically, so has the push for quality and accountability. There has been a growing emphasis on the quality of care provided to a health plan's enrollees. Increasingly, agencies are expected to gain accredited status, to examine and publicly report outcome and satisfaction-with-care data, to demonstrate positive impact on the health and disease status of the population of patients served, and to manage their providers so that agency care equals or exceeds identified standards for treatment of specific disorders. These types of quality mandates require the agency manager to work collaboratively with staff members to ensure they understand and support the need to examine, improve, and publicly report findings about the agency's quality of care. Every mental health agency should have an explicitly stated scope of care that defines what it does and does not do. What an agency says it does, it should do well. Its scope of care should set quality parameters. Furthermore, the agency's quality improvement process should examine all services offered within the agency's scope of care and detect opportunities for enhancements.

Role of the Manager

Clearly, the pressure to increase both efficiency and quality can strain the relationship between management and staff if not handled thoughtfully and openly by all involved. Achieving these twin goals requires an honest partnership and a true communitarian viewpoint. How well the manager helps staff deal with the opportunities and threats nested in the demands for efficiency and quality will have a lot to do with an organization's overall success. Every mental health service manager will find it quite challenging to determine first the appropriate thresholds for efficiency and quality and then the balance when one conflicts with achieving the other.

The Need for Continuous Process Improvement and Internal Stability

Because processes are at the heart of making products, manufacturers understand that both prosperity and survival are based on a fearless and open attitude toward modifying the processes used to produce their products. They realize that continuously improving processes through refinement or technological breakthroughs both gives them a competitive edge in efficiency and allows them to enhance quality. Consequently, manufacturers devote resources and energy to understanding and modifying their core processes and ensuring a smooth transition to the contemplated adjustments. The mental health agency manager can benefit from this approach.

Creating a Change Culture

Often, change brings with it opportunity and loss, both of which create some degree of internal instability in systems and in interpersonal relationships within an agency. Essentially, the manager of a mental health agency must create a change culture or climate in which members of the agency staff agree with the importance of constantly adjusting procedures to comply with state-of-the-art developments and also appreciate the need to adapt their functioning to incorporate desired process improvements. Herein lies one of the critical tasks of the manager: how to get staff to embrace change and then lead the agency through the change while not temporarily degrading service quality or inviting staff resistance or dysfunctional competition.

How efficiently a manager balances the press for improving processes with the ability of staff to incorporate those changes without morale problems is critically important to the smooth functioning of an agency. Every organization has a "bearing capacity" for change beyond which—no matter how well intentioned or needed the changes are—it will not be able to implement those changes successfully. This means that agency managers must be astute readers of how much change their organization can master before the staff is overwhelmed and agency functioning is immobilized. It is not simply a question of the number of changes, as many process improvements, the ones that simplify everyone's work, are easily incorporated and embraced by all. Rather it is more a question of understanding the difficulty staff will have in incorporating the changes into daily practices.

Administrative Processes

Processes that need to be subjected to continuous improvement in mental health agencies can be categorized into two types: administrative systems or processes, and caregiving processes. The administrative processes, such as client scheduling systems, billing systems, and record-keeping procedures, have been subjected to far greater systematic scrutiny than have the care-providing processes.

Therapeutic Processes

The notion that discernible gains in the therapeutic endeavor can be made by subjecting caregiving processes to process analysis has been slow to penetrate the human service profession. Therefore it has been only relatively recently that managers of mental health clinics have begun to grapple with the thorny problem of subjecting psychotherapeutic processes to the same degree of scrutiny for improvement that has been done for administrative systems.

More and more mental health clinic managers are recognizing the importance of clarifying and improving the fundamental therapeutic processes staff members use in treating agency clients. Clarified psychotherapeutic processes produce two key benefits: they help practitioners focus and channel judgment and they reduce substandard practices and unhelpful treatment variations across practitioners. The need for agencies to understand and improve caregiving processes is at an all-time high as the knowledge base informing practice rapidly expands, new pharmacological aids are approved, specializations proliferate, syndrome-specific treatments are developed, competition for clients becomes outcomes based, and other changes occur. It has become increasingly difficult for the individual practitioner to be the master of everything and weigh all factors when making judgments about care. Processes that provide systems for channeling judgment or metrics for solving problems can unburden practitioners and reduce what are known as "common cause" variations in performance due to substandard practices of individual providers.

Key Elements in Therapeutic Process Improvement

The ability of the clinic manager to improve psychotherapeutic processes has been hampered by the fact that few treatment processes have been detailed enough to serve as a basis for continuous improvement activities. Fundamental to the improvement of any processes are the following key elements. First, the people who are part of a process must function as a team by which discrete efforts are merged into a system of coherent functioning. Second, the component elements of the larger process must be clearly identified. Third, the agency's performance on each of the elements must be analyzed to determine opportunities for improvement. Fourth, once areas of opportunity are identified, an organization must develop procedures for modifying its processes. Last, once desired enhancements are made the effects of the change must be evaluated.

With more to know, integrate, and translate into practice, the greater the press to discover and understand the processes undergirding treatment of specific disorders. In an expanding knowledge base, failure to show progress on improving an agency's treatments jeopardizes both the practitioners and the agency because the greater the complexity the more chances there are for errors in judgment that could compromise a patient's treatment.

Understanding the value of continuous process improvement for the practitioners and the agency can lead the manager of a mental health clinic to lose sight of the burden change places on an agency and its staff. The challenge to the manager is to pace and sequence changes so that internal stability is not unduly compromised while the agency strives to provide the best care it can and maintain its competitiveness.

Balancing Accountability and Autonomy

At the agency level, autonomy is something that is typically earned. In general, the better an agency functions the more autonomy it is granted to achieve its mission. A central task of the clinic manager is to be able to strike the proper balance between achieving the autonomy the agency and its providers require to function and the need to be accountable for its actions to its patients and funding sources.

Accountability and autonomy are inextricably linked. If autonomy is granted without a foundation it serves little value. If withheld, quality and satisfaction are constrained. The agency manager must seek enough legitimate authority from funding or governing bodies for the agency to function effectively. At the same time, the manager must negotiate with staff to surrender some autonomy to ensure that the requisite level of accountability is established to support continued autonomy. Properly balanced, autonomy and accountability support each other. When out of balance, inefficiency, poor morale, and conflict result.

A task of the leader for the agency as a whole is to develop and manage an accountability system that does not unnecessarily constrain the autonomy and authority of the agency to develop innovative practices, utilize efficient treatment modalities, and exercise necessary professional judgment. Such an accountability system must also achieve a balance between holding staff accountable (e.g., for providing care, ethical functioning, meeting legal practice requirements, and continuing professional development) and providing it with the proper amount of autonomy and support to carry out its duties.

Balancing the competing yet complementary dimensions of autonomy and accountability require the leaders of a mental health clinic to use good negotiation processes to work through the needs espoused by consumer representatives, governing body members, agency staff, and accreditation bodies. Once balanced, maintaining harmony depends on achieving continued cooperation from these parties on the need to have some rational relationship between accountability and autonomy.

MAINTAINING THE AGENCY'S EFFECTIVENESS

This chapter conveys the message that continuous process monitoring and continuous improvement are at the very heart of successful management. Most of the fundamental processes that structure the work of an agency are fluid. Like all processes, if they are not attended to they will deteriorate or change in unintended ways, creating greater variation in performance. Additionally, mental healthcare is in a period of rapid and profound change which inevitably requires that the bedrock processes of an agency be continuously monitored and enhanced to ensure that they reflect state-of-the-art performance. Managers must also keep in mind that the core processes are interrelated and constantly compete for the attention of the manager and the resources of the agency. Successful managers are people who can balance competing demands, determining which processes must take precedence given the circumstances.

REFERENCES

Accreditation Association for Ambulatory Health Care. (1993). *1994/1995 Accreditation handbook for ambulatory health care.* Skokie, IL: Author.

Austin, L. A. (1979). *Zero-base budgeting.* New York: American Management Association, AMACOM.

Barker, J. (1992). *Future edge: Discovering the new paradigms of success.* New York: W. Morrow.

Deming, W. E. (1986). *Out of the crisis.* Cambridge, MA: MIT, Center for Advanced Engineering Study.

Emery, F. E., & Trist, E. L. (1965). The causal texture of organizational environments. *Human Relations, 18*(1), 21–32.

Gitlow, H. S., & Gitlow, S. J. (1982). *The Deming guide to quality, productivity, and competitive position.* Cambridge, MA: MIT, Center for Advanced Engineering Studies.

Hersey, P. (1984). *The situational leader.* New York: Warner Books.

Johnson, R. S. (1993). *TQM: Leadership for the quality transformation.* Milwaukee, WI: ASQC Quality Press.

Joint Commission on Accreditation of Healthcare Organizations. (1995). *The joint commission 1995 MHM accreditation manual for mental health, chemical dependency, and mental retardation/developmental disabilities services.* Oakbrook Terrace, IL: Author.

National Committee for Quality Assurance. (1997). *Accreditation standards for managed behavioral healthcare organizations.* Washington, DC: Author.

Odiorne, G. S. (1995). *Management by objectives.* New York: Pitman.

BIOGRAPHY

David J. Drum   David J. Drum received his Ph.D. from The American University, Washington, D.C., in 1969 and is a Diplomate of the American Board of Professional Psychology. For over 30 years he has managed university mental health centers. At The University of Texas at Austin, Dr. Drum is Associate Vice President for Student Affairs for Health Care, Director of the Counseling and Mental Health Center, and Professor of Counseling Psychology. He is a fellow of the American Psychological Association and in 1997 he received the Distinguished Service to the Profession Award from the American Board of Professional Psychology.

4

UNIVERSITY HOSPITAL ADMINISTRATION

RONALD B. MARGOLIS AND C. ALEC POLLARD

*Saint Louis University School of Medicine and
Saint Louis Behavioral Medicine Institute, Saint Louis, Missouri 63110*

INTRODUCTION

Besides having to keep pace with a rapidly changing healthcare system, numerous other challenges await nonphysicians administering mental health programs in academic healthcare centers (AHCs). Hospital-based psychologists, for example, are often strangers in a strange land, working in a system that does not understand the nature or value of psychological services and research. Despite these challenges, more psychologists work in AHCs than ever before (Litwin, Boswell, & Kraft, 1991; Sweet, Rozensky, & Tovian, 1991). Yet, very few resources in the literature directly address the needs of psychologists and other mental health professionals involved in university hospital administration.

The purpose of this chapter is to discuss issues relevant to mental health administrators and managers working in AHCs, with particular emphasis on challenges facing psychologists and other nonphysician mental health professionals in administrative positions. Among the topics addressed are the various ways in which mental health services can be organized within university hospital systems, the nuts and bolts of clinical program development, and the task of integrating academic activity with administrative and clinical responsibilities. Though it is not possible to address the needs of every professional in this position, it is hoped the issues discussed in this chapter are relevant to the vast majority of mental health administrators working in academic medical environments.

ORGANIZATIONAL MODELS

Mental health programs are administered in a variety of organizational settings and no two administrators' situations are identical. It is helpful for administrators to be familiar with the advantages and disadvantages of various organizational models. With this knowledge, administrators developing new programs are likely to make more informed organizational decisions and those with established programs can better manage the strengths and limitations of their program's organizational structure.

There are several alternative organizational models for psychologists working in AHCs, some of which have been discussed at recent meetings of the American Psychological Association (Pollard, 1995). One model is to organize psychologists into an independent department. John Arnett and Robert Martin (1995) from the University of Manitoba School of Medicine and Rosalyn Cartwright (1995) from Rush Medical College have discussed their experiences as chairs of independent departments of psychology situated in medical schools. Not all AHC psychology departments, however, are in medical schools. Nathan Perry (1995) chairs a department of clinical and health psychology at the University of Florida Health Sciences Center, but his department is located in the school of allied health. Another model has been described by Robert Thompson (1990) from Duke University School of Medicine. In this model, psychologists are organized as a division within a psychiatry department. This model is more common and usually less difficult to implement than the departmental model, but offers less autonomy to psychologists. Margolis and Pollard (1995) describe an alternative and less common division model operating at the St. Louis University School of Medicine. Their model is a multidisciplinary, behavioral medicine division headed by psychologists. This division was in the psychiatry department for many years before moving to the department of community and family medicine. One final model is the one presented by Danny Wedding (1995), who directs the Missouri Institute of Mental Health, an affiliate of the University of Missouri School of Medicine. An independent institute affiliated with a medical school, such as the one directed by Wedding, offers psychologists another viable organizational model.

At a meeting at Georgetown University, the Working Group on Governance and Administration (WGGA) of the Association of Medical School Psychologists (AMSP) decided that a common descriptive language was needed in order to discuss, evaluate, and compare how psychologists are organized at various healthcare centers (Margolis & Pollard, 1997). Instead of describing prototypes (e.g., department vs division in a department, etc.), the group identified ten key ways in which different organizational units of psychologists may vary:

1. *Type of Unit* (e.g., division, department, institute, college, or center)
2. *Host Unit* (e.g., medical school, other school in an academic health center, department in a medical school)
3. *Discipline Composition* (e.g., psychology only vs. multidisciplinary)
4. *Services* (e.g., research, clinical service, teaching/training, or public policy)
5. *Reporting Relationship* (To whom does the head of the unit report? The department chair, dean, division chief, vice president, etc.)
6. *Funding Source* (Where does funding come from? Is there more than one source?
7. *Clinical Privileges* (e.g., inpatient, outpatient, none)
8. *Degree Granted* (e.g., doctoral, master's, none)
9. *Advanced Training* (Does the unit train interns, practicum students, fellows, residents, etc.)
10. *Administrative Control* (To what extent are budgets, policy, practices, etc., determined by psychology?)

The WGGA concluded that no perfect organizational prototype exists that is universally applicable to all AHCs. Each center has its own history, political climate, resources, and competing services, and each psychology leader has his or her own supporters and detractors.

All of these factors are important to consider when making decisions about program organization. In reality, many psychologists working at AHCs are scattered about various departments with few or no organizational ties. Although some individuals have certainly succeeded in this situation, the WGGA did not feel that having psychologists work in isolation is optimal. The group stressed the value of having some organizational structure for psychologists working in the same AHC, and encouraged the development of at least informal ties whenever possible. Furthermore, given the vulnerability of psychologists in systems dominated by physicians, the group urged psychologists to develop organizational units with as much administrative control as possible. The stability and quality of psychology programs are best ensured when budgets, practice guidelines, and working conditions are determined by psychologists. It may not be possible or even desirable for all psychologists to be organized as independent departments, but they should be aware of the risks of practicing without administrative control and some formal structure.

CLINICAL PROGRAM DEVELOPMENT

Because most mental health administrators working in AHCs are either directly or indirectly involved in the provision of clinical services, we have devoted a large section of this chapter to clinical program development. The single greatest challenge currently facing developers of clinical programs is keeping pace with the rapidly evolving healthcare system. As the trend of integrating AHCs into larger healthcare delivery networks continues, for example, there will be increased reliance on mai.aged care and capitation contracts for service delivery. A clear impact of this trend is a greater need for managers to understand and actively navigate the shift in culture from purely academic or service values to a more business-oriented environment. Developing and directing clinical operations within an AHC requires administrators to gain expertise in multiple areas of healthcare delivery and organizational management (Yenney & American Psychology Association Practice Directorate, 1994).

The following subsections discuss several key issues relevant to the development of clinical programs in university hospital settings. Broad guidelines are provided because settings will vary greatly in terms of managed care penetration, network development, emergence of integrated delivery and financial systems, for-profit status, and many other factors.

Academicians and Clinicians as Managers

When academicians and clinicians are challenged to address business issues, there are several common reactions (Margolis, 1997): "If I do good clinical work, the program will do well"; "If I wanted to worry about budgets, I would have become a CPA"; "All I want to do is sit in my office and do research"; and "I find that quality cannot be measured, but I know what it is when I see it." All of these comments are reactions to the intrusion of business values onto the academic or clinical mission. While these responses are understandable, administrators must learn to consider their program as a business as well as an academic or clinical enterprise. Failure to ignore or fully understand the fiscal realities of an AHC places the administrator in a potentially vulnerable situaiton. Academic institutions simply do not have unlimited resources and faculty can no longer assume someone else is paying the bills. This challenge is certainly not limited to nonphysicians. For example, the following statement is from an address given by a physician at a medical society meeting (Norland, 1997):

> The take home message is that physicians can compete in a managed care market, but we see the money that the for-profit companies suck out of the system vanishing. We need resources; we need actuaries; we need to understand risks; we need to know how to manage risk; we need computers; quality assessment and business managers. Physicians must rapidly master the business part of the healthcare system. It is very similar to the airline industry where the pilots are the CEO's. We all entrust our lives to physicians and pilots. We have to know that they always have our best interests in mind. (p. 7)

Only after clinicians and academicians in administrative roles accept the business aspects of healthcare can they effectively take on the challenge of balancing the missions of research, education, service, and fiscal responsibility. In the current climate, failure to grasp this fundamental reality will jeopardize the viability of a program.

Human Resources

The success of any clinical endeavor in mental health service delivery is clearly dependent on people. Traditionally, university healthcare delivery systems have staffed key positions primarily with faculty. In part, this has been in response to the need to address the missions of research, education, and training in addition to service. As AHCs struggle for fiscal survival, relying more on clinical revenue than ever before, there is increasing tension between administrators and faculty over issues of clinical productivity. Naturally, many faculty clinicians perceive a clash between academic mission and the pressure to generate clinical revenue. They are concerned that teaching and research time will be less valued and less protected than in the past. To complicate matters, AHC leadership often gives mixed messages regarding how faculty should budget their time. The press for higher levels of clinical productivity is not always accompanied by the admission that less will be accomplished academically. Under these conditions, it is not surprising to hear some faculty comment on the lack of differentiation between their "academic positions" and those of their colleagues in the private sector.

One solution to the need for greater revenue from faculty is to place salaries at risk and create incentive systems tied to clinical revenue (e.g., the university only guarantees 50% of faculty salary with the remaining percentage tied to clinical productivity). Another solution is to change the personnel mix, shifting to more nonfaculty clinicians and an academic leadership that represents a minority of the clinical department. When doctoral level providers are needed they can be recruited as clinicians rather than faculty. They may be given adjunct or clinical appointments, but their primary role would clearly be defined as clinical service. Revenue generated by nonfaculty can help protect academic time for faculty, the business equivalent of recognizing that a research and development department is a critical part of any business, particularly an academic center. Faculty research and development is simply a cost of doing business in a field in which it is important to be on the cutting edge.

There are, of course, many other human resource challenges that are not unique to AHC mental health administrators. Like most managers, they must deal with staff recruitment, performance evaluations, job descriptions, incentive systems, corrective counseling, documentation of employee performance, and termination of staff. It is important for academic managers to appreciate the importance of these tasks in managing a successful organization. It is not sufficient to say that the hospital has a human resource department to take care of these things, because this would be an abdication of administrative responsibility. The administrator's close working relationship with the human resource and legal departments is crucial to a successful operation.

Assessing the Environment for Program Development

In the delivery of healthcare, an administrator has to continuously evaluate and assess the external environment. Although it is important to understand national trends in healthcare, it is even more crucial to understand what is happening in the local marketplace. The administrator needs to monitor changes in the community, such as new alliances, buyouts, mental health carve-outs, mergers, global capitation agreements (i.e., medical and psychiatric payments are combined and made prospectively on a per member per month basis with the risk assumed by the provider), and privatizations of the public sector. The maturity of each of these trends in the marketplace differs greatly across communities and healthcare systems.

In addition to understanding marketplace trends, it is helpful to know about existing community services relevant to the administrator's program. Thorough analysis of competing "products" can influence an administrator's decision to modify the development of a program, to start a new program, or to join with an existing program in the community. A competition analysis also helps administrators determine whether there is a market for their program at all.

In a university hospital, analysis of the internal environment is equally important. The administrator will need to find the answers to several key questions. For example, administrators should find out who is ultimately responsible for program development. Generally this will not be one person and can range from department chairs to chief financial officers, practice managers, hospital CEOs, and university management committees. There will also be factions with vested interests in the AHC that will view the development of a new program as either an asset or a threat. With increasing emphasis on cost reduction, the internal environment assessment should also ask whether the proposed program duplicates existing services within the hospital. To complicate matters further, if the hospital is currently part of either an affiliated or merged network, questions should also be raised about duplication within the network. Finally, keep in mind that the process of internal assessment is not just an opportunity to evaluate receptivity within the hospital, it is the starting point of "selling" a program to the internal market.

Product Definition and Development

A crucial step in developing programs is understanding and defining the product to be delivered. The administrator must clarify both the nature and the scope of the product before developing and marketing the program. This step should involve input from various sources. Furthermore, defining the product is an ongoing process that usually involves multiple revisions throughout the life of the program. For example, to be responsive to managed care, an administrator may develop an acute 23-hour, hospital-based clinical service to provide a temporary and safe environment for patients and avoid costly hospital admissions. The process of defining this product would likely involve input from AHC personnel familiar with hospital regulations, nursing administration, insurance and reimbursement specialists, and the hospital's emergency department. The process might also include feedback from patients, healthcare providers, managed care companies, and other potential consumers of this new service. Gathering input and seeking collaboration not only help define the product, but also identify the administrator as sensitive to the community's needs, rather than as an "ivory tower academician" out of touch with the marketplace.

Budgeting

Academicians and clinicians in the role of administrator have often been willing to rely on their business consultants and chief financial officers to create budgets. For most of these mental health administrators, training in budget management was not part of the graduate school curriculum. Nonetheless, it is crucial to understand the budgetary process, in particular, the principles involved in allocating expense and revenue. A helpful strategy for the "budget-challenged" administrator is to develop an ongoing, collaborative relationship with a fiscal manager who can educate the administrator about program management from a fiscal point of view.

One important part of a budget is the expenses, which can be subdivided into direct and indirect expenses. Direct expenses in AHC budgets are largely the same as those in other business budgets. For example, the following items are frequently included under direct expenses: salaries and benefits, consultants, supplies, minor equipment, capital equipment, maintenance of equipment, recruitment, marketing, telephone, professional development, space, and legal. Each institution will have its own specific guidelines for designating expense items.

A more politicized category of budgeting is indirect expense. Indirect expense is the overhead sometimes attributed by the university or hospital to cover activities of the dean's or university president's office, maintenance of the physical plant, and other general expenses. Institutions vary in how they allocate such costs. Clearly, academic institutions have legitimate overall administrative expenses that require funding. However, determining what is a reasonable amount of indirect expense and what is an equitable distribution by department or program is often a source of great contention. At many institutions, these issues have not always been discussed openly. However, with the growth of university practice groups managed by faculty, there is increasing demand for open review of this kind of fiscal information. Administrators may never be thrilled with the "dean's tax," but understanding the basis for it may lessen any mistrust.

Revenue, like expenses, can also be divided into direct and indirect revenues. Direct revenue is the dollars tied directly to the provision of clinical service and other sources of direct income. Direct revenue calculations frequently involve assumptions regarding concepts such as gross revenue, contractuals (i.e., discounts given to payors such as insurance companies and managed care organizations as part of a contractual relationship), and bad debt (i.e., accounts/amounts written off as uncollectible). These terms are not always understood by mental health administrators, but are crucial to the fiscal management of a program. Administrators should become familiar with these general concepts as well as their AHC's specific assumptions regarding bad debt, contractual allowances, calculation of deductibles, and other financial terms. Knowledge of these concepts and assumptions can help guide some program policy decisions. For example, an institution may assume that revenue not collected after 180 days should be written off at 100%. This assumption should be considered when deciding how a program will handle patients in litigation for payment that may not be received for several years.

Indirect revenue refers to the amount of money generated by other departments of the hospital that is in some way attributable to a program. Although not always in a program's ongoing financial statement, indirect revenue is often considered in the decision to start or maintain a program. For example, a clinical service may triage patients to other parts of the hospital. This program has then indirectly generated revenue for the institution by creating business for other departments. Another example is Medicare allowances for education. Such items do not always appear directly on the budget, but do fiscally benefit the institution.

Finally, it should be noted that many of the assumptions regarding expense and revenue significantly change under a capitated reimbursement system. For example, in a capitated environment, a program with high patient utilization that was once a substantial source of revenue may now be viewed as a significant expense to the organization. Under capitation, a greater focus is placed on management of expense in evaluating the fiscal impact of a program. Thus, budgeting assumptions depend greatly on the market and on the model of reimbursement and service delivery.

Information Systems

The administration of mental health services relies on information systems (see Freeman, this volume). Given the sophistication of these systems, the availability of experts within the university is an advantage for managers in AHCs. It is nonetheless important that administrators be educated consumers and understand the powerful role that information systems can play in the management of patient registration, billing, marketing, data gathering, utilization review, quality assurance, and many other facets of operation. Electronic records and electronic billing may in the near future be a required part of clinical practice. Efforts to integrate clinical practice and research will also be greatly facilitated by the newer information systems. Information management requirements, particularly for the operation of large-scale programs, are significant. Consumers of information include clinical staff, patients, administrators, hospitals, insurance companies, utilization reviewers, and case managers. A user-friendly, nonduplicative information system can be an enormous advantage in the competitive marketplace.

Marketing

Although some university systems still view marketing as merely public relations, most recognize the comprehensive nature of this endeavor. Marketing is an essential component of programs that succeed in a competitive environment (Pollard & Margolis, 1993). The first step of marketing is to identify a program's customers. In mental health delivery, customers can include patients, community agencies, employee assistance programs (EAPs), managed care companies, primary care physicians, and businesses. Each of these customer groups becomes the target of specific marketing strategies.

Most marketing strategies are simply different ways of communicating with customers. Methods of communicating to markets include academic publications, advertising, brochures, stories in the media, newsletters, presentations, telephone calls, meetings, and, more recently, the internet. University hospital-based systems have an advantage in communicating with television and print media because faculty are often the experts in a given area. Research can play a dual role of advancing the academic mission and bringing public attention to a program. A market niche for AHCs is as a center for cutting-edge treatments, tertiary services, and university experts.

A key component of any marketing plan should be personal contact. Ultimately, the objective of other communication strategies is to bring principal customers (e.g., physicians, case managers, EAPs, etc.) in contact with the mental health experts at the university hospital. Most programs cannot afford to wait for customers to come to them. A challenge for administrators is therefore to move providers out of their offices and into the offices of referral sources. Furthermore, in the competitive marketplace in which most AHCs are trying to survive, marketing cannot be something done only by those willing to do it. The institution's culture must promote active, continuous referral development as the responsibility of all staff.

Quality Management

Another advantage of AHCs is the availability of utilization review (UR) and quality improvement (QI) departments (see McDonel et al., this volume). However, although hospital UR and QI programs have long been helpful for the delivery of inpatient care, they frequently have had less experience with outpatient services. Quality and utilization issues are obviously just as crucial to outpatient programs as they are to inpatient services, a fact increasingly recognized by regulatory agencies.

Administrators cannot view UR and QI as simply the job of the utilization manager. Quality requires that administrators attend to all aspects of service delivery, including the patient's first call on the phone, the suitability of parking, how patients and visitors are greeted in the waiting area, the efficacy of treatment, and the efficiency of the billing process. Admittedly, control over many of these aspects of operation is elusive in a university hospital system. Nonetheless, administrators need to monitor UR and QI and to exert whatever influence they have to ensure their program provides high-quality service. There are many consultants, workshops, and books available on customer service and total quality management that present methods pioneered in other industries that are applicable to mental health delivery systems (e.g., Drucker, 1990; Peters, 1987).

Managed Care Negotiations

Development of managed care contracts and delivery of contracted services requires constant attention, relationship building, and the ability to deliver on agreements. In many university hospital systems, managed care negotiations are centralized by a hospital management team. Unfortunately, in this situation mental health services frequently become a secondary priority compared with other high-dollar managed care services (e.g., transplants). Thus, it is crucial for managers of mental health programs to play an active role in negotiations, either by serving on managed care contracting committees or by taking over contracting functions for mental health with the support of the hospital system. Many managed care organizations have mental health professionals in key administrative roles. This obviously places mental health administrators in the best position to understand and intelligently discuss issues addressed in a mental health contract.

It is important to recognize that approaching managed care from a university hospital base may have some disadvantages for a managed care contractor. Medical centers are historically viewed by managed care as expensive, inflexible, and biased toward overtreatment, particularly in inpatient care. Further complicating negotiations is managed care's refusal to pay for services delivered by trainees. This is an evolving issue that could have a significant impact on the future of professional training and one that currently places hospital-based mental health systems at a disadvantage. Another potential point of conflict with managed care is the AHC mission of developing new, more effective treatments. Cutting-edge treatment may in fact be efficacious and reduce costs, but frequently such procedures are not yet covered by managed care. The challenge is to convince managed care companies of the merits of these new interventions, which requires clinical outcome data presented in a way that is easily understood by managed care representatives.

AHC programs may have some advantages in negotiating with managed care, particularly university hospitals that have joined larger healthcare delivery networks. Managed care often wants relationships with healthcare systems that are comprehensive, cost-effective, and offer one-stop shopping. University hospitals that have joined networks offer tertiary, specialized treatment while also providing the full spectrum of care and desirable geographic coverage. Whether university-based or not, one key to working successfully with managed care is understanding that the contract phase is only the beginning. The contract is just one phase of an ongoing relationship that requires review of contract performance and continuous feedback between the managed care company and the AHC.

INTEGRATING ACADEMIC ACTIVITY

With greater reliance on clinical revenue, it is increasingly difficult for faculty to achieve the academic mission of AHCs. The old model of faculty working in the clinic for six hours and devoting the rest of the week to academics is no longer a viable practice for academia. In terms of protected time for education and research, there is clearly a loss with the new environment. Administrators need to search for different ways to protect time for training and for advancing the science of mental health, while continuing to deal with the fiscal realities of healthcare.

One possible solution discussed earlier involves changing the mix of clinical staffing in AHCs, with less reliance on faculty. This strategy reduces the cost of overhead and protects more time for a smaller number of academically productive faculty. Another option is to look at clinical services as a major focus for research efforts and to tailor information systems and clinical protocols to advance the goals of research. Given the emphasis on development of clinical pathways and practice guidelines, AHCs are well positioned to develop empirically derived treatment models currently in greater demand than ever before.

Another significant concern for AHC mental health administrators is their training mission. As more public sector healthcare delivery systems are privatized, opportunities for training are diminishing. In the private sector, managed care has been reluctant to approve trainees as providers of care. The current lack of funding support for training represents a major threat to our healthcare system. AHCs cannot afford to wait until leadership in managed care understands the need for academic training. Administrators need to become active advocates for training. This role includes working with state government, mental health management systems, and the court of public opinion to take corrective action before the nation's healthcare system faces a serious shortage of trained professionals.

ADVOCACY WITHIN THE AHC

As we have indicated previously, there is no single blueprint for a successful organizational unit applicable to all AHCs. Each administrator needs to adapt principles of administration and management to his or her own institution. One priority for all administrators, however, should be to educate their AHC about the nature and value of mental health services. The better an AHC understands mental health and the psychological aspects of physical health, the greater the chances are that a mental health program will survive in that organization. In addition, the quality of a program will depend in part on the extent to which an AHC appreciates the conditions under which mental health programs are most likely to thrive.

To address this issue, the WGGA developed seven organizational guidelines for AHCs (Margolis & Pollard, 1997). The group proposed that AHCs that employ psychologists should strive to do the following:

1. Provide high-quality psychological services that are cost-effective in reducing symptom distress and improving patient functioning and that are accessible to all relevant patients.
2. Ensure that psychologists participate in governance and are granted faculty rank and status with rights and opportunities equivalent to those of any other doctoral level healthcare profession.
3. Facilitate the participation of psychologists in all aspects of the AHC academic mission, including teaching, training, and research.
4. Make psychological expertise and knowledge accessible to all relevant categories of students and trainees in the AHC.
5. Have an internal system of quality control for the practice of psychology that is determined and monitored by psychologists.

6. Ensure that psychology meets nationally recognized standards for the profession of psychology.
7. Create a distinct budget for psychology under the direction of a psychologist that is evaluated according to the same principles of cost–benefit analysis as are applied to the budgets of other disciplines within the AHC.

These guidelines outline an ideal environment for psychologists working in a university hospital. They are based on the premise that stable and effective services are more likely to occur when the program's leadership actively participates in the organization and is granted authority over and accountability for a program's operations. It should be noted, however, that few healthcare centers currently meet these guidelines fully. The recommendations provide a model for AHCs to use in making organizational decisions. Although the AMSP has pledged to educate AHCs about the guidelines, mental health administrators need to work proactively to actualize these guidelines at their respective healthcare institutions. To the extent these guidelines are not met, the quality of programs, as well as the quality of life of those who administer them, will be diminished.

FINAL COMMENTS

As AHCs scramble to find an organizational model to move them successfully into the future, road maps for mental health administrators may be hard to find. AHC administrators will have to cope with numerous unpredictable changes in their organization's structure, policies, and priorities. They will also have the predictable tasks of managing faculty who long for the good old days when chairs were more interested in academics than clinical revenue and dealing with clinicians who do not like the world of managed care. Do all of these changes mean an end to science, faculty roles, clinical training, and cutting-edge mental health service? No, the sky is not falling, but it is definitely changing and administrators will need to adapt.

There is little doubt that AHCs will look significantly different ten years from now. The "true faculty" will become smaller in number, as clearer distinctions are made between the roles and functions of different types of staff. In the clinical world, the current emphasis by third-party payors on cost may eventually return to quality, but not until clinicians have had to survive several shifts in the way in which services are reimbursed. Throughout the entire process, mental health administrators will be called on to manage these changes effectively. Creative, risk-taking administrators who can adapt without abandoning their academic and clinical values will help define the AHCs of the future.

REFERENCES

Arnett, J. A., & Martin, R. M. (1995, August). *Discussant presentation for symposium entitled "Survival in university medical settings: Alternative organizational models for psychology.* Paper presented at the meeting of the American Psychological Association, New York.

Cartwright, R. D. (1995, August). *A psychology department in a school of medicine.* Paper presented at the meeting of the American Psychological Association, New York.

Drucker, P. F. (1990). *Managing the Nonprofit Organization.* New York: HarperCollins.

Litwin, W. J., Boswell, D. L., & Kraft, W. A. (1991). Medical staff membership and clinical privileges: A survey of hospital affiliated psychologists. *Professional Psychology: Research and Practice, 22*(4), 322–327.

Margolis, R. B. (1977). Building and maintaining clinical programs. *Journal of Clinical Psychology in Medical Settings, 4*(1), 35–40.

Margolis, R. B., & Pollard, C. A. (1997). Report of the Working Group on Administration and Governance. *Journal of Clinical Psychology in Medical Settings, 4*(1), 29–33.

Margolis, R. B., & Pollard, C. A. (1995, August). *A behavioral medicine division repositioned within a university healthcare network.* Paper presented at the meeting of the American Psychological Association, New York.

Norland, C. C. (1997, January). Inaugural Address. *Metro Medicine,* pp. 6–9.

Perry, N. (1995, August). *A psychology department in a school of allied health.* Paper presented at the meeting of the American Psychological Association, New York.

Peters, T. (1987). *Thriving on chaos.* New York: Alfred A. Knopf.

Pollard, C. A. (Symposium Chair). (1995). *Survival in university medical settings: Alternative organizational models of psychology.* New York: American Psychological Association.

Pollard, C. A., & Margolis, R. B. (1993). Marketing psychological services based in a university medical center: Practical and ethical considerations. *Psychotherapy in Private Practice, 12,* 15–22.

Sweet, J. J., Rozensky, R. H., & Tovian, S. M. (1991). *Handbook of clinical psychology in medical settings.* New York: Plenum.

Thompson, R. L. (1990, August). *Perspectives from a medical psychology division in a psychiatry department.* Paper presented at the meeting of the American Psychological Association, Boston.

Wedding, D. (1995, August). *An independent institute affiliated with a psychiatry department.* Paper presented at the meeting of the American Psychological Association, New York.

Yenney, S. L., & American Psychological Association Practice Directorate. (1994). *Business strategies for a caring profession.* Washington, DC: American Psychological Association.

BIOGRAPHIES

Ronald B. Margolis   Ronald B. Margolis, Ph.D. is a professor in the Department of Community and Family Medicine at Saint Louis University School of Medicine and Director of the Saint Louis Behavioral Medicine Institute. Dr. Margolis's professional interests and publications are in the areas of administration and management of behavioral health services, family therapy, chronic pain, and cognitive functioning in the elderly.

C. Alec Pollard   Dr. Pollard is a professor in the Department of Community and Family Medicine at Saint Louis University School of Medicine and Director of the Anxiety Disorders Center at the Saint Louis Behavioral Medicine Institute. In addition to being widely published in the field of anxiety disorders, Dr. Pollard has written about a number of key issues relevant to the administration and management of mental health services.

5

MANAGING A MANAGED CARE ORGANIZATION

NICHOLAS A. CUMMINGS

Foundation for Behavioral Health, Scottsdale, Arizona 85251

INTRODUCTION

This chapter deals with the creation of a new industry, financing and implementing the first company protype, and then building it within seven years to become the largest company of its kind. More to the point, it is a case study in entrepreneurship rather than just management, which may be of considerable value to many mental health practitioners as they become energetically involved in the formation of a broad range of new and unique enterprises. These include not only managed care companies (MCOs), but also contract research organizations (CROs)—which, as outside companies, can perform the credible outcomes studies all MCOs need—telecommunications companies that service the communications needs of the current health industry, and provider-driven networks that contract with MCOs or with the regional purchasing consortia of employers. Other practitioners who developed their knowledge and skills in employment with successful start-up companies have formed consulting services to help practitioners form their own enterprises and to provide the management, financing and marketing skills that are not readily acquired in the conventional education and training of the mental health practitioner.

MANAGEMENT VERSUS ENTREPRENEURSHIP

I founded American Biodyne, proximal to the so-called Silicon Valley in California, and had the opportunity to get to know many of the legendary figures who made the Golden Age of the Silicon Valley. I also had the opportunity to get to know the venture capitalists who financed their unique start-ups, from whom I learned as much regarding entrepreneurship as I did from knowing the entrepreneurs themselves and by being one of them. As a group, they have two things in common: 1) the founder of a start-up already *knows* how he or she will make it work, and sees this successful outcome when no one else can; and 2) founders of start-ups are essentially entrepreneurs and not managers. An entrepreneur must listen to only his or her own voice, because everyone else is telling the innovator that the idea is unworkable, too risky, and even preposterous. Listening to others' advice will cause the entrepreneur to question his or her own belief that the risk is irrelevant inasmuch as the implementation and subsequent success are obvious. The manager, on the other hand, must listen to everyone, distill all that has been heard, and accordingly make an appropriate and correct management decision.

Successful entrepreneurs usually make terrible managers, and timing is important: at the point the company is no longer a start-up, the entrepreneur must pass the reins of the mature company over to the next generation of (professional) managers. Many, if not most entrepreneurs are incapable of letting go of their creation, forcing their venture capitalists or stockholders to evict them. This befell Steve Jobs, the brilliant founder of Apple Computers, who resisted all advice to resign as CEO and was painfully thrown out of his own company by Arthur Rock, the country's foremost venture capitalist who had financed him and had become his close friend. Job's successor, John Sculley, all but destroyed Apple Computers before he, in turn, was thrown out—but that is another story. The fact is that such corporate bloodletting is avoided when the founder intuitively recognizes it is time to step down. There are enough exceptions (e.g., David Packard of Hewlett-Packard, Armand Hammer of Occidental Petroleum, and perhaps Bill Gates of Microsoft) to persuade the unwilling entrepreneur that he or she will be the one-in-a-hundred exception to the so-called rule.

CREATION OF AN INDUSTRY

Background

During the 1970s and 1980s the inflationary curve for healthcare began to spiral out of control, often exceeding the inflation rate of the general economy by two and three times. The federal government grew increasingly concerned and through a series of unsuccessful initiatives, such as monetary incentives to increase the supply of physicians in the expectation this would increase competition and reduce fees, sought to reduce the rate of inflation in healthcare costs. It was not until the mid-1980s before any of these government interventions affected costs, and then only medical and surgical costs. The cost of mental health and chemical dependency (MH/CD) services accelerated sharply, nullifying the savings in medicine and surgery and driving the continued spiral of inflation. There are reasons why these initiatives succeeded or failed, but all were influential in the creation of managed care and particularly managed behavioral care, both of which were new industries.

Supply and Demand

When the government discovered that the shortage of physicians that plagued healthcare in the United States during the decades of 1940 to 1970 was about to come to an end, public policy began to rely heavily on the economic "laws" of supply and demand to curtail healthcare costs. There were enough physicians in the pipeline to not only terminate the shortage, but also result in a glut of physicians. When the era of physician surplus arrived, to everyone's dismay healthcare costs not only continued to increase, but the rate of increase even accelerated. Soon it became apparent that the reason for this was that physicians controlled both supply and demand: as each physician experienced a reduction in patient clientele, he or she merely increased the number of billable procedures for each patient and for every condition. Not only was the temporary loss of income short-lived, physician incomes climbed to new heights. It was not until the late 1980s when physicians lost control of healthcare in favor of those who pay the bills (employers, taxpayers, government and third-party payors in general) that healthcare began to respond to the laws of supply and demand.

Federal HMO Legislation

The prototype of the modern health maintenance organization (HMO) was founded shortly after World War II and grew rapidly. This Kaiser Permanente Health System from the very beginning drew the wrath of the medical profession, which retaliated by refusing to allow the Kaiser physicians to belong to the county medical societies. On the other hand, it captured the favorable interest of health economists. During the Nixon administration legislation was enacted that allowed the federal government to encourage and fund the formation of HMOs which until 1975 had been largely a California and Minnesota phenomenon. The White House saw HMOs as the possible solution to the healthcare economic crisis. Senator Edward Kennedy, who chaired the U.S. Sentate Subcommittee on Health, saw HMOs as bringing the nation one step closer to nationalized healthcare. With this empowerment, HMOs proliferated from less than 1% of the insured population to their current status as the dominant healthcare system in the nation. Unfortunately, HMOs did not deliver behavioral care very efficiently, and sought to control costs by either providing crisis care only or by capping the benefit at 10 or 20 sessions. The exception was Kaiser Permanente in Northern California, which experimented extensively with efficient/effective psychotherapies, later known as Brief, Intermittent Psychotherapy Throughout the Life Cycle, or just "HMO Therapy" (Cummings & Sayama, 1995; Cummings & VandenBos, 1981).

Enactment of DRGs

Frustrated by the continued high inflationary curve in healthcare, in the mid-1980s, Congress placed into effect the table of diagnosis related groups (DRGs) for Medicare and Medicaid reimbursement to hospitals. This mandated a set number of days of hospitalization for each of almost 400 conditions. If the hospital exceeded the allowance, it lost money. If it used less than the allowance, it made a profit. Soon the insurance industry emulated the new cost structure and hospitals found themselves with as much as a 50% empty bed rate in medical and surgical services. Hospitals were used to a reimbursement rate of cost plus 15% and under the new rules they fell into financial difficulty. Many closed their doors, and many more were sold to proprietary chains. Nonetheless, for the first time in history medical and surgical costs were tethered and the inflationary spiral was slowed.

In direct contrast, MH/CD costs spun to their highest level ever. Alert hospital administrators, seeing that there were no DRGs in psychiatry, converted all of the empty beds to MH/CD services and huckstered new 30-, 60-, and even 120-day programs in television commercials. Within three years, MH/CD costs doubled, with the greatest increases going to new and highly touted adolescent programs. There was suddenly a remarkable behavioral healthcare cost crisis in America.

Turning the Private Sector Loose

Unable to construct DRGs for MH/CD, the federal government tacitly decided to let the private sector solve the problem. It was at this point that what is now known as managed care was born. Decades of laws and regulations restricting the so-called corporate practice of medicine were at first ignored, then either repealed or struck down by the courts. Companies sprung up to help HMOs and the new managed care companies (MCOs) manage their MH/CD costs, essentially using utilization review (UR) as the primary tool. Essentially, UR is the process by which a payor company reviews utilization practice patterns and compares physicians who provide a relatively high intensity of services with those who are ostensibly more efficient. This results in a chilling effect known as the sentinel effect." The new industry known as managed behavioral care, working as an efficient and effective delivery system, was yet to be established.

Conceptual Predecessors to Managed Behavioral Care Delivery

Several events preceded the MH/CD cost crisis and DRGs that had an impact in the conceptualization and implementation of what was to become the nation's first behavioral health delivery system. These were the discovery of the medical cost offset effect, the Bethesda Consensus Conference, and the Hawaii Medicaid Project.

Medical Cost Offset

In the mid-1950s Kaiser Permanente discovered that 60% of its physician visits were by persons who had no physical disease, or whose medical condition was being exacerbated by stress and emotional conflict (Cummings & Follette, 1968;

Cummings, Kahn, & Sparkman, 1965; Cummings & VandenBos, 1981; Follette & Cummings, 1967). This was later verified as a general finding within the medical system of the United States, and the collateral finding that behavioral interventions could significantly reduce the overutilization of medical and surgical services became the focus of research by the National Institute of Mental Health and the Health Economics Branch of the then Department of Health, Education and Welfare. This medical cost offset effect was important in persuading the health insurance industry to include psychotherapy as a covered benefit for the first time, and set the stage for the continued development of HMO Therapy, a focused and brief therapy model.

The Bethesda Consensus Conference

In 1979, the federal government published a compilation of all the medical cost–offset research available (Jones & Vischi, 1979) and subsequently convened the Bethesda Consensus Conference (Jones & Vischi, 1980). Reviewing all of the research findings, this conference concluded that medical cost offset savings were greatest in organized settings and increased proportionally to the degree the behavioral interventions were innovative and focused. At the same time, the Healthcare Financing Administration (HFCA) was becoming concerned with the escalating cost of Medicaid, which was significantly exceeding that of the run-away costs in the private sector. It was decided to conduct an extensive research and demonstration project in Medicaid.

The Hawaii Medicaid Project

Hawaii was chosen as the site. This seven-year, $5.5 million project was funded and supervised by HCFA, and the contract required annual renewal, enabling the government to end the project at any time if it were shown to be unsuccessful or problematic. I served as the principal investigator and created a nonprofit delivery system named the Biodyne Centers, after two Greek words meaning "life change." It was here that what came to be known as the Biodyne Model was refined and, in response to Congressional legislation encouraging researchers to take federally funded results into the private (proprietary) sector, American Biodyne was launched in 1985.

Interestingly, after the Hawaii Project results were widely disseminated, HCFA drastically altered its regulations to permit the states to contract their Medicaid services to managed care (Cummings, Dorken, Pallak, & Henke, 1993). For the second time, medical cost offset significantly affected national public policy.

The Vision

A description of the new industry, along with the business strategy, was presented in a major address to the American Psychological Association, coincidental with the founding of American Biodyne, and published one year later (Cummings, 1986). I tried to give away the technology and indicated that I would cap American Biodyne at 500,000 covered lives, leaving opportunity for another 49 such companies. American Biodyne would serve as a model, where psychologists could come to learn and train in the new industry, and then go out and emulate it with their own companies. In this way practitioners would own managed behavioral care delivery, thus guaranteeing it would remain clinically driven.

The prediction that this model would attract 25 million enrollees is modest in hindsight, inasmuch as the industry surpassed 100 million enrollees in some form of managed behavioral care within the first decade. Nonetheless, practitioners considered the plan grandiose, and leaders in the profession predicted it was nothing but a passing fad (Wright, 1992). I kept my promise to cap American Biodyne for three years, at which point I realized no one was going to accept my offer. I then marketed the company aggressively for the first time, and within five years achieved an enrollment of 14.5 million. This success did not go unrecognized by business interests. The model was widely emulated, with dozens of competitors emerging within a brief period. This was in keeping with original predictions (Cummings, 1986), but the industry has not been cognizant of a companion prediction that these "carve-outs," as they came to be known, would serve a useful purpose for about ten years. They were necessary because health plans were unable to curtail their own MH/CD costs. Once the technology was known to all, it would be unnecessary to have outside companies performing the task, and it would be time to "carve back in." Rightfully, behavioral health belongs with and as a part of primary care (Cummings, Cummings, & Johnson, 1997).

FOUNDING THE COMPANY

Three tasks must be completed before it can be said the company is launched. Once the company has been conceptualized, it is necessary to prepare a business plan, assemble the team, and obtain capital. Although interdependent, each is critical to the successful start-up, and each must be performed equally well.

The Business Plan

The business plan with its financial projections is integral to the start-up (Cummings, 1996). Most mental health professionals have never so much as seen a business plan, and that is an excellent starting point. Assemble as many business plans from successful start-ups as one can borrow. These do not have to be in the same industry, but they should resemble one's own start-up in size and scope. Fortunately there is now software which will help in the organization and preparation, but it will not write the business plan.

The business plan must tell a compelling story. It must showcase the founders, emphasize the competitive edge, and have numbers that will make sense when potential investors crunch them. It must clearly determine the mission, goals, and strategies of the company, and honestly present problems and solutions. There have been great ideas with poorly constructed business plans, and poor ideas with excellent business plans, neither of which is viable. The business plan produced in preparation for the launching of American Biodyne was the best presentation of an excellent idea that I could muster. It told the story well: why a new industry was timely and why the assembled team could accomplish the mission. It presented one-, two-, three-, and five-year financial projections which were conservatively optimistic and believable. It is better to exceed the original financial projections, especially in the early years. If a company should require a second tier of funding for expansion or even reformulation, having fallen short of expectations will render the task of tapping additional capital, or even a loan, more difficult.

Once the business plan has been written to its best possible presentation, it is then given to the lawyers to insert the necessary legal disclaimers, such as, "This is a risky new business that has never before been attempted, and the investor may lose his or her investment in total." When I saw this and the large number of other blood-curdling insertions required by the legal aspects of the process, I was appalled. But I soon learned that seasoned investors ignore these legal disclaimers and make their own experienced judgment as to the potential of the company.

Most sophisticated potential investors, and especially venture capitalists (VCs), will not explore a deal beyond the business plan. If it is lacking either in presentation or conceptualization, they will distance themselves without ever telling the founders why. It is literally the *key* to the start-up.

The Team

Although sophisticated investors and venture capitalists (VCs) look mostly to the principal founder, they firmly believe it requires a team to make a company successful. They shy away from what they refer to as "Lone Rangers," and look to a team that has a number of critical characteristics.

Overcoming Risk Aversion

Most mental health professionals are highly risk aversive, and as such would never undertake a start-up company. A surprisingly impressive number, however, are currently proving this may become far from typical. No matter how entrepreneurial the principal founder may be, the team of founders must also have overcome their own risk aversion.

Many VCs have confided in me that their decisions are based only 25% on the excellence of the idea, and 75% on the ability and confidence of the founders to pull it off (Cummings, Pallak, & Cummings, 1996). The ideal founder is a David Packard, working 18 hours a day in a rented garage because he was too poor to rent an office-workshop, who goes on with his partner Hewlett to form one of the fortune 500 companies. Few practitioners can match the confidence and dedication of a Dave Packard, Steve Jobs, or Bill Gates, and investors do not expect this ideal. Yet they are put off when the would-be entrepreneur desperately retains his or her faculty position, government appointment, or other full-time job. This behavior telegraphs to the potential investor that the practitioner has little confidence in his or her own ability or idea, and the concept has been relegated to the status of an exciting hobby which deserves capitalization. The investors in American Biodyne years later told me that they were most impressed by my determination to start the company at age 62, risking retirement savings with little opportunity to regain them if the venture should collapse. When questioned by them, I responded, "This idea is so good that if I can't make it work I deserve to live my old age in poverty." This one response turned a liability (the relatively advanced age for founding a start-up) into an asset.

The Fire-in-the-Belly

The zeal known among VCs as "the fire-in-the-belly" is mostly expected of the principal founder, but they also look for a somewhat lesser manifestation of it in the members of the team. American Biodyne was fortunate in recruiting three co-principal founders who not only left prestigious and well-paying positions, but were eager to accept low salaries in exchange for an equity position comprising 1% or more of the company. For an income substantially below their previous levels, the operations officer left a vice presidency in a national medical supply corporation, the finance officer left a lucrative position with a world-class accounting firm, and the clinical officer resigned a senior post with the nation's largest HMO. All three were in their mid-thirties in age and knew that since equity was the reward, if they each did not make the company succeed they would have nothing ten years later.

Risk-taking and fire-in-the-belly are never touted in the business plan, but their existence is readily apparent in the manner in which the compelling story is told.

Eschew the Few

Most successful business executives or clinicians will not leave a status position to join a start-up, but occasionally there are a few so willing because they have accumulated enough wealth to mitigate the risk. They may want the greater reward possible in a start-up, or they may seek the excitement absent in their present dull but lucrative job. The fire-in-the-belly is not only absent, but they are also not taking the chance of losing all that may be characteristic of the young competent executive who has not yet "arrived." These applicants should be carefully screened. As American Biodyne grew, it was believed that the company would prosper by hiring these prestigious and established types. Of several so hired, not a single one remained long with the company, usually leaving by mutual consent.

It is never comfortable making sweeping generalizations, but it is almost as important to know what not to look for as it is to be aware of what is needed. The following characteristics, admittantly unfair to the many exceptions, should be regarded as signs necessitating further inquiry. The longer and higher a business executive has climbed the corporate ladder, the less useful he or she is likely to be. Such a person is used to the prestige, the perks, the authority, and the high salary. Similarly, the longer one has been cloistered in academia, especially in a tenured position, the less likely he or she will adapt to the ambiguities and insecurities of a start-up. And the least desirable prospects are found in government, where competence must take a back seat to politics. It must be emphasized that once American Biodyne learned these lessons and interviewed such applicants with a wary eye, it found excellent personnel from all three venues.

Positioning the Company

There are essentially three ways to position a company, and this must be done at the outset as it is difficult to change once the company has succeeded (or failed): a start-up with exit strategy, a start-up in perpetuity, or an options-open strategy.

Exit Strategy

Most start-ups have as their goal an initial public offering (IPO) within five years. VCs insist on this as their best means for cashing-out. It also makes the founder's stock liquid and raises a war chest to use for acquisitions, finance expansion, and wipe out debt. At this point, ownership shifts from a closely held private company to one that is publicly traded, in the health industry usually on the NASDAQ. If this is the strategy, it should be positioned in the business plan with factors that would signal the successful initiation of an IPO.

In Perpetuity

Although the preceding strategy is sought in almost every start-up, there is an unusual kind of group, seemingly limited to healthcare, for which the goal is one of perpetuation without an exit strategy. The outstanding examples are the several Permanente Medical Groups that contract with the nation's original and largest HMO, the Kaiser Health Plan. The purpose is to provide a stable, practitioner-owned environment in which to practice for one's entire career. This strategy, of particular attraction to the practitioner, is more fully discussed elsewhere (Cummings, 1996).

Options Open

In the third type of strategy, the original intent may be to have a group practice in perpetuity, but the company can be positioned from the beginning so that it can keep open the option of being acquired or going public. American Biodyne positioned itself from the beginning to keep its options open. It was anticipated that as long as the intention was to cap the company at half a million enrollees, it would be an exciting atmosphere for a "family" of practitioners to enjoy a successful career. When it became apparent the mental health professional community was not going to take advantage of the technology and own it, the subsequent spectacular growth to 14.5 million enrollees supplanted the "family" congeniality and made an IPO all but mandatory.

Capital Formation

The most formidable hurdle for practitioners is the acquisition of capital of sufficient magnitude to launch the company. Often the task is so daunting that founders are tempted to move ahead with minimum capitalization and risk jeopardizing the project, as under-funded companies seldom succeed. Yet if all the foregoing have been accomplished, this may actually be the easiest part of the project. The amount of venture capital available is vast, far exceeding the number of start-ups worthy of investment. At the present time start-ups are fueling this nation's economy and differentiating it from all other industrialized nations, which lack such resources and facilities.

Source and Level of Capitalization

Whenever practitioners contemplate obtaining capital, they immediately conclude that they should immediately seek out the VCs. Actually, the source of funding depends on the amount needed; venture capital is seldom for small projects. The founder of a start-up should roughly consider the following schedule. (a) For up to about $250,000 in either capitalization or seed money, the best source can be wealthy, interested friends. This resource is both overlooked by worthwhile projects and abused by unworthy concepts that have been turned down by everyone else. (b) From $300,000 to $1 million the best sources are the venture capital clubs composed of successful entrepreneurs who are interested in funding the next generation of start-ups. They rely on their own entrepreneurial talent and experience in assessing a business plan and usually are fascile in their discernment. (c) Finally, projects over $1 million are more suitable for consideration by VCs.

Characteristics of Venture Capitalists

Practitioners are not generally aware that VCs differ widely from one another. Most VCs tend to specialize, for example, in technology or healthcare. For some VCs, certain industries are shunned, whereas these same industries are favored by others. If the potential entrepreneur has not done his or her homework, even the most compelling story will fail if the VC does not capitalize within the business sector represented in the business plan.

Venture capitalists range from those who choose an investment and then trust their judgment by staying out of management's way to those who are very involved, perhaps even intrusive. A seat, or even seats, on the board of directors is a frequent demand, and the history of start-ups reveals that it is usually the VCs who are instrumental in dislodging and replacing the founder. Some VCs even have the reputation of replacing as much as 95% of founding management, whereas others would rarely intrude. Finally, in the rush to cash-in, some VCs pressure a company toward a premature IPO, when waiting one or two years would result in greater market valuation for the company. Clearly, there are great differences in degree of intrusiveness among VCs, and entrepreneurs need to assess investors with whom they might have to live for a number of years. American Biodyne was fortunate in attracting a surplus of capital. I interviewed potential investors for compatibility and decided to avoid VCs altogether. I relented somewhat in the latter decision when I was advised that it would benefit the company if the legendary Arthur Rock was allowed to take a minor investment position.

A frequent and reasonable requirement is that there be two forms of stock at the outset: common stock for the founders and *preferred stock* for the investors. This arrangement requires that if a distressed company is liquidated, the preferred stock (the investors) will be paid first.

Big Problems with Big Solutions

Venture capitalists like big problems, because this signals the potential for big solutions. Behavioral healthcare is a $60- to $80-billion industry, with several times that amount in such annual costs as suicide, absenteeism, disability, and human suffering. There is room for big companies providing big solutions for big problems. If an industry has a less than $5 billion portion of the economy, VCs are generally not interested.

Avoid Going Back to the Well

Overcapitalizing a company can be almost as bad as undercapitalizing it. In the latter, the company will run short of operating capital and find itself having to go back to VCs and suffer dilution. In an overcapitalized company the temptation is to make expenditures prematurely or unnecessarily. This, too, can result in having to seek additional capital, along with the fact that initially too much of the company was given to the investors to obtain the excess capital.

The American Biodyne Experience

American Biodyne was capitalized at a modest sum: $500,000 in preferred stock to the investors and $1 million in common stock to the founders. With a total initial valuation of $1.5 million, the "sweat equity" of those who founded the company was two-thirds, a very enviable position. The company never returned to the well. Rather, each contract financed future contracts, and the initial capital formation was never spent. It remained ready to be used as part of a future acquisitions war chest.

MANAGING THE COMPANY

Managing the initial phases of a start-up often requires defying conventional wisdom, and for this reason the entrepreneur is often the best person upon whom ultimate decisions should rest. These entrepreneurs are seldom trained managers, and need the advice of a good MBA to whom they must listen and from whom they will learn. Then they must have the courage to reject the advice on critical, but rare occasions. The founder is the CEO, whose lack of skill will result in a number of management mistakes, none of which will be fatal. On the other hand, the conventional wisdom that would have certainly damaged the company will have been avoided. The energy of a start-up team is its enthusiasm. There is a firm belief that it is not disgraceful to make a mistake, but it is unforgivable not to recognize it and correct it. The founder/CEO treats the team as family, and the team will follow him or her anywhere. All have risked their careers; the formula is succeed or die.

The First Year

Only 20% of all start-ups make it to the fifth year, the traditional benchmark of success. Of those that fail, 40% will do so in the first year and another 40% will seem to succeed, only to meet their demise in the third year. Venture capitalists know this and calculate it in their formula: the one in five that succeeds will have a ratio of investment to reward of 25:1 or more, making it all very worthwhile to the VC (Cummings, 1996).

The Struggle to Guarantee Clinical Preeminence

American Biodyne almost died the first year because I have unwarranted credence to conventional wisdom. Wanting to ensure that the company would always be clinically driven, yet recognizing the lack of management acumen among clinicians, I accepted the advice of my MBA-degreed operations officer. A parallel, dual management system was implemented in which those managing the clinical part of the enterprise reported up the ladder to the CEO, while those directing the operations side (i.e., day-to-day management, finance, human resources, etc.) reported ultimately to the chief of operations. This worst of all possible systems almost destroyed the company. Authority and responsibility fell between the cracks, and each side blamed the other. Very quickly the faulty system was dismantled.

Faced with the dilemma of ensuring sound business practices while maintaining the clinical preeminence of the company, there were only two choices: either train business managers to be clinicians, a plan deemed by all as impossible, or train clinicians to be business managers, deemed highly improbable but not impossible. The latter plan was adopted. In each state and in each region doctoral-level practitioners were placed in charge of both clinical services and operations. They were accorded release time to pursue seminars and courses in management and finance, and they were encouraged to enroll in part-time or evening MBA programs. All received the requisite training, and several obtained the MBA degree.

No matter how high on the ladder the clinician/manager was, he or she was required to spend two full days per week in hands-on treatment with patients. This included me, as all were admonished to promote and implement sound business practices which would always be subordinate to clinical imperatives. This worked well and the company not only flourished, but never had to resort to the artificialities of session limits, utilization review, and preauthorization. Simply, the effective clinician is an efficient clinician.

Clinical Retraining

It was evident during the Hawaii Medicaid Project that even after choosing the best clinicians, they would have to be retrained in focused psychotherapy. A 130-hour training module was developed which was limited to 35 clinicians and conducted in a two-week span. The training was done on an as-needed basis after each new contract, but it averaged 10 training modules per year. Literally more than 1000 clinicians were retrained during the first seven years of the company's history.

It was also ascertained during the Hawaii Medicaid Project that in spite of the retraining, if clinicians were then left to practice without follow-up, they would soon revert to their original training. Consequently, intensive on-the-job supervision and continued training was mandated which included two hours per week of supervision (one hour of individual and one dyadic) and three hours per week of clinical case conferencing during which psychotherapists were expected and encouraged to present their most baffling cases. Of the clinicians' time, 15% was spent perpetually in quality assurance.

Finally, each Biodyne Center, composed of six to eight clinicians, was subjected to an intensive three-day annual clinical audit. The audit team sat in individual and group sessions, supervisory sessions, and business meetings. The patient charts and all aspects of the center received intense scrutiny, at the conclusion of which an audit report discussed the strengths and weaknesses of the center and listed its deficiencies, which required a six-month plan for correction. Center directors spent six months preparing for and then six months recovering from each audit.

During the first two years, I conducted all of the retraining and all of the clinical audits, each time involving a team so that at the end of this period others could conduct both audits and retraining.

On the surface, the system may seem rigorous and to some even harsh. It cannot be overemphasized that the exact opposite was true: the atmosphere was so accepting and rewarding that clinicians clamored for the opportunity to present their therapeutic failures. I was constantly bombarded with requests for help. Many consultations were conducted on the telephone, but in the majority of cases the individual clinicians received attention during my frequent visits to the centers. In later years, there were master clinicians available to continue this tradition even though the company had hundreds of fulltime psychotherapists.

Marketing Strategy

The marketing of a totally new delivery system is difficult, because the health industry moves slowly and conservatively. Several unconventional strategies were adopted with stellar success. For the first four years, I did the marketing. As the founder, I was best able to describe the system and its advantages, and I had the credibility of having created the mental health system at Kaiser Permanente at a time when no insuror covered psychotherapy. I also had an impressive track record in research and in the creation and management of several previous enterprises. My being a former president of the American Psychological Association was important in identifying me as having credibility among my peers.

The product being marketed was not only capitated, but also the provider was at risk to provide the agreed upon coverage for all of the MH/CD treatments of a particular third-party payor, be it a health insurance, Blue Cross/Blue Shield, HMO, or government plan. The coverage included hospitalization, outpatient treatment, and a continuum of MH/CD services. It was a staff model with centers spaced geographically so that no patient would require more than a 30-minute drive in normal traffic. The MH/CD services were what came to be known as a "carve-out," and patients had freedom of choice, but only among Biodyne providers.

Because of the newness of the concept, marketing was conducted not by brochures but face-to-face, and only with the CEO of the company being marketed. Subordinates in the health industry seldom possess the knowledge to assess innovation, and never have the authority to implement it. The CEO-to-CEO marketing was inordinately successful when it took place. If a particular CEO being marketed assigned the meeting to a subordinate, Biodyne would decline.

As part of the overall strategy, only contracts of over 100,000 enrolees were sought, and preferably those approaching 500,000 potential covered lives. It is as much work to implement a program for 10,000 lives as it is for 500,000.

Financial Strategy

American Biodyne's "black box" was its ability to reduce the then bloated psychiatric and chemical dependency hospitalization by 95%, leaving much of the capitation for expansion of the innovative outpatient programs that made this possible. Nonpsychiatric clinicians were trained in 24-hour coverage and in the importance of seeing a presenting patient in the middle of the night before admission. Psychiatrists of the era typically would respond to an emergency room call saying, "hospitalize the patient and I'll be there in the morning." The following morning, by virtue of having spent the night in a crazy place, every patient needs hospitalization. The assessment by its very nature is only possible at the time of presentation. If at that hour the patient responds to outpatient techniques, then that treatment is continued on a daily and even twice daily basis, with hospitalization having been avoided (Pallak & Cummings, 1992).

Using doctoral psychologists with additional training to perform this emergency service was highly successful. In seven years, there was not one mortality or liability suit, all of which enraged beleaguered hospital administrators and the psychiatrists that were thus preempted. American Biodyne was the first, and therefore the most controversial managed behavioral care company to address successfully the national crisis of psychiatric overhospitalization.

The second financial strategy contributing to the company's success was the decision to create centers and services only *after* a contract was in hand. This prevented a drain on capital, as the revenue stream and the service expenditures were concurrent. However, this always necessitated a scramble to create new centers, recruit and train the clinicians, and prepare all of the required logistics, regularly within 60 days and twice within 30 days. The company never failed to meet the time constraints of its many turnkey operations, and saved millions of dollars in setup costs.

Managing beyond the First Year

The crises of the succeeding years included having to manage a consistent 200% annual growth and having to shift beyond the staff model. The successes were reflected in the company's several acquisitions, its going public, and its eventual sale.

Staff-Network Model: Another Innovation

The staff model in which the practitioners are salaried and work out of a center is far more efficient than the network, but it bears some formidable difficulties. The first is the need for critical mass, making it impossible to implement centers in rural areas. Another is the resistance of many patients who feel managed coming to a staff center but do not feel managed sitting in a network provider's private office. The third difficulty is that most providers do not wish to be on a salaried staff, preferring to work as part of a network. As the company continued to expand, it became apparent that growth would be stymied under a staff model. Rather than convert to a soley network model, a new model was created: the staff-network arrangement. In this model the staff conducts the clinical case conferences, covers the emergencies, manages the network, and treats the most problematic cases. This arrangement served the company well as the clinical culture continued to be reflected in the staff, while engaging what eventually was to be 14,000 contracted providers.

The staff of each center was always able to identify the best providers in the network, which the company then encouraged to form group practices and serve as "prime" or "core" providers treating exclusively American Biodyne referrals. In some cases the company also supplied the capital as well as the encouragement for the formation of such provider groups.

Managing 200% Annual Growth

The company found itself in the enviable position of having runaway growth. This was met with the decision that although difficult, the company could manage 200% annual growth without jeopardizing quality. Growth was capped at that figure, and potential client organizations were given a time estimate of when they could be serviced. Rather than hampering the growth, this decision rendered the company more attractive and perpetuated the inordinate growth beyond the point when it might have abated.

Acquisitions

There are four reasons why a successful company makes acquisitions: a) to acquire market share, b) to penetrate new geographical areas where it has been shutout, c) to acquire new technology, and d) to obtain a distressed company at a bargain price and then turn it around. American Biodyne used all of these strategies. For example, obtaining the California HMO license involves two to three years of red-tape and as much as $2 million. By acquiring a small California company having such a license, American Biodyne then filed a revision and thereby substantially reduced the complexity of the task. It acquired a new technology by purchasing a national employee assistance program (EAP), and in buying several other companies it entered arenas that would have been difficult to penetrate with traditional marketing.

The acquiring company always assures the acquired company that senior management will not be altered and downsizing will not occur. This promise can never be kept, as duplication must be eliminated and a new company culture must be infused. Founders of a company that is considering being acquired should take this inevitability into consideration.

Initial Public Offering

Criteria for an IPO are formidable and usually require five years of successful operation. Among these criteria are three consecutive quarters of profitability, with the fourth quarter demonstrating a projected annualized income of at least $1 million. The growth and revenues should resemble a staircase: there should be an overall upward trend even though at points it may be flat. The initial market capitalization should be at least $40 million in an industry that is on the scale of $1 billion. The company should be experiencing at least 35% annual growth with increasing margins. These criteria will bring the required institutional support for the IPO (Cummings, 1996).

American Biodyne far exceeded these criteria. In fact, the company was profitable from its first quarter and every quarter thereafter, a rare track record. Its determination to go public was postponed one year by the Gulf War, and the expensive and exhaustive legal, underwriting, and other preparations had to be performed twice at a price exceeding $1 million. The IPO was successful at a split of three times for each share. Opening at $10 per share, it never faltered and continued to steadily increase to $34 before the company was sold less than two years later.

Once a company is publicly traded, its quarterly reports are made public and become a management obsession. Falling short of expectations in such a report depresses the stock, and the company must constantly educate stock analysts about the company to ensure proper analysis of the stock. A stock that loses 25 to 30% of its opening value will very likely incur a stockholder's suit alleging that the company misrepresented the stock on the prospectus. Once such a suit is filed it becomes a self-fulfilling prophecy as the stock plunges even further because stock analysts downgrade a company under such litigation.

Sale of the Company

American Biodyne received a number of overtures from large corporations wishing to buy it, but it was only after I reached age 70 that such offers were seriously considered. The company was now covering 14.5 million lives in all 50 states. Furthermore, the time was nearing when my initial prediction as to the lifetime of the "carve-outs" was maturing. It would soon be time to carve in, heralding the end of an industry (Cummings, 1997).

Along with the spectacular growth, the maintenance of high quality, and having defined an industry, American Biodyne had two national acknowledgments: the December 1990 issue of *Inc Magazine* named it number 42 in "America's 500 Fastest Growing Private Companies," and the May 25, 1992, issue of *Business Week* listed it as number 14 in "America's 100 Hot Growth Companies." American Biodyne's successes brought a good price on a stock-swap with MedCo Containment Services which, one year later, was acquired by Merck. Those who invested $1 in 1985 and held on to all three of the successive stocks (American Biodyne, MedCo, and Merck) in 1996 realized over $150 in value.

CONCLUSION

The decade of 1985 to 1995 demonstrated that doctoral-level mental health practitioners can apply their education and training, augment it with additional training and experience, and become leaders in healthcare. Several hundred psychologists who were with American Biodyne its first seven years have gone on to become the captains of the industry, from CEOs and vice presidents of successful companies to founders of their own innovative companies. Many have created new concepts within the reconceptualized health industry, while others have applied their ability to predict and control costs to the formation of new clinically driven companies and regional group practices. They attribute this success to their early training and experience as pioneers with American Biodyne, and at a recent informal gathering in Dallas these practitioners named those years the "Biodyne bootcamp."

In addition to the research and clinical education and training of a sound doctoral program, these practitioners have several characteristics in common: a shared vision, enthusiasm for change, skepticism for conventional wisdom, risk-taking ability, an optimistic view of the future, innovativeness, and self-confidence. In a word, they are entrepreneurs who have lifted the barriers for those mental health practitioners in the future who possess or can acquire these qualities.

REFERENCES

Cummings, N. A. (1986). The dismantling of our health system: Strategies for the survival of psychological practice. *American Psychologist, 41,* 426–431.

Cummings, N. A. (1996). The search for capital: Positioning for growth, joint venturing, acquisition, and public offering. In N. A. Cummings, M. S. Pallak, & J. L. Cummings (Eds.), *Surviving the demise of solo practice: Mental health practitioners prospering in the era of managed care* (pp. 205–216) Madison, CT: Psychosocial Press.

Cummings, N. A. (1997). Behavioral health in primary care: Dollars and sense. In N. A. Cummings, J. L. Cummings, & J. Johnson (Eds.), *Behavioral health in primary care: A guide for clinical integration.* Madison, CT: Psychosocial Press.

Cummings, N. A., Cummings, J. L., & Johnson, J. (Eds.). (1997). *Behavioral health in primary care: A guide for clinical integration.* Madison, CT: Psychosocial Press.

Cummings, N. A., Dorken, H., Pallak, M. S., & Henke, C. J. (1993). The impact of psychological intervention on health care costs and utilization: The Hawaii Medicaid project. In *Medicaid, managed behavioral health and implications for public policy: Vol. 2. Healthcare and utilization cost series* (pp. 3–23). South San Francisco: Foundation for Behavioral Health.

Cummings, N. A., & Follette, W. T. (1968). Psychiatric services and medical utilization in a prepaid health plan setting: Part 2. *Medical Care, 6,* 31–41.

Cummings, N. A., Kahn, B. I., and Sparkman, B. (1965). *The effect of psychological intervention on medical utilization: A pilot project.* Oakland, CA: Kaiser Foundation Reports.

Cummings, N. A., Pallak, M. S., & Cummings, J. L. (Eds.). (1996). *Surviving the demise of solo practice: Mental health practitioners prospering in the era of managed care.* Madison, CT: Psychosocial Press.

Cummings, N. A., & Sayama, M. (1995). *Focused psychotherapy: A casebook of brief, intermittent psychotherapy throughout the life cycle.* New York: Brunner/Mazel.

Cummings, N. A., & VandenBos, G. R. (1981). The twenty-year Kaiser-Permanente experience with psychotherapy and medical utilization: Implications for national health policy and national health insurance. *Health Policy Quarterly, 1*(2), 159–175.

Follette, W. T., & Cummings, N. A. (1967). Psychiatric services and medical utilization in a prepaid health plan setting. *Medical Care, 5,* 25–35.

Jones, K. R., & Vischi, T. R. (1979). Impact of alcohol, drug abuse and mental health treatment on medical utilization: A review of the literature. *Medical Care, 17* (Suppl.), 1–82.

Jones, K. R., & Vischi, T. R. (1980). *The Bethesda Conference on Medical Cost Offset.* Washington, DC: ADAMHA Report.

Pallak, M. S., & Cummings, N. A. (1992). Inpatient and outpatient psychiatric treatment: The effect of matching patients to appropriate level of treatment on psychiatric and medical-surgical hospital days. *Applied & Preventive Psychology, 1,* 83–87.

Wright, R. H. (1992). Toward a political solution to psychology's dilemmas: Managing managed care. *Independent Practitioner, 12*(3), 111–113.

BIOGRAPHY

Nicholas A. Cummings   Nicholas Cummings is President of the Foundation for Behavioral Health, Chair of The Nicholas & Dorothy Cummings Foundation, and Distinguished Professor of the University of Nevada, Reno. Dr. Cummings is also founding CEO of American Biodyne (MedCo, now Merit Behavioral Care). He is a former President of the American Psychological Association and founding President of the four campuses of the California School of Professional Psychology. Dr. Cummings was a Chief Psychologist (now retired), for Kaiser Permanente Health Plan and founding President of the National Academies of Practice in Washington, D.C. He was the founder of the National Council of Schools of Professional Psychology (NCSPP) and the founder of the American Managed Behavioral Healthcare Association (AMBHA). Dr. Cummings was formerly an Executive Director of the Mental Research Institute in Palo Alto, California and the President and Executive Chairman of U.K. Behavioural Health, Ltd., in London, England. Dr. Cummings received his doctorate in 1958 from Adelphi University.

6

MANAGING QUALITY IMPROVEMENT AND CLINICAL OUTCOMES IN BEHAVIORAL HEALTH SETTINGS: A NEW ROLE FOR PSYCHOLOGISTS

ELIZABETH C. McDONEL, L. DIANE ASHLEY, AND MICHAEL A. ASHLEY

Grant Blackford Mental Health, Inc., Marion, Indiana 46952

GRACE LONG

Quinco Behavioral Health Systems, Inc., Columbus, Indiana 47202

GORDON GIBSON AND ARMEN SARKISSIAN

Center for Behavioral Health, Inc., Bloomington, Indiana 47401

SHARON KRAUS

Tri-City Mental Health, East Chicago, Indiana 46312

KIRK WHEELER

Adult & Child Mental Health, Indianapolis, Indiana 46227

INTRODUCTION

A NEW PERSPECTIVE FOR MENTAL HEALTH PROFESSIONALS

STARTING THE COLLABORATION

CHOOSING A METHOD FOR IMPROVING SERVICES
AND MEASURING OUTCOMES: CLINICAL PATHWAYS

STRUCTURING THE COLLABORATION

CURRENT STATUS OF THE PROJECT

THE ROLE OF CLINICAL PSYCHOLOGISTS IN TECHNOLOGY
TRANSFER AND CREATING CULTURAL READINESS FOR THE
MANAGED CARE ACCOUNTABILITY MOVEMENT

INTRODUCTION

The managed health care movement has created a climate of increased competition and accountability for providers of behavioral health services. The pressure has caused headaches for mental health administrators but may also bring opportunities for clinical and research-trained psychologists who have a sense of adventure, tolerance for rapidly changing environments, and an interest in seeing their work lead to immediate systems changes. As we introduce the challenges and opportunities facing healthcare service providers, and describe the roles of the professional workers engaged in this field, we also provide an overview of managed care principles. We demonstrate how psychologists' training enables them to provide unique assistance in meeting these challenges.

A NEW PERSPECTIVE FOR MENTAL HEALTH PROFESSIONALS

To summarize what changes in the behavioral healthcare marketplace mean to mental health professionals, imagine that you are the CEO of a community mental health center (CMHC). With a $14 million budget and 200 employees, you serve a client population that tends to be seriously mentally ill and economically disadvantaged. You've been traveling along a stable course for many years. But with the advent of managed care, you find that the fundamental values and virtues of your field of discipline are now in question. There are no clear road maps. You have to cut your own path.

First, you have to accept the new language. Formerly, you worked in the area of *mental health,* or possibly *community mental health.* You are now in *behavioral health* and *managed behavioral healthcare.* The new terminology is a refrain of accessibility, acceptability, quality, accountability, customer satisfaction, outcomes, and data-based decision making. You no longer serve *patients* or *clients,* but *customers* and *consumers.* Some of these concepts make sense. Of course customers must know they are getting the best care for the most reasonable price. Although some of these terms may sound like new lingo for standard practices, other words give semantic license to practices with which you may be uncomfortable (e.g., rationing services).

You begin to examine the unavoidable consequences to your organization of these changes. In the last decade, managed care organizations have burgeoned to provide an ever greater variety of services to the payor; most of these focus on cutting costs. You know that most privately insured persons have some form of managed care incorporated into their health plans (Freeman & Trabin, 1994) and that over two-thirds of all states are incorporating managed care principles into their publicly funded service delivery systems (Sherman, Zahniser, & Smukler, 1995; see also Feldman, 1992, for an overview of the penetration of managed behavioral health care into the public sector).

To consider how your organization will adapt to and even make the best of this revolution, you turn to the voluminous array of information available. Stacks of brochures for conferences pile up on your desk with titles such as *Advances in Managed Behavioral Health Care: Success in an Era of Increasing Competition* and *Capitation and At-Risk Contracting: An Intensive Executive Education Program for Behavioral Healthcare Providers, Community Mental Health Center Administrators and Delivery System Managers.* You subscribe to impressive publications such as *Behavioral Healthcare Tomorrow, Behavioral Health Management,* and *Health Data Management.* Your colleagues regularly scan many of the bulletin boards on the internet devoted to behavioral health outcomes and managed care. Your competitors, you read, are gaining ground on you in the race to simultaneously lower costs and raise quality of care. Even more worrisome is that they are gathering hard evidence—actual data—to substantiate these claims of low cost and high quality. The competition is using powerful computers and even electronic medical records to replace cumbersome paper medical charts. Well, you scarcely have time to evaluate all of these advances wisely. A quick scan is about all you can manage.

Your guides? Some are vendors, cashing in on the new trends; some offer legitimate advice. They talk about providing you with methods for *outcomes management* or *report cards.* Is this science or marketing? How do you know the difference between a sincere outcomes expert and a consultant who offers a quick survey that eats up one-third of your profit for the year? Some of the new outcomes companies that were hot last year just went out of business this year. Can you afford to hire someone to do this in-house? What about getting help from the local universities? In academia, integrity has traditionally been held sacred over the dollar. No, you decide that the response to changes must be immediate, and your past experience is that academia moves more slowly, savoring the esoterics before getting down to the urgencies of survival.

At this point you waver. Perhaps the job of being a CEO of a community mental health provider organization has become too complicated. But then you've always been in this field for what you can do for persons with mental illness. That's still what it's about. And you have a personal investment: you not only have an MBA, but a master of social work degree as well. So you keep in mind the dual perspectives of the business person and the clinician.

You discuss with your colleagues, who are CEOs and upper management of similar provider organizations, the real threat that some major managed care organization will soon buy up all of the provider agencies, stripping out the management levels while keeping the clinical staff, who will then be managed by the policies, procedures, and protocols of this giant. More than a dozen large managed care organizations (MCOs) have the reputation, power, and economies of scale to negotiate contracts from your former payors. You worry that the state dollars for care of persons with serious and persistent mental illness and for care of persons with addictions could be diverted into profit-oriented interests. The Employee Assistance Programs (EAPs) you've negotiated are starting to migrate to providers in the networks of the MCOs. Insurance companies won't let you put your clinicians on their provider networks without cutting rates or making other concessions, such as precertifying your clients before you start treatment or telling you what type of assessment and treatment you are allowed to give. You accept that the managed care revolution has been successful in weeding out some of the unnecessary care, but you have also heard about incidents when needed care was wrongly restricted or delayed with deleterious effects. The demand for your business is waning with competition increasing and access to treatment being monitored by managed care entities. Survival depends on beating or joining your competitors.

Competition in your niche of healthcare is especially alien, mental health being one of the final frontiers of the managed health care movement, which has by now penetrated all other areas of healthcare. Mental health had been considered so complex and distinct from other forms of healthcare that it was carved out separately from general managed healthcare plans for many years. Furthermore, community mental health centers have long-standing traditions: they were born in 1963 with President John F. Kennedy's landmark Community Mental Health Centers Act (Public Law 88-164, Title II) and were intended in part to fund and accelerate the recent movement toward deinstitutionalization of chronically mentally ill patients. In later years, federal mandates and revisions of this law provided further seed funding and oversight for CMHCs (Rochefort & Logan, 1989, 1993). Indiana has 30 CMHCs that developed out of these federal initiatives between 1963 and the 1980s. State government cooperated with and assisted in implementing this federal vision. In fact, the government prevented competition in the past by dividing a state into "catchment areas," which were regions of protected turf with boundaries that other provider agencies were not supposed to cross.

What happened? In the period of a few years, during the early 1990s, your state, along with a wave of others, and with the blessing of the federal government, blew up the old rules. New mental health reform legislation has been passed at the state level. In Indiana, for example, the governor championed legislation to introduce competition and accountability to state-funded mental health services (McDonel, Meyer, & DeLiberty, 1996). That represents about half of the typical CMHC's business. Federal politics in the 1990s emphasized shrinking government (e.g., Osborne & Gaebler, 1993), accelerating a trend that began in the 1980s toward federal retrenchment with respect to community mental health (Rochefort & Logan, 1993), which was consistent with the downsizing movement in American corporations of the 1990s. All forces point inescapably toward acceptance of hard realities. Your state acknowledges that some mental health providers will fold, while others will merge, consolidate, and weed out unneeded staff. Rumors circulate that some state mental health officials have a hit list of less-favored CMHCs they hope will close up shop. Your state intends to conduct independent surveys of customers' satisfaction with your services. A consumer manual will be published and data will be collected to show which providers have the best ratings.

The Psychologist in a Managed Care Context

To examine this new territory of competing values, we'll look through the eyes of some who came to managed care by a route different from our CEO. We'll show how seven psychologists of different backgrounds turned their training and talents to the creation of a consortium in response to managed care pressures. The goal of this collaboration was to create a quality improvement and outcomes measurement system for their 14-member CMHCs. The collaboration was called the Indiana Clinical Pathway Collaboration Project and used a methodology known as *clinical pathways* (also known as *critical pathways*) to structure its efforts. The collaboration was committed to collecting and analyzing data, on a larger scale than ever attempted before in this system, to measure the impact of services provided to their customers. The psychologists involved in the collaboration embraced research-validated and accountable clinical practices. One of them is the first author of this chapter (McDonel), a research-trained clinical psychologist whose career had moved away from academia and toward applied research and training efforts in the governmental and private nonprofit mental health sectors. This professional journey brought her to co-lead the pathways collaboration. One psychologist served as the project's entrepreneur and business manager and was a chief of clinical operations (COO) within executive management of one of the member CMHCs (M. Ashley, third author). The five other clinical psychologists involved in this project (Gibson, Long, Wheeler, Sarkissian, and Kraus) were employed by CMHCs in this consortium prior to the onset of the project, and four had been active in Indiana's CMHC system for many years. These psychologists held positions with varying mixtures of clinical and administrative duties.

The Research-Trained Psychologist in the New Behavioral Health Management Environment

Like other research-trained psychologists around the country, McDonel believed that the future assured stable funding of psychological research. Graduate training had supported this belief. But just as the world had turned upside down for our hypothetical CEO, similar changes occurred in universities, industrial research laboratories, and other research-oriented institutions. In the late 1980s, the downsizing of federal government brought a crunch in federally funded research, not just in behavioral science, but also in the physical and biological sciences. The recurrent reform theme of accountability was reflected in the call for relevance in federally funded research. Park (1996) details the decline in federal and private research funding and research capacity in both academia and industry, and expresses concerns about continued trends.

In the 1990s, "talented young Ph.D.'s, once courted by both academe and industry, find themselves shuttling from one temporary position to another—or shut out of science altogether" (Park, 1996, p. 18). Tobias, Chubin, and Aylesworth (1996) offer an array of statistics to illustrate the oversupply of scientists and the competition for jobs. They note, too, that there is a growing segment of scientists who have developed migratory lifestyles, taking temporary positions as they can get them. It is not unusual now for some tenure-track academic positions to attract up to 1000 applications. Tobias et al. (1996) recommend a series of reforms in the educational system to help make graduates more employable in nontraditional settings (for a review of these funding problems and a view on why this happened, see Tobias et al., 1996). In psychology, this might include training to function in management careers in the behavioral health industry as our psychologist-authors have done.

These trends, along with an interest in systems change and mental health policy, affected McDonel's career odyssey and choice of employment settings. As with many other research-trained colleagues, new opportunities for nontraditional funding of research beckoned. She made the initial leap from more traditional laboratory research in psychology to mental health services and policy research in collaboration with the Indiana state government. This was an area where her work would have an immediate impact on service systems, because lawmakers at state and federal levels were interested in applied research on community-based psychosocial interventions for persons with severe mental illness whose healthcare was typically funded by government. In making this leap, McDonel discovered how radically different are the two cultures of government and academia. A two-year postdoctoral fellowship in mental health services research and policy, funded by the National Institute of Mental Health (NIMH) and organized by the National Association of State and Mental Health Program Directors, helped prepare her for the culture shock, so that she could communicate bilingually and navigate between the two worlds. Conducting state-sponsored research while in a soft-money academic position exposed McDonel to the differing viewpoints of academia and state policymakers. Major issues for the policymakers were the direct relevance of research to taxpayers and constituents and the potential for practical applications of the findings. Quick turnaround of data was needed to address these issues. Elected officials want evaluations that can bring answers during their own terms in office. Sometimes the findings are not what they want to hear, and the researcher cannot support the politicizing and censoring of the data. Boundaries must constantly be negotiated to safeguard against threats to the integrity of the scientific data being generated. The relentless pursuit of truth and the values of science, when it disconfirms the value of a pet theory or policy, are not warmly welcomed. In a highly political arena, conflict can also arise about credit for work, authorship rights, and ownership of data. Graduate school had prepared McDonel more for the narrow culture of university-based, investigator-initiated research than for alternative environments. Park (1996) notes that national legislators have been critical of such curiosity-driven research in the more basic sciences and have recently increased their interest in funding initiatives that are more strictly germane to national goals. The need for psychological research that is more relevant to consumers' and practitioners' needs in the real world of clinical practice in a managed care environment has been recently addressed by many in the field (e.g., Newman & Tejeda, 1996; Seligman, 1995).

Cultural conflicts surfaced during a study of the discharged population of Indiana's oldest state-operated psychiatric hospital that was slated for closure and again in a separate analysis of concurrent mental health reform legislation in Indiana. McDonel collaborated with a team of university-based researchers to evaluate the effects to the hospital's discharged patients of closure (Deci et al., 1997; McDonel et al., 1996; McDonel, Wright, Pescosolido, Miller, & Elbracht, 1994; McGrew, Wright, Pescosolido, & McDonel, 1998; Pescosolido et al., 1996). McDonel was a co-principal investigator in this research program that received combined state and federal funding as part of a five-year NIMH research infrastructure support (RISP) grant in mental health services research. Although the government provided funding in this hot area and temporary soft-money positions were available, university psychology faculties were slow to consider mental health services and policy research as a needed complement to the academic repertoire, and tenure-track positions in this field were rare. The cultural bias of many top university psychology departments has been to revere and reward research that is basic rather than applied or evaluation projects that are controlled and not correlational, investigator-initiated and not dictated to any degree by other parties, and performed solo or with a few colleagues rather than in a collaborative spirit. "Evaluation" or "program evaluation" targets applied and pragmatic questions, such as the long-term educational outcome of children in a Head Start program or the effect of a media program to increase monthly self-breast examinations for early detection of cancer. Evaluation research has its own set of journals, a trade association, ethical guidelines, parlance, methodology, and a long tradition. Yet the purer, more basic research hypotheses can often be layered into an evaluation project, as happened with the study of the state psychiatric hospital closure (Pescosolido et al., 1996). At the same time that practical public policy questions were addressed, such as whether the ex-patients were better off now than before, research questions were also asked about how the density, interconnectedness, and valence of social ties within patients' social networks affected their illness careers both inside and outside of the hospital. A full discussion of the boundaries between research and evaluation and between types of evaluation is beyond the scope of this chapter, but these are important conceptual distinctions in applied research. Scriven (1996) gives some definitions and contrasts the forms of evaluation.

Indiana's mental health reform legislation opened up new opportunities for evaluation research in mental health services. The legislation was a high-profile project for the state's governor, Evan Bayh. The issue received constant attention in the news media and was hotly debated among all stakeholders (see McDonel et al., 1996, for a full description of the development of the legislation and the hospital closure). The main tenets of the now widely accepted philosophy of managed healthcare were incorporated into law, affecting the provision of all state-funded mental healthcare. For CMHCs, managed care was encroaching, through private insurance companies on the one side and now from stewards of the public mental health dollar on the other. Of special interest to Indiana's CMHCs was that, over the next several years, more than a third of the savings from the hospital's closure (the hospital's total budget was about $23 million) would be reallocated to funding intensive community-based care for discharged patients. The state forced CMHCs in the hospital's region to compete for this business and to demonstrate that services were appropriate. This brought opportunity, but also new requirements for accountability. Major political forces further demanded that directors of nonprofit, private sector behavioral healthcare organizations collect and analyze data, measure outcomes, provide training, adopt scientifically validated and efficacy-based treatment approaches, and access and critically evaluate the scientific and policy literatures. McDonel's evaluation efforts in these areas prepared her both substantively and culturally, and opened the door for subsequent work with Indiana's mental health services providers.

Ironically, visionary, research-oriented psychologists had long ago begun preaching accountability in their own discipline and had forewarned of the time when external policing mechanisms would be forced on mental health service providers if they did not adhere to empirically validated treatment modalities (e.g., Hayes, 1987, 1989; McFall, 1984, 1991; Rotter, 1971). Accountability was at the heart of a major split within the American Psychological Association during the late 1980s, leading to the formation of a new organization, the American Psychological Society (APS), which strongly embraced the values of a scientifically based practice of psychology. Many of our colleagues failed to heed the early warnings and are being brought around only now through the managed healthcare movement.

Whereas some psychologists resisted accountability, even those who accepted it were beset by practical challenges. For example, under administrative pressure, practitioners may slip into a habit of giving tests for which reimbursement is available but which have little utility for planning treatment (e.g., Glueckauf, 1993). The integration of science with practice requires organizational structures that foster rather than conflict with efficacy-based practice. Lee Sechrest (in Hayes, 1989) observed that even the most thoroughly trained and scientifically oriented psychologists would often drift into delivering unvalidated forms of care after spending time in the clinical practice arena. He advised clinicians to network and to receive regular monitoring and peer review, the feedback loops that are now part of the methodology of managed care.

After leaving school, many clinicians face institutional environments that provide little or no support for continuing education and honing skills. Information is available, but has been so overwhelming in scope and quantity that clinicians cannot routinely tap into it. A substantial body of technology for changing behavior sits on library shelves, but has been slow to be discovered and applied at the front line. Laboratory studies abound to demonstrate efficacy in treatment in everything from depression to attention-deficit disorder, with many researchers continuing to churn out even more assessment and treatment studies. But there has been a bottleneck between the literature and everyday practice. Given the reserve of underemployed psychologists, shouldn't some time and labor be devoted to this interstitial role of translating technology into applications?

To address technology transfer, a literature has been accumulating on the difficulty of disseminating mental health technologies from the laboratories and library shelves into applied field settings. Articles in journals such as *Applied and Preventive Psychology* provide examples of technology transfer. The federal Agency for Health Care and Policy Research (AHCPR) was founded by Congress in 1989 with the mission of enhancing quality, effectiveness, and accessibility to healthcare (VanAmringe & Shannon, 1992). AHCPR has taken a position of leadership and has made enormous contributions toward information and technology dissemination. The organization has sponsored initiatives to create clinical practice guidelines and health technology assessments for providers in a variety of health care areas, including a guideline on treating depression in primary health care settings (AHCPR, 1994a, 1994b). AHCPR contracted nonfederal, multidisciplinary expert panels to review the literature on specific clinical conditions and to create guidelines to help digest and make accessible the overwhelming amount of information available for the most common medical practices (AHCPR, 1993; McCormick & Fleming, 1992). In 1996, AHCPR shifted its efforts to supplying scientific evidence to provider groups so that they can develop their own guidelines. AHCPR (1996) cites substantial evidence that the guidelines it has sponsored have increased quality and reduced costs. AHCPR has funded a variety of dissemination-related research projects and a major conference in 1991 on the effective dissemination of clinical and health information (described in VanAmringe & Shannon, 1992).

Other professional associations in behavioral health have developed or plan to develop practice guidelines. For example, the American Psychiatric Association has published guidelines for the treatment of bipolar disorder and major depression (APA, 1993, 1994). Yet the movement to formalize treatment recommendations in guidelines has not seen harmonious agreement. The American Association of Applied and Preventive Psychology, an affiliate of APS, has criticized the American Psychiatric Association's guidelines as too biased toward pharmacological treatment (Hayes, 1996) and not created in partnership with MCOs which have the power to authorize the specified care. Some guidelines have been developed largely within a single discipline, such as the American Psychiatric Association, whereas others are clearly more multidisciplinary in nature, such as those by AHCPR, or the newly published guidelines in The Expert Consensus Guidelines Series (e.g., Treatment of Schizophrenia: McEvoy et al., 1996; Treatment of Bipolar Disorder: Kahn, Carpenter, Docherty, & Frances, 1996). Some of these guidelines may conflict from one sponsoring group to another.

This confluence of factors—changing funding patterns for researchers, call for relevance in research, efficacy-based behavioral treatment approaches, mental health policy initiatives and the managed healthcare movement, and basic science training, including digesting the research literature and data collection and analysis—created a fit between the training of our psychologist-authors and the emerging need of Indiana's behavioral health service providers to demonstrate accountability. We describe first the quality improvement and outcomes project that evolved to meet this new pressure and then highlight the roles that some psychologist-managers took to help make this project successful.

The task facing our collaboration was to translate and implement abstract policies generated by state government and by the philosophy of managed care into the specific practices at the provider level. Psychologists in the project created decision-support mechanisms to help the provider access, digest, and critically evaluate the avalanche of relevant information and to measure the subsequent impact of interventions. Mental health administrators now had strong external incentives to reconfigure their systems to support the managed care goals of accountability and efficacy-based services. The concurrent movement to provide increasing assistance to providers for transferring technologies into practice through mechanisms such as practice guidelines greatly supported this goal.

Let's go back to our representative CEO. As the environment for psychologists has substantially changed in the last decade, psychologists can now relate to the concerns and challenges of the CEO. McDonel knew many community mental health CEOs and had engaged in an ongoing dialogue with them about state-supported research and how it affected their interests. Many CEOs expressed interest in the evaluation research but were concerned about not getting enough help with research questions of their own. (Most CEOs do not understand how university faculty obtain external funding to pursue particular research interest.) Over time, McDonel came to appreciate the apprehensions of the executive management of these companies. M. Ashley, a COO (a psychologist-manager and the third author), brought McDonel together with a group of colleagues at a state-level meeting. The idea was raised of a self-funded collaboration of CMHCs to address the concerns of all CMHCs. Hiring a research psychologist would provide additional infrastructure to support administrators in learning how to collect, analyze, and use data. Although descriptive data were constantly being generated in spreadsheets, few people understood the need for inferential statistics or other research methodology in collecting and interpreting data. The rigorous search for alternative explanations for findings was an unfamiliar concept, and there was need for additional sophistication in sifting through and critically evaluating information in scientific journals and trade publications. Some staff, who had degrees of expertise in these activities, had no time allocated to them. On an agreement to provide collaborative support, McDonel was hired by the third author as an "outcomes and evaluation specialist."

STARTING THE COLLABORATION

One of the first issues that the CMHCs made clear is that they wanted the research psychologist to be one of them—a corporate citizen—and not just a consultant or independent contractor. This, of course, has both advantages and disadvantages.

On the positive side, an insider role would encourage investment and an in-depth understanding of the culture and loyalty to the organizations involved. Disadvantages could be less credibility of findings to any external agency and the risk that the evaluator would lose objectivity by being a member of the organizations involved. McDonel reached an understanding with the CMHCs that learning the truth about the degree of quality and then reporting it accurately was desirable, even when distressing. Only then could they use these data to fix the system and gain the edge they were seeking against their competition.

In the evaluation methodology literature, ongoing measurement of process and outcome data for the purpose of continuous improvement has been called *developmental evaluation* (Patton, 1994, 1996). Developmental evaluation interlaces two more classic forms of evaluation originally described by Scriven (1967) as *formative* (focused on measuring process components to improve a program) and *summative* evaluation (measurements of the outcomes, merit, or value of the program). In developmental evaluation, the program is never expected to reach a steady state of acceptability, but will always be subject to frequent improvements and adjustments. Quality control systems can be expensive to plan and implement; once in place, it is desirable in most settings to make it a permanent component of business operations. Where evaluation is ongoing, long-term, and focused on what is commonly called *continuous quality improvement* (CQI), the evaluator often becomes part of the system under evaluation.

Although Indiana's new legislation set into motion a report card to be developed by state officials, this and similar report cards to be offered by private vendors had an obvious drawback from the provider's perspective. Although it would offer the consumer useful information and meet the state's need for an objective method for comparing providers, report cards typically collect little or no process data to correlate with the outcomes. Suppose the state reports that your CMHC is below average on customer satisfaction with services, ease of locating the center, comfort of the facilities, and degree of relief from symptoms. In fact, this report card is a good example of a purely summative evaluation. Unfortunately this information yields no clues to help administrators know where to begin to correct the system. We labeled this the *context problem* with outcomes data and it has been addressed by others measuring outcomes in health care facilities. Pigott and Broskowski (1995) argue that outcomes data are virtually useless to providers without simultaneously measuring the inputs and systems processes that contributed to the outcomes; they illustrate how this approach is also at the core of Deming's well-known and well-disseminated approach to quality control in manufacturing. An American, Deming's work was first tested in Japanese automobile manufacturing with stellar results (Deming, 1986). One of the core tenets of Deming's *total quality management* (TQM) approach is to measure the variability surrounding a manufacturing process and to reduce that variability to improve outcomes. This is repeated continuously in a CQI format. In healthcare, the service delivery process and systems and clinician variability can be measured; once identified, unproductive sources of variation can be modified, and subsequent effects on outcomes evaluated. For example, delays in the time that it takes for clients to be seen for their first appointments are a source of variability that might be attributable to having too few clinicians to meet demand, poor management of vacation time, or not enough clerical assistance to process intake paperwork and reimbursement information. Once these sources of variability are identified and corrected, outcomes (latency to first appointment) can be measured again to gauge improvement.

Our collaboration group reasoned that evaluation would occur in a two-tiered format. On one hand, the state and managed care companies would proceed with their report cards and utilization studies to provide external and independent feedback to the system (summative evaluations). On another level, we would conduct our own internal developmental evaluation that would not only reveal our strengths and weaknesses, but would include enough process and systems information to help us pinpoint the source of the problems. Ultimately, both forms of evaluation need to be conducted concurrently to yield the best results for consumers. We had a further long-term goal of using our evaluative efforts in direct negotiation with MCOs, insurance companies, or other payors to authorize needed care or to establish contracts based on our track record.

Quality Improvement and Its History and Methodology in Nursing

Near the start of the collaboration, McDonel paired up with a quality improvement (QI) specialist at one of the partner CMHCs (D. Ashley, second author). This QI specialist is a nurse and has the training and background typical of a QI specialist in a healthcare facility. The traditional function of the QI specialist (also known as quality improvement analyst, quality manager, and similar titles) includes an array of activities. Healthcare facilities are subject to accreditation by a variety of regulatory agencies. A QI manager's job duties and responsibilities correspond to the domains of focus for the major accrediting bodies. The Joint Commission on the Accreditation of Health Care Organizations (JCAHO) is the predominant agency in behavioral health care, but there are several other major agencies and regulatory bodies that set standards and requirements for behavioral healthcare providers, including Medicaid, Medicare, and the National Committee for Quality Assurance (NCQA) (e.g., 1995), and the Commission on the Accreditation of Rehabilitation Facilities (CARF) (e.g., 1992). Quality improvement managers address risk management issues such as the safety of patients and staff with respect to infection control, exposure to bloodborne pathogens or toxic substances, and violent outbursts by patients. They often must help the organization's human resources manager to meet Occupational Safety and Health Administration (OSHA) requirements and also monitor the competency of staff and document the appropriateness and veracity of professional credentials. Accrediting agencies such as JCAHO look at the stated mission and values of the organization and verify that policies and procedures of the organization operate to foster these goals (e.g., JCAHO, 1994, 1996). Quality managers focus on the consistency of procedures with the organization's mission and ensure adequate documentation of its operations. Quality improvement managers also collect data known as quality indicators and give the organization feedback and descriptive summaries of trends on a regular schedule. Mortality and suicide rates, for example, will be closely monitored. Rates of patient seclusion, use of physical restraints, and patient and staff injuries will be recorded and reviewed. Medication errors (e.g., wrong medication, wrong dose, wrong time, or delays in administration) or overuse of particular types of medications are typically monitored. For instance, medications that can be addictive or abusable such as the benzodiazepines for anxiety symptoms or Ritalin for attention deficit symptoms might be tracked. Average lengths of stay or intensity of service utilization could be assessed for circumscribed diagnostic groups or classes of patients, or broken down by clinician for individual feedback. *Utilization management* (UM)—the ongoing effort to control overuse or misuse of tests and services is an increasingly important function of the QI manager. The QI role also includes ongoing training of staff and ensuring that the organization provides adequate consumer education. Most recently, monitoring client and system outcomes and surveying customer satisfaction have come under the purview of QI.

Traditional Training for QI Managers in Healthcare

The QI position is usually filled by persons with a degree in nursing, which suits them well to QI responsibilities. Occasionally those with degrees in medical records technology or social work fill this role. Traditional core concepts in the training of nurses encompass what is collectively referred to as the *nursing process,* defined by these steps: a) observation and assessment, b) planning, c) implementation, and d) evaluation. Some of these principles are as old as the nursing profession itself, evolving from the work of such early champions as Florence Nightingale during the era of the Crimean war and after. She was first to codify and professionalize the nursing role, which began as a trained physician's helper on the battlefields of war. Nurses' roles widened to make functional assessments of patients, to respond to emergencies, to develop and refine medical documentation systems, and to teach patients about the nature of their illnesses and the course of care. The American Nursing Association has refined this conceptual scheme over time and has influence licensure laws of each state through the development and fine-tuning of nurse practice legislative acts. Quality improvement processes evolved naturally within the nursing role: Evaluation of quality of care and client outcomes were firmly entrenched in the nursing process tradition. The evaluation phase was a critical part of the nursing role—not only were nurses charged with delivering doctors' orders, but were also responsible for the continuous monitoring of the patient's condition and well-being. Information about these outcomes were needed for regular reporting back to the attending physician.

There are various levels of training for nurses: Licensed practical nurses, nurses with associate's, bachelor's, and master's degrees, and doctorate-level nurses. Professional certification can be acquired at the bachelor level and above through the American Nursing Association in areas like psychiatric nursing/

mental health, geriatrics, pediatrics, or oncology. Clinical specialties are offered through advanced practice nursing at the master's level and above. Bachelor's level nurses typically receive research and statistics training and are often responsible for collecting such systems data such as service utilization and for writing descriptive summaries for the purpose of pinpointing problems. Conducting consumer satisfaction surveys is another recently revitalized role from the early days of nurses, asking patients how they liked their stay in the hospital or if they understood the demonstration they received for their wound care. Nurses frequently conduct retrospective chart reviews to look for patterns of service associated with certain problems. Most of the statistical functions used by QI managers are descriptive rather than inferential. Although there has been an impressive surge of scientific research in nursing at the master's and doctorate levels in the last two decades, significance testing and proposing and testing of causal inferences are typically beyond the scope of the generalist nurse quality assurance (QA)/QI manager, except in the most sophisticated of settings and with advanced or continuing education. Although the average healthcare provider does not have the resources to fund advanced QI initiatives, the pressures of the managed care movement continuously push against this threshold (e.g., Spath, 1995). Now that the job description of QI analyst has evolved to include more complexity in handling data, the standard nurses' training begins to fall short. Either additional statistical and research training is required for the QI manager or collaboration with someone with this expertise may be required for advanced projects. In our case, the latter solution worked well. Larger MCOs and providers have the infrastructure to conduct technically advanced data collection and analysis (Rosenstein, 1996). As managed care continues to penetrate the marketplace, the curriculum of nursing schools may come to overlap the scientific training of psychologists. If psychologists want to fill this niche in a collaborative role with nurses, the time is now to establish a claim on this new territory.

With the growth of large databases comes an exciting opportunity for health services researchers to mine archival data and plan large prospective studies. Some MCO databases document millions of covered lives. As medical records are converted to electronic platforms, and the computer automates problem identification, opportunities for evaluators and researchers give rise to fresh system dilemmas for providers. As QI managers increasingly detect problems through automation, the capacity for finding solutions to those problems may lag behind. Here too is a possible new role for psychologists. As staff or as consultants to management in behavioral health settings, psychologists will not only be needed to evaluate, but also to identify, generate, and implement remedies for systems flaws.

In our consortium, the collaboration between the research psychologist and the QI manager capitalized on the skills of both nursing and research psychology. Some skills overlapped, regarding clinical knowledge, teaching experience, familiarity with managed care philosophy, and mental health policy issues. But there were also separate areas of expertise: the research psychologist had more experience with advanced statistics, critical review of scientific literature, research and evaluation methodology, and writing scientific papers and reports; whereas the QI nurse had a wider background in medical records rules and traditions, typical sources of systems variance, and requirements of accrediting and other regulatory bodies.

CHOOSING A METHOD FOR IMPROVING SERVICES AND MEASURING OUTCOMES: CLINICAL PATHWAYS

After reviewing the literature for state-of-the-art concepts that might guide our own QI efforts, we chose an approach known as the *clinical pathway* method. Clinical pathways (also known as *critical pathways*) are healthcare decision support tools drawn from sources of expert information that have been shown to increase quality, reduce unwarranted practice variation, and control costs (e.g., Spath, 1994). Pathways can be written to help identify those providers who engage in unorthodox, outdated, unvalidated, or unnecessary procedures. Clinical pathways are formatted as a checklist or guideline to describe site-specific plans of care that are typical for patients grouped within a specific diagnosis, DRG, or functional problem area (see Fig. 1 for an excerpt of a critical pathway developed by our collaboration). A pathway is a road map for clinician, administrator, and client that projects a trajectory of care for a routine episode of illness or medical procedure (Brandt, 1994). Yet pathways should not be construed as mandates or standards of care, rather, they are reminders or heuristic devices for staff about practices that are likely to benefit the client. It is a managed care methodology to ensure timely, cost-efficient quality care (e.g., Crummer & Carter, 1993).

Primary benefits expressed for paths in the QI literature are improved client outcomes, reduction of unnecessary or duplicate services, reduced lengths of stay or intensity of services, and decreased costs. Critical pathways enable the monitoring and reduction of unproductive variations (i.e., error variance) in service delivery (Hart & Musfeldt, 1992; Spath, 1994, 1995). For example, some clinicians may give tests that absorb client's time and resources but do not lead to enhanced treatment. On the other hand, for certain clinical problems, insufficient testing might lead to poor differential diagnosis and inappropriate treatment. Variations among testing practices by an organization's clinicians can be monitored to see what types of tests with what frequency and timing lead to what types of outcomes for which types of clients.

Pathways Are Location-Specific Guidelines

For a given group of clients, pathways translate general, laboratory and field-tested knowledge into specific, concrete, and locally viable recommendations for care. The practice guidelines being published in behavioral health by a variety of organizations cannot be simply dropped into any behavioral health setting. For example, some settings may not have the staff or resources to put into place all of the recommendations made in a practice guideline. In settings where mental health

Grant-Blackford Mental Health, Inc.

ALCOHOL INTENSIVE OUTPATIENT PROGRAM (I.O.P.)
CRITICAL PATHWAY

Path Elements	Diagnostic Phase Week 1	Acute Intervention Phase Week 2-7	Transition Phase Week 8
RESOURCE ACQUISITION	1. Admission Recertification [Admitting Therapist] 2. Obtain Demographic Information [Admission Representative] 3. Consent for Treatment [Adm. Rep.] 4. Release of Information for Insurance [Adm. Rep.] 5. Releases for Previous Treatment and Referral Source [Adm. Rep.] 6. Client Rights [Adm. Rep.] 7. Complete Payment Agreement [Adm. Rep.] 8. Orient Client to Scheduling and Payment Expectations [Adm. Rep.]	9. Recertification, as necessary [IOP Staff] 10. Monitor for Payment & Attendance [Scheduling Clerk]	11. Evaluate Need for Additional Releases of Information [IOP Staff] 12. Monitor for Payment & Attendance [Scheduling Clerk]
CLINICAL ASSESSMENT	1. I.O.P. Assessment [Case Coordinator] 2. Psychosocial History [Case Coordinator] 3. Health/Nutritional Assessment [Case Coordinator] 4. Medical History Questionnaire (Complete the above items if not already done on Inpatient) [Adm. Rep.; Client Completes; Reviewed by Therapist & Physician] 5. Administer S.A.S.S.I. [IOP Staff] 6. Mental Status Exam [Case Coordinator] 7. Assess Need for New Diagnosis Summary [Case Coordinator] 8. Determine GAF [Case Coordinator] 9. Identify Target Population [Care Coordinator]	10. Random Urine Screen [IOP Staff Completes; Inpatient Staff Witness Specimen Collection] 11. Random Breathalyzer Screens [IOP Staff]	12. Random Urine Screens [IOP Staff Completes; Inpatient Staff Witness Specimen Collection] 13. Random Breathalyzer Screens [IOP Staff]

. . .

CLIENT OUTCOMES	1. Can Verbalize Basic Understanding of Program and Expectations [Client; IOP Staff monitor] 2. Demonstrates Participation in Treatment Planning by Giving Signature [Client; IOP Staff monitor] 3. Participates in completion of Outcome Measures [Client; Witnessed by IOP Staff]	4. Consistently Attends Program - Is Able to Identify Level of Addiction 5. Maintains Sobriety 6. Agrees to Family Involvement 7. Identifies Relapse Triggers and Risk Behaviors 8. Regular Attendance at Self-Help Group [All Steps in this Phase are Responsibility of Client; Monitored by IOP Staff]	9. Completes Relapse Prevention Plan 10. Shows Evidence of Abstinence 11. Completion of Assignments [All Steps in this Phase are Responsibility of Client; Monitored by IOP Staff]

FIGURE I   Excerpt of a critical pathway for outpatient intensive alcohol treatment.

consumers are poor, the newer, pricier, yet more effective medications may not be the treatment of choice over less expensive substitutions (e.g., this is often the case with pharmaceutical formularies in prison settings). Although practice guidelines have helped enormously to digest and summarize scientific and expert information, their translation into a local version is still necessary, as well as their evaluation at the local level.

Adapting Pathway Methodology to Behavioral Healthcare

Pathways arose from the nursing literature, with its emphasis on streamlining documentation of the nursing process and systematizing the QI process. When we began our collaboration, these tools were widespread in general medical–surgical inpatient settings, but were uncommon in outpatient and behavioral health settings. A recent survey of 1100 hospitals showed that 81% were using pathways, the most common of which were for total joint replacement, open-heart surgery, pneumonia, vaginal delivery, and congestive heart failure (*Health Systems Review,* 1996). We extended the concept to chronic care, as most pathways we had read about dealt with short-term acute care. Our project is still in progress, and its development and preliminary findings are summarized next. A more detailed literature review of the pathway concept and a description of our findings is given in a separate paper (McDonel et al., 1998).

STRUCTURING THE COLLABORATION

Thirteen CMHCs contracted with one CMHC as the lead agency.[1] M. Ashley handled contract negotiations and many of the entrepreneurial and business aspects of the project. His success at this role was likely enhanced by his long history in a variety of positions at several of the participating CMHCs. He had been a clinical site director in a large NIMH-funded research demonstration project to evaluate two community-based treatment interventions for persons with severe mental illness and substance abuse problems (Bond, McDonel, Miller, & Pensec, 1991). For our project, he developed a business plan delineating its scope, its intended impact, and its intended beneficiaries. With each CMHC as a shareholding member of the collaboration, our broad collective goal was to implement efficiently state-of-the-art methods for quality improvement and to measure the effects of these ef-

---

[1]The collaboration consists of the following organizational partners in Indiana: Adult and Child Mental Health Center, Indianapolis; Center for Mental Health, Anderson; Cummins Mental Health Center, Danville; Grant-Blackford Mental Health, Marion; Howard Community Hospital, Kokomo; Madison Center, South Bend; Porter Starke Services, Valparaiso; Quinco Behavioral Health Systems, Columbus; South Central Community Mental Health Centers, Bloomington; Southlake Center for Mental Health, Merrillville; Southwestern Indiana Mental Health Center, Evansville; Swanson Center, Michigan City; Tri-City Community Mental Health, East Chicago; and Tri-County, Inc., Center for Family Counseling, Carmel.

forts on client and system outcomes. Furthermore, we wanted to create a database to compare the cooperating organizations' performances. Early on, the shareholder CEOs envisioned that once pathways were developed and had undergone a first-run validation, the project would enlarge to include new organizations as customers and would broaden in scope as its own infrastructure grew. Legal expertise was needed to address intellectual property rights and to ensure that staff of participating agencies did not purposely or inadvertently divulge proprietary materials. One of the goals of the collaboration was to build QI tools that would give us a competitive edge against organizations outside of our consortium. Getting this number of CMHCs to collaborate and to trust one another in the current environment was a considerable challenge and had rarely happened on this scale before in Indiana outside of collective lobbying efforts. It took the entrepreneurial efforts of M. Ashley and several detailed workshops on the proposed project given by McDonel and D. Ashley before the consortium was formally initiated in May of 1995.

The 14 participating CMHCs each created pathway teams of five to seven members. All pathway teams had chairpersons who convened once a month to form an advisory council. Four of the teams were led or co-led by psychologists (Wheeler, Kraus, Long, Gibson, and Sarkissian). The advisory council members received intensive training from McDonel, D. Ashley, and M. Ashley, which they, in turn, shared with their team members. Training was supplemented with extensive site visits and telephone and fax communication.

Developing Critical Pathways

Our 14 CMHCs developed pathways in broad diagnostic areas including bipolar disorder type I, major depression (acute, recurrent, and a third track combining all depressive disorders together), adjustment disorder, alcohol abuse and dependence disorders (an inpatient detoxification path as well as three outpatient tracks differentiated by levels of functioning and severity at admission), panic disorder, chronic schizophrenia (both acute and maintenance tracks), borderline personality disorder, conduct disorder co-occurring with oppositional defiant disorder in children, attention deficit disorder in children, and oppositional defiant disorder comorbid with attention deficit disorder in children.

Before we developed our pathways, we collected baseline data that revealed current practice patterns and served as a needs assessment to justify creating provider-based tools to better control utilization of services. Each CMHC submitted data on high-volume and high-risk diagnostic categories. The most commonly treated illnesses, or those with the highest perceived risk, were chosen from this list. Each CMHC picked a diagnostic area to target for pathway development. All teams conducted a chart audit to review strengths and weaknesses of their current practices, with each CMHC auditing 30 to 65 charts within its target diagnostic category. McDonel and D. Ashley, with feedback from the advisory council, created a chart review protocol for collecting these data; McDonel analyzed these audit data and wrote interpretive reports for each team.

We found a variety of service patterns that could improve or benefit from better coordination (summarized in McDonel et al., 1998). Average lengths of stay and service intensity measured in number of outpatient visits were computed for diagnostic areas to determine reasonable target lengths of stay for the pathways, in combination with data from literature reviews. Lengths of stay showed wide variability within each diagnostic domain for a particular center, suggesting that further efforts to predict and differentiate short-term from long-stay clients might be productive. Some interesting and useful findings turned up: some were expected and some were a surprise. From a database of 730 total cases, we found that two-thirds of discharges were nonmutual—that is, clients dropped out of treatment without formally terminating with the therapist. Comorbidity was high. Primary diagnoses changed about one-third of the time over the period of admission to discharge. Over half of all clients were on at least one psychiatric medication; these rates were higher within certain diagnoses. Disconcerting to the psychologists on the teams was the finding that psychological testing and neuropsychiatric testing were rare, although CMHC staff could easily cite the reason for this—no reimbursement, no testing. Less than half of the cases had Diagnostic and Statistical Manual (DSM) IV-Axis V or Global Assessment of Functioning (GAF) scores improve from admission to discharge; an unknown was whether this effect was real or caused by inconsistent and unreliable use of the GAF. No-show rates were high on average, occurring once for every three outpatient visits. Over half of the cases had at least one no-show during the treatment episode. No-shows are costly and an important source of variation to measure and modify. Medication use for clients was strongly associated with other service intensity. We also found evidence of inappropriate use of pharmacology in some cases. Overuse of benzodiazepines and underuse of antidepressants occurred for some disorders. Also, the data alerted some psychiatrists to the relationship between overuse of polypharmacy or too frequent switching of medications and treatment complications.

The pathway teams then conducted literature reviews on their target diagnoses, again with assistance from McDonel and some of the psychologists. Many staff had not been to a university library in years and needed help in conducting computerized literature searches. Once articles were located, further help was needed in reviewing, consolidating, and digesting this information. Although these efforts were initially intimidating for some, we reasoned that CMHC staff needed to step through this process for themselves with assistance, rather than having it done for them. We felt that not only would this enhance expertise for future efforts, but that it would greatly increase ownership and buy-in that would facilitate implementation of the pathways. Furthermore, we felt that teaching staff new skills in information gathering was consistent with state-of-the-art management philosophies espousing "learning organizations" as more competitive and resistant to obsolescence (e.g., Senge, 1990).

Pathways went through numerous drafts as the group reached consensus about the best common format for all pathways. In the process, we learned which elements made chronic-care pathways different from short-term pathways. Each pathway outlined recommendations for staff in the following domains: resource acquisition (i.e., precertification for insurance, explaining discounts and sliding scales to clients), assessment and testing, medications, treatment plan, consumer education and family orientation, discharge planning, referrals and consults, client outcomes, and system outcomes. An excerpt of one of our pathways for outpatient intensive alcohol treatment is presented in Figure 1. The time windows for chronic paths were not measured in days, as are the typical acute care paths, but in time phases specified by the literature for each diagnosis. For example, in the literature on major depression, three phases emerged with approximate lengths of duration suggested for each: acute, stabilization, and maintenance. The application of pathways to outpatient chronic mental health care was uncharted territory and therefore presented some conceptual challenges. One fundamental struggle was to trim a diagnostic category down to a level for which a pathway is appropriate and then to define an episode of care. We had to differentiate between pathways for a first break of an illness or a recurrence, as in major depression. Eligibility criteria for a pathway were further constrained by the presenting level of severity. One team created pathways for alcohol abuse and dependence that combined diagnostic and functional criteria to determine pathway eligibility: Three pathway levels for alcohol treatment were developed, one each for mild, moderate, and severely impaired functioning. With input from the research psychologists, the teams selected simple systems and client outcome indicators for their paths, created an implementation plan, and trained front-line staff in the use of the pathways.

Responding to variability in lengths of stay or intensity of service contracts discovered in our baseline audit, several pathway teams developed separate tracks for groups with different expected lengths of stay or number of service contacts. The schizophrenia team developed acute and maintenance tracks of their pathway and eligibility criteria to determine client appropriateness for each track. The team looking at dysthymia was perplexed by intensive service utilization and so broadened their pathway to encompass all types and subtypes of depressive disorder. Within their single megapath, target rates of service utilization and differential expectations were created for depressive subtypes (e.g., dysthymia vs. single episode of depression). This pathway also concentrated on detecting psychiatric and physical comorbidity and ensuring appropriate access to medication early in the episode, as well as generating reevaluation criteria when there is failure to improve.

First-Run Validation of the Pathways

To validate the pathways, we created an evaluation audit instrument. This instrument records outcome measures combined with adherences to each recommendation on the path. Documentation of the occurrence and timing of all of these process variables is known as *variance reporting*. Clinicians can record reasons for departing from the pathway; subsequent review by the provider's QI manager can determine whether these variances or departures from pathways are warranted.

Three types of systematic practice variation can be coded from a clinical pathway and analyzed to improve practices: patient/family, system, and community (Crummer & Carter, 1993). In *patient variance,* a deviation from the pathway occurs because of a patient-related factor such as a suicide attempt, medication intolerance, declining treatment, or failing to understand treatment. *System variances* arise from organizational problems, such as a delay in the availability of a service or a clinician, or computer problems. A *community variance* occurs when a patient remains in inappropriate or more restrictive care because services needed outside the organization are unavailable, such as insurance coverage or beds in the state hospital. Variances of all types can be recorded and analyzed over time, helping an organization to know where to mobilize resources against barriers to pathway implementation. As a guideline, the path allows latitude for exceptional or extraordinary care for those who need it. Practitioners should feel free to vary from the pathway as their clinical judgment warrants. The only difference from traditional care is that, on a pathway, practitioners must justify or explain why they made deviations from the prototypical care outlined on the path. Thus, there are favorable and unfavorable variances from pathways. A warranted variance occurs when more intensive services are initiated to handle an unforeseen complication. An unfavorable variance would occur when a psychotherapist fails to monitor for suicidal ideation in a depressed person. When a clinician engages in variances that are more likely to achieve positive than negative outcomes, that ratio might be taken as a type of index of advanced clinical skill. By engaging in productive variances, these skilled clinicians may help the system to identify flaws in the pathways which can be remedied by a QI team.

Because each pathway's outcome measures are uniquely matched to the clinical problem at hand, they are more sensitive to change than outcome assessments that cover a wide spectrum of disorders and problems. This method is also more client-friendly, in that clients are not spending time answering assessment questions of little relevance to the problem being treated, and we are not spending time measuring things we do not expect to change with treatment. Most importantly, the outcomes are temporally linked to the system context and process elements, so that one knows how to fix the system when the outcomes report card is unfavorable. Some of the outcome measures selected for the paths were short and simple and were scheduled to be repeated at intervals throughout the course of care. Measurement required by pathways may differentiate subtypes of patients for whom less-than-optimal outcomes might be expected at the outset. Some variances in provider practice patterns may be correlated with either positive or negative consumer outcomes. This strategy of linking outcomes to pathway adherence or variance will enhance providers' capacity to predict what types of consumers will benefit most from the path and to revise and refine pathways over time (see Pigott & Broskowski, 1995, for a more in-depth discussion).

CURRENT STATUS OF THE PROJECT

Teams began implementation between January and April of 1996 and ended implementation in early 1997. The average rate of adherence to each pathway's recommendations ranged from 65 to 81% across the 11 centers that have completed data to date. In-depth analysis and further project description is reviewed in McDonel et al. (1998). Anecdotal data so far have provided valuable evidence of the pathways' utility for identifying system problems. For example, the team that focused on adjustment disorder discovered a glaring gap between the literature and reality. They found that it was unrealistic to plan for five- to seven-visit lengths of stay. A sizeable number of clients came for only one visit, and sometimes two. This team is now looking for a briefer treatment modality and a method to identify these clients a priori to better serve them. Another team focusing on creating a path for attention-deficit disorder discovered that the inclusion of stricter differential diagnosis criteria and the addition of intensive diagnosis-specific testing reduced the number of clients initially thought to have attention deficit disorder/attention deficit hyperactivity disorder (ADD/ADHD) by half. We are looking forward to using this type of data in negotiation with MCOs and payors to authorize reimbursement for testing, as we are now able to demonstrate its utility for increasing quality and decreasing unnecessary services. In fact, we have had two instances when a clinician authorized more care from an MCO by describing the pathway and its rationale to the MCO case manager. Some CMHCs have used their pathways in contending for state-funded contracts for addictions services. We expect much more interaction of this type with external managed care entities as our project grows. Ultimately, our goal is to subsume many of the managed care functions under our own QI efforts, and, with our own documentation of pathway merits, contract directly with employers and insurance plans, bypassing the for-profit MCO that often serves as a middleman. Some have expressed concerns about providers falsifying these data. If risk-based or capitated contracts are awarded, providers will suffer the consequences of having inaccurate data, and so it is in their best interests to pursue QI efforts with integrity. We know that the consumer will pay for managed care one way or another, and that managed care is here to stay. We believe in a model that can incorporate managed care principles at the provider level, perhaps competing directly with the function of some MCOs. To accomplish this, providers will have to affiliate into large networks themselves.

Our next step in this project is to link paths with menus of even more specific treatment protocols appropriate for persons on the path, much like subroutines in a computer program. We believe that one important benefit of our paths when linked to treatment protocols is that medical records are reformatted into quantifiable checklists, removing most of the routine narrative reporting. With pathways, narrative documentation is completed only by exception when an unusual circumstance has arisen. This not only shrinks charts to a workable size for entry into computer databases, but also makes searching for and analyzing data in medical records much more efficient. In fact, we envision that with pathways and protocols on a computer platform as part of an integrated medical record, much of these QI and evaluation efforts can be done concurrent to treatment rather than retrospectively, fulfilling one of the ambitious expectations that JCAHO has for the healthcare facilities it accredits (one CMHC has already received a commendation by JCAHO, in part for its pathway efforts). Also underway in our collaboration is the planning for expansion to other partners (e.g., software companies for automation) and provider organizations. M. Ashley has contracted with new customers, including two new CMHCs and Indiana's Department of Education to use the pathway concept to achieve multiple system integration to serve the state's most severely emotionally disabled children.

THE ROLE OF CLINICAL PSYCHOLOGISTS IN TECHNOLOGY TRANSFER AND CREATING CULTURAL READINESS FOR THE MANAGED CARE ACCOUNTABILITY MOVEMENT

The needs of the provider community in addressing managed care issues seems an ideal match to the skills of both research-trained and clinically trained psychologists working in management. Most doctorate-level psychologists receive fundamental research training as part of their graduate training. Thus the clinical psychologists in our project played a role in helping other front-line clinicians and staff accept the culture changes that were necessary to implement clinical pathways. They assisted in the roles of technology translators and trainers in research values and philosophy, and as role models for using data as feedback to change clinical practices. Five psychologists each led or participated in teams to establish the clinical pathway project in their centers. Wheeler, an administrator and former university professor, is a psychologist who focused on the problem of institutional readiness for change. His center, a well-established and traditional suburban CMHC, chose to define a pathway for borderline personality disorder. Wheeler joined this team after development of their path, but before the implementation phase. This development team had underestimated the degree to which the clinical staff would resist changes in their traditional practice patterns. These clinicians had been accustomed to practicing solo with little institutional monitoring. Wheeler addressed this resistance through training in structured implementation of performance improvement tools. He further helped to familiarize clinicians with the philosophy of using data for decision support. His team is now ready to implement a new pathway in their CMHC.

G. Gibson, an administrator at The Center for Behavioral Health in Bloomington, Indiana, has provided leadership for developing a behavioral health care delivery system driven by scientifically supported treatment interventions. Prior to the inception of the pathway project, Gibson was involved in establishing several organizational, infrastructural, and cultural conditions that were necessary for generating widespread commitment to building and providing efficacy-based treatments (Chard & Gibson, 1994; Gilkey, Gibson, & Chard, 1995). One important precursor to the success of the pathway project was the establishment of a board-approved center policy reinforcing the use of procedures and interventions supported by the research literature. Gibson consulted with clinicians to assist them in adhering to their new policy. This center developed a computerized treatment efficacy database with 1200 studies on the effects of a variety of interventions. To further strengthen their new policy, the center developed a personnel selection system that takes into account professional training and work experience in empirically validated treatment programs and interest in practicing in an organizational culture with strong commitments to science and accountability in clinical practice. Gibson also provides technical support for measuring outcomes and performance indicators: his center now has more than 50 measures in use (Gibson, 1995; Morrison, 1996). These activities created a supportive atmosphere for implementing pathways.

A. Sarkissian is a counseling psychologist who served as Director of Utilization Management at The Center for Mental Health in Bloomington, Indiana. He has provided the interface between this organization's own efforts to improve treatment and to measure outcomes and his role in managing relations with approximately 20 managed behavioral health care organizations and contracts with these companies. Sarkissian helped to reengineer a treatment protocol already developed in-house for treating children with ADHD by weaving it into a clinical pathway. Sarkissian provided oversight for staff training on this pathway and specifically dealt with issues of compliance or fidelity to the pathway and problems created by staff turnover. In particular he dealt with the problem of turnover of psychiatrists at his center. Sarkissian met the challenge of training psychiatrists in the ADHD pathway/treatment protocol and working with psychiatrists who had been committed to the sole use of pharmacological interventions, an approach at odds with a pathway that emphasized a parent training component. Sarkissian addressed an internal rift between the clinicians who supported using efficacy-based pathways and protocols and those who resisted. Nonsupportive clinicians were asked to conduct a pilot study in another diagnostic area and to create and test their own protocol. This side project was successful and helped to change attitudes of the formerly resistant clinicians, who now became converts to the center's efficacy-based policy and "legitimizers" of pathways and protocols for others. Consistent with the continuous quality improvement approach used in the pathway process, Sarkissian fostered ongoing modification of the pathway to increase compliance and to coordinate utilization management activities of the center with the pathway.

S. Kraus was a clinical psychologist who served as clinical director at Tri-City Community Mental Health Center in East Chicago, Indiana. She was concerned about the variability in practice her center as it related to the treatment of the dually diagnosed seriously mentally ill (SMI) and substance abuse clients. Significant staff turmoil arose over the differences in treatment philosophy between those who espoused confrontational stances regarding SMI clients' use of substances and those who were more gentle in their approach. Kraus had previously participated in evaluation studies of programs developed for the SMI in her center, including in-home case management and an NIMH-funded initiative in outreach to the homeless mentally ill. She believed that a literature review and the developmental process of building a pathway in this area might help her team to reach a consensus regarding treatment philosophy. She and several psychology interns at her center were instrumental in doing the literature search and interpreting the quality of research for the Tri-City pathways team.

G. Long, a clinical psychologist at Quinco Behavioral Health Systems, Inc., in Columbus, Indiana, led that center's clinical path team. The center's organizational structure is team-based. Each team functions with relative autonomy in delivering a unique set of services. Thus, the goal was to gain buy-in by one or two target teams. The corporate culture emphasized change and improvement of service quality and style in the effort to meet the rapid revolution in the healthcare environment. Although administrative support was evident, the goal was to achieve approval and support at the team level. Long volunteered to lead the critical pathway project at her organization. As the psychologist in charge of organizational outcomes, critical pathways were the means to provide outcome data, utilization review, and quality improvement, and to increase the organization's readiness for the demands of managed care. In her role as pathway team leader, she organized the development of the pathway, educated and trained pilot team members, and directed the implementation process. She frequently relied on individual and group clinical skills to ease clinician's emotional responses to the pathway. Persuasion skills, logical reasoning, empirical data, and cajoling, combined with the use of meaningful incentives, were the tools she used to gain guarded staff cooperation and acceptance. Long's pivotal role was as a mediator. Recognizing the resistance of clinical staff to administrative directives regarding provision of services, it was necessary for her to facilitate pathway implementation in such a way that it met the needs of the pathway project, the clinical team, and the administration. She mediated between the pilot team and the pathway team, between the pathway team and the organization's QI council, and between the administration and both the pilot and pathway team. Her psychological background lent credibility and expertise in the fundamental areas of empirical support and research; her clinical skills and knowledge (especially of group dynamics) were critical assets in the development and implementation of critical pathways in her organization.

CONCLUSION

The managed behavioral health care movement has vastly changed the landscape for service providers and administrators. We believe that psychologists have unique training to apply toward solving some of the dilemmas faced by behavioral health providers and are best poised to serve as effective guides through this new, complex, and sometimes hostile territory. We have provided one innovative example of how psychologists' skills were tapped to guide management in meeting the increasing accountability pressures from payors and managed care entities. As there is less and less room for doctorate-level clinicians in a managed care environment in behavioral health, and as the funding and opportunity for more basic psychological research has declined, the role of psychologist as applied researcher or as administrator in behavioral health services organizations is a new one that many in the field may well want to consider.

REFERENCES

Agency for Health Care and Policy Research (AHCPR). (1993). *AHCPR-supported clinical practice guidelines* [Fact sheet] (Publ. No. 93-0050). Rockville, MD: U.S. Department of Human Services.

Agency for Health Care and Policy Research (AHCPR). (1994a). *Depression in primary care: Vol. 1. Detection and diagnosis. Clinical Practice Guideline, No. 5* (PHS Publ. No. AHCPR93-0550). Rockville, MD: U.S. Department of Human Services.

Agency for Health Care and Policy Research (AHCPR). (1994b). *Depression in primary care: Vol. 2. Treatment of major depression. Clinical Practice Guideline No. 5* (PHS Publ. No. AHCPR93-0551). Rockville, MD: U.S. Department of Human Services.

Agency for Health Care and Policy Research (AHCPR). AHCPR-sponsored guidelines help users increase quality and cut costs. *Research Activities, 194,* 10–11.

American Psychiatric Association (1993). Practice guideline for major depressive disorder in adults. *American Journal of Psychiatry, 150* (April supplement).

American Psychiatric Association (1994). Practice guideline for the treatment of patients with bipolar disorder in adults. *American Journal of Psychiatry, 151* (December Supplement).

Bond, G. R., McDonel, E. C., Miller, L. D., & Pensec, M. (1991). Assertive community treatment and reference groups: An evaluation of their effectiveness for young adults with serious mental illness and substance abuse problems. *Psychosocial Rehabilitation Journal, 15,* 31–44.

Brandt, M. (1994). Clinical practice guidelines and critical paths—roadmaps to quality, cost-effective care (Part I and Part II). *Journal of AHIMA95.*

Chard, K. M., & Gibson, G. (1994). *Research management support for efficacy-based interventions in mental health service settings.* Paper presented at the American Psychological Society, Washington, DC.

Commission on the Accreditation of Rehabilitation Facilities (CARF). (1992). *Standards manual for organizations serving people with disabilities.* Tucson, AZ: Author.

Deci, P., McDonel, E. C., Semke, J., Hadley, T., Hogan, M., Wright, E., & Pescosolido, B. A. (1997). Downsizing state-operated psychiatric facilities. In S. H. Henggeler & A. B. Santos (Eds.), *Innovative services for difficult to treat populations.* Washington, DC: American Psychiatric Press.

Deming, W. E. (1986). *Out of the crisis.* Boston: MIT, Center for Advanced Engineering Studies.

Feldman, S. (1992). *Managed mental health services.* Springfield, IL: Charles C. Thomas.

Freeman, M., & Trabin, T. (1994). *Managed behavioral healthcare: History, models, key issues and future course.* Rockville, MD: Center for Mental Health Services.

Gibson, G. (1995). *Efficacy based interventions in behavioral health care settings.* Symposium of the National Convention of the American Psychological Association, New York.

Gilkey, W. A., Gibson, G., & Chard, K. M. (1995). *Organizational support for empirically based interventions in a community mental health setting.* Paper presented at the American Psychological Association, New York.

Glueckauf, R. L. (1993). Use and misuse of assessment in rehabilitation: Getting back to the basics. In

R. L. Glueckauf, L. B. Sechrest, G. R. Bond, & E. C. McDonel (Eds.), *Improving assessment in rehabilitation and health.* Newbury Park, CA: Sage Publications.

Hart, R., & Musfeldt, C. (1992). MD-Directed critical pathways: It's time. *Hospitals, 66(23),* 56.

Hayes, S. C. (1987). The gathering storm. *Behavior Analysis, 22,* 41–45.

Hayes, S. C. (1989, July). An interview with Lee Sechrest: The courage to say "We do not know how." *APS Observer,* pp. 8–10.

Hayes, S. C. (1996). Practice guidelines: The course ahead. *Scientist Practitioner, 5*(2), 23–24.

Health Systems Review. (1996, January/February). The prognosis for pathways: A study of clinical path trends in healthcare. *Health Systems Review.*

Joint Commission on the Accreditation of Health Care Organizations (JCAHO). (1994). *1995 MHM: Accreditation manual for mental health, chemical dependency, and mental retardation/developmental disabilities services,* (Vol. 1). Oakbrook Terrace, IL: Author.

Joint Commission on the Accreditation of Health Care Organizations (JCAHO), (1996). *1997–1998 Comprehensive accreditation manual for behavioral health care.* Oakbrook Terrace, IL: Author.

Kahn, D. A., Carpenter, D., Docherty, J., & Frances, A. (1996). Treatment of bipolar disorder: The expert consensus guidelines series. *Journal of Clinical Psychiatry, 57,* Suppl. 12A.

McCormick, K. A., & Fleming, B. (1992, December). Clinical practice guidelines. *Health Progress,* pp. 30–34.

McDonel, E. C., Ashley, L. D., Ashley, M. A., Wheeler, K., Gibson, G., Long, G., & Beeler, S. (1998). *Critical pathways in managed behavioral health care: An integrated approach to implementing practice guidelines, conducting continuous quality improvement and outcomes management, and automating the clinical record.* Monograph contracted by U.S. Substance Abuse and Mental Health Administration, Center for Mental Health Services, Washington, DC.

McDonel, E. C., Meyer, L., & DeLiberty, R. (1996). Implementing state-level mental health policy reforms in Indiana: Closing a state-operated psychiatric hospital and passing major mental health reform legislation. *International Journal of Law and Psychiatry, 19*(3/4), 239–264.

McDonel, E. C., Wright, E. R., Pescosolido, B. A., Miller, J., & Elbracht, D. (1994, September). *The Central State Hospital Discharge Study: Tracking Report,* Bloomington: Indiana University, Institute for Social Research.

McEvoy, J. P., Weiden, P. J., Smith, T. E., et al. (1996). Treatment of schizophrenia: The expert consensus guidelines series. *Journal of Psychiatry, 57,* Suppl. 12B.

McFall, R. M. (1984, November 2). *Clinical science and clinical professionalism: Are they incompatible?* Presented at the 18th annual convention of the Association for Advancement of Behavior Therapy, Philadelphia.

McFall, R. M. (1991). Manifesto for a science of clinical psychology. *Clinical Psychologist, November,* 75–88.

McGrew, J. H., Wright, E. R., Pescosolido, B. A., & McDonel, E. C. (1999). The closing of Central State Hospital: Long-term outcomes for persons with severe mental illness [Special issue]. *Journal of Behavioral Health Services and Research,* in press.

Morrison, D. P. (1996). Clinical outcomes assessment. In C. Stout (Ed.), *The complete guide to managed behavioral healthcare.* New York: Wiley.

National Committee for Quality Assurance (NCQA). (1995). *Standards for accreditation.* Washington, DC: Author.

Newman, F. L., & Tejeda, M. J. (1996). The need for research that is designed to support decisions in the delivery of mental health services. *American Psychologist, 51,* 1040–1049.

Osborne, D., & Gaebler, T. (1993). *Reinventing government: How the entrepreneurial spirit is transforming the public sector.* New York: Plume.

Park, R. L. (1996, May/June). Fall from Grace: The deep gash in science funding suffered in the great Washington budget war is just the latest insult in a long decline. *The Sciences,* pp. 18–21.

Patton, M. Q. (1994). Developmental evaluation. *Evaluation Practice, 15*(3), 311–320.

Patton, M. Q. (1996). A world larger than summative and formative. *Evaluation Practice, 17*(2), 131–144.

Pescosolido, B., Wright, E., McGrew, J., Mesch, D., Hohmann, A., Sullivan, P., Haugh, D., DeLiberty, R.,

& McDonel, E. C. (1996). The human and organizational markers of health system change: Framing studies of hospital downsizing and closure. *Research in the Sociology of Health Care, 69*–95.

Pigott, H. E., & Broskowski, A. (1995, May/June). Outcomes analysis: Guiding Beacon or Bogus Science? This "now darling" of the behavioral health field has a piece missing, i.e., critical pathways. *Behavioral Health Management,* pp. 22–24.

Rochefort, D., & Logan, B. (1989). Federal retrenchment, block grants, and state control. In D. Rochefort (Ed.), *Handbook on mental health policy in the United States* (pp. 143–172). New York: Greenwood Press.

Rochefort, D., & Logan, B. (1993). Federal retrenchment, block grants, and state control. In D. Rochefort (Ed.), *From poorhouses to homelessness: Policy analysis and mental health care* (pp. 65–94). Westport, CT: Auburn House.

Rotter, J. B. (1971). On the evaluation of methods of intervening in other people's lives. *Clinical Psychologist, 24,* 1–2.

Scriven, M. (1967). The methodology of evaluation. In R. W. Tylor, R. M. Gagne, & M. Scriven (Eds.), *Perspectives of curriculum evaluation.* Chicago: Rand McNally.

Scriven, M. (1996). Types of evaluation and types of evaluator. *Evaluation Practice, 17*(2), 151–161.

Seligman, M. E. P. (1995). The effectiveness of psychotherapy. The *Consumer Reports* study. *American Psychologist, 50,* 965–974.

Senge, P. (1990). *The fifth discipline: The art and practice of the learning organization.* New York: Doubleday/Currency.

Sherman, P., Zahniser, J., & Smukler, M. (1995). *S.M.H.A.'s managed care practices. Resources for Human Services Managers, Evergreen, CO.* Prepared under contract with the West Virginia Office of Behavioral Health Services.

Spath, P. L. (1994). *Clinical paths: Tools for outcomes management.* Chicago: American Hospital Publishing.

Spath, P. L. (1995, March/April). Quality data: The foundation of healthcare performance improvement. *Quality Resource,* pp. 1–4.

Tobias, S., Chubin, D., & Aylesworth, K. (1996, July/August). Chutes and ladders: In an unstable market for new Ph.D.'s, success in science must be redefined to include careers outside the ivory tower. *The Sciences,* pp. 17–21.

VanAmringe, & Shannon. T. (1992, December). Awareness, assimilation, and adoption: The challenge of effective dissemination and the first AHCPR-sponsored guidelines. *Quality Review Bulletin,* pp. 397–404.

BIOGRAPHIES

L. Diane Ashley   L. Diane Ashley, BSN, RN, LSW, is Executive Vice President of Quality and Marketing of Behavioral Pathway Systems, a company within Grant-Blackford Mental Health, Inc., in Marion, Indiana. She has over two decades of experience in quality management in mental health care. She remains involved in the development of the pathway project, including training other providers in the use of pathways, and in the expansion of the pathway concept into quality management of children's services systems funded by the state of Indiana Department of Education.

Michael A. Ashley   Michael A. Ashley, Ph.D., HSPP, is a licensed clinical psychologist and Executive Vice President of Operations and Technical Development of Behavioral Pathway Systems, a company within Grant-Blackford Mental Health, Inc., in Marion, Indiana. He has held management positions in several of Indiana's community mental health centers over the last two decades and has participated in NIMH-funded research demonstration projects. His current clinical and administrative interests focus on further development of the clinical pathway project, including approval by the Joint Commission on Accreditation of Healthcare Organizations (JCAHO) for some elements as performance indicators under its ORYX initiative, and on establishment of a software platform for the pathways (see http://www.behavioralpathwaysys.org).

Gordon Gibson Gordon Gibson, Ph.D., is Director of the Center for Behavioral Health Research in Bloomington, Indiana. Dr. Gibson and the psychology staff have developed a computerized treatment efficacy database and multiple outcome measurement systems for use with the center's behavioral healthcare interventions. They use empirically supported manualized treatments with 20% of their patients and efficacy-based interventions with the other 80%.

Sharon Kraus Sharon Kraus, Ph.D., HSPP, is a licensed clinical psychologist and is currently Associate Director of Clinical Services at Tri-City Community Mental Health Center, in East Chicago, Indiana. She is a member of the Society of Psychologists in Management and she also manages a small group practice in the Chicago suburbs. Her primary clinical interest is in family therapy.

Grace Long Grace Long, Ph.D., HSPP, is a clinical psychologist and director of the predoctoral psychology internship at Quinco Behavioral Health Systems, in Columbus, Indiana. She provides clinical services at an adult outpatient facility, coordinates the clinical supervision program, and administers the training activities for the predoctoral internship program. Dr. Long plans and implements outcomes activities at Quinco. She has integrated program evaluation components into the internship training experience and has facilitated the implementation of clinical pathways in two separate programs at Quinco.

Elizabeth C. McDonel Betsy McDonel, Ph.D., HSPP, is currently an Evaluation Specialist at the Center for Mental Health Services, Substance Abuse and Mental Health Services Administration, U.S. Public Health Service, in Rockville, Maryland. She is a clinical psychologist and was an NIMH-funded postdoctoral fellow in Mental Health Services and Policy Research at Indiana University—Purdue University at Indianapolis. Her research has been in the areas of psychiatric rehabilitation services for persons with severe and persistent mental illness, implementation of managed mental health care policies and quality improvement practices, and behavioral assessment.

Armen Sarkissian Armen Sarkissian, Ed.D., HSPP, is the Director of Utilization Management at the Center for Behavioral Health, in Bloomington, Indiana. He is licensed as a Health Service Provider in Psychology in Indiana and California. He is also Adjunct Professor in the Department of Counseling and Educational Psychology at Indiana University—Bloomington.

Kirk Wheeler Kirk E. Wheeler, Ph.D., is the Chief Operating Officer of a community mental health center in Indianapolis. A clinical psychologist, Dr. Wheeler has experience with the care of children, adolescents, adults, and older adults in a variety of settings. His work experience includes academic medicine, hospital practice, clinical and administrative roles in for-profit psychiatric facilities, and formation/oversight of group practices. His present research focuses on outcome measurement and best practice protocols.

PART II

HIGHER EDUCATION ADMINISTRATION AND MANAGEMENT

7

HIGHER UNIVERSITY ADMINISTRATION

CHARLES A. KIESLER

University of Missouri, Columbia, Missouri 65211

INTRODUCTION
DIFFERENCES AMONG UNIVERSITIES
THE MULTIPLE CULTURES OF A MAJOR UNIVERSITY
HELPFUL HINTS
WHERE DOES THE MONEY COME FROM?
INTERNAL DECISION MAKING IN UNIVERSITIES
PERCEPTIONS OF SIGNIFICANT OTHERS
USING POWER
SOME ADVANTAGES OF A PSYCHOLOGICAL BACKGROUND
BIOGRAPHY

INTRODUCTION

I have always thought of myself as a scholar first and foremost and, as a young psychologist, marveled that anybody would pay me to do research, something I would have been willing to do for nothing. On the other hand, I have, from the very beginning of my professional career, maintained other responsibilities as well. While still an assistant professor, I was also chair of an undergraduate major at Yale, and the following year took on as well the directorship of the graduate program in personality and social psychology. Having carried out both roles simultaneously led me to bristle somewhat at the terms "administrator" and "administration." Those terms have always brought to mind such phrases as "due diligence" and "do no harm." For me, administration has always meant "having an impact," "creating new models or visions," or "meeting a personal challenge." I apply the same thinking skills to administration that I apply to my research interests. In this view, what others might see as an administrative crisis and therefore an emotional upheaval, I would see as a challenge and an intellectual puzzle, something to which I would almost look forward.

A psychological background has some real advantages in university administration, and I will discuss some of them at the end of this chapter. Let me start by discussing some of the differences among universities that affect their administration, as there is far more variation among them than people typically think. At the same time, there is far more similarity to some other types of organizations than people typically give credit. In between these two end points, I want to discuss some of the issues that make a better administrator in higher education.

DIFFERENCES AMONG UNIVERSITIES

Universities versus Colleges

What distinguishes universities from colleges is their emphasis on research. I am stressing categories rather than names, because many schools that use the term university to describe themselves place no emphasis on research. I can think of one little private school that had no graduate education at all. With a $250,000 gift, it started a business school with a masters of business administration program and immediately changed its name from college to university. In my view, the name was all that changed.

When a university has research as a high priority, the culture is very different from other institutions of higher education. Some of the cultural differences of research institutions drive small-minded administrators wild. For example, in doing research, one has difficulty telling how hard the faculty are working on a week-to-week basis. Furthermore, when research has an outcome and is published, it is often difficult for a nonexpert to tell how good it really is. However, these differences are relatively trivial. The most important aspect of a university emphasizing research is that it is emphasizing creativity. A creative work culture is a more emotional one, it is more driven and certainly more disdainful of appointed leaders (administrators). A leader or administrator who is a scholar has a tremendous advantage in this environment. I want to come back to this issue of culture later, but for now, note that an institution emphasizing research is a much different organization from one that emphasizes only teaching. Indeed, the degree of emphasis on research makes a difference.

First Tier versus Second Tier Universities

Within the institutions that emphasize research, there is a considerable difference in culture, depending on how uniform the quality of the faculty is. The top 60 or so universities are different than the others. The last time I looked, the Association of American Universities had 56 members. Membership is by invitation only and one of the criteria is the number of research dollars from sources outside the university. The better the university, the more uniformly the faculty play leadership roles (and are expected to play leadership roles) in their disciplines at a national and international level. One can look at someone's vita and pretty much tell whether they are a star or a budding star in their field. Independently of one's own knowledge of the field itself, one can tell because of the accolades that peers give to the faculty member. In the case of a star, one can see invited colloquia at the nation's best universities, presidencies of disciplinary groups, national and international research awards, as well as, of course, a substantial number of publications in the best journals. This does not mean that someone who has not accomplished all of these things is not first rate, it is just less clear. However, the criteria used to judge quality of the faculty must be external to the university.

In the best universities, these external criteria for excellence pervade the place. One knows one's colleagues are very good. You know yourself that you are very good. The important distinction here is that in trying to sense one's own worth (or have other people sense it), one uses criteria external to the university. In an institution that is less uniformly high in quality these external criteria are less clear. When any of the criteria become internal to the university, it can lead to a lot of petty jealousies and acting out on the part of individual faculty. The sort of petty jealousies and campus politics that one sees in movies and novels that have universities as a central setting do not occur (or occur much less often) in the nation's best universities, at least in my experience. When I was a new and young department chair I noticed that one of my faculty had been paid a small amount of money more than another faculty member for the better part of 20 years. When I inquired why, it became clear to me that this defined the local pecking order in ways that had nothing to do with performance. At the end of the first year, I equated the salaries, and the one formerly more highly paid was furious with me. But that was the beginning of a very much needed change of local culture. An administrator has a very different job to the degree that the criteria for excellence of the faculty are not external to the campus.

Public versus Private

Public and private research universities are very different creatures, but the better the public university the more it shares certain characteristics with private universities. The faculty in the major private universities are paid substantially more than those in the major public universities, and often have better fringe benefits. However, the faculty in a public university receive much more in terms of the research infrastructure than do faculty in private universities. For example, when I was chair of the psychology department at Carnegie Mellon, only about one-third of our overall budget for the department came from university funds. Phrased a different way, the money we received from the university (typically called "hard money") was equivalent to the salaries of the faculty and one secretary. The other two-thirds of the budget was produced by the faculty through grants. To take another example, in 1992, I moved from being provost at Vanderbilt University (a private school) to being chancellor at the University of Missouri-Columbia (a public school). At that time the average full professor at Vanderbilt was paid about 40% more in salary than the average full professor at Missouri (the difference has decreased since then). On the other hand, at Vanderbilt, there was not a single post-doctoral research associate paid for with university funds, whereas at Missouri there were literally hundreds of them. The tendency of public universities to pay less, but provide more of the infrastructure leads to very different cultures between public and private universities. The private research university is a much more scrambling, entrepreneurial environment, more pressing, and probably a more stressful one. There are probably higher and more clearly stated expectations for success (both on an annual and on a long-term basis), and the higher salaries are offered as the primary rationale. The top half-dozen or so public universities pay more than their peers, but their expectations of the faculty are more like the private ones as well. The difference in cultural requirements can lead to substantial differences in administrative approaches. For example, at Vanderbilt, I was once recruiting a top faculty member from a first-rate public university. When I inquired as to his needs in order to become a colleague, he responded that he wanted to have a new assistant professor to help him with his research. I replied that we didn't do that but I offered him a $250,000 research fund to be used at his discretion and which could be used for a research assistant if he wished. He thought I was being extraordinarily generous. I wasn't. I knew that even if the assistant professor never became an associate professor, I would end up spending at least twice as much over the course of those intervening years than the $250,000. In a public university, I probably would have greater access to an additional faculty line than I would have to finding a pocket of money of a quarter of a million. In a public university, I probably would have been more attuned to the cost of the package in the current year rather than the total cost over multiple years. That is one of the differences between the major public and private universities. There is typically greater budgetary flexibility in a private university; then when an administrator has a dollar he or she can spend it on a greater variety of things. The drawback, of course, is that the administrator probably has to raise the dollar.

The use of public funds in the public university leads to different public groups feeling that they have an ownership position in the university. By that I don't mean simply the legislature and the governor's office, but also alumni and parents and the taxpaying public. All feel they are part owners. At the University of Missouri-Columbia, almost 80% of our total budget came from nonlegislative sources. I once calculated, given that fact and the typical economic multiplier effect of new money into the state, that the university accounted for more new taxes paid to the state than it received in its legislative appropriation. We were a profit center for the state. It became quickly obvious to me however that except for a few economists, no one thought that fact had any importance whatsoever for our budget, and I quit bringing it up.

Public and private major research universities are very different, and the demands on their leaders are very different as well. On the other hand, the major public research universities are probably more like their private peers than they are like the state colleges that emphasize teaching. And the small, church-linked private college is probably different from all others. When one talks about administration in higher education, it is important to understand that one is not speaking of a single type of organization. An organization that is very large is fundamentally different from one that is very small, and an organization that makes substantial use of public funds is very different from one that does not. And one whose core purpose for being is permeated with demands for creativity is very different from one that is not. However, even for the university that is ostensibly creative in nature, there are very substantial differences in subcultures within the organization.

THE MULTIPLE CULTURES OF A MAJOR UNIVERSITY

C. P. Snow once wrote a book entitled *Two Cultures*. The two cultures he was referring to were the sciences versus the arts and humanities. He felt the thought processes in these two groups were very different and so were the values. He also concluded that the scientist knew more about the arts and humanities than vice versa.

Snow had a point, but I think there are larger and more important cultural differences. I refer to the differences between the academic and research side of a university and the business side. The business side includes some real businesses. As chancellor, I had 46 different little suborganizations called auxiliaries, everything from the power plant to the bookstore to the TV station. Each of these auxiliaries had a requirement that they be "stand-alone" organizations. This means that they don't cost more than the income they produce. The business side also includes accountants, the building and grounds people, those focused on insuring the university, those concerned with legal issues and potential law suits, and the like. The business side of a university is much more like a nonuniversity business than it is like the academic side of the university. (Sometimes the two get confused. I once had an accountant tell me that I was interfering with his academic freedom. I said, "Son you have that wrong. You don't have any academic freedom." He seemed nonplused.) There are often clashes between these two groups. The faculty will often regard the business people as being "bean counters" who are trying to interfere with their rights, and the business people often regard the faculty as a little crazy and unwilling to be team players. Indeed, I once had a senior administrator who never used the word "faculty" without preceding it with the word crazy ("Do you know what the crazy faculty have done now?"). One group tends to be nine-to-five, always tries to routinize the workload, and always addresses the bottom line. The other group talks about the quality of ideas and intellectual freedom, and never wants to talk about the bottom line. As an extreme example of the latter, I once had a dean who had a strong tendency to overspend his budget. In exasperation I once told him, "Here is Kiesler's rule: Don't spend money that you don't have." He responded quite seriously, "Oh! Nobody ever told me that before." In this case, I was the one that was nonplused.

Managing these two different groups in ways that keeps both productive and with high morale can be quite challenging. I frequently maintain that managing a major university is more difficult than managing a business. In a university, you have all of the requirements of running a major business, and have in addition a major overlay of creativity and personal freedom. In some nontrivial ways, managing a university has more in common with managing the national symphony than it does with managing General Motors.

Space does not allow for detailed discussions of administering higher education, but in the next section I try to give some hints on productive administration pulled from 30+ years of experience.

HELPFUL HINTS

Stress Your Own Strengths

This first recommendation involves something that I see very few administrators of any organization trying to accomplish. The point is that high-level positions in higher education, perhaps more than those in other organizations, have some flexibility in how they approach the job. A perceptive, self-analysis of your own strengths and weaknesses can lead to somewhat of a restructuring of your position to emphasize your own strengths. As a personal example, I am not a "schmoozer." That is, making small talk in a one-to-one environment is not one of my strengths. Even when I do it acceptably, I don't enjoy it. On the other hand, I am a good public speaker. This led me as a provost and a chancellor to reconstrue some of my day-to-day behavior. I tried not to have situations in which my passive attendance at a meeting or a gathering was all that was required. My senior staff was instructed that if I were to show up for some sort of gathering, say a faculty reception, I would like to say a few words from the front of the room. In this way, my presence was always noted, my presentation was something I do well, and it allowed me to repeatedly iterate my vision and goals for the university. It furthermore saved me time. Instead of making my way around the room shaking hands with each person and making some small talk for an hour or two, I could frequently come in and fulfill my obligation in 15 or 20 minutes. I encourage you to think of the various personal attributes that are advantageous for your position, and then to do a very tough-minded self-assessment of what your strengths and weaknesses are. To the extent that you have authority to do so, I suggest that you try to "tilt" your position so that what others expect of you are things that you do very well, and the things that you don't do so well are delegated to others who do. If you don't handle numbers well, then don't put yourself in the position of attending one budget meeting after another. If you write well, but don't speak well, then do a lot of personal note writing and try to stay away from public speaking. If you are self-conscious about your lack of height, try to arrange it so you always speak from a raised dais. And so forth. You will be happier and more productive to the extent that your everyday activities are things that you both enjoy and do well. This does not mean that you can totally restructure your position and only do things that you enjoy. However, it does mean that there is greater flexibility in many of these positions than most people think.

Your Priorities and Goals

Many administrators get so focused on their organization's priorities and goals that they forget their own. I have always tried to lay out my goals on an annual basis. In doing so, I have always differentiated between the goals from the organization for which I hold responsibility and the goals for myself in which I played a unique role. The latter are not separate from the organization's goals, but can be thought of independently in terms of time commitment. They might include such things as spending more time with the faculty, trying to close more deals with donors, showing more personal support for intercollegiate athletics, or trying to devote more attention to showing the accomplishments or contributions of women and minorities.

I write these personal goals down at the beginning of each year. At the end of the year, I try to do a careful assessment of what we were able to accomplish. So far so good. Many people do this, Where I am different is that I then do an analysis of my calendar for the year. I try to see how much time I actually spent in various activities. It not infrequently occurs that even though I had a set of activities to which I attached a high priority, I still didn't spend a lot of time accomplishing them. In fact, this kind of outcomes analysis, if you will, can be quite surprising. In retrospect, it can feel like you spent a lot more time on something than in fact you did. There is a good reason for this of course. If something is a priority with you, then you are likely to remember all of the occasions on which you spent some time trying to accomplish it. This form of self-assessment can provide an effective private feedback loop.

Having assessed whether your time commitments followed your priority lists, you can then try to restructure some things that you do. At one point I found myself spending a lot of time in front of faculty groups talking, but very little time listening and discussing in detail some of the issues facing the university. I planned to spend more time at small gatherings or to drop in on more meetings. However, I did not have enough flexibility in my schedule to just drop in on things on an ad hoc basis. Because my information was that the faculty also wanted me to spend more time doing this, I finally decided I would have to schedule it to make it happen. I set up a twice-a-week lunch with a dozen faculty, randomly chosen, to discuss a variety of issues facing the university and to allow me to hear the concerns of individual faculty. Some weeks I couldn't accomplish this but over the course of a couple of years I really heard and talked to a large number of faculty in small group settings. It was a large enough group so that schmoozing wasn't a critical variable, but a small enough group so that each faculty member was able to say whatever he or she wished. It not only met a goal, but it turned out to be thoroughly enjoyable as well.

The suggestion here is not only to organize your time, but also to see whether the time you spent matches up well with your priority list.

WHERE DOES THE MONEY COME FROM?

Many university administrators decry the lack of flexibility in their budgets and complain that even though they have clear priorities, they can't find enough money to fund them. I have a couple of small suggestions that can add up to major impact. One is to get involved in the details of your budget. In my experience, almost any academic unit, from department to university, can extract and pile up about 2% of the total budget, and in ways that no one notices. This involves finding out where you are spending money that nobody cares whether you spend it or not. This can involve small but important sums of money. For example, as a department chair I was consistently hit with the request to buy new journals. We had no money to do so. When I requested a printout of all of the psychology-related journals that the library bought, I discovered we were still taking journals for a specialty in psychology that we no longer had. All of the faculty in that specialty, by design, had either left or retired. The library still took all of those journals (and resisted canceling them). Once we stopped taking those journals, we had plenty of money to buy the new journals the faculty wanted to have. The faculty didn't care about continuing the old journals, and were actually unaware that they were still being purchased. As far as they were concerned the new money came at no cost to them. This approach can also add up to big dollars. When a $600 or $700 million budget, finding 2% of it for flexibility adds up to a great deal of money. At Missouri, we captured millions in that way and invested it in quality. I once spent over $15 million on faculty research niches, but it probably would have taken me over an hour to tell you the many places where I got the money.

So the rule of thumb is that one can recapture about 2% of an academic budget without anybody really being aware of it happening. A similar rule of thumb is that one can capture about 5% of the budget with people aware of what you are doing but not complaining. As a department chair, I once thought that we were spending astronomical amounts of money on long-distance calls from the faculty. In looking at the bills, I came to the judgment that the majority of these charges were not really professional, but more personal in nature. I issued a policy of requiring my signature for any long-distance calls charged to the department. Over the course of a couple of years, the money saved was very substantial, and I never once disapproved a request. In retrospect, I would go about that a little more diplomatically, but it was effective.

INTERNAL DECISION MAKING IN UNIVERSITIES

In my experience, decision making in universities tends to be irrational. By irrational I don't mean to imply that one can't predict what the decisions will be. One can. However, there is not much conscious thought that goes into them. Some of the cynical adages about faculty regarding administrative decisions turn out to have more truth in them than one would like to see. One such adage is that of the "squeaky wheel." University administrators, who have typically received no formal training in administration whatsoever, often don't know how to judge the merit of an administrative request. Frequently, they substitute the persistence of the requesting unit for any kind of rational basis to a decision. They reason that if the unit is so convinced of their case that they will come back with their request several times a year and several years in a row, there must be some merit to the request. It might indeed have merit, but the requesting unit also might understand the squeaky wheel principle. Furthermore, administrators typically distrust the numbers underlying any request and don't know how to judge what the right numbers should be. Consequently, there is a strong tendency among university administrators to cut any requests for money in half. As a young department chair, I always found the latter bias to be particularly galling, because one was forced to lie in order to end up with an adequate response to a request. Suppose, for example, that the department chair has made a request for new desktop computers for all of the faculty in his or her department, and has made an honest proposal on how much this would cost. If the dean to whom the request is directed decides to honor the request but only gives half the money, it could be worse than saying no altogether. In a setup like computing, if one has only half the money needed, then one can either give desktop computers to only half the faculty (and thereby live with conflict which may go on for years) or more to a cheaper brand of equipment and a less adequate service. The latter is particularly a problem, because one will surely not be able to get up-to-date equipment and it will be years before one's unit has another computing request approved. The department could well be stuck in a time warp of mediocrity, while the administrator feels good about approving its request.

I have always recommended trying to undercut both of these phenomena, which are very natural ones and are likely to play a role if not actively resisted. One technique is to never approve a request for funding with less than full funding. I have always publicly stated to faculty and other administrators that upon request I will either give them what they have requested or zero, but never anything in between. I add that if I believe their request is inflated, the amount that I will give is definitely zero. This strongly encourages people to be honest in their recommendation and if a leader is successful in developing this kind of culture of honesty, his or her life will be easier.

The other recommendation is to face up to the ambiguities inherent in a budget request. It is not unusual to be uncertain whether you should or should not approve a request. Universities are so complicated these days that uncertainty may be the typical and realistic response of an administrator. The real issue is what you do then. I have always recommended that the administrator ask him or herself, "What do I need to know to make this decision rationally and confidently?" This leads you down different avenues. For example, you might ask yourself some of the following questions. What do units of similar quality in competitive universities have? This addresses the question of whether it is needed to compete with similar schools. What do similar departments in this university have? This addresses the question of whether approval of the request is fair inside the university. What happens if I say no? Am I really permanently dooming a solid and promising department? What happens if I say yes? Is the unit able to make a substantial leap in quality and national competition? Will it more successfully recruit the very best new PhDs to its faculty? Will its productivity increase? I have found that asking oneself these kinds of questions really can help to sharpen the basis on which you could or should make a decision. Furthermore, by sharing this information with the requesting unit—essentially saying here is what I have to know to give a rational response to your request—you can really sharpen the argument underlying the request.

When one looks at the details of a university budget one is struck by the illogic of it all. Resources that various units have in the university are a patchwork of irrational decisions spanning years. When one asks why a particular unit is so well funded in supplies and expenses money, and why another is not, one reveals some of this lack of rationality. For example, one answer I received to such a question is that a particular unit happened to make the request in a year in which there was more money available. Or another unit tried to make its request repeatedly but it was during the time when the legislature was cutting the university's budget, so they couldn't be accommodated. The combination of these lucky or unlucky coincidences, and the administrator's penchant for simply passing on whatever moneys they receive (e.g., a 3% increase in supplies and expenses and a 4% increase in salary), these differences can really become magnified over time, until there is no rhyme or reason to their existence.

A lack of explicit rationality to the decision-making process can be quite debilitating to the morale of the faculty and staff. Faculty and staff can live with less-than-ideal budgets if they understand the reason for it and think the budget resources are fairly allocated. Furthermore, if they believe that the decision-making process is rational, then they also probably believe that any inequities will be smoothed out in the future.

The bottom line here is that by asking yourself, what do I need to know to make this decision confidently, you will develop a more rationally based and appreciated set of decisions.

PERCEPTIONS OF SIGNIFICANT OTHERS

Psychologists understand that the perceptions of others are important and that they don't necessarily reflect reality. This becomes important in decisions, because the decisionmaker's actions may be perceived quite differently from his or her intent. This can go either way, with a good decision being perceived as a bad one, or a bad decision received positively. Suppose a university administrator rejects a request from faculty and staff to increase some fringe benefit (a wellness center for example). The administrator could have done this with an eye to approving an even better solution, say a solution that involves putting the same amount of money into salaries. For example, I have always leaned toward minimizing hidden benefits and maximizing salary money. The reasoning is that fringe benefits are not uniformly useful to faculty and staff. Free tuition benefits for the children of faculty and staff are only beneficial to those faculty and staff who happen to have college-age children. I have always thought the best avenue was to put as much of this money into the paycheck of every faculty and staff member and let them make their own decisions about their personal and family priorities.

The point is that an administrator, for very good reasons, could reject a request to increase a fringe benefit that is not uniformly useable, and thereby produce a fairly uniform furor on campus. The best antidote to this sort of situation is always to ask yourself, when about to make an important decision for others, How will others perceive it? I have fairly often changed the details of a complicated decision when I thought that significant others would misperceive it. Sometimes the misperceptions relate to a trivial aspect of the overall decision, and therefore it is easy to fix in advance of announcing the decision. Sometimes the aspect about to be misperceived is an important part of the decision. In that case, it is best to talk to the affected individuals in groups in advance of making the decision.

I have found it useful over the years to adopt a strategy of saying publicly, "I am thinking of doing X for the following reasons. What do you think?" In essence, invite a critique of your decision in advance of making the decision. It allows you the luxury of making a better decision without having to deal with the misperceptions of others. In the case of an important decision such as fringe benefits, this might well involve consultations with a number of groups on campus, and the administrator working a little harder to get other people's opinions in advance. Both of these steps can help build better relationships between the administrator and concerned others.

Note that there is an added benefit to this technique of asking how others will perceive a potential decision: You can't give a decent answer to the question unless you know how the significant others think about the issue and related issues. You can't know that unless you have been listening to them in the past. The added benefit is that this kind of strategy is of great value in keeping an administrative leader from becoming too isolated in his or her position.

There is another added benefit if you clearly and repeatedly make an effort to understand how other people think about a problem: It makes it easier to teach other people how *you* think about problems. Consider the typical scenario of requests made to a university administrator. A person or group writes the administrator (or telephones) stating that there is a problem, describes perhaps some basis for the problem, and requests a face-to-face meeting. Administrators routinely do approve such meetings, and the result is a multiperson meeting with what can be a fairly lengthy document outlining the problem, the request, and some justification. The initial result of this for the administrator is to distrust the numbers that are presented and to be relatively unsure about whether to agree to the request or not. The most typical outcome of such a meeting is that the administrator critiques what is presented, expresses some distrust, and requests further documentation and justification. It is not unusual for this process to be repeated several times.

Now suppose a different scenario, namely, that the administrator has taught the relevant faculty and staff how he or she thinks in response to such requests. What should be taught is the administrator's question to him or herself, what do I need to know to approve this request confidently? Above, I made the point that the astute administrator needs to understand how significant others think about particular issues. Now I make the point that it is a great advantage for an administrator to teach others how he or she thinks about an issue. If one can do that successfully then the typical result is that the requesting unit will spend a lot more time preparing the initial request, anticipating the kinds of questions that would be asked and the thoughts that might be concealed and addressing them up front. The ideal result is that instead of repeated meetings that increasingly become frustrating and perhaps rancorous, the request and the decision to approve can take place in a single meeting. (Note that you can not have a reputation for disapproving all such requests and still get this kind of culture going.) The immediate result is that the administrators, many of whom believe that most of their lives are spent in such meetings, save an enormous amount of time: One meeting accomplishes what previously took several meetings to accomplish. Furthermore, there are fewer requests. That is, if the potential requester walks through the kinds of questions the administrator will have when the request is made and discovers that in all honesty he or she does not have the adequate responses, then the request will probably not be made in the first place. This outcome means that the administrator will have fewer requests for scarce resources, and fewer meetings for each request. Morale of others will be higher, because at least they understand the basis for decision making. Their world therefore becomes more predictable, and their requests are more likely to be successful (assuming there is some justification for them).

Paying attention to the perceptions of others, and teaching them how to perceive you, are the two basic processes underlying all of these recommendations.

USING POWER

The short form of this topic is, don't—or at least try not to. Let's face it, many people are attracted to higher-level university administration because they perceive these positions to be ones of power. This is exactly the sort of people that should be encouraged to go into other fields. A major reason for thinking this way has to do with the culture of a major university. As I have described it before, it is a place primarily of creativity, of ideas. Bureaucracy in general and the use of power in particular tends to cast a pall over these activities. Disproportionate talk of budgets or costs has a similar tendency. Universities are not really meritocracies, but the faculty and administrators of the best universities find it useful to act as if they were. Faculty tend to think that the very best universities are meritocracies (within reason) and mediocre universities are not. Therefore, when an administrator flagrantly uses his or her power, the inference is obvious and the thought of it, to faculty, staff and students alike, is depressing.

So the recommended course of action is to act as if you had little or no power. Act as if you were persuading people to do the right thing. Is that possible? I think, for the most part, it is. If you are doing your homework—analyzing your decision alternatives, looking closely at costs and implications, thinking about how others will perceive a particular decision, and modifying it so it will not be misperceived—and you are legitimately acting in the long term best interests of the university, signaling in advance what you are thinking of doing, you probably have a very good case for arguing that you are doing the best thing possible. In which case, everybody (almost everybody) will accept the decision as a reasonable thing to do. They won't argue against it, and they won't fight putting it into place.

SOME ADVANTAGES OF A PSYCHOLOGICAL BACKGROUND

There are many aspects of a psychological background that are very useful in administration and higher education. For example, universities are first and foremost learning environments. Even research, as complicated as it can be, is a method of learning or discovery. Being aware of the fundamental processes of learning, in and out of the classroom, is an advantage. The statistics and methodology background of psychologists is an advantage as well. An amazing array of statistics flow across the desk of any administrator in higher education. Concepts like reliability and validity, indeed even measurement error, are very useful. Concepts of reliability and measurement error address the question of when is a statistic worthy of attention (Is the graduation rate going up or not? Is the small decrease in graduation rate this year a trend line or simply a blip on the screen?).

I have thought for decades that the most fundamental question in psychology was that of measurement, in particular the measurement of change. These concepts are at the core of any discussion relating to the proper array of required courses (the so-called canon), the attributes that one needs in the job market, or the things one needs to learn to be a long-term productive citizen. Trends in this national debate emphasize the need to communicate well, both orally and in writing, and to have analytic ability, particularly of the quantitative sort. One sees a lot of argument in the literature about which schools do the best and which have the right idea. The national press reports hot discussions of what is the best required writing program. One sees very little discussion of how writing ability or writing achievement would be measured, and the correct answer is that there aren't very good measures of writing achievement or writing ability. Even if one could measure it reliably (and in my opinion there are no first-rate tests), would the measurement be valid as well? That is to say, if it can be demonstrated that writing achievement has improved in college X, does that mean a graduate can now claim that his or her ability to communicate in the workplace has been enhanced? That becomes more a question of validity, but it's a very important question and one that is not being very well addressed in discussions affecting higher education.

Knowing about and understanding the concept of role is important. In mentoring others, I stress repeatedly that people's reaction to them and relationships with them are more focused on the role they occupy than on their identity as people. It is not unusual, for example, for a faculty member to make an appointment to see an administrator and upon arrival express extreme anger and hostility about some issue of which the administrator is completely unaware. The faculty member may have a just cause but was rebuffed at various organizational levels along the way. In fact, in these kinds of circumstances it is almost surely true or he or she wouldn't have come to your office. People see you as responsible, and indeed often are distressed by your claim that you know nothing about a particular issue, and they may go on to think that even if you don't know anything about it, you are still in a position to have allowed the injustice to occur (because you are in charge of the system). Over the years, I have seen a lot of administrators respond with anger to expressions of anger, to respond with a great sense of unfairness because someone has accused them of something of which they are unaware. That expression of anger will ultimately come at great cost to that administrator, and others' long-term impression will likely be that he or she has a short fuse and has little sympathy for the problems of others. Firmly understanding the concept of role and understanding that many people's reactions to you and relationships with you rest on the role they see you play, rather than on your personality attributes, can make you a lot more effective as an administrator. Having, for example, a clinical background in which recognition of acting-out behavior is not unusual also might help.

The social-psychological concepts (and database) regarding group conflict, attitude and opinion change, and resistance to change are very useful. Not many days go by without my being able to use the existing data on these three topics, although I seldom say anything out loud about them.

In this chapter I have tried to describe a bit of the variation among higher education institutions, and how the meaning and demands of commonly named positions among these institutions can vary substantially. I have also discussed how the university is not a single culture, and how life can become easier for the administrator who understands that. I have tried to offer some of the advice and counsel I give other budding administrators as a mentor and friend. This requires using concrete examples which I hope have been useful. Lastly, I have tried to indicate what there is in the intellectual and educational background of the mental health professional that is directly useful in carrying out administrative duties. I believe that there is a great deal there.

BIOGRAPHY

Charles A. Kiesler   Dr. Kiesler received his undergraduate degree from Michigan State and his Ph.D. from Stanford in Social Psychology. He has been a leading scholar and administrator all his career. He was a Program Director at Yale, a Department Chair at Kansas and Carnegie-Mellon, a Dean at the latter, Provost at Vanderbilt, and Chancellor of the University of Missouri, Columbia. He also was Executive Director of the American Psychological Association. He has received several awards for his research, including the American Psychological Association Award for "Distinguished Contributions to Research in Public Policy" (1989) and the American Evaluation Association's Gunnar Myrdal Award in "Recognition of contributions to the advancement of evaluation practice in health service delivery" (1989). He is a member of the Institute of Medicine of the National Academy of Sciences. He currently is the Thomas Weil Distinguished Professor of Health Services Management at the University of Missouri, Columbia.

8

DIRECTING A CLINICAL TRAINING PROGRAM: A TASK ANALYSIS

ADELE S. RABIN AND SHARON L. FOSTER

California School of Professional Psychology, San Diego, California 92121

> *Directors . . . provide leadership, guidance and direction, coordination, and inspiration—setting the climate in which the program operates. The training director is also expected to be an appropriate professional role model for other faculty and students.*
>
> *—APA Accreditation Handbook, 1986, p. 9*

INTRODUCTION

One important administrative role that clinical psychologists play in academic settings involves directing doctoral training programs in clinical psychology. Directors of clinical training (or DCTs) oversee the development, implementation, and evaluation of a systematic educational program designed to educate clinical psychologists. Usually these programs are housed either in a department of psychology or in a free-standing or university-based professional school setting, and offer either a doctor of philosophy or doctor of psychology degree.

Management and Administration Skills for the Mental Health Professional

To date, very little research examines either the role of the DCT or the skills required for successful execution of this role. Therefore, in this chapter we couple our own observations and experiences with the experiences of our colleagues and with survey data collected from DCTs by Cone (1997) and Wisocki, Grebstein, and Hunt (1994) to provide a detailed task analysis of the DCT position. We also speculate on qualities that we believe promote success with these tasks, and itemize particular challenges of the position. As empirical clinicians, however, we recognize that many of our observations warrant future empirical corroboration or disconfirmation.

DIRECTOR OF CLINICAL TRAINING: A JOB DESCRIPTION

First and foremost, the DCT is the leader of a training program. Directors of clinical training plan and oversee faculty recruitment and retention; graduate student recruitment, retention, advising, and tracking; accreditation site visits and reports; and program and curriculum development and evaluation. They are also responsible for materials that describe the program, such as catalog descriptions and recruitment materials. Often they are responsible for producing or revising a graduate student handbook, which describes the program, its policies, and procedures in detail. Some DCTs manage budgets related to the training program and secure clinical placements for students. Some must find and negotiate financial support (e.g., scholarships, awards, tuition waivers) for students. They also handle student problems and advise graduate students who are having difficulty in the program. Most DCTs have staff reporting to them who assist in the day-to-day administrative tasks of the program.

The authority and related number of responsibilities of the DCT vary as a function of the setting in which he or she serves, the number of students in the program, staff resources available to the DCT, and the department or school's traditions with regard to decision-making authority and process. In general, DCTs who administer programs housed in departments of psychology have less authority and administrative responsibility, fewer students, and fewer resources than the DCT in a free-standing professional school. Although DCTs in professional schools typically have larger faculty and student bodies to manage, they more often are able to delegate or assign responsibilities for large chunks of administration and record keeping to other staff (e.g., a clinical placement coordinator, financial aid officer).

In addition, a DCT is also a faculty member, and usually has at least some of the duties associated with that role. Therefore, DCTs may also teach classes, supervise research, sit on departmental and school-wide committees, provide national service, pursue their own scholarly interests, advise undergraduate and graduate students, and see clients. In this chapter, we focus primarily on administrative rather than faculty duties. As we discuss later, however, the dual administrator–faculty role underlies one of the most challenging aspects of the directorship: balancing the multiple demands of the position.

KNOWLEDGE REQUIREMENTS OF THE POSITION

Knowledge is a key element to effective program management and the successful program is certain to have an informed DCT. The effective DCT must have or develop a knowledge of issues and regulations pertaining to accreditation and licensing, and of financial and legal issues which may impact program management. He or she must have knowledge and skills in sound business practices, in addition to the ability to function as a solid professional role model.

Training Models

Understanding the traditional models of training in clinical psychology is important for seeing the "big picture" that should underlie the development, implementation, and evaluation of a coherent training program. The predominant models that underlie most training programs in clinical psychology currently are the Boulder or scientist–practitioner model (APA Committee on Training in Clinical Psychology, 1947) and the Vail 1973 practitioner model (c.f. Korman, 1974). Variants of these models also exist in specific graduate psychology programs. The National Council for Schools and Programs of Professional Psychology (NCSPP) has advanced a competency-based curriculum (c.f. Peterson et al., 1991) which can be used alone as a training model, but which is more commonly used in conjunction with either the Boulder or Vail training model. A version of the NCSPP competencies for professional psychology has been recently incorporated into American Psychological Association (APA) program accreditation criteria (APA, 1996).

Advocates of each of these models have proposed training philosophies, competencies, and experiences that should be incorporated into training models that follow each philosophy. The philosophy a given program adopts should be tied closely with program goals and should answer the following questions: For what careers does the program prepare the student, and in what settings? What are the relevant knowledge and skill requirements? The answers to these questions will have bearing on the training model selected and the program developed. Even if a program espouses a nontraditional training model, it is important for the DCT to be clear about the goals of the program and how these fit into the traditions that have guided training programs in the field.

Accreditation Guidelines

Most clinical training programs either have or desire accreditation by the American Psychological Association. Knowledge of current accreditation criteria and guidelines is mandatory for these programs. Even directors of clinical programs that do not seek APA accreditation should be cognizant of this information, as many states require that applicants for licensure have completed an APA-accredited program or its equivalent before the applicant may take the state licensure exams.

The APA (located in Washington, DC) maintains an Office of Program Consultation and Accreditation and publishes guidelines that indicate the criteria programs must meet or exceed for accreditation (APA, 1996). In addition to reading these guidelines, new DCTs can also review previous accreditation reports to see how the program has presented itself in the past, how its curriculum and training experiences fit with accreditation requirements, and how the program has traditionally presented its goals and evaluated its performance in relation to those goals. Volunteering to become a site visitor for a regional or national accrediting body, attending site visitor workshops, and talking with colleagues about their accreditation experiences are also good ways to become more familiar with the accreditation process.

Because regional accreditation is a prerequisite to APA accreditation, the DCT should be familiar with regional as well as professional accrediting bodies. Regional accrediting bodies such as the Western Association of Schools and Colleges accredit institutions as a whole. Most DCTs in university settings will have (and need) little knowledge of these bodies and their requirements; university administrative offices, such as Academic Affairs, typically oversee the activities involved in site visits for regional accreditation. Because regional accreditation typically involves assessing the university as a whole, rarely do accreditors concern themselves specifically with the clinical training program. In contrast, in smaller schools or in free-standing professional schools in which the clinical training program is a core part of the educational mission of the institution, DCTs may participate in regional accreditation site visits and document preparation. New DCTs in these settings should inquire about regional accreditation and become familiar with issues raised in previous accreditation visits that pertain to the clinical program.

Licensing Requirements

Because programs must prepare students for future careers, knowledge of the entry-level requirements for those careers is important both for program development and for advising students. At a minimum, DCTs should be familiar with the licensing requirements in the state in which the program is located; even better is to have information about other states' requirements that students can consult as needed. Although there is considerable similarity among states in their licensing requirements, there are also unique requirements and idiosyncracies in interpretation of students' academic preparedness. It is important to monitor and to document difficulties encountered by graduates as they prepare for licensure in states other than the state in which the program resides. Careful documentation can later save the DCT and the registrar considerable time and effort.

Clinical Internship Policies and Procedures

Because students in most programs apply for APA-accredited internships, it is also important to keep abreast of requirements for internship applications. Rules and regulations that govern the type of contact between internship agencies, student applicants, and DCTs are particularly important to investigate, for several reasons. First, breaching these guidelines constitutes at best unprofessional and at worst unethical behavior on the part of the transgressor. Second, the DCT is generally held responsible for the conduct of the graduate students in his or her program, and internship sites have been known to reject future applicants from a program based on unprofessional behavior from a previous applicant or DCT. Third, these guidelines can change from year to year as internships seek to improve the application and selection process. In addition to reviewing APA program accreditation domains for internship training, the Association of Psychology Postdoctoral and Internship Centers (APPIC) publishes a directory of training centers and rules and regulations for participation in them (e.g., APPIC, 1995)

Specialty Training Guidelines

While most clinical training programs are designed with the assumption that solid generalist skills are the appropriate entry-level goal, some clinical training programs also offer specializations. These specializations, or tracks, may in time develop into new programs that are independent of the clinical program from which they emerged. Partnerships between programs, institutions, and industries are a current training trend in education generally. In psychology, these alliances can result in specialty programs which broaden the roles psychologists can serve. Examples include partnerships between law and psychology and medicine and psychology giving rise to forensic psychology and health psychology programs, respectively. The marriage of cognitive psychology and information technology informed a new training model now called distributed (or distance) learning, and the productivity, downsizing, and reorganization demands of business and industry coupled well with psychology to give rise to a variety of organizational development programs and dual clinical–organizational psychology programs. Faculty sometimes integrate clinical child and developmental psychology into programs in developmental psychopathology; neurosciences and clinical psychology may meld into training in clinical neuropsychology. As these specialties form, they are often accompanied by conferences and resulting publications outlining recommended classes and training experiences for students. These written materials provide important information on professional consensus about what specialty programs should entail, and are particularly useful when a DCT is considering the development of a new program.

Societal Trends

The terrain of clinical training has changed considerably over the past two decades. The proliferation of professional school training models and programs coupled with significant societal changes have encouraged the expansion of training models and opportunities. Changes in the way healthcare is funded (e.g., managed care) have changed the ways in which clinical services are provided.

Programs, no matter how well established, should not be static. As the field develops and changes, the DCT must keep abreast of societal, marketplace, and higher education changes to which a graduate program should be responsive. For example, divorce rates have lifted the issues of custody evaluation and impact of divorce on child adjustment to the forefront of clinical service. Runaway healthcare costs have resulted in a managed care environment that directly affects psychological service delivery by limiting access and coverage, and by attempting to choreograph care. The resultant opportunities and responsibilities for clinical psychology are enormous. Changes in healthcare delivery put the burden squarely on the discipline to continue to develop empirically supported treatments that can be standardized and disseminated. Knowledge and skills related to disaster responsiveness and gang warfare may be demanded by today's social environment, as are competencies to serve a multicultural community. Advances in technology, communication, and travel have resulted in an international marketplace of many services, including higher education. In short, the landscapes of higher education as well as mental health service delivery are changing rapidly and the successful DCT is an informed DCT.

Societal trends in financial areas related to graduate training are also important to follow. Types and levels of funding available to students are useful to assess in the interest of obtaining departmental and school resources for recruiting and retaining talented students. National norms in faculty salaries are also useful to obtain; the APA routinely publishes salary information on psychology faculty, broken down by region, type of program, and rank. When the DCT is responsible for recruiting adjunct faculty and negotiating their contracts, he or she should develop an awareness of current salary ranges in the geographical area, as well as nonrevenue resources available to sweeten the offer or to reward faculty loyalties.

Ethics, Legal Issues, and Due Process Requirements

One of the most enjoyable aspects of the DCT position involves interacting with students to maximize their success and with faculty to help advance their careers. One of the least enjoyable aspects of the position involves dealing with student and faculty academic and professional difficulties. Students occasionally fail classes, thesis or dissertation defenses, or comprehensive examinations. Others show serious deficiencies in clinical performance, or engage in unethical or felonious behavior. In most of these cases, the faculty will wish to take some action. Common actions include developing a plan for the student to remediate the problem, placing the student on probationary or "warning" status in which further similar problems will lead to termination from the program, and/or terminating the student from the program. Faculty may also conduct themselves inappropriately, with the most common student complaints against faculty (in our experience) involving sexual harassment issues, unethical romantic involvements between faculty and students, and sexist or racist comments.

Handling these difficulties effectively requires knowledge of APA ethical guidelines (APA, 1992), school and departmental policies about appropriate student and faculty behavior, and appropriate legal guidelines or definitions related to equal opportunity, discrimination, sexual harassment, dual relationships, and so on. A DCT must also be extremely knowledgeable about due process requirements involved in different courses of action that can be taken in response to student and faculty problems. Many a good decision has been rendered unenforceable or has been overturned because the individual guiding the process failed to follow due process requirements. Equally important, the DCT should understand the type of documentation and evidence necessary to substantiate complaints and to record formally the process by which the complaint or problem was handled (e.g., was the alleged troublemaker informed of the problem and allowed to have his or her say?). The DCT should also know and inform faculty about legal guidelines and confidentiality issues regarding access to and the contents of student files.

The discipline's code of ethics also has specific components related to training. For example, it specifically requires professional psychologists in charge of training programs to ensure that the academic program is consistent with training objectives and that written materials provided to current and prospective students provide accurate representations of the program and its requirements for successful completion (APA, 1992; see also Fisher & Younggren, 1997). These requirements were added to the code to protect the consumer given the proliferation of different training models and degree programs.

SKILL REQUIREMENTS OF THE POSITION

As should be apparent by now, the DCT must have good leadership, organization, and management skills. The DCT must also demonstrate a number of additional competencies, many of which are characterized by active information seeking, hypothesis testing, assessment, and intervention. These skills are often associated with the scientific method, which, in turn, is typically associated with traditional, Boulder model clinical training programs. However, continual changes in the knowledge base, societal problems, and the service delivery environment demand a larger, more responsive repertoire from the professional psychologist whether he or she functions in an academic, clinical, or industrial setting.

More than 20 years ago, the preference for models of clinical training other than the single-hat, Boulder model was clearly established with the Vail Conference and subsequent survey research. The majority of DCTs of newer programs felt strongly that clinical training programs should be more professionally oriented than the traditional programs that existed at that time (Shemberg, Keeley, & Leventhal, 1976). This resulted in the establishment of a new complement of clinical training programs with, for example, multiple tracks, an emphasis on applied research, and a community psychology focus.

Several years ago, the NCSPP published a broader set of core professional competencies which have been proposed as curriculum guides. These six competencies are a useful framework for describing the skills needed to function successfully as a DCT. Competence in relationship building, assessment, intervention, research and evaluation, consultation and education, and management and supervision have been proposed as goals of a professional psychology curriculum (Peterson et al., 1991). These same clinical competencies can also be used to describe the duties and challenges of the role of DCT.

Relationship Building

This competency concerns the ability to develop and maintain constructive working relationships and is the foundation upon which all other competencies depend. When applied to the DCT, this means that the DCT should be able to form good working relationships with faculty, staff, and students. In fact, in a survey of clinical psychology graduate students and faculty, it was found that relating well to students was considered a very important characteristic of a successful DCT, as was a high level of integrity (Cone, 1997). The majority of relationships formed by a DCT demand sensitivity to issues of power and authority and should model their responsible use.

The DCT sets the climate of the program and ideally this is an environment in which people work together in an atmosphere of mutual respect. Relationship skills are as prerequisite for the working alliance as they are for the therapeutic alliance. Neither the clinician nor the DCT can perform successfully in their roles without a working knowledge about relationships and the skills necessary to establish and maintain them.

Relationships with Students

Relationships with students begin with the initial admissions interviews and welcoming orientation sessions. Because the DCT is the person to whom the clinical graduate students will turn and upon whom they will rely for academic guidance, students must accept and trust the DCT. Specifically, the DCT should relate well with students, be available to them, and advise them effectively. These characteristics of the successful DCT were among the top ten characteristics faculty and students rated as critical for the position (Cone, 1997).

Students should feel comfortable approaching the DCT with problems and concerns. This is particularly important to avoid crises that occur when small problems blossom into major headaches because they are not nipped in the bud. Approach is generally more likely if the DCT is available to students (i.e., is on campus regularly, returns calls in a timely fashion, schedules student appointments promptly). Good clinical skills such as listening, reflecting, and responding nondefensively also help the students to trust the DCT. Reasonable advice on how to handle systemic problems or faculty–student difficulties also goes a long way toward building student trust, as does prompt intervention to correct difficulties or mistakes that fall within the DCT's scope of responsibility.

We have found that a proactive stance is a productive one when it comes to problem prevention. A DCT who takes the initiative to discuss in student forums potential pitfalls that might be encountered in the program will find that problems occur less frequently, and when they do inevitably occur, they can be handled smoothly and expeditiously. For instance, town meetings dedicated to topics such as faculty–student relationships, academic honesty, mentoring expectancies, and so forth, model and inform direct communication, ethics, and professionalism.

The DCT should also build skills for judiciously confronting and challenging students who encounter clinical or academic problems, or who fail to take responsibility for their contribution to a problem. The DCTs are often the individuals who must tell fledgling clinicians that they will be asked to leave the program if they fail their comprehensive examinations again, that their clinical work is inadequate, or that the faculty recommends that they take a leave of absence to resolve personal difficulties before continuing with the program. In addition, the DCT often must prompt students to discuss the circumstances surrounding performance problems, eliciting sufficient information to assess the source of the difficulty, and must advise students on how to remediate their problems. Although many of these situations are difficult, it is important to handle them in a timely fashion, using direct communication sprinkled liberally with tact and empathy.

Just as in clinical work, a few behaviors can seriously interfere with relationships with students. Students often find it extraordinarily difficult to approach an authority figure with a problem, and as a result have heightened sensitivity to the DCT's response to their concerns. Automatically dismissing a student's concern, responding defensively, or failing to follow through on a promised course of action may communicate to the student that his or her risk was not worthwhile, and may be relayed in such a way as to discourage other students from approaching the DCT.

Relatedly, it is important for the DCT to remember that perceptions can easily drive reality. Good perception-management skills can be critical for the DCT's mental health and political survival. It is also important not to underestimate the power of student and faculty gossip. One student's experience with the DCT will likely be communicated to others, sometimes in a distorted fashion. Similarly, a student problem can become a juicy tidbit for a departmental rumor mill. Therefore, discretion is key in dealings with students. The DCT should inform faculty about student problems on a need-to-know basis and should avoid gossiping with students about other students. Favoritism should also be avoided in the name of fairness, equity, and due process.

A DCT should also avoid becoming triangulated in problems that concern the student and others. Students will often approach a DCT with an interpersonal or professional problem with a colleague, supervisor, or faculty member, and expect the DCT to "do something about it." The temptation, especially for the inexperienced administrator, is to step in and solve the problem. Often, however, a much better choice is to discuss the problem with the student and coach the student in how to handle the problem directly with the other person involved. If the student is too frightened to do this, even after coaching, a meeting between the student and the faculty member (or colleague or supervisor) in which the DCT acts as a facilitator may serve as an intermediate step. Such actions teach the student appropriate ways of handling the sorts of challenges they are likely to encounter in professional life. They also highlight the fact that the DCT serves not only as an administrator but also as a role model for both students and faculty, and therefore he or she should behave in ways that deserve emulation.

Finally, as diversity in the student body increases, DCTs should increase their sensitivity to the experiences and concerns of students from different backgrounds. The impact of belonging to certain minority cultures may be such that students refrain from seeking help from peers, faculty, and administrators alike. For example, a lone student of color in a largely white department may be reluctant to raise concerns about a faculty member's unwittingly offensive habit of asking the student for his or her opinion repeatedly as "the representative of your race." Proactive administrative practices can save these individuals from feelings of isolation, attenuate fears of failure, and may heighten the probability of academic success. For example, it is important to establish support groups and mentorship programs for students of color, international students, gay and lesbian students, and so on. It is also important that class schedules and special campus events be planned with respect for religious customs and practices. In our experience, a diverse student population adds vitality to a program and to campus life, and enriches students' academic and interpersonal experiences. The DCT has a responsibility to his or her faculty, staff, and student body to obtain and implement continuing education in the area of diversity to foster an environment characterized by inclusion and respect.

Relationships with Faculty

The personality and emphases of a program are usually a direct reflection of the faculty who maintain the program. For a program to function well, it should reflect the strengths and interests of the faculty and involve faculty with students in ways that are beneficial to both. The director should encourage a sense of program "ownership" among faculty both to encourage a positive esprit-de-corps among colleagues and to promote faculty involvement in and responsibility for the program.

A DCT's relationships with faculty are complicated by the fact that in many instances the DCT is both a peer and a supervisor of faculty colleagues. Thus, the DCT may work side by side with colleagues as an equal on dissertation, thesis, and faculty committees. The same DCT may have considerable power in assigning incoming graduate students to faculty labs and in determining the courses that faculty teach in the graduate program. In some programs, the DCT has a large role in evaluating faculty performance and determining faculty year-to-year merit raises. The maintenance of appropriate professional and interpersonal boundaries is critical in navigating the multiple relationships the DCT can experience in the professional setting.

Many of the skills required for success with students also serve the DCT well in relationships with faculty colleagues. Diplomacy, interpersonal sensitivity, and fairness are crucial to success with colleagues. Good communication is also important: faculty particularly appreciate early warnings about upcoming duties and potential problems.

Relationships with Other Administrators

The DCT must also form and sustain appropriate relationships with other administrators. These administrators may be other program directors, deans, program heads, provosts, chancellors, and presidents. Often, meetings with other administrators place another set of demands on the DCT: protecting program constituents within the broader context of institutional advancement. It is important, therefore, to be aware of one's program needs and resources, and to see how these fit within the general structure of the organization.

We have been in meetings in which other administrators used various methods to gain power, control, or validation and approval. More frequently, we have found that successful managers, from middle manager to chief executive officer, most often bring diplomacy, sensitivity, and a sense of fair play to the table. Good assertiveness skills are essential when dealing with the occasional resource-hungry or manipulative colleague. The importance of clear professional boundaries mentioned earlier is also important to recognize again, as administrators are likely to serve on committees together, provide evaluations of one another, and appear publicly together for institutional advancement activities.

Relationships with Support Staff

Given the multiple demands of the DCT position, it is important to streamline program management and to delegate responsibility for clearly identifiable aspects of the program. Many DCTs have an administrative assistant. Some DCTs also have administrative faculty or staff to whom they delegate management of practicum and internship experiences. DCTs must also interact successfully with personnel from departments of recruitment and admissions, registration and records, student affairs, financial aid, and so on. Solid interpersonal skills and an appreciation for the team efforts that are involved in the management of an institution will be well received.

In sum, the DCT is a highly visible individual within the program and that visibility may extend to relationships with the professional and lay communities. Because the DCT is the program's emissary, and because his or her behavior reflects directly on the program, there is constant pressure to behave only in ways that deserve emulation by colleagues and students.

Assessment and Intervention

Assessment is involved in every aspect of the role of a professional psychologist, and for the DCT assessment is an ongoing activity. So is problem solving. Effective DCTs know how to assess problems and design effective interventions. They have the skills to design, select, and implement a variety of assessment strategies.

Program assessment differs from typical assessments in clinical work in that issues are generally systemic, rather than individual. DCTs should suspect systemic problems when the same complaints or problems arise repeatedly across students or over time. Several types of systemic problems are relatively common: policy problems, procedural problems, record-keeping problems, personnel problems, and communication problems.

Policy problems occur most commonly when a program lacks a policy for dealing with issues that arise regularly. For example, faculty may complain regularly to the DCT that they are overloaded with student responsibilities, while others shirk their duties because no formal policy exists for ensuring even division of faculty supervision duties. Students may complain about unfair treatment in assigning placements or financial aid because the process is haphazard. Formal, written policies are particularly important for dealing with matters of academic integrity and ethics; student admission, probation and dismissal; complaints and grievances; and allocation of resource issues.

Procedural problems can occur for several reasons. One instance arises when policies are in place but procedures are not specified clearly or are outmoded. For example, faculty bylaws may give responsibility for a decision to a faculty committee that has not been convened in years. Students may be told that they have the right to appeal a decision, but not how to go about it or to whom to appeal. In these cases, the clear solution is to develop procedures consistent with the policy, write and circulate those procedures, and follow through to see that the procedures are implemented correctly and consistently. Depending on the program and department, development of procedures may be the responsibility of a standing committee, an ad hoc committee, the DCT, or the chair of the department or professional school equivalent (e.g., dean, provost, chancellor).

A second type of procedural problem arises when procedures are clearly specified but not followed consistently. This can occur when faculty write procedures that fail to specify who is in charge of their implementation. For example, a grievance procedure may specify that students should approach a "faculty representative," but no faculty member has been appointed to serve that role because the procedure fails to specify how the appointment should be made. Writing procedures in active rather than passive tense forces faculty to avoid such ambiguities: an admissions policy that states "the admissions secretary will review files for incomplete information" clearly specifies who will do the review task, whereas the statement "files will be reviewed for missing information" does not. Specifying who is in charge of what, when people should convene to make group decisions, and the processes by which policies translate into action can all make procedures run much more smoothly.

A final procedural problem occurs when a procedure is clearly specified and in place, but the person responsible fails to follow through or does so inconsistently. For example, procedures may specify that an advisor meet yearly with students, but the faculty member fails to do so. Guidelines may indicate that students turn in their dissertation proposals by the end of their fourth year, but some students fail to comply. In some cases, a friendly reminder may be all that is needed. In the case of consistent failure to follow a procedure, a serious talk with the offender may be in order. When this fails to work, or if the problem is more widespread, more in-depth assessment may be needed to determine whether the procedures are unworkable or whether systematic consequences may be needed to bring the offender(s) into line. For example, some programs routinely place students on probation for failing to meet deadlines for completing program milestones such as comprehensive examinations and thesis defense.

A particular challenge is presented in the case of faculty noncompliance with policy and procedures, particularly when it is chronic or when the rights of others are jeopardized. There are few tangible rewards that can be manipulated contingent on faculty performance in the academic setting, particularly in a setting in which the faculty member has tenure. Clearly, increasing the nature and intensity of verbal feedback may be one way to shape the desired behavior via social approval or disapproval. Should this mechanism fail, the consequences for the noncompliant faculty member become quite serious, as the only major consequences that remain concern salary increases based on merit and promotion, which may not be under the control of the DCT. In the rare event of chronic noncompliance by a faculty member, we have found that clear written feedback that specifies the consequences for further noncompliance (e.g., absence of merit-based salary increase) typically results in the desired behavior change.

Noncompliance with clear policy and procedure can be a major resource drain for the program and the department or school. For example, the student who does not complete the dissertation in a reasonable period of time drains faculty resources and prevents access to the mentor by other students in need of that faculty member's expertise. The faculty member who is chronically late in turning in grades or student evaluations creates a burden for staff who record the grades, update the transcripts, and follow procedures for identifying students who are experiencing academic or clinical performance difficulties. Thus, one faculty's noncompliance with procedure results in a considerable waste of valuable time and energy which otherwise would have been directed at program maintenance and improvement efforts.

Record-keeping problems are closely linked to both policy and procedural matters. It is important to keep records of student admissions, student progress and performance in the program, student evaluations, and student clinical experiences.

Licensing boards from states around the United States may contact the program for documentation to indicate that a student's experiences do (or do not) meet their specific requirements. A program with erratic or incomplete records will be hard-pressed to provide this documentation. It is particularly important for programs that lack APA accreditation to provide complete documentation about students' experiences, as students may be called on to prove in detail that they received the equivalent of an APA-accredited degree. The same is true when students participate in non APA-accredited internships. Some licensing boards have even been known to request syllabi and reading lists from past courses. Keeping files up to date and documenting faculty actions are also crucial when students are having difficulty with the program, so that faculty can review exactly what they told problem students about their performance, the remedial action required, when the students' status would be reevaluated, and the consequence if the problem continued.

It is important not only to have record-keeping policies and procedures, but also to ensure that those responsible for the materials to be placed in the records do so in a timely fashion. This is not always easy, because in one semester students may receive grades from faculty members, evaluations of comprehensive examinations or other requirements, and clinical evaluations from on-site and faculty supervisors. Students also generally receive from faculty yearly written evaluations of their overall performance. Placing a staff member in charge of distributing, collecting, prompting forgetful faculty, and monitoring files for completion greatly assists in systematizing this process—as does development of a schedule by which the staff member routinely implements these procedures.

A DCT also occasionally must deal with personnel problems. A secretary may routinely respond rudely to students. A faculty member may fail to return student phone calls and may not appear for scheduled appointments. The DCT will make, or cause to be made, a careful assessment of the situation and intervene as necessary, taking care to document what was found; what is required of the individual; when, how, and by whom reevaluation will occur; and the consequences should the problem continue. In many cases, bringing attention to the problem is sufficient for its correction. Due process, administrative support, and a paper trail of clear feedback are necessary should the need for probation or termination arise.

A final systemic problem occurs because of communications problems. One of the most common of these is the failure to inform students or faculty of matters likely to affect them. A DCT may solve a teaching problem by assigning Dr. Jones to teach a different course for the next year, but fail to discuss the issue with Dr. Jones. A practicum site may ask for a student to be moved from one service to another and the DCT approves the move without discussing the matter with the student. A DCT plans an upcoming party for an important colloquium speaker without informing faculty of her visit until a few days before the visit, then is angry and hurt when only two colleagues and three students come to the colloquium and social event.

Decision making and planning without consulting or informing those involved can have several negative consequences. Assertive faculty and students will come immediately to the DCT's office to complain or to refuse the assignment. Those who respond more passively may be silently resentful. Insufficient advance notice may also result in faculty or student absence from voluntary events, either because they already have other commitments or as resistance in response to constraints on their autonomy. Faculty and students like to have some say in matters that will affect them directly. At a minimum, they need to be informed of decisions that may affect them. Involving and talking with faculty and students, although time consuming, promotes the view that the DCT cares about the individuals involved in the program and will take their opinions into consideration in making decisions.

Giving advance notice is also important when a program changes its requirements, policies, or procedures—the further in advance the better. Because faculty and students rarely read or attend to everything they hear or find in their mailboxes, we generally try to inform students and faculty of important decisions in at least three ways: in person and orally (e.g., in meetings), via posted announcements (e.g., on bulletin boards or on doors), and via memos in their departmental mailboxes.

The DCT, along with the program faculty and other administrators, must assess from time to time the extent to which the program faculty are able to deliver up to-date knowledge and skills. Are faculty members teaching in their areas of major strength? What additional resources might the program require (e.g., additional faculty expertise in the form of new faculty or professional development)? The DCT is responsible for identifying current and future needs of the program and its constituents and for attempting to gather the identified resources, whether these involve special courses for the faculty, faculty recruitment, library additions, or major equipment purchases. In order for new program goals to be realized, the appropriate resources must be firmly in place. Thus the DCT must monitor the extent to which the needed resources are available, and if they are not, the DCT must either develop a specific plan to acquire them, or modify or abandon the goal.

Research and Evaluation

Programs are not static, or at least they should not be. Rather, they should be sufficiently flexible to respond to societal changes, accreditation directives, and consumer preferences. Thus, program development, implementation, and evaluation are skills required of any DCT.

Although several models of clinical training exist, there are currently no direct outcome data that identify which model is most successful in preparing professional psychologists to function successfully in a changing mental healthcare environment. The DCT must be able to assess the effects of program alternatives and to adopt the alternative that produces the best outcomes. For example, different models of research training may produce different outcomes depending on the faculty and institutional resources available. Similarly, different instructors or different methods of teaching a particular subject matter may result in differentially prepared students. The DCT is responsible for assessing the various components of the training program and for shifting strategies when outcomes are unsuccessful. Making data-based and not personality-driven decisions maximizes program improvements and minimizes the risks of misattribution or misinterpretation.

The need for ongoing assessment of program objectives is clearly important for maximizing the quality of education and training students receive and the environment in which they receive it. The DCT and accrediting bodies need to know whether program outcomes are consistent with the program model and mission; whether students are tracking through the program in a timely manner; how the performances of core and adjunct faculty are evaluated and what use is made of the information; and the extent to which the program is sufficiently sensitive and responsive to diversity-related issues, trends in education, resource allocation demands, and so forth. Program evaluation and quality improvement practices should be ongoing and the DCT is responsible for developing and implementing relevant databases and schedules for updating them.

Accrediting bodies require the program to submit a detailed self-study at various intervals. The self-study is highly labor intensive. No matter how well planned, preparing for and going through an accreditation visit is disruptive to students, staff, and faculty and drains valuable resources. Well-documented and continuous program evaluation efforts lessen the burden of preparing a self-study by allowing the authors to summarize and convey existing data. Ongoing program evaluation and improvement activities demonstrate the program's ability to govern itself and to strive to meet or exceed discipline standards.

Consultation and Education

Just as the clinician is sought as an expert in the resolution of "problems of living," so the DCT is likewise sought when problems of living develop within the context of the institution. The DCT provides leadership in the form of consultation, education, and effective role modeling.

Consultation always involves the transmission of information to others. The DCT consults and collaborates with colleagues, students, other administrators, agencies, and industries to effect change, although the DCT is not typically the ultimate agent of change. Sometimes this consultation is informal, as when a colleague who is new to the DCT role consults an established DCT at another institution for information or guidance. Sometimes it is more formal, as when a DCT serves as an APA site visitor to another institution (and, technically speaking, serves as a consultant to the APA with regard to the program's compliance with accreditation guidelines). Thus, incumbent on the DCT is the responsibility to stay abreast of models and new methods of consultation and aids to education. The DCT must be able to advise effectively whether the consultees are individuals, groups, programs, or institutions.

The DCT position often affords opportunities to serve on professional committees, community boards, and so on, to advance the discipline, educate the public, and bring recognition to the program and its host institution. Although the time demands of the DCT position can be considerable, the judicious choice of extracurricular professional and community activities can result in several potential benefits. By virtue of interpersonal connections, the DCT may be able to recruit potential students or faculty, identify new opportunities for increasing revenues, learn new styles of leadership, learn new solutions to old problems, and so on. The DCT is often sought by local agencies, media representatives, and professional groups to consult on a wide range of issues and may be of enormous benefit to end consumers.

Consultation and education go hand in hand, as one goal of consultation is to impart specific competencies to the consultees. Consultation is primarily a problem-solving endeavor, and as such it is important that the DCT have excellent skills in this area. Problems that are too vaguely defined or inaccurately conceptualized rarely lead to effective solutions. Problem conceptualization demands that a DCT obtain historical and contextual information about factors that may be relevant to problem maintenance. Skills that elicit and facilitate brainstorming are needed as are negotiation, decision-making, and conflict resolution skills in order to assist consultees in evaluating alternative solutions. In sum, in addition to solid social skills, the successful DCT will also possess knowledge and skill in consultation, behavior analysis, systems analysis, and effective teaching practices.

In addition to the roles DCTs may play as consultants, DCTs also use consultation. For example, in order to retain strict confidentiality, a DCT at one institution might consult a DCT at another institution about a student or faculty problem. A consultant might be employed to help faculty learn to infuse the curriculum with diversity-related materials. Consultation might also be needed when designing new tracks, special programs, or workshops, or when preparing for accreditation evaluation.

Management and Supervision

Management activities for the DCT include directing, organizing, and controlling educational services and those who deliver them. Although most clinical training programs do not offer formal coursework in management principles, management issues consume a significant proportion of most professional psychologists' time (Rickard & Clements, 1981).

Management and supervision skills are often learned on the job. Given the complexity of the DCT position, most DCTs endorse mentoring their successor into the position. However, most DCTs also report that they had no mentor for the DCT position (Wisocki et al., 1994). Whether the new DCT plans to continue in academic administration or is just holding the fort until a successor can be named, we recommend that she or he consider taking a general course in management principles—particularly if no local mentor in the department is available. Business schools and departments are excellent resources and faculty are usually exempt from paying tuition in their own institutions. DCTs with career goals involving longer-term academic management may also take advantage of specialized programs and summer institutes in higher education management. In the absence of formal classroom training, a trusted colleague with good management skills and common sense can provide a valuable sounding board for discussing ways in which to handle difficult program issues. Usually this person should hold a senior academic rank and/or hold (or have held) a similar position in order to avoid any impressions of favoritism and unfair faculty privilege.

Supervision can be viewed as a subset of management skills that usually involve a more individualized focus and a directive approach. Part of a successful supervisor–supervisee relationship concerns mutual understanding the demands of the role. New supervisees often need to be taught how to use supervision. For instance, the supervisor may encourage active participation, an open and inquisitive attitude, solid preparation, and a nondefensive orientation. When issues of culture, personality, or differing values arise within the context of the supervision relationship, these must be attended to in an objective and collegial fashion. In addition, a clear sense of purpose and action, conveyed with solid communication skills, good teaching abilities, and a collegial attitude will serve the novice supervisor well. Like management skills, many training programs do not systematically build knowledge and skill in the area of supervision. Books and articles about supervisory practices, both within and outside professional psychology, may help the novice supervisor.

One important part of management is conveying positive feedback for jobs well done. The reward schedule in academia tends to be a thin one. Faculty need to be appreciated and acknowledged for their accomplishments. Teaching excellence, scholarly productivity, efforts to shape the successes of their graduate students, community service, and national visibility all warrant compliments—especially public ones. Similarly, graduate students should be congratulated on achieving program milestones and staff members thanked for consistent and competent efforts. Tangible rewards are always welcome, but approval and recognition can also motivate colleagues and students by letting them know that the DCT and others notice and appreciate their efforts.

Faculty management frequently requires team-building skills. Even one program faculty member who is uninvolved in decision making, obstreperous to progress, or detached from faculty socialization can adversely impact the remaining faculty and the student body. Early and consistent team-building efforts pay off handsomely when program faculty must work together in difficult or demanding endeavors such as cost cutting without sacrificing educational quality, admitting the next incoming class, developing plans for students experiencing academic difficulty, or designing new educational opportunities for students.

Faculty members usually formulate program decisions within the context of a program meeting. Increasing the probability of reaching consensus quickly can streamline these meetings and encourage teamwork. Individual discussions between the DCT and faculty members before meetings provide one way to access different perspectives and also allow each member to have an equal voice. Just as science is advanced by persuasion, so too is faculty consensus advanced by individual, persuasive meetings. Group e-mail now makes it possible to have interfaculty discussions of program issues before meeting formally to discuss them.

Faculty meetings serve several important functions, not the least of which are program management and faculty cohesion. We recommend that meetings be called regularly but that they only be called when there is significant business to conduct. No one likes wasted time, and meetings tend to fill whatever time is allocated for them, independent of the agenda. We further recommend that the DCT enter each meeting with specific goals and outcomes for the meeting in mind and leave each meeting with specific action plans. It is also helpful to circulate written proposals in advance of the meeting in which they are to be discussed.

The DCT should give some thought to which program issues should be considered by the clinical faculty as a group and which issues should be handled individually by the DCT. This will depend in part on faculty preferences for involvement in decision making versus freedom from meetings. We say this because democratic decision making takes time. Clearly, one should involve the faculty in major program and policy-making activities and avoid burdening faculty with small implementation decisions. At an intermediate level are decisions regarding exceptions from academic policy, development of procedures for implementing policy, and handling student-related concerns. In less democratically oriented programs, the DCT will handle most of these alone. With highly democratic programs, these issues may be discussed and resolved in program faculty meetings. In general, we prefer to take issues with policy implications (i.e., development, modification, rules for exceptions) to the faculty almost always, to take procedural issues to the program faculty when they are complex or involve faculty members' time and effort but not when they are straightforward, and to handle individual student concerns outside of faculty meetings, unless these concerns involve academic dismissal or ethical misconduct.

Keep in mind that academics place a high premium on their individual autonomy. Relationship building and maintenance, along with the DCT's consistency (Staw & Ross, 1980), help the DCT to move programs and program faculty in new directions. This is no small challenge, as moving faculty in a new direction is, as someone once said, akin to herding cats.

MORE THAN THE SUM OF THE PARTS: PUTTING THE JOB TOGETHER

Most readers of this chapter are probably either prospective or new DCTs. In light of previous data (Wisocki et al., 1994), we expect that this chapter may provide the closest thing to mentorship into the position that the reader may experience.

Thus, we conclude the chapter with information, observations, and experiences that put the tasks described earlier in context.

Characteristics of the Average DCT

We could find only one study that assessed demographics of incumbents and descriptive statistics about the DCT position. Wisocki et al. (1994) surveyed DCTs of APA-accredited, university-based programs who were members of the Council of University Directors of Clinical Psychology (CUDCP). We do not know the extent to which the information obtained by Wisocki et al. are generalizable to DCTs of APA-accredited programs housed in professional schools, to DCTs of nonaccredited programs, or whether the findings are equally applicable to directors of both Ph.D. and Psy.D. granting programs. We also cannot know from the current data the extent to which the findings generalize to women or to other minority groups who occupy the DCT position, because only 19% of the sample was female and only 3% were ethnic minorities. Thus, the findings are somewhat limited in generalizability, and additional studies are necessary before a fully informed profile of the DCT incumbent and position can be offered.

According to the Wisocki et al. data, the average DCT is best described as a 45-year-old (range = 32–69 years), Caucasian (97% of sample) male (81% of sample) full professor (71% of sample), who received his training in a clinical psychology program (89%) with a cognitive–behavioral or social learning theoretical orientation (40%). The average size of the clinical training program represented by the DCTs was 55 graduate students and 10 clinical faculty housed in a department of an average of 26 faculty and 550 undergraduate students. The major reasons DCTs gave for accepting the position were, "to make a positive change in the program" (86%), and because they "were the best qualified" candidate for the position (70%).

The time the institution allocated to DCT responsibilities varied in the sample. Seventy-eight percent of respondents held year-round contracts, with 41% indicating calendar year contracts for 10 to 12 months, and 37% having academic year (9-month) contracts plus summer compensation of an average of 15% of their academic year salary. Salaries ranged from $30,000 to $89,900. This salary range is likely restricted given that a large proportion of DCTs (55%) did not include information on summer salary supplements when responding to this question despite the fact that 78% of respondents claimed year-long compensation. The major systemic resources reported by the DCTs were a reduced teaching load (95%) and secretarial assistance (82%). Only 22% of DCTs had a program budget and this was very small (mode = $15,000) and not perceived as particularly under their control.

Given a typical workload of 32 to 40 hours per week, the DCT position in a university department of psychology was a half-time to full-time position for 80% of respondents, with 21% involved in administration for 16 to 20 hours a week, and 59% reporting 21 hours per week or more devoted to program administration

(Wisocki et al., 1994). In comparison, we have observed that DCTs of professional school programs may have full-time administrative responsibilities, higher compensation, larger student and faculty bodies, often have very large budgets ranging from several hundred thousand to several million dollars, and exert modest to considerable control over their budgets.

Pros and Cons of the Job

Wisocki et al. asked DCTs to describe their job satisfaction and to identify the major positive and negative aspects of the position. The vast majority of respondents stated that they were glad they had accepted the DCT position (94%) and most stated that they would accept another term of office (74%). The positive aspects of the position were most frequently identified as working with the students, the opportunity to contribute to program development, and the opportunity to influence the program and the profession. Negative aspects of the position identified most frequently were the amount of paperwork and trivial tasks associated with the position, lack of support from faculty, and that the position demanded too great an investment of time for the product.

The impact of the position on respondents' careers was both positive and negative. Seventy-five percent of respondents indicated that the position resulted in less time for personal work and research, with 67% indicating that the position had an adverse impact on their research productivity. Career benefits of the position were that it expanded one's horizons, resulted in increased respect and recognition, increased one's administrative experience, increased involvement in the program, increased one's sense of accomplishment, increased awareness of professional issues, and resulted in increased power and influence. DCTs also reported that the position resulted in increased levels of stress and increased conflicts with faculty.

In addition to influencing aspects of one's professional role, the position of DCT also affects one's personal life. The position was described by DCTs as resulting in less personal time, higher levels of stress and burn-out, adverse effects on personal relationships and health, increased cynicism, and increased distance from students. On a more positive note, DCTs endorsed greater job satisfaction, greater sense of accomplishment, and greater personal awareness. Thus the position of DCT can be very rewarding professionally but perhaps at a cost to personal relationships and physical health.

Personal Qualities Necessary for the DCT

Wisocki et al. asked DCTs to indicate the personal qualities they believed were important for the position. The ability to be a well-organized administrator and to be people oriented, empathic, and a good listener were endorsed by 45% and 36% of respondents, respectively. More specific information about important characteristics of the DCT was found by Cone (1997), who administered a survey to 124 fac-

TABLE I   Top Ten Behavioral Characteristics of a DCT as Selected by Faculty and Students[a]

Characteristic	Mean	(SD)
Shows problem-solving skill and diplomacy	5.61	(0.66)
Is committed to the maintenance of APA standards and other generally accepted professional criteria	5.56	(0.72)
Relates well to students	5.54	(0.73)
Advises students effectively	5.46	(0.77)
Knows how to develop programs	5.44	(0.75)
Makes self available to other faculty and students	5.43	(0.81)
Is accepted and trusted by clinical students	5.38	(0.93)
Shows concern for student issues	5.33	(0.81)
Knows how to evaluate programs	5.38	(0.91)
Shows a high level of collegial integrity	5.11	(1.15)

[a]From Cone, 1997. Used with the permission of John D. Cone.

ulty and students of clinical psychology doctoral programs. Respondents were asked to rate 42 DCT characteristics on a seven-point, likert-type scale, in which zero was "not important at all" and six was "extremely important." The top ten characteristics endorsed by respondents as the most important are listed in Table 1. Table 1 shows that problem-solving skills, people skills, program development skills, and program evaluation skills were endorsed by students and faculty as most important for DCTs.

Professional Support

Just as difficulties in practice are most likely to plague the isolated practitioner, so is the isolated DCT at risk for uninformed decision making, litigation, and early burn-out. Opportunities to interact with other administrators are usually available in one's department or school, and other opportunities can easily be made. Professional school-based programs may send administrative and faculty representatives to NCSPP meetings. The organization convenes twice annually, once in January and again in August (just prior to, and in the same location as, the APA convention) to address issues relevant to the education of professional psychology. A support system of helpful colleagues is easy to obtain at the NCSPP and APA meetings, and these relationships extend throughout the year, facilitated by e-mail access. Clinical training programs that are housed within universities send representatives to the Council of University Directors of Clinical Psychology (CUDCP). Attendance and participation at these and other professional association meetings can result in the acquisition of valuable information, networking, and support resources.

This chapter would not be complete without mention of the importance of time-management skills for anyone in or contemplating the DCT position. Many DCTs are recruited into the position because they are productive teachers and scholars, and they may want to retain these roles while serving as an administrator. Yet the needs of students, faculty, staff, and program evaluation can result in many occasions when it seems that 60-hour weeks are insufficient to fulfill the demands of the position. Although availability is important, having an "open door policy" does not mean the door literally has to be open whenever the DCT is in. It is helpful to have an assistant protect the DCT's concentrated work efforts as needed. Setting aside time for teaching, research, clinical work, and writing—and sticking to the schedule—is another way to protect time for important activities that can easily be displaced by the day-to-day demands of administration. Thus, the DCT can teach colleagues and students that, "Tuesday morning is my writing morning," or that, "Friday is my research day," and then stick to the schedule. This will only work, however, if the DCT either works some of the time off-campus or intersperses research and clinical time with times that she or he is readily available—otherwise, so-called "emergencies" will regularly consume this valuable time. Because the position is inherently stressful, stress management skills used liberally are also excellent protection against fatigue and burn-out.

It is easy to take the DCT position then try to add administrative duties on top of an already full professional schedule. Adding new duties simultaneously adds extra hours to the 24-hour day, however. It is useful before assuming the position to take a hard look at the time the position will consume, and to see what activities must be stopped, put off, or modified to make time for the demands of the position. Otherwise, time for family, exercise, friendships, and hobbies may gradually diminish as the DCT tries to run the program, teach, direct research, write grants, edit journals, and conduct a clinical practice. As with most things in life, there is a balance to strike between professional and personal goals. This is probably one of the most challenging aspects of the position.

In summary, being a successful DCT poses multiple challenges and requires a wide repertoire of skills. It provides opportunities to develop new skills, to exercise leadership, and to contribute to the development of one's colleagues, students, and the profession. The DCT position may serve as a stepping stone to higher education management for some. For others, the ultimate goal of taking the position is to return to the faculty as soon as possible. Whatever the goal, the DCT leaves the position with the knowledge that his or her contributions to colleagues, students, and the institution have been substantial.

In closing, one caution: we have provided a good deal of descriptive information and many suggestions in this chapter. The wise reader will consider these cautiously. Because of the dearth of data on this position, our observations are largely unsystematic, and anecdotal rather than based on data. Although we believe many of the duties of the DCT are reasonably consistent across institutions, this awaits empirical scrutiny—as does the effectiveness of many of the suggestions we offered liberally throughout this chapter.

REFERENCES

American Psychological Association (APA). (1992). Ethical principles of psychologists and code of conduct. *American Psychologist, 47,* 1597–1611.

American Psychological Association (APA). (1995, February). *Guidelines and principles for accreditation of programs in professional psychology.* Washington, DC: Author.

American Psychological Association (APA). (1996). *Guidelines and principles for accreditation of programs in professional psychology.* Washington, DC: Office of Program Consultation and Accreditation.

American Psychological Association Committee on Accreditation and Accreditation Office. (1986). *Accreditation handbook.* Washington, DC: Author.

American Psychological Association Committee on Training in Clinical Psychology. (1947). Recommended graduate training program in clinical psychology. *American Psychologist, 2,* 539–558.

Association of Psychology Postdoctoral and Internship Centers (APPIC). (1995). *APPIC directory* (24th ed.). Washington, DC: Author.

Cone, J. D. (1997). *Selecting directors of clinical training using idiographic assessment procedures.* Unpublished manuscript, United States International University, San Diego, CA.

Fisher, C. B., & Younggren, J. N. (1997). The value and utility of the 1992 Ethics Code. *Professional Psychology: Research and Practice, 28,* 582–592.

Korman, M. (1974). National conference on levels and patterns of professional training in psychology. *American Psychologist, 29,* 441–449.

Peterson, R. L., McHolland, J. D., Bent, R. J., Davis-Russell, E., Edwall, G. E., Polite, K., Singer, D. L., & Stricker, G. (Eds.). (1991). *The core curriculum in professional psychology.* Washington, DC: American Psychological Association and National Council of Schools of Professional Psychology.

Rickard, H. C., & Clements, C. B. (1981). Administrative training for psychologists in APA-approved clinical programs. *Professional Psychology, 12,* 349–355.

Shemberg, K. M., Keeley, S. M., & Leventhal, D. B. (1976). University practices and attitudes of clinical directors. *Professional Psychology, 7,* 14–20.

Staw, B. M., & Ross, J. (1980). Commitment in an experimenting society: A study of the attribution of leadership from administrative scenarios. *Journal of Applied Psychology 65,* 249–260.

Wisocki, P. A., Grebstein, L. C., & Hunt, J. B. (1994). Directors of clinical training: An insider's perspective. *Professional Psychology: Research and Practice, 25,* 482–488.

BIOGRAPHIES

Sharon L. Foster   Dr. Sharon L. Foster is a professor at the California School of Professional Psychology in San Diego. Her scholarly work deals primarily with children and families, although she has also authored several book chapters and articles related to research methodology. Among her many professional activities, Dr. Foster coordinated the Ph.D. Clinical Child Psychology Training Program at West Virginia University, and directed the Ph.D. Clinical Training program at CSPP-SD.

Adele S. Rabin   Dr. Adele S. Rabin is an associate professor and the Director of the PhD program in Clinical Psychology at the California School of Professional Psychology in San Diego. In addition to academic administration, teaching, and research, her professional activities include program development, implementation, and evaluation in business, industrial, and academic settings.

9

ACADEMIC ENTREPRENEURSHIP

LINDA J. HAYES, RAMONA HOUMANFAR, MONICA M. GARLOCK, PATRICK M. GHEZZI, W. LAWRENCE WILLIAMS, AND JAMES E. CARR

Department of Psychology, University of Nevada, Reno, Nevada, 89557

INTRODUCTION

Higher education is facing a number of serious challenges. The days of expanding budgets are long since over and with them has gone the leisurely pace of life once so typical of the ivory tower. Coupled with these changes are threats to institutional autonomy. Government agencies are imposing more restrictive rules and regulations and the courts are enforcing them. Accountability of a much higher order than ever before is being demanded. Additional resources have not accompanied these demands, however, and few universities see themselves in a position to allocate their already limited resources to meet them in a satisfactory manner. Instead, many have responded to the challenge to "do more with less" by adopting an entrepreneurial stance. This stance is communicated in a number of ways, among which include establishing partnerships with business and industry, assisting in technology transfer, encouraging faculty to seek external support for research, and fostering fee-for-service contracts.

Despite its apparent necessity, academic entrepreneurship has not been met with full support from all of the university's constituencies. Academic faculty, in particular, resist this move and argue against it on a number of grounds. A common argument of faculty in the humanities, for example, is that opportunities for revenue generation are not available to them. Others argue that these sorts of activities are not included in their role statements, nor are they properly weighed in promotion, tenure, and merit reviews. Still others argue against such strategies on the grounds that they lack the skills to undertake them or they are philosophically opposed to them.

The changes taking place in the university merely reflect the rather massive changes already underway in society at large. Hence it seems highly unlikely that any of these arguments will be effective in thwarting this same transition in higher education. Neither are they likely to thwart the entrepreneurial pursuits of academic administrators. On the contrary, those departments and individual faculty who make good faith efforts at income generation are highly likely to gain administrative favor, along with the support and resources that come from favored status.

In this chapter, we describe our adventures in academic entrepreneurship. In 1990, the University of Nevada-Reno accepted our proposal to establish a doctoral program and a professional master's program in behavior analysis at virtually no cost to the university. This is our tale of how that was done and where we are today. Our purpose in telling this tale is to foster similar efforts elsewhere.

PROGRAM INITIATION

The details of how our plan to self-capitalize a graduate training program came about and some of our outcomes by the end of the fourth year of operation have been published elsewhere (Hayes et al., 1995) and we will not reiterate them here. The core idea of self-capitalization and its most critical elements are worthy of some further clarification, however.

Self-Capitalization

Three things are necessary to self-capitalize a graduate training program. First, you need to find or cultivate a receptive and reasonably flexible institution in which to house the program. Second, you must be able to provide a needed service for a fee. And, third, you must have a means of leveraging the fees received. The first of these three elements has been described in Hayes et al. (1995) in some detail; hence we will focus on the second and third elements here.

Providing a Needed Service for a Fee

If the resources to establish a new program are not coming from the university, they have to come from somewhere else. In this model, they come from the community on a fee-for-service basis. Consequently, you must be able to provide a needed service for a fee. Although the present model might be adapted for implementation in virtually any academic discipline, some disciplines are inherently better suited to the model than others. Specifically, those disciplines with powerful applied branches are most suitable.

The mention of "service" in this specification is not incidental. Product-oriented applied disciplines are not as well suited to the model because of the capital outlay typically required for the production of the product. Likewise, the mention of "need" is not insignificant. It is not sufficient merely to be able to provide a service, if no one needs that service. Neither is it sufficient merely to provide a needed service. There must be a buyer. Someone must be willing and able to pay for it. Behavior analysis is particularly well suited to this model. We have been able to sell a variety of needed services to the community.

Leveraging the Fees Received

It is one thing to operate a human service agency. It is quite another to operate a human service agency for the purpose of funding a graduate training program. To do the latter, it is necessary to have a means of leveraging the fees received. In our model, this leverage comes from the salary savings generated when graduate and undergraduate students deliver our services in exchange for academic credit. The involvement of students in this manner is essential to the workability of the model.

How It Works

In essence, we offer undergraduate field-experience classes in which students received hands-on training in service delivery with clinically relevant populations. These trainees make up our front line-service staff, generating the bulk of our billable hours. The undergraduate trainees are supervised by graduate students who are participating in this capacity in exchange for graduate credits in clinical and organizational psychology. These trainees make up our managerial staff. Faculty members in the program, whose salaries are paid not by the university, but rather by the fees generated by the services provided by students, supervise the graduate students. These fees, when properly leveraged, are also sufficient to fund graduate stipends, support staff, and other requirements for the operation of a graduate training program.

Faculty Circumstances

Faculty are hired, through regular hiring processes at the university, into nontenure track, academic positions. They have slightly reduced teaching loads to compensate for their entrepreneurial activities. Most of their teaching is done at the graduate level: They are solely responsible for delivering the graduate curriculum in behavior analysis. They have offices in the department and full voting rights in all departmental matters with the exception of tenure decisions. Like other academic faculty, they are expected to be active in research and service, and are eligible for promotion and merit raises.

Unusual Characteristics

Some features of this arrangement are more characteristic of a business than a university. For example, faculty hires can be initiated as soon as the resources are available to do so. A faculty hire is an expensive proposition relatively speaking, hence it might seem that there ought to be some caution with hires in a self-capitalized program. Quite the contrary, a faculty member's salary is not viewed as a program expense, but rather as an investment: Faculty members develop service businesses, which bring into the program considerably more revenue than is necessary to pay their salaries. As can be seen in Figure 1, the program's gross revenue pattern matches that of its faculty hires. Revenues increase with each new hire (within some limits, of course).

Likewise, a graduate stipend is ordinarily viewed as an expense. In a self-capitalized system, however, graduate students are running the businesses developed by the faculty members. It is in the program's interest to admit as large a cohort of qualified applicants as can be accommodated.

Finally, under ordinary circumstances, faculty tend to prefer small classes for various pedagogical reasons as well as for the work-load reduction typically associated with smaller classes. Contrary to this, our faculty actually recruit undergraduates into their classes.

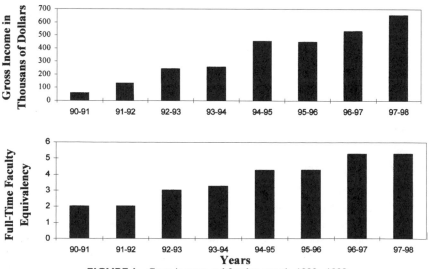

FIGURE 1   Gross income and faculty growth, 1990–1998.

University Contributions

It is not true that the addition of a graduate program in a self-capitalization model involves no cost to the university, nor in our view should it. It is true that the university makes only a small contribution toward faculty salaries. For example, the program has in total only .64 of a full-time faculty equivalency. The university pays a portion of faculty salaries for undergraduate teaching. Similarly, the university allocates only a small number of graduate stipends to the program, the remainder is the program's responsibility to generate. These contributions have increased over the years (Fig. 2).

Still, however, the university has contributed to the program substantially in other ways. For example, it provides office, lab, and clinic space for the program, as well as office services and supplies. Secondly, it does not recover indirect costs from the grants and contracts, which capitalize the program (with some legitimate exceptions). In addition, all of the program's grants and contrasts, as well as most of its other financial operations are managed through university offices and functions.

Benefits of the Self-Capitalization Model

The benefits of this model are substantial for all concerned. The community benefits from having its needs met in an exemplary way at a reasonable cost. The university benefits from the addition of a graduate training program for a small additional cost. Graduate programs generate revenue for the university in the form of tuition and fees, by way of producing credit hours in cases of formula funding, and

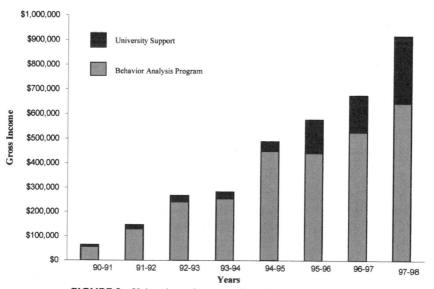

FIGURE 2 University and program financial support, 1990–1998.

through their efforts to obtain external support. More indirect benefits also accrue if those graduate programs develop national visibility. The faculty benefit from the opportunity it affords for academic appointments, through which the academic program may be developed and students may be trained.

Although student labor supplies the means by which all of these benefits for others are achieved, students also benefit enormously from this model. They receive high-quality, job-related training, which is otherwise unavailable to them. This increases students' opportunities for employment as well as graduate training. Our program has also grown in such a way that we now employ more undergraduate students (approximately 80 per academic semester) than any other unit on campus. Consequently, one outcome of students' credit labor has been to make opportunities for them to earn wages.

Graduate students also benefit immensely from the model. They gain more applied experience than their counterparts in other graduate programs and much of this experience is in roles at a much higher level of responsibility than is ordinarily the case for graduate students. Advanced students become administrators of the service businesses operated by the program. Furthermore, the managerial services afforded by graduate trainees provide the means by which graduate stipends are generated. All students are funded by the program for the duration of their training. Finally, the students benefit from the basic curriculum and research training that is also funded by service revenues.

With this understanding of how the program operates, and its value to those involved, we move on to describe some of these functions in more detail, as well as various outcomes achieved by this model over the past eight years.

PROGRAM GROWTH AND DEVELOPMENT

Under ordinary circumstances, the growth of graduate programs, as measured in faculty positions, graduate stipends, and support staff, depends on patterns of resource allocation from the central administration, which in turn, depend on overall university budgets enacted by state legislatures. In other words, programs typically have little direct control over their own growth. In contrast, a self-capitalized program has full control over its own growth in the sense that its growth depends entirely on the program's success in generating the resources needed to support it. This difference in control and the program's success in generating the resources needed to take advantage of it have resulted in rather substantial program growth over the past eight years. For example, since its initiation, the Behavior Analysis Program has added four faculty lines and two support positions compared with almost no growth in either category in the other three departmental programs combined over the same period. Student growth has been particularly dramatic, increasing tenfold in eight years (Fig. 3). These accomplishments in the human resource domain are enabled by and correspond to similar patterns of accomplishments in the financial domain. The gross income of the program has increased

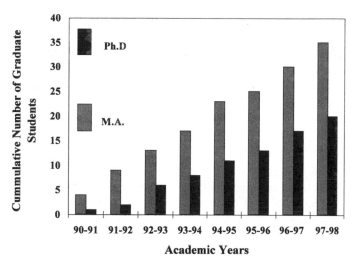

FIGURE 3   Cumulative number of graduate students, 1990–1998.

from $53,000 in 1990 to approximately $650,000 in 1998, representing a 12-fold increase.

Although growth and development are always priorities for new programs, they were absolutely essential for the survival of our program owing to their part in a complicated set of interlocking financial, academic, and political contingencies to which we have already alluded, and were, for this reason, our top priority from the outset. Although other issues have emerged as priorities in more recent times, growth and development remain important to the program's well-being. Our strategies for producing program growth and development and the outcomes achieved through them are described next, along with some of the challenges we have or are currently facing.

HUMAN RESOURCES DEVELOPMENT

As previously described, the faculty have two sets of responsibilities, one academic and one entrepreneurial, the latter providing the opportunity for the former. Implied by the faculty's willingness to abide by this arrangement is their passion for teaching and research. The opportunity to engage in these activities is what their entrepreneurial activities buy them. It goes without saying, then, that means of attracting qualified students and fostering their development as scholars are central concerns of the faculty.

The curriculum calls for more than just scholarship or "knowing about," it also includes "knowing how." In short, the program is also about getting things done and one of the things that must get done is to ensure the survival of the program and with it the livelihoods of all those dependent on its survival. The survival of the program is critically dependent on student resources. As explained earlier, the fees for services provided by nonsalaried student employees provide the leverage needed to sustain the workability of the self-capitalization model. Without the salary savings from credit labor, the program could not survive. Hence the development and effective use of student resources are also of utmost importance.

Graduate Student Recruitment

Like many other programs, we have marketed the program to our colleagues and potential students through the distribution of program brochures and posters, and by exhibiting the program at regional and national professional meetings. We expect our current students to participate in recruitment efforts through their presence and intellectual participation at those meetings. In addition, the novelty of our program provided an opportunity for marketing by way of professional presentations and publications. Finally, we have cultivated a reputation as a rather unusual program—one that is regarded as both productive and playful–serious—which seems to appeal to students and faculty.

As a result of these marketing efforts, and the national visibility for the program they have created, we have seen a steady increase in the number of applicants to the program. We have also been quite successful in having students accept our invitations to interview, a success fostered by our provision of partial travel expenses.

Our capture rate of applicants has also increased over years. Students have reported many different reasons for selecting our program over comparable alternatives, including the breadth of training available, the opportunity for applied experience, the social climate—even its self-capitalization strategy. Our ability to offer financial support to incoming students, however, is probably our most effective means of recruitment, and this ability increases every year as a benefit of self-capitalization.

Student Quality

Student growth has not been accomplished at the expense of student quality. An increasing proportion of students applying to the doctoral program have presented at professional meetings and published in professional journals. Also, an increasing number of masters' program applicants report having had experience in applying behavior analysis. In addition, graduate record exam scores and grade point averages of students admitted to the doctoral program show a slightly increasing trend over the years, while the scores of students admitted to the masters' program have remained relatively stable[1] (see Figs. 4 and 5).

---

[1]These data were collected by Peter C. Dams and Sean M. Coriaty.

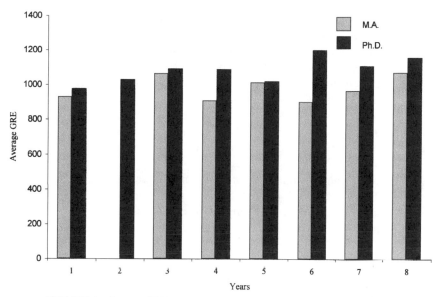

FIGURE 4 Average GRE scores of masters and doctoral students, 1990–1998.

Student Productivity

A number of measures reflect student productivity, some of which are not able to be reported adequately due to the youth of the program as well as other confounding factors, including insufficient faculty resources. Significant among such measures is time to graduation. Preliminary indications are that time to graduation

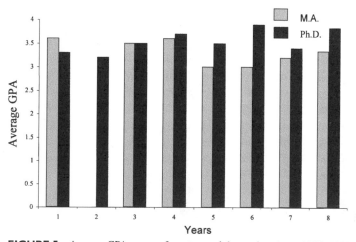

FIGURE 5 Average GPA scores of masters and doctoral students, 1990–1998.

is decreasing with each subsequent cohort. For example, students admitted with bachelor degrees during the first two years of the program are taking an average of seven years to graduate with doctoral degrees, whereas students in the third and fourth cohorts are graduating in five years on average.

Student productivity is also measured by the number of student conference presentations and professional publications (see Fig. 6). The total numbers of first-authored paper and poster presentations by students since the inception of the program are 195 and 106, respectively.[1] The total numbers of first-authored and other-authored publications by students over the life of the program are 10 and 7, respectively.

These totals translate into relatively high rates of presentations and relatively low rates of publications per student. Because publications are viewed more favorably than presentations by most employers, one of our challenges is to focus a greater proportion of our students' energy on preparing their work for publication.

Student Placement

Student placement upon graduation is perhaps the most important indicator of a program's success in that it is the means by which the discipline and profession profit from the program's efforts. Of the six doctoral graduates, one has taken an academic appointment, one has taken a university administrative appointment, two have taken research and development positions in the private sector, one has taken a clinical position, and one a post-doctoral fellowship. Of the eight masters' graduates, two have gone on to advanced training, three have taken clinical positions, and three have taken organizational positions. In short, all are either gain-

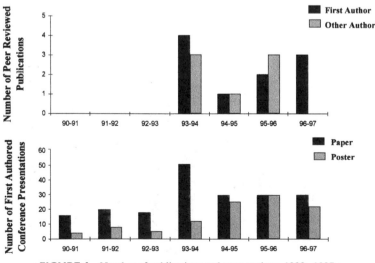

FIGURE 6   Number of publications and presentations, 1990–1997.

fully employed as behavior analysts or are pursuing advanced training in the discipline.

The fact, however, that none of the doctoral graduates has taken an academic appointment in a doctoral degree granting program is problematic for the future of the program. This circumstance is not unique to graduates of our program but represents a problem in the field more broadly. There are relatively few doctoral programs in behavior analysis across the country and openings are few and far between. To develop the means of making our students more competitive for the few positions available is not a long-term solution to this problem. The solution is to build more behavior analysis doctoral programs to hire the graduates of the various programs producing them. Generations of student potential will be lost if we wait for the resources to be allocated by universities for this purpose. The solution to the problem of replicating doctoral-level training is to build behavior analysis programs on the self-capitalization model. One means of achieving this goal is to train graduate students in the essential characteristics of this model and the means by which it might be implemented elsewhere. We are currently providing this training to our students and we are making it available to others by way of professional workshops and publications such as this one.

Graduate Student Retention

Student retention became a problem during the third and fourth years of the program. A second faculty member joined the program somewhat late in the third year, leaving three cohorts of students under the direction of a single full-time faculty member for a period of time long enough to discourage a number of students. In addition, we were developing a number of new projects over this period and our human resources were stretched thin, a circumstance that worsened with each student loss. Seven new doctoral students and four new masters' students left the program during these years. Since then, we have added two additional faculty members and have lost an average of only one student per year.[2]

Having been unable to make a suitable hire this past year, and having admitted a large class on the promise of having made one, we are in some danger of losing some members of our newest cohort.

Undergraduate Student Recruitment

Undergraduate majors in psychology are required to take a direct-learning course to give them an opportunity to learn job-related skills. Among the courses available to fulfill this requirement is "Field Experience in Behavior Analysis." Most of the students selecting this course are placed in the human services businesses operated by the Behavior Analysis Program, where they receive training and experience as front-line service workers. As previously explained, the salary savings

---

[2]These data were collected by Peter C. Dams and Sean M. Coriaty.

afforded by student labor in these businesses are essential to the program's survival under the self-capitalization plan. Hence, it has been important to develop effective recruitment strategies and a number of different strategies have been implemented over the years, although without evaluation as to their relative effectiveness or their costs of implementation. As a result, particular practices tended to be favored over other practices without good reason. For example, the strategy of sending personal letters of invitation to potential students was assumed to be effective enough as a recruitment tool to justify its unusually high cost of implementation.

Recently, graduate practicum hours were allocated for an evaluation of these practices.[3] A survey of faculty and graduate students as to the most likely source of new recruits revealed this to be "faculty advisement." This was an interesting finding given that none of the respondents were formally involved in undergraduate advising and relatively little effort had been made to inform advisors of the opportunities available. Fourth on the list was "personal letters," which accounted for only 13% of the new recruits. Overall, all of the practices were thought to account for roughly the same percentage of the new recruits (Fig. 7).

Subsequently, undergraduate students enrolled in the Field Experience in Behavior Analysis class over the same semester were asked to report the principal means by which their participation in these classes had been recruited. These data are shown in Figure 8. As can be seen in this figure, the course catalog and class presentations are responsible for 75% of the new recruits. These data, needless to say, have focused our recruitment efforts on class presentations.

Undergraduate Student Retention

It is not enough to recruit students into field experience classes. It is also necessary to retain them, and this has been problematic, particularly when placements have been made in adult services. For many undergraduates, this class constitutes their first exposure to developmentally disabled people, and many of those served in the adult programs exhibit challenging behaviors of various sorts. Many students are frightened, saddened, disgusted, or otherwise overwhelmed in this work environment and respond by withdrawing from the class, often after the dates at which full tuition reimbursement is available and other classes may be added without a late fee. More than these losses, though, is the loss of a valuable learning experience.

The loss of a trainee also impacts the Behavior Analysis Program by reducing the value of salary savings achieved. The financial impact of field experience retention failure is substantial, as shown in Figure 9. These data[4] have prompted the development of stronger supports for trainees in these classes, including more extensive training and better supervision of trainees in these placements.

---

[3]This study was conducted by Jill Pellicciarini-Hilton and Amanda C. Nicolson.
[4]This study was conducted by Ramona Houmanfar.

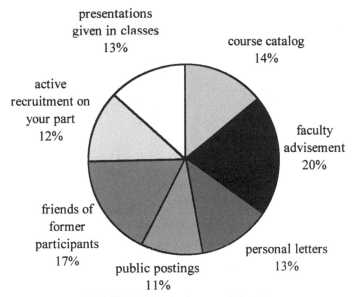

FIGURE 7   Perceived sources, Fall 1997.

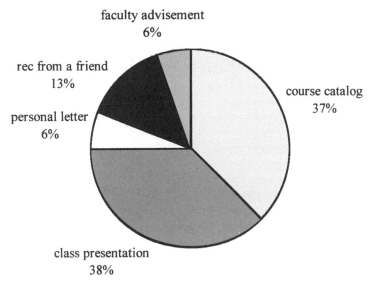

FIGURE 8   Sources of recruitment, Fall 1997.

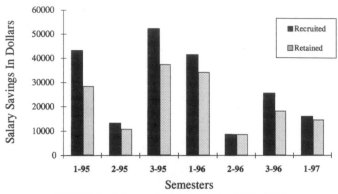

FIGURE 9   Salary savings by semester, 1995 – 1997.

Faculty Recruitment

The recruitment of faculty has presented somewhat of a problem. A nontenure track appointment in a new graduate program, operating by way of an unheard of and unproven financial strategy, has been a difficult sell. It was not only the program's novelty and its uncertain future that made for difficulties. More than this, the demands of faculty in this program are extraordinary: They are expected to handle all of the responsibilities of regular academic appointments, namely teaching, research and service, *as well as* manage businesses through which sufficient revenue can be generated to pay their salaries.

On the other hand, academic appointments in behavior analysis graduate programs are rare opportunities. Likewise, the potential benefits of providing services through a business operated by a behavior analysis graduate program are considerable. At least for these reasons, and possibly many others, we have been able to make successful hires. Now that the program is going into its ninth year of operation, with all faculty lines still intact, we anticipate fewer difficulties in this regard.

Quality

The unusually large demands placed on the faculty in our program might have been expected to undermine their quality ratings as academics. This has not been the case. All of the faculty are reviewed annually for merit raises along with other departmental faculty, and with no provision for enhancement of their ratings out of consideration for their entrepreneurial activities. All of the program's faculty have routinely received departmental ratings in the commendable to excellent range, placing them in the upper third of the group.

Faculty Retention

Our most threatening issue in this domain has to do with job security in the event of a financial disaster. Although we have assurances from the university that the program will be sustained under such conditions, these assurances, like many others, have been given informally and not all of the faculty are fully convinced of the university's commitment to the program or its faculty.

A second problem concerns benefits of one sort or another. For example, nontenured faculty are not eligible for certain types of internal grant support. These eligibility rules were established to prevent nontenured, grant-supported clinical and research faculty, who are not responsible for academic programs, from absorbing these funds. Our faculty do not fit into this category—indeed they do not fit into any regular faculty category—yet because of their nontenured status, they are denied eligibility for these sources of support. Second, start-up packages for new faculty are not available from the university and must, instead, be generated by the program. As such, they have been minimal.

Raises, by way of merit and promotion, are also a sore point among the faculty. They are evaluated for these benefits in the same manner as all other university faculty. For a faculty member in a self-capitalized line, earning a merit raise is a mixed blessing, however. It means that despite having earned it, in order to get it, the faculty member has to earn the additional money to pay for it by way of his or her own entrepreneurial efforts.

We are working on all of these problems. For the time being, however, they remain problems and their persistence may eventually impact faculty retention.

FINANCIAL RESOURCES DEVELOPMENT

The financial history of the program is best characterized as having gone through a series of five phases distinguished by particular interventions. These interventions and some of their outcomes are discussed next.

Phase 1: Financial Obliviousness

During the first several years of the program's existence, our energies were spent developing new contracts. Our thought was that if we could just generate more revenue, somehow it would be enough to cover our expenses, whatever they might be and about which we had no timely information. In short, we didn't know what we were doing and neither did the university. As the years went by, however, the potentially disastrous consequences of our ignorance weighed more and more heavily upon us. As a result, in 1995, we began what has turned out to be a continuous process of professionalizing our financial operations. Fortunately, this process, beginning with the Phase of Financial Awareness, was underway by the time we and the university simultaneously discovered our accumulated $68,000 dollar shortfall.

Phases II, III, IV, and V were not independent interventions but rather components of a more comprehensive financial management strategy, known in the literature as Open Book Management (Case, 1995; Stack & Burlington, 1992). The aim of Open Book Management is to create a company of business people who see themselves as partners in business, who are ready to take responsibility for the well-being of the company, and who expect to share in the company's profits for doing so. The principal objective of companies operating under this model of financial management is successful growth.

Open Book Management is based on the following logic. First, unless employees are informed as to the effects of their actions on their company's financial status, they cannot be expected to take responsibility for nor direct their actions in such a way as to impact that status favorably. Hence, to hold employees responsible for their actions in this manner, it is necessary to open the company's books to employee inspection and to provide training such that employees understand these documents.

Second, unless employees are given feedback about the effects their actions are having on the company's financial status over time, their performances in this regard cannot be expected to improve. Hence, to produce improvements in performance, it is necessary to provide feedback in the form of frequent contact with the company's finances.

Third, unless employees are given opportunities to share the profits achieved by the company as a result of their actions, they cannot be expected to continue to work in the interests of the company. Hence, to sustain employees' motivation to participate, it is necessary to provide them compensation commensurate with the company's profits.

We bought this logic, and implemented the following component phases sequentially over a four-year period. Within each phase, a number of modifications also occurred as a result of various observations and investigations. Some of these investigations and their outcomes are described.

Phase II: Financial Literacy

In the spring of 1995, the program director attended a workshop on Open Book Management conducted by Jack Stack and his colleagues, after which the concept was introduced to the faculty and graduate students in the program, as well as to the university administration. Subsequently, a number of the program's administrative staff were also trained on this management system and, on the basis of this training, balance sheets documenting the monthly profits and losses of the program were developed. We also developed a customized database program for the management of billing and payroll data, and from which reports could be automatically generated. These various financial documents were distributed to the faculty on a monthly basis and were reviewed with the program director and administrative staff during training committee meetings for the remainder of that fiscal year. A sample balance sheet is shown in Figure 10.

Beginning in the fall of 1996, these reports were also distributed monthly to all of the graduate students in the program, although only those who were working in revenue-generating clinical projects received explicit training in financial literacy during that year.[5] This training was provided by the program's administrative staff in the context of the various projects' monthly administrative meetings.

[5]The exclusion of students working in non-revenue-generating projects of other sorts was merely a practical matter.

REVENUE SOURCES	Jul-97	Aug-97	Sep-97	Oct-97	Nov-97	Dec-97	Jan-98	Feb-98	Mar-98	Apr-98	May-98	Jun-98	Year To Date
Autism	$12,208.82	$11,346.65	$14,119.33	$15,302.33	$13,362.33	$13,362.33	$13,682.33	$13,379.50	$13,379.50	$13,333.14	$12,920.14	$12,920.14	$159,349.37
Children Services	$8,695.23	$6,667.90	$7,381.07	$7,440.30	$7,206.15	$7,206.15	$7,132.25	$7,537.09	$8,667.50	$8,271.50	$7,500.85	$8,053.52	$98,406.96
CILA	$4,196.92	$4,019.74	$2,561.21	$2,702.61	$2,787.70	$2,434.00	$2,883.91	$0.00	$1,904.69	$2,094.25	$0.00	$0.00	$26,345.03
FAS	$0.00	$312.50	$525.00	$525.00	$525.00	$525.00	$525.00	$525.00	$525.00	$525.00	$525.00	$0.00	$5,037.50
LH Other Activities	$0.00	$0.00	$0.00	$0.00	$0.00	$0.00	$0.00	$0.00	$0.00	$0.00	$0.00	$0.00	$0.00
P4TH	$15,355.02	$15,159.24	$13,976.56	$14,015.64	$10,164.75	$10,565.46	$11,494.05	$11,385.15	$15,179.14	$14,403.54	$15,237.69	$15,237.69	$164,579.89
PCI	$6,147.31	$5,552.20	$5,990.05	$7,147.30	$5,592.10	$6,013.42	$7,819.68	$8,320.10	$9,023.36	$9,618.17	$8,758.00	$10,071.72	$98,134.60
Behavioral Safety	$0.00	$0.00	$0.00	$0.00	$0.00	$0.00	$0.00	$0.00	$0.00	$0.00	$0.00	$0.00	$8.00
OMRP	$5,254.80	$1,280.40	$1,412.40	$1,510.40	$1,260.40	$1,260.40	$1,260.40	$480.40	$480.40	$0.00	$0.00	$0.00	$14,532.80
SRC	$403.25	$435.69	$275.71	$549.23	$498.08	$268.83	$363.85	$475.83	$393.98	$219.17	$196.99	$1,095.71	$5,476.29
Trinity Master's Prog	$11,725.40	$3,834.00	$3,834.00	$3,834.00	$3,834.00	$5,481.40	$5,481.40	$5,481.40	$5,481.40	$5,481.40	$5,481.40	$5,481.40	$43,783.20
Trinity West	$999.54	$2,183.95	$2,183.95	$2,183.95	$2,183.95	$2,183.95	$2,183.95	$2,183.95	$2,183.95	$2,183.95	$2,183.95	$2,183.95	$25,022.99
Waukee School	$0.00	$312.40	$325.00	$325.00	$325.00	$301.88	$285.94	$525.00	$710.48	$956.47	$912.18	$408.73	$6,468.87
TOTAL	$65,684.38	$52,604.35	$55,677.70	$47,137.41	$47,975.41	$52,813.76	$53,094.25	$57,939.89	$60,336.70	$52,082.85	$55,532.04	$58,456.60	$658,856.60
EXPENSES													
Professional Wages	$12,738.16	$12,738.16	$11,938.16	$11,938.16	$11,938.16	$11,938.16	$10,938.16	$14,438.16	$14,208.16	$14,208.16	$14,208.16	$14,208.16	$154,437.91
Wages/ Grade	$16,090.67	$15,954.59	$17,972.80	$19,293.44	$17,073.64	$14,458.59	$12,438.02	$12,892.44	$12,581.12	$13,299.37	$13,170.72	$13,769.75	$182,033.13
Wages/ Undergrade	$14,454.96	$12,904.36	$11,811.68	$12,777.94	$11,956.18	$14,012.49	$12,508.81	$14,237.37	$13,170.42	$12,193.34	$16,963.03	$16,963.03	$158,374.45
Operations	$2,882.08	$1,767.05	$3,048.23	$3,848.04	$2,734.80	$3,647.92	$3,733.54	$4,332.11	$6,247.30	$1,144.03	$4,638.39	$4,638.39	$41,330.01
Tuition & Fees	$0.00	$1,266.43	$1,266.43	$1,266.43	$1,266.43	$1,266.43	$1,266.43	$1,266.43	$1,266.43	$1,266.43	$1,266.43	$0.00	$13,644.23
Travel (Autism)	$394.44	$363.30	$448.38	$491.79	$408.69	$482.64	$689.43	$435.57	$671.19	$607.47	$357.21	$416.82	$5,766.93
SDS	$366.56	$343.11	$357.41	$314.86	$342.31	$205.07	$341.41	$305.30	$322.06	$317.64	$304.39	$392.79	$4,084.90
FICA and Medicare	$1,334.17	$978.18	$333.13	$326.36	$411.61	$221.21	$211.18	$179.79	$217.31	$59.82	$66.10	$46.98	$0.00
TOTAL	$48,361.83	$46,217.57	$47,176.22	$50,327.01	$45,387.22	$42,371.08	$45,545.02	$45,010.03	$47,855.74	$49,176.60	$42,712.36	$53,435.93	$47,370.48
NET INCOME	$17,435.15	$4,886.79	$5,508.14	$5,350.77	$1,750.39	$5,604.34	$7,267.73	$5,076.21	$10,064.78	$11,150.10	$10,169.67	$3,096.94	$47,370.48

FIGURE 10 Example of a balance sheet.

As a group, academics are not particularly interested in financial matters. In fact, many would claim that having little or no responsibility for such matters in the context of their academic appointments is one of the most attractive features of academic life. Graduate students tend to be of the same mind on this issue. Our group was not unusual in this regard, which is to say, we met with some initial lack of enthusiasm for, if not outright resistance to, financial literacy training. One rather convenient response to this circumstance was to believe that frequent exposure to financial reports would eventually result in their understanding them despite an absence of formal, systematic training. It became increasingly obvious, however, that no such understanding was accumulating in the group as a whole, and this realization prompted a study of the group's financial literacy.

In the fall of 1998, the financial literacy of the graduate students and faculty, as it pertained to time logs, revenue, and expenses, was assessed by way of an unannounced, anonymous, multiple-choice questionnaire distributed during a regular program meeting.[6] The average score for graduate students on this test was 77.2, with a range of 52.5 to 92.5. As a group, the students were most well informed about time log issues and procedures. This was not surprising given that the payroll records were based on time log reports and all students were responsible for completing them on a regular basis. They were less well informed about issues related to the program's revenue. This finding was also understandable in the sense that revenue generation, in the form of contract negotiations, is largely a faculty responsibility. Cost savings, on the other hand, are largely issues of human resource management for which graduate students have primary responsibility and over which they have significant control. It was in this financial category, however, that graduates students were least well informed.

Our previously mentioned "convenient belief" in the learning gains to be achieved by frequent exposure to financial statements suggested that the longer students had been in the program, the more they would understand about the program's finances. In addition, it seemed reasonable to assume that those who were involved in revenue-generating clinical projects were more likely to score higher on the literacy test than those in other sorts of projects. However, a subsequent analysis of these data,[7] in which these two variables, namely students' years in the program and their involvement in revenue-generating clinical projects versus other sorts of projects, revealed a more complicated picture. Preliminary analyses showed that more years in the program did not predict better scores on the financial literary test unless those years had been spent in revenue-generating clinical projects. For students in non-revenue-generating projects, the longer they had been in the program the poorer their scores on the literacy test.

In summary, we have not provided adequate financial training to our graduate students. Neither have we arranged contingencies whereby learning gains achieved are sustained over time. These shortcomings are just now beginning to

---

[6]This study was conducted by Cristin D. Harrison.
[7]This study was conducted by Monica M. Garlock, Thomas S. Higbee, and David A. Wilder.

be addressed.[8] This fall, for the first time, all incoming graduate students and all current students moving into administrative roles in revenue-generating clinical roles will receive formal, systematic financial training. As a result of this training, they should be able to explain all of the numerical entries on the monthly balance sheet and other financial reports, as well as describe actions that might affect those numbers in both positive and negative directions. This intervention, however, will not solve all of the problems we are facing in this domain.

Phase III: Financial Responsibility

Although the faculty have always been responsible for the program's finances, this responsibility was made more explicit in the fall of 1996. As of this date, the faculty agreed to add to the monthly program meeting agendas a review of the monthly balance sheets for all of the businesses operated by the program, as well as for the program as a whole. During these reviews, faculty members were obliged to present and comment on the financial status of their businesses, explaining and celebrating unanticipated profits, as well as explaining and discussing strategies to make up for unanticipated losses. The balance sheet for the program as a whole was presented by the program director.

Initially, the graduate students—particularly the new students—tended to say very little at these meetings apart from cheering at the sight of profits, especially unanticipated profits. As it turned out, these cheers appeared to have an impact on the reports made by the faculty. From the standpoint of Open Book Management logic, the purpose of reporting the financials as frequently as is practical is not just to ensure accountability for what happened but, more importantly, to make it possible to affect what will happen. In short, the emphasis is not so much on explaining what happened during the previous month but on forecasting what will happen in the next month and what might be done to ensure a good outcome. Accordingly, one aspect of each faculty member's financial report was a forecast of the next month's income and expense figures for his or her business, and each month the figures forecasted for the previous month were compared to the numbers actually obtained that month. Obviously, the goal is to forecast these figures as accurately as possible, accuracy being a measure of the extent to which the variables affecting these figures are known. Forecast accuracy did not improve over time, however. On the contrary, it got increasingly worse: expenses and profits were increasingly underestimated. Our analysis of this finding was that inaccurate forecasting was being shaped by audience approval in that the greater the difference between the forecasted and obtained numbers—in these particular directions—the louder the cheer. We have not pursued this line of research, despite its implications for organizational effectiveness.

---

[8]Brief training sessions conducted by Cristin Harrison, involving a high degree of interaction and guided notes, were found to produce slight improvements on financial literacy test scores in each of the three areas of time logs, revenue, and expenses.

As of the fall semester of 1998, presenting the financial reports at program meetings became the responsibility of graduate students in administrative roles in these businesses. This practice has not only fostered greater financial sophistication on the parts of those presenting the data but, in addition, has engendered greater participation by the student group as a whole.

Four of the businesses that produce a majority of the program's income are human service oriented. These include the PATH (Prevocational Assessment and Training Rehabilitation) project, PCI (Progressive Community Integration) project, the Child Intervention program, and the Early Childhood Autism program. The PATH project is a community day training center providing functional life skills for adults with severe developmental disabilities. PCI is a community inclusion program for developmentally disabled adults and transitioning youth. The Child Intervention program is an intensive, early intervention program for children with autistic behavior and related disabilities. The Early Childhood Autism program serves young children with autistic behaviors and their families by providing early, intensive home-based intervention.

The profitability of these businesses depends on their ratios of billable to nonbillable hours. Billable hours are direct service hours in which the client is present. Nonbillable hours are those required to administer the processes by which billable hours are delivered in a competent manner. For the most part, they represent management and training activities. We examined these ratios across four of our human service businesses as well as the program as a whole.[9] These ratios are presented in Figure 11. This abscissa shows months of the fiscal year with 1 representing July of 1996, 12 representing June of 1997. The bottom panel shows that for the program as a whole, we operate at a ratio of approximately seven billable hours to three nonbillable hours. We have not attempted to compare this ratio to industry standards, which would be a useful benchmark. All of our businesses are operating close to this ratio with the exception of the Child Intervention program, which is operating closer to a ratio of five billable to five nonbillable. This observation provided an opportunity to address this issue, in the course of which we concluded that not all businesses are operating under the same constraints whereby their ratios would be similar. We also realized that nonbillable hours is a rather gross category in which is included several different sorts of activities, among them development, management, and training. It also raised awareness of the possibility of inefficiencies that might be corrected, the possibility of charging higher fees for these services, and so on.

Having appreciated the character of the nonbillable hours category, we then examined its makeup. Figure 12 shows the proportions of nonbillable hours that were consumed by training and by management. We assumed that training hours would increase with the start of each semester, as new trainers joined treatment teams, and decrease rather abruptly until the next semester onset. The bottom panel illustrates this pattern, with training hours up during months 2 and 3 (August

---

[9]These analyses were conducted by Monica M. Garlock and Mark R. Dixon.

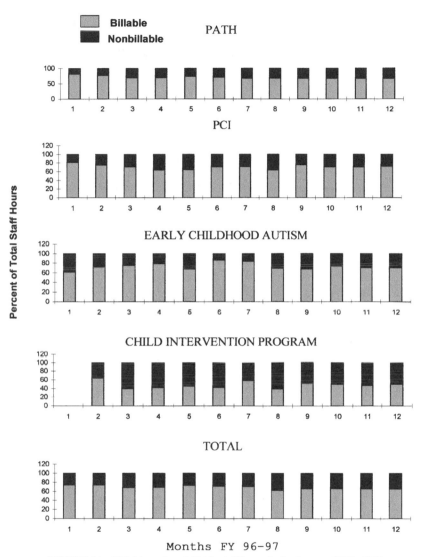

FIGURE 11 Billable and nonbillable staff hours for businesses, 1996–1997.

and September), declining rather quickly until months 7 and 8 (January and February), then increasing once again in months 11 and 12 (May and June) for the summer session.

The same pattern is reflected in all of the individual businesses as well, although there were some notable anomalies. For example, PCI shows considerable training activity in month 9 (March); likewise, for the Child Intervention program in month 4 (October). The most noticeable deviance from the expected pattern oc-

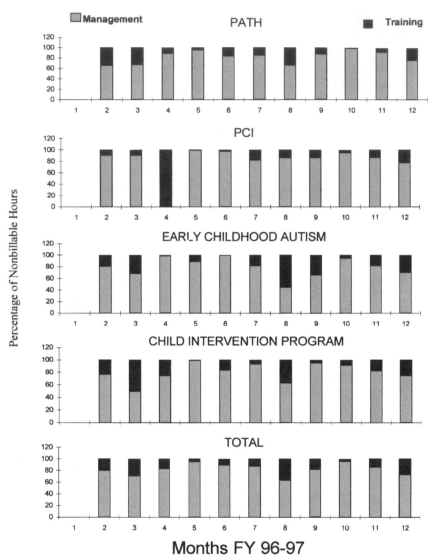

Months FY 96-97

FIGURE 12   Percentage of nonbillable staff hours for businesses, 1996–1997.

curred in the Autism business. Training activity occurs at relatively high levels through March. Although there were many different reasons for these findings across programs, collecting and discussing the data allowed the reasons to be formulated and promoted problem-solving activity.

One other observation is worthy of mention because it relates to the importance of seeing the program, in addition to its individual businesses, as an important unit of analysis. Figure 13 shows the percentage of total salaries saved by trainees' labor for each of the four businesses as well as for the program overall. These savings constitute just less than 40% overall, as seen in the bottom panel. The variability across projects is enormous, however. PCI, in particular, leveraged salaries very little, in contrast to the Child Intervention program. Again, there are many reasons for these differences. Nonetheless, the distribution of salary savings across all of the businesses is important for ensuring a wide range of training opportunities for students. Having access to these data also informs recruitment processes.

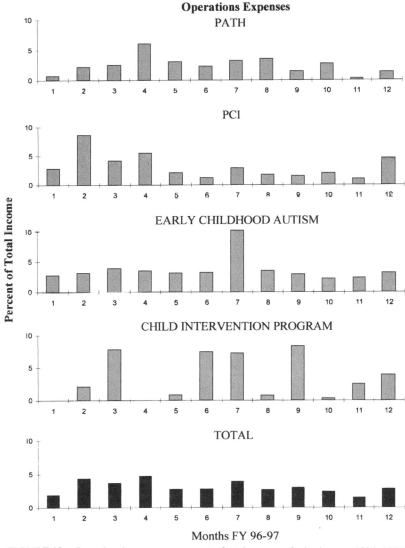

FIGURE 13 Operational expenses as percent of total expenses for businesses, 1996–1997.

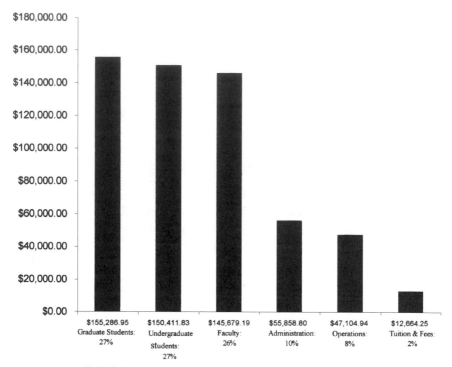

FIGURE 14 Program expenses, July 1, 1997–June 30, 1998.

In summary, by giving faculty and graduate students responsibility for examining financial data and the processes that bring them about, opportunities for affecting finances in favorable directions are made more obvious.

Phase IV: Impacting the Numbers

Assuming responsibility for the numbers is one thing. Changing them is another and it has only been within the past year that we have been in a position to effect change. In any service business, wages and salaries constitute a significant proportion of business expenses. This proportion is even greater in the case of the behavior analysis program due to the fact that, among lesser cost categories, the university does not charge the program rent for the space required for its operations. Figure 14 shows the program's major expense categories and their dollar values for the fiscal year 1997–98. The first four categories, namely graduate student wages, undergraduate student wages, faculty wages, and administration costs make up our personnel costs and they account for 90% of the program's expenses. This means that our business opportunity centers on cost-effective personnel management.

Inefficiencies in management practices are not always obvious, however. In addition, they may be particularly difficult to detect by those closest to them. To provide assistance to managers in this regard, we allocated 20 hours of graduate practicum resources to management consulting. The students serving in these consulting roles were given the task of observing the practices of particular businesses from a more objective perspective, particularly as those practices affected personnel costs, and to report their observations and suggestions to business managers. Essentially this arrangement meant that graduate students were consulting to faculty for the most part, a rather unusual arrangement to say the least.

These consultations had varying degrees of success in the sense of bringing about financially significant changes in business operations. On the whole, though, they were useful enough to have been approved for continuation, even enhancement, next year. One example of the sort of work the consultants performed is the revision of the time log system for the Early Childhood Autism project.[10]

The Early Childhood Autism project provides intensive, in-home services to children with autism and their families, for which the families pay privately under contract with the Behavior Analysis Program. These contracts specify a number of service hours to be delivered each month. A lead tutor is assigned to each family, the responsibilities of whom include coordinating, monitoring, and reporting on the delivery of services to that family. Billing reports for services delivered are based on lead tutors' reports of service hours delivered. The services are delivered by tutors who are employed by the program. These students are paid on an hourly basis, as reflected in their time logs. In summary, there are three sets of numbers relevant to service delivery in this system: the number of contracted hours, the number of hours billed, and the number of hours paid out in wages.

If the system is operating effectively, these three numbers should be identical. The baseline segment of Figure 15, however, shows they were not identical. The implication of this finding was that one or more of the following circumstances was prevailing on a regular basis: 1) fewer or more service hours were being provided than were specified in contracts; 2) fewer or more service hours were being billed to families than were being delivered; and 3) fewer or more hours were being paid out in wages than had been worked.

The consultant's observation of business practices revealed that lead tutors were monitoring service hours delivered on the basis of incomplete tutor sign-in sheets, supplemented by hours assumed to have been delivered on the basis of the tutor work schedule. On the basis of this calculation,[10] they were coordinating service delivery in excess of contract specifications, or short of them. The payroll, on the other hand, was being calculated on the basis of tutors' time logs, which were being submitted independently. The solution was to eliminate both the lead tutor's log and the tutors' independently submitted payroll logs, preserving a revised sign-in sheet as the source of data for all three reports. The effect of this intervention is seen in the left panel of Figure 15.

[10]This study was conducted by Melany P. Denny.

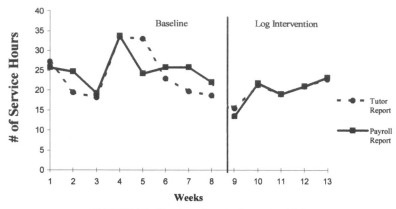

FIGURE 15   Number of service hours provided.

Phase V: Bonus Compensation

As previously indicated, the principal objective of companies operating in accordance with the Open Book Management model is successful company growth. This was also our objective in adopting this model. Because a much higher level of involvement and responsibility for managing our businesses would be required to grow the program than had been required merely to be aware of its financial status, we drafted a plan to compensate program members for their efforts in this regard. A bonus compensation plan (BCP) was ratified by the entire program later that summer and contracts, in which the details of the plan were carefully specified, were signed by all program members.

The BCP has been in operation continuously since that time, although with a number of relatively minor modifications designed to eliminate what we later recognized as ambiguities or inequities, and with a modified payout schedule designed to overcome some of the difficulties inherent in operating in the context of a state university. The details of the original plan and the logic behind its various features are presented, followed by two years of financial outcomes achieved with a bonus plan in place.

Bonus Compensation Plan

The first set of questions to ask in constructing a bonus compensation plan are how much money will be set aside as the bonus pool? and where will this money come from? The experience of Stack and others in the business sector suggested that a bonus of less than 3% of an employee's annual salary was ineffectual. Consequently, to deliver a bonus equal to 6% of a graduate student's annual salary, and somewhat less than this for faculty, we needed a pool of approximately $35,000. This money would have to come from the increase in net profits achieved. Consequently, the payout contingency specified that the bonus would be paid out only if the growth target was achieved. That is, no bonus would be paid out if the target was not achieved. Furthermore, given that the intent of the plan was to grow the program, it would be senseless to pay out all of this increase in bonuses. We decided to pay out only half of the increase in bonuses, returning the other half to the program. This decision meant that we needed to make $70,000 in net profits by the end of the year, which translated as a 15% increase in net profits over the previous year.

A second set of issues had to do with eligibility. Although all faculty members have the same opportunity to affect the program's financial status, the same is not true for graduate students. Opportunities in this regard vary with their stipend and practicum placements. These placements are determined by the faculty. Moreover, the BCP was intended as a means of growing the program as a whole in which all are participants regardless of their ability to impact its growth. By this rationale, all faculty and all full-time graduate students were made eligible to participate in the plan. Part-time students were also eligible to participate, although their bonuses were prorated.

How often payouts should be made became the next issue. Most of the businesses operating by way of the Open Book Management model were paying out twice a year. Our behavior analytic sensibilities suggested that they be made as often as possible, however, and we agreed on a quarterly schedule. There are risks associated with this schedule, however. If profits are not evenly distributed across quarters, and early quarters are particularly good, substantial payouts may be made only to discover that the year-end target has not been achieved and more has been paid out than has been brought in to pay for it. Our net profit data over the past three years is irregular in this aspect, as may be seen in Figure 16. To maintain a

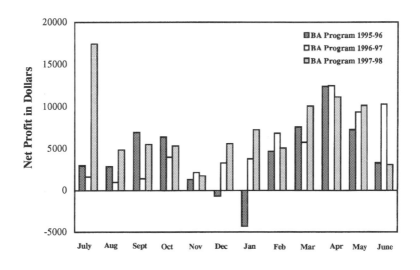

Months

FIGURE 16 Net profits by month, 1995–1998.

relatively rich quarterly schedule while also protecting the program from the risks associated with it, we increased the proportion of the bonus pool available for payout across quarters. Ten percent of the pool was available at the end of the first quarter if the net profit target for that quarter had been reached, followed by 20%, 30%, and 40% over the next three quarters, respectively. Finally, to avoid undermining motivation to participate in the event of poor early quarters, we allowed bonuses not paid out at any quarter to roll over to the next quarter. This procedure permitted the entire pool to be paid at the end of the year only if the year-end target was achieved.

As articulated up to this point, all program members were to benefit equally if the program as a whole achieved its year-end net profit target. In other words, there were no incentives for especially worthy performances on the parts of particular individuals built into the plan. To provide for these, we established a contingency whereby increases in net profits beyond 15% and up to a maximum of 35% would be available for proportional contributions to faculty on the basis of the contributions of their businesses to the total profits achieved. Net profit increases in excess of 35% were to be returned to the program. The rationale for this was that should the program have an unexpected windfall, these monies would be used to hire additional faculty, rather than be paid out as additional discretionary bonuses.

Fiscal Performance

As shown in Figure 17, none of the first three quarterly net profit targets were reached during FY 96–97 and no bonuses were given out until the final quarter. One hundred percent of the bonus pool was delivered at the end of the year.

As shown in Figure 18, a payout was made at the end of the first quarter of FY 97–98, but no payouts were made at the end of either the second or third quarters. This left 90% of the bonus pool to be paid out at the end of the fourth quarter if the year's target is reached. This appears highly likely, although the actual net profit was necessarily an estimate at the time of this writing.

Phase VI: Accrual Accounting

For most of the program's history, the greater part of its income has come from government sources. Although payments from these sources may be delayed, they will eventually be paid. More recently, however, a greater proportion of the program's income is coming from private sources. As this has happened we have been confronted with delayed and unpredictable payments as well as uncollected debt, all of which have contributed to cash flow problems of a magnitude we had not previously had to solve. To protect the program and make its members more fully aware of the program's financial status at any given time, we have begun to include cash flow data on our monthly balance sheets.

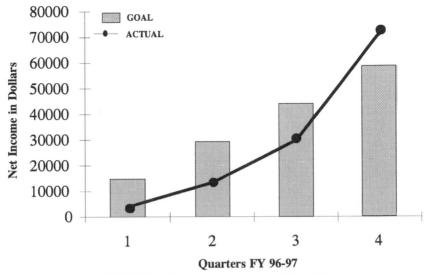

FIGURE 17   Net income over quarters, 1996–1997.

FUTURE PLANS

Our plans for the future, in the most general terms, are to survive as an outstanding graduate program in behavior analysis. Described below arc two intiatives: the first pertainig to program quality improvement, the second to program survival.

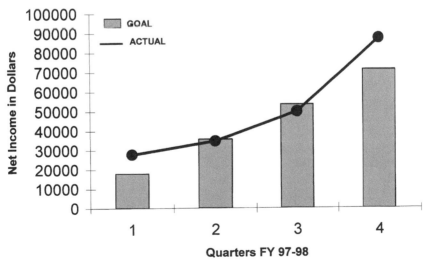

FIGURE 18   Net income over quarters, 1997–1998.

Bonus Compensation for Quality Improvement

Although it might seem sensible to begin a program with a well-articulated mission and objectives, in actual fact, this rarely happens. Instead, program missions tend to evolve after the fact, more or less descriptive of what the program has come to be about. This is how our mission and objectives have arisen and why we are discussing them under the heading of "future plans." Over the past year we have been developing a formal mission statement for our academic program, accompanied by more concrete goals and objectives, as well as strategies by which they may be achieved and how their achievement might be objectively measured. We are also collecting data on relevant outcomes, reanalyzing old data according to new criteria, and reconstructing historical practices and procedures from archival files for the purpose of developing a baseline assessment of program outcomes since its inception.

As an example of a process measure, our program handbook specifies a timeliness for the completion of various academic requirements, such as comprehensive exams. The baseline assessment will show us the extent to which this timeline has been followed. The handbook also specifies that one of these comprehensives, completed in the form of a manuscript, must be submitted for publication in a peer-reviewed journal. As a quality outcome measure, we will be assessing the degree to which these submissions have been accepted for publication in these journals.

Our goal in all of this is to complete the baseline assessment before the end of the current fiscal year. With these data in hand, we intend to set a target for improvement in a collection of particularly significant outcomes (e.g., student publications) exactly as we have for our financial outcomes, and arrange to provide bonus compensation to all program members if we reach our target by the end of the fiscal year. We will be tracking these numbers at our monthly program meetings, along with our financial data.

Securing Our Future

As noted in previous sections of this chapter, we have identified a number of problems to tackle in order to secure the future well-being of the program. Significant among them are issues of job security for faculty members in the event of a substantial, unpredictable, and unavoidable financial loss, and the implications of such a loss for the program as a whole. We are working on several fronts in this regard, two of which are described next.

Diversification of Revenue Sources

Most of the program's revenue comes from fees for services provided to people with disabilities. This revenue, and hence the program's survival, is subject to disruption as a result of government action at either the state or federal level. It also depends on our ability to compete successfully with other regional providers. Both of these circumstances have provided funding in the past and may be expected to do so in the future. Our best strategy to ensure the program's survival, then, is to diversity, and we are making a concentrated effort to do so.

Trading Credit Hours for Faculty Lines

The University of Nevada, Reno, is formula funded, meaning that its state-supported institutional budget is calculated on the basis of the number of student credit hours it produces. At present, the university is under considerable pressure to meet its projections.

We have found a way to make ourselves useful toward this end, and plan to trade our assistance for financial security. Specifically, one of our entrepreneurial efforts has been to deliver our masters' degree program to a cohort of 17 students in another state by contracting with a large human-services agency in that state. This arrangement has worked out well for everyone concerned. More than this, though, it generates student credit hours and these credit hours, coming from out of state, are unquestionably new credits. In other words, they cannot be interpreted as credit hours recruited out of other existing programs on campus.

With our first out-of-state cohort graduating, we have another 30 students in line to join a second cohort. Thirty graduate students in a 30-credit masters' program produces a significant number of new credit hours, more, in fact, than many existing graduate programs on campus. Moreover, this particular delivery of the masters' program is only one such initiative, of which there are two others in various stages of development It seems likely that the university will trade portions of faculty lines for credit hours generated in this way. Faculty salaries make up one quarter of the program's expenses, hence any relief in this category constitutes a significant opportunity for the program.

EPILOGUE

Our experience shows that it is possible to develop a successful graduate training program on the model of self-capitalization. The model requires an ability on the part of the academic discipline involved to provide a needed service for a fee, a means of leveraging the fees earned, and a flexible academic institution in which to situate the program. Fulfilling each of these requirements involves its own set of challenges. Our strategies for cultivating a supportive institutional home for the program have been described in detail elsewhere (Hayes et al., 1995) and have, as such, not been the focus of the present chapter. Neither have we devoted much space to detailed descriptions of the services provided by our program other than to emphasize their need and their ability to generate fees. A great variety of services may fit this pattern. Instead, we have focused on the means by which fees for services delivered have been leveraged in such a way as to support the growth and development of the academic training program. Beyond this, we have described our strategies for engaging all program participants in these efforts, and the means by which we are working as a group to enhance the quality of the program.

Higher education appears to be undergoing a transition, the outcome of which promises to be considerable institutional support for the development of training programs on an entrepreneurial model such as the present one. We are convinced of the workability of this model, and have tried to demonstrate our conviction by the way of detailed descriptions of our outcomes in a number of critical domains. More than this, in the course of pursuing the model of self-capitalization, we have discovered some of its advantages over traditional practices. Among them are a significantly greater potential for program growth and development, and a much greater opportunity for the comprehensive training of students.

We continue to face a number of challenges, and meeting them will merely establish conditions under which new challenges will arise. Meeting these new challenges will depend on our ability to foresee them and on the resources we have accumulated to address them, both of which are favored by ongoing outcome assessment and a conscious emphasis on continuous improvement. In short, we are well positioned to respond quickly and effectively to a wide range of potential problems. The only problem that we are unlikely to solve is that of being unlike a traditional graduate training program in every way. The cost of solving this problem is much too high.

ACKNOWLEDGMENTS

This chapter was written in collaboration and with the support of Steven C. Hayes and Sidney W. Bijou. The authors also acknowledge the contributions to the manuscript by the students in the program, particularly, Sean M. Coriaty, Peter C. Dams, Melany P. Denny, Mark R. Dixon, Cristin D. Harrison, Thomas S. Higbee, Jill Pellicciarini-Hilton, Amanda C. Nicolson, and David A. Wilder. Finally, appreciation is extended to the Department of Psychology and the University of Nevada-Reno for their continuing support for the Behavior Analysis Program.

REFERENCES

Case, J. (1995). *Open book management.* New York: HarperCollins.
Hayes, L. J., Hayes, S. C., Ghezzi, P. M., Bijou, S. W., Williams, W. L., & Follete, W. (1995). A self-capitalization model for building behavior analysis graduate programs. *Behavior Analyst, 18,* 331–339.
Stack, J., & Burlington, B. (1992). *The great game of business.* New York: Doubleday.

BIOGRAPHIES

James E. Carr James E. Carr is currently an Assistant Professor in the Behavior Analysis program of the Department of Psychology, University of Nevada. His current research interests include the assessment and treatment of tic disorders and of severe behavior problems displayed by individuals with developmental disabilities and college teaching and teacher training. He has published over two dozen articles on the application of behavioral principles to the assessment and treatment of clinical problems

Monica M. Garlock   Monica Garlock is a doctoral student in the Behavior Analysis Program at the University of Nevada, Reno.

Patrick M. Ghezzi   Dr. Ghezzi is an associate professor of psychology at the University of Nevada, Reno (UNR). He also serves as the director of UNR's Early Childhood Autism Program. His current interest is in early intensive behavioral interventions for young children with autism.

Linda J. Hayes   Dr. Hayes is a professor of psychology and director of the graduate programs in behavior analysis at the University of Nevada, Reno (UNR). She also serves as the Director of University Assessment at UNR. Her basic research focuses on complex human behavior, verbal behavior in particular. Her applied work is in the area of organizational behavior management and system analysis. She is best known for her work in the area of behavioral theory and philosophy.

Ramona Houmanfar   Dr. Houmanfar is the coordinator of the graduate program in behavior analysis at the University of Nevada, Reno. Her basic research interests focus on complex human behavior with an emphasis on the analysis of cultural phenomena. She is best known for her work in the area of organizational behavior management and the interrelated areas of behavioral system analysis and performance management.

W. Lawrence Williams   W. Larry Williams received his Ph.D. from the University of Manitoba in 1977. Larry helped design and implement and then chaired from 1978 to 1984 the first Master's degree program in special education at the University of Sao Carlos in Sao Paulo, Brazil. From 1984 to 1994, he directed several clinical behavior analysis programs in developmental disabilities at Surrey Place Centre in Toronto. As an Associated Professor of Psychology at the University of Nevada, Reno, his teaching and research interests are in developmental disabilities and organizational behavior analysis.

PART III

GOVERNMENTAL
ADMINISTRATION

10

PUBLIC POLICY ADMINISTRATION AND THE PSYCHOLOGIST

ROBERT L. DYER

Criterion Health, Inc., Bellevue, Washington 98008

INTRODUCTION

The psychologist who assumes a policy development and administrative role in government is on a course to experience a very exciting and at the same time frustrating opportunity. The distinct differences between theory and practice are never more apparent than when policy impacts, with beautiful or terrible consequences, the life of someone you know.

The process of government policy development and administration is tedious and fraught with compromise. It should not be entered into lightly. The stakes are quite high. Senior management in mental health, substance abuse, corrections, or welfare all have the potential to make a real and profound difference in people's lives.

An important and often overlooked caveat to the topic of this chapter is the basic role of the executive branch of government. The positions I describe exist in

Management and Administration Skills for the Mental Health Professional
Copyright © 1999 by Academic Press. All rights of reproduction in any form reserved.

the executive branch of government. The executive branch administers public policy—it *does not* make public policy. This means that most of the time and energy an administrator expends is in behalf of existing public policy—for good or ill. My purpose in writing this chapter is to chronicle the array of potential activity and probable experience that a psychologist entering the role of county or state administrator of public behavioral health benefits may profit from knowing. My experience reflects the move from managing a large private-sector service enterprise to becoming a state mental health department director.

BENEFIT VERSUS SERVICE: SCOPE OF WORK

Probably the single greatest insight awaiting the neophyte psychologist/administrator is the rarely discovered fact that the role of the public steward is to manage a program of taxpayer funds that assure eligible citizens receive eligible services for a fair rate at an acceptable standard of quality, all done with adequate checks and balances to ensure a reasonable level of administrative performance. This task is not about intuiting what constitutes the greatest way to deliver services. You are administering a procurement system, overseeing millions of your fellow taxpayers' hard earned dollars. The system needs to address the following questions:

- What is the need in the covered political area for mental health services?
- How is that need attended to? Who delivers what?
- Who pays for it?
- Who can't receive what they need? For what reasons?
- How is the public protected from unethical, unscrupulous, and incompetent practitioners and programs?
- Who will the tax dollars be utilized to benefit? How will they be recognized?
- When is it the citizen's responsibility to purchase care?
- When does a citizen's behavior exceed the community standards so greatly they must receive care against their own wishes?
- What practitioners and programs will be eligible to receive funds in support of publicly supported citizens?
- What standards of performance must those practitioners and programs maintain to continue receiving funding in support of eligible citizens?
- How are the targeted recipients of benefits faring as they impact related agencies of government, i.e., housing, rehabilitation, corrections, welfare, education, and so on?
- What administrative systems are in place to ensure satisfying other governmental units' standards of accountability for taxpayer stewardship?

Throw in assorted issues such as rights of parents and needs of children, and so on, and a myriad of lawsuits aimed at the role and responsibility of government, and you have the main role and function of the administrator pretty clearly framed. You are running a public insurance company for a very large and contentious board of directors. Your clinical skills will be put to good use in staff meetings and with special interest groups—not planning or conducting therapy. The opportunity cost of focusing on delivering care or becoming significantly involved in planning or evaluating care would be to the detriment of other issues.

AUTONOMY VERSUS TEAM ROLE

Psychologists tend to work in environments conducive to autonomous activity. Traditional roles of therapy or teaching assume great degrees of freedom for the practitioner. A public policy official is working for a senior (usually elected) official, who most probably is not a behavioral health professional, that is, a governor or county executive, and so on. If you are the mental health director, you are one of many department heads, fitting into a role and set of evolving priorities. Your budget is constrained by both history and a rigorous and ritualistic process assuring minimal change. All commitments, contractual or policy based, are reviewed (and usually drafted) by attorneys. All initiatives must be approved by intermediaries or the senior administrators themselves (i.e., governors, chiefs of staff, etc.). All significant changes in policy, funding, or benefit coverage are likely to require legislative branch approval, that is, a new law.

It should be noted that at the state level mental health is one of the top ten departments by budget size and number of employees. Historically the administrator is a mental health professional, often one with significant government mid-level management experience. Seldom is the mental health agenda on the list of priorities for change. Administrators are usually not part of the senior planning team for all administration initiatives. (When they are, as I was privileged to be, it's a much more interesting "ride.")

I found that awkward reporting relationships existed between the governor's office (an aide), the budget office (a deputy in the division answering to a deputy of the budget director), the attorney general's office (three staff attorneys in the division), the human resources department (many specialists in the division reporting to different people in the state bureaucracy), and the legislature (a deputy outside the division initially carrying the agenda). Each of these individuals were bright, capable, and experienced. None of them were behavioral health professionals. All of them had ambitions for advancement in government. None of them were solely concerned about mental health issues. Personal priorities and communication styles loom large.

It takes many individuals to administer public policy. Attorneys, accountants, physicians, as well as mental health professionals, consumer advocates, professional writers, software specialists, and so on. It is "a big tent." Inclusion must be the rule. Coordination, as would seem obvious, is always an issue. Internal and external teams must be created. Teams needed include:

<u>Internally</u>

• Resource management. Dedicated people must be on the lookout to secure funding. Additionally this team must ensure that appropriate safeguards exist to retain funding.

• Public policy. This group has the responsibility of securing a biennial needs assessment. Who was receiving care? Who needed care? Who delivered it? and so on. They also represent and coordinate all external groups. Many different groups with unique agendas are lobbying for their issues. These must be distilled into manageable, prioritizable, definable, and budgetable initiatives for change.

• Contract management. The basic business of the agency is procuring benefits. Contracting with provider entities, monitoring performance, and assuring value are the main tasks of a specially assembled staff. A conscious goal here was to move from ever-changing process regulations to an outcome orientation. This move from attention to how business is performed to what the purchases accomplished on behalf of consumers and taxpayers was very difficult for many department personnel, and surprisingly, at least to me, for many providers.

• Service management. Most governmental agencies still conduct some direct service, whether state hospitals or case management. A special team to administer services is needed to assure coordination and focus. In our state, their task was to ensure common performance standards, acceptable quality, and appropriate coverage of all low-incidence, specialized services.

• Special projects group. In government great pressure exists to assure constancy. Change is difficult. Dedicating personnel to coordinate and implement initiatives is imperative to implementing anything new into the system. Communication, contracts, reports, and problem solving all require dedicated personnel to begin new systems and to assure a successful transition.

<u>Externally</u>

Current providers, provider guilds, advocates, consumers, and representatives of taxpayers all need input and feedback. Their respective agendas are not always appropriate to merge. Typically, many groups already exist that are agenda based, for example, state psychological associations and mental health associations. Often these have very prescribed priorities and agendas. Groups of professionals such as current contractors or guilds usually have full-time dedicated staff to lobby their issues. Customer advocates and consumer groups usually are not as well funded to carry their message.

Good stewardship requires assuring a balance to voices heard.

• Provider groups. Current contractors need to be blended with guild representation. Guild groups such as state psychiatry, psychology, or social work associations are always working a legislative agenda. Contract providers are almost always seeking both more money and increased protections for their minimally competitive relationships. Blending both needs is a great way to bring to bear the need for reasonable technology and accountability. None of the involved parties are likely to desire to share their purpose with others whom they perceive as competitors; yet in truth, only by banding together is it likely that the consolidated agenda will be prioritized adequately to result in significant change. The public administrator is not in charge of such groupings but rather needs a way to offer a common platform for the planning and distillation of common means and methods of performance.

• Consumers, consumer advocates, and taxpayer representatives need special protections and support. Professional advocacy groups exist with dedicated staff and a national agenda but many more local groups exist which carry important messages with a "tiny voice" of funding and media awareness. Current political correctness ensures a visible role for some advocates, but government seems to lose sight entirely of the need to assure ongoing input from consumers and taxpayers about the benefits they receive. I support independently sampling the individuals who utilize the services on issues such as accessibility, acceptability, impact, and value. Results can be used for provider profiling and give a different picture from relying exclusively on consumer advocates for results of care.

STEWARDSHIP

Government impacts the access and delivery of behavioral healthcare in many ways. In reviewing the total healthcare expenses in America, 60% of the expenses of behavioral healthcare are provided by the government in one form or another. So we see the role of government as both insurer and purchaser of care.

Government has the role of protecting the public in credentialing, certifying, or licensing practitioners or providers, and by administering laws that deny citizenship rights in favor of forced care.

Government purchases care for needy citizens as well as for government employees and their dependents. Given the boundaries of what constitutes behavioral health range over several governmental areas, public policy must be made to coordinate governmental programs and ensure internal consistency between administering agencies and levels of government. The range of concerns that the state mental health authority must address include:

• Behavioral Health parity/inclusion in state health plans approved by the state
• Determination of needy citizens' access to state-supported behavioral healthcare
• Determination of needy citizens' personal and financial support for cosupport of behavioral health services accessed
• Coordination of other governmental programs:
    Housing
    Disability
    Education
    Corrections
    Medicaid
    Medicare
    Welfare

- Care administered in state-supported facilities
- Protection of the public from fraudulent or exploitative practices
- Procurement practices for state-supported recipients: needy citizens, employees, and their dependents
- Loss of citizen rights and forced care, commitment

SYMBOLISM

I was unprepared for the symbolism in the role. The executive branch administrator is a major source of revenue for many individuals. Current contractors certainly want to curry favor. Potential contractors desire to show the advantages of doing business with them. Current utilizers of the system have ideas for improvement and seek acknowledgment for inadequate or just plain "bad" service. Stakeholders need attention for potential changes in the system. Internal governmental officials seek attention from their peers for any policy-related issues.

At the beginning of my tenure mail was delivered twice daily. I had an administrative assistant and an office manager. They assisted me gallantly, yet more than one foot of "appropriate" mail reached me daily. Over 20 groups built in an expectation that the director would attend meetings they offered. The majority of the day along with several evenings a week were given to representation at meetings. About one month into the job my agenda reflected 32 hours of fixed meetings per week. Change had to occur to actually do any work. NOTE: Introverts need not apply. Extemporaneous presentations along with formal presentations are a necessary part of representation. You will not be effective if you are unable to verbally handle a very diverse set of issues.

FOCUS

As can be seen, the myriad of tasks can be daunting. There is a strong need to focus resources to accomplish improvements in the system. Neither people's access to your calendar nor the contrived priorities of special interest groups should be allowed to create the priorities of the unit. A formal planning process, inclusive of national research, consumer sampling, and balanced focus groups should identify the top priorities.

Mental health issues tend to be confusing (like any service issues) in a political arena. Politicians are not certain of why they should tamper with services to a needy population if no major budget savings will occur. Complex issues must be distilled into recognizable metaphors. Our state was changing from a funding model dedicated to certain well-established providers to a system that identified a set of benefits to all eligible citizens from an array of providers. The phrases "dollars follow the patient" and "patient voice and choice" communicated a code for the solution to complex changes in the way the state solved citizens' mental health needs. Implied in the code was a set of changes that included

- A system of eligibility for citizens and a way to check eligibility at all service sites
- A written set of benefits and potential providers
- Providers offering a long vertical array of services to encourage "one stop shopping" and to avoid transfers of care
- Elimination of catchment areas in which citizens had no choice of providers. (What was "caught" in catchment areas were dollars with no competition and no consumer choice. These are not necessary when plenty of choice in providers exists.)
- The creation of performance criteria to measure the effectiveness of provider organizations delivering care
- The common platform of contracting for all publicly purchased care. This implied commonality in purchasing of behavioral healthcare across various state departments. That is, Medicaid, children's protective services, rehabilitation, education, mental health, and drug abuse would use common procurement criteria.
- The consolidation and simplification of the state budgeting process. Instead of "line items" for all contracting agencies, fund pools for eligible populations were created. (All manner of "porkbarrel" concerns were "kicked off" with this change. Providers seeing their monopolies threatened appealed to elected officials. Consumer advocacy groups had to prevail with their beliefs in the improvements of choice and quality to move the issue. "Follow the money" is a useful phrase. Do it and you will see why certain issues are "stuck." Set up your system with strong attention to financial incentives and disincentives. Changing the biennial budget process was truly "where the rubber hit the road." We changed the system when we changed the budgeting process.)

OUTCOME ORIENTATION

Government typically engages in a quality initiative called process regulation. Regulations are created which specify that certain procedures are followed. When an industry is new and outcome standards are not known, it provides a loose method of standardization. Given that publicly funded mental health services emerged from a period when access to care and standards of care were quite limited, it is no surprise that a process regulatory-type of oversight represented the method of stewardship of the day.

Process regulatory systems of oversight are cumbersome. They require on-site inspections and massive documentation of both policy and procedure along with documentation samples to prove compliance to internal documentation. It is easy to blur the lines between oversight and management, for example, specifying caseload size, membership in governance, and so on. Bad processes, decreasing new providers' interest in the field due to the regulatory "price" of entry, inhibiting new benefits from occurring because they don't conform to existing regulations, inefficiencies, and a stifling of creativity unfortunately are the unintended side effects of process regulations—"yellow waxy buildup" of deadening procedures, all with initially good intentions.

A switch to an outcomes orientation reflects a change in emphasis. Providers still must satisfy health and safety standards. They still must have credentials indicating education or policies and procedures reflecting standards of practice (i.e., Joint Commission on Accreditation of Healthcare Organizations, Council on Accreditation of Rehabilitation Facilities, Council of Accreditation, etc.). Additionally, they must exhibit performance on certain key indicators above a certain standard of their peers (e.g., be below 75% of their peers on no more than 3 of 15 items). This outcome shift allows sharing performance data. It ensures some attention to results. It encourages a common language around the items chosen to measure performance.

Choosing the parameters of outcome is quite difficult. Little agreement exists about clinical outcome instruments. This has been a common agenda for psychologists. Thousands of studies have been conducted. Clinical outcome isn't the appropriate standard. In public stewardship the standard of concern is the comparable use of tax dollars, i.e., what proof exists that the dollars have resulted in value? Mental health competes with education, roads, sports arenas, and so on. Can you show political "professionals" value for their dollars? By using independent sampling of consumers along with results of tax consumption and contribution of pre- and postservice usage you provide a proof of stewardship that is meaningful to elected officials. Note, the "right" outcome for tax dollars is tax consumption or tax contribution (tax conservation). Mental health services can have a major impact on these measures. Annually sampling 2% of consumers and then comparing their tax consumption pre- and postintervention provides a tremendous amount of useful information. Mental health can influence working, housing, education, and health, all items with tremendous impact on tax dollars and all trackable. The equivalent of "medical offset" is very obvious in public mental health.

MANAGEMENT

The management environment is very difficult. Managing multiple tasks simultaneously is a necessity. Human resources are strained. The senior executive "inherits" problems that are long standing and visible. Tools for remediation are limited due to the nature of government. Personnel issues are extremely cumbersome; creating jobs, hiring, motivating, and firing are all rigidly defined. Procuring technical assistance is not easy. Changing contract requirements or finances are tightly prescribed.

The administrator must be knowledgeable and facile with essential business management techniques. You are leading people. You are working in a contract environment. You are responsible for significant amounts of taxpayer moneys. Of all of the management training I have experienced, the concepts of participatory management and project management seemed the most useful. Creating and working from a public, data-based strategic plan was a marvelous aid for focusing resources. A biennial report with data-based needs assessment and prioritized areas for focus created a public method of addressing the most important issues and for planning the outcome orientation necessary for "unsticking" the system.

COMMUNICATIONS AND THE MEDIA

The one place the mental health administrator desires not to be is on page one, with a picture above the crease. This almost certainly means bad news. Whenever a mental health tragedy exists the media goes to the people who are charged with oversight. The buck as Harry Truman said, stops with the administrator (if not, it may have to go to the governor—a really bad thing for a mental health issue). It should be noted that regardless of vigilance, tragedies do occur in a system that serves 1.9% of the population, in our case over 160,000 people a year. All deaths in state facilities were reported to me when they occurred. Routine, methodical, and thorough reviews occurred (quite quickly). Systems had to be instituted to assure prompt, accurate reporting. The administrator needed to see facilities where care occurred (no small feat with 11 state facilities and 470 contract entities). The administrator was held accountable for issues the media identified, for as long as the media chose to focus on them. The media wants quotes from the top.

A surprising lesson was the partisanship of the media. The major urban newspaper supporting the opposition party of the governor for some strange (tongue very firmly in cheek) reason was able to report negative innuendoes on stories that no one else identified. It honestly hurt me personally to have intentions questioned and culpability or results distorted. My personal finances were reported by this paper along with business interests unrelated to the position, all with negative innuendo in the lead paragraph.

The most amazing thing about the potency of the media in a political environment is its ability to define the issue. My state implemented a program in which the eligible citizens chose the providers. This change resulted in a restructuring of programs closer to consumers. Our state had been second in the nation in inpatient bed days per citizen. This was because the dollars had been designated for programs not patient needs. The changed financing system meant more outpatient and supportive care services and fewer inpatient beds needed. Our evaluations found quicker access, increased satisfaction, and an ability to serve more than three people in rich, wraparound care in their community for each person who previously would have had to stay in state facilities because of a lack of community-based care. Most people identified as a good thing quicker access for more people to richer programming in less disruptive settings. The repeated lead story from the "loyal opposition" paper was the loss of service caused by the closing of one of two state facilities in one city. The staff at our Christmas party conducted a most humorous skit on this paper's headlines to our greatest accomplishments of the year. While it rallied the staff, it unfortunately had an adversarial effect on public understanding. Thick skin is probably a necessary feature for public administrators.

POLITICS

I was politically naive. Politics had never been on my radar screen of what was important. My internal stance was the job had to be accepted with the understanding that if ever asked to do something "political" that clashed with personal ethics then quitting was the only option. Simple, but internally clear.

It never happened. I was treated with courtesy, graciousness, support, and appreciation—by the administration. My burden was to find ways to make the agenda for improving the mental health system worthy of attention to those outside mental health administration. Change requires the attention of the attorney general and the budget director (among others). It became obvious that visibility in other agencies was necessary to represent our constituencies well. Being on the inner circle for policy change in the administration was the best way of influencing the mental health agenda. We identified personnel, issues, and solutions to assist Medicaid, welfare, corrections, disability, housing, and education. System synthesis and integration led to improvements in many areas. Each of those areas has its own arcane rules, methods, and priorities (as well as interesting personalities). You must focus on their agenda to advance yours. Simple concept—tough application.

RESOURCES

Many resources can assist the transition. A few that I found valuable include:

- American Managed Behavioral Healthcare Association, 700 13th Street NW, Suite 590, Washington DC 20005.
- American Public Welfare Association, National Office of Medicaid Directors, 810 1st Street NE, Suite 500, Washington DC 20002-4267.
- American Society of Addictive Medicine, 5225 Wisconsin Ave. NW, Suite 409, Washington DC 20015.
- Bazelon Center for Mental Health Law, 1101 15th Street NW, Suite 1212, Washington DC 20005.
- Center for Mental Health Services, SAMSA, 5600 Fishers Lane, Rooms 15–105, Rockville, MD 20857.
- Center for Substance Abuse Treatment, 5600 Fishers Lane, 6th floor, Suite 840, Rockville, MD 20857.
- Institute for Behavioral Health, 1110 Mar West Street, Suite E, Tiburon, CA 94920.

- Managed Health Care Association, 1401 "I" Street NW, Suite 900, Washington DC 20005.
- National Alliance for the Mentally Ill, 200 N. Glebe Road, Suite 1015, Arlington, VA 22203-3754.
- National Association of State Mental Health Program Directors, 66 Canal Center Plaza, Suite 302, Alexandria, VA 22214.
- National Council for Community Behavioral Healthcare, 12300 Twinbrook Parkway, Suite 320, Rockville, MD 20852.
- National Institute on Drug Abuse, 5600 Fishers Lane, Parklawn 10-05, Rockville, MD 20857.

BIOGRAPHY

Robert L. Dyer   Bob Dyer is the president of Criterion Health in Bellevue, Washington. Criterion is a behavioral health management services company specializing in accountability services, creating and overseeing provider-owned managed care systems, and disease management programs. Bob is active with the National Council for Community Behavioral Healthcare and the Institute for Behavioral Health, presenting regularly at national and regional conferences. Bob has been chief executive officer of a managed care company, a state mental health commissioner, a psychiatric hospital administrator, a corporate benefits manager, and a private practice clinical psychologist.

PART IV

OTHER ADMINISTRATIVE ACTIVITIES

11

MANAGING A PROFESSIONAL ASSOCIATION

RAYMOND D. FOWLER

American Psychological Association, Washington, DC 20002

INTRODUCTION

Very few people, if any, enter the field of psychology to become association executives, and fewer still take graduate courses designed to train them for such a position. But graduate work in psychology, particularly in the applied areas such as clinical, counseling, and industrial–organizational psychology, is excellent preparation for managing a professional organization. This chapter considers some of the unique challenges and opportunities of managing a professional association and how psychology training can contribute to the effectiveness of an association executive.

ASSOCIATIONS

The French writer Alexis de Tocqueville who visited the United States in 1835 noted the American tendency to band together in voluntary association:

Americans of all ages, all conditions, and all dispositions constantly form associations. They have not only commercial and manufacturing companies, in which all take part, but associations of a thousand other kinds, religious, moral, serious, futile, general or restricted, enormous or diminutive. (1835)

No other country has an association sector as well developed as the United States. Seven out of ten adult Americans belong to at least one association and one out of four belong to four or more. The United States currently has more than 23,000 national associations and more than 141,000 state, local, and regional associations or chapters (Ernstthal & Jones, 1996).

Associations exist for a great variety of purposes. The most common types are trade associations and professional associations. *Trade associations,* which evolved from the medieval merchant guilds, have companies or businesses as members. Members of *professional associations* are individuals who voluntarily come together to promote their professional interests. This chapter focuses on professional associations. Although such groups vary greatly, they have some elements in common.

THE PROFESSIONAL ASSOCIATION

Professional associations can trace their roots back to the late Renaissance when scientific societies were formed to collect and disseminate knowledge (Ernstthal & Jones, 1996). The oldest American scientific society, the American Philosophical Society, was founded by Benjamin Franklin in 1743. The American Association for the Advancement of Science was founded in 1780 and represented most of the scientific disciplines until the last half of the nineteenth century when a number of other scientific and professional societies were formed.

The term *professional association* encompasses those societies that strive to advance the body of knowledge in their fields, to keep their members informed of professional developments, and to provide a variety of services to their members and to the general public. They include scientific societies such as the American Chemical Society and the American Psychological Association, medical societies such as the American Medical Association and the American Psychiatric Association, and learned societies such as the Modern Languages Association and the American Philosophical Association.

Elements of a Professional Association

The principal elements of a professional association are *membership, leadership, governance, executive, staff,* and the *public.* The roles and responsibilities of each element should be clearly differentiated.

Membership: The members of the association, who may be classified according to level, such as full members, less than full members, and members with distinction, are made up of individuals whose professional qualifications meet the requirements set by the association.

Leadership: The leadership consists of those individuals who take an active part in the association as committee members and volunteers.

Governance: The governance of a professional association consists of members of the leadership who are elected to positions of responsibility. Governance ordinarily centers on a board of directors and officers who are elected by the membership or by representatives of the membership.

Executive: The senior executive of an association may be called director, executive director, or other title, depending on the size and preferences of the association. In this chapter, the term chief executive officer (CEO) will be used. The CEO holds a unique position between the membership and the staff. The CEO's role, which includes both leadership and staff functions, will be examined in some detail in another section.

Staff: The staff of a professional association may or may not be members of the association. Typically, the chief executive of the association, who is selected by the board of directors, selects and supervises the staff members of the association. The CEO and staff members ordinarily do not vote for officers or on structural and policy issues. Their job is to facilitate the work of the officers and to implement the policies determined by the board of directors or the membership.

Public: Making a contribution to the public is an important part of the mission of professional associations. The favorable tax status that many professional associations have is based on their service to the public. Many associations maintain public information programs and some include public members on committees.

Comparisons to Businesses

Professional associations generally have a corporate structure similar to a business, but there are important differences. Ernstthal and Jones (1996) suggest some comparisons:

- Size. Most associations would fit in the small business category. Only 12% of associations have revenues that exceed $10 million annually and only a handful reach the level of mid-sized business (revenues of more than $50 million).
- Mission. The ultimate purpose of a business is profitability. An association may make a profit on some of its operations, but its purposes are generally stated in terms of the advancement of the profession and service to the public.
- Structure. Businesses tend to have a clearly defined hierarchy with power centered at the top and sometimes little input from the owners (stockholders). Associations have a much more diffuse distribution of power in which the members (stakeholders) may participate actively in the governance of the association through committees, representative bodies, and elected officers. The interactions between staff and stakeholders in an association can be quite complex.

- Markets. Business may expand their base of stockholders and customers as they choose. Associations, although they may provide services to the general public have a membership or stakeholder group that is more narrowly defined by their mission statement and their membership requirements.

Although professional associations differ from businesses in significant ways, there is no reason that a professional association cannot be run in an efficient and businesslike manner. Members of a professional association have the right to expect that their dues and the assets of the association will be managed responsibly.

The American Psychological Association: A Case Study

The principles of association management can be best presented in a specific context. As the American Psychological Association (APA) is the association with which I am most familiar, I will draw my examples from my APA experiences. The APA is larger and more complex than most professional associations, but the management principles are similar for all but the very smallest associations.

A Profile of the American Psychological Association

The APA is a scientific and professional association incorporated in the District of Columbia, with a membership of 150,000 members and affiliates. The 85,000 members are mostly doctoral level psychologists employed as faculty members or as practicing psychologists in a variety of settings. The affiliates are mostly graduate students, but there is a significant number of high school teachers of psychology, and 5000 are psychologists in other countries.

The APA has annual revenues in excess of $60 million, about half of which comes from publishing journals and books. Dues account for 19% of the revenues; most of the remainder comes from advertising, the annual convention, grants and contracts, interest, and investment income. The APA is the world's largest behavioral science association.

The APA owns an eleven-story building located near the U.S. Capitol which houses its 500 employees and all central office activities. About 65% of the space is occupied by the APA and the remainder is rented to provide income.

A Brief History of the APA

The APA was founded in 1892 with a membership of 38 and grew very slowly for the next half century. At the beginning of World War II, the membership was only around 3000, and nearly all were college and university faculty members. Only a few APA members were concerned with applications of psychology to human issues.

Almost a third of the members of the APA served in uniform in World War II and many were involved in screening, selection, and placement of military recruits and working with neurological and psychological war casualties. Many veterans who had worked as assistants to these psychologists went to college and graduate school on the G.I. bill and became the first generation of clinical psychologists.

Before 1946, the APA had no central office. Like many other small professional organizations, it was administered out of the office of the Secretary/Treasurer, wherever that person might live or work. In 1946, the association reorganized to take in some smaller groups that had split off from APA. The reorganization (in effect, a merger of several associations), led to a decision to establish, for the first time, a central office, which marked the beginning of the modern APA.

After several moves to larger quarters, the association built and moved into its own building in downtown Washington in 1965. In the following years, two small additional buildings were purchases in Northern Virginia to house the publishing operations and the finance office.

By 1983, the association had achieved a comfortable financial status with three rapidly appreciating Washington-area buildings, a portfolio of equity investments, and a successful publishing business. In 1983, APA purchased *Psychology Today*, a national circulation magazine that had been an important voice for psychology but had fallen on hard financial times. It was generally believed that the magazine could be turned around and made again into an editorial and financial success.

The content of the magazine improved rapidly, but operating costs escalated. The association was saddled with millions of dollars of debt and the net worth of the association steadily drained away. By the late 1980s, the net worth of the association had reached a minus figure, and bankruptcy loomed as a distinct possibility. Selling the buildings was a painful but necessary decision, but the *Psychology Today* drain continued.

In early 1988, the situation reached crisis proportions. The deficit in 1987 had been $6.2 million, more than all of the previous deficits of the association's history combined, and 1988 was projected to be worse. The chief executive officer, having lost the confidence of the board, resigned. The APA had no CEO, no finance officer, heavy debts, and very little respect from its members.

My first experience in assuming management duties for APA began in 1988. As president and chairman of the board of directors in 1988, I shared with the board the responsibility of rebuilding a badly damaged organization. We instituted a series of drastic measures including a freeze on expenditures, salaries, and new hires. In May 1988, *Psychology Today* was sold. By the end of 1988, the finances of the association had been brought under control, and the association began to dig out of the financial ruin that it had faced. A search was initiated for a new CEO. I was invited to be a candidate, and in June 1989, I was selected as the new chief executive officer.

MANAGING APA

My background before becoming CEO of APA was seven years as director of a university-based psychological clinic, and 20 years as a psychology department chairman. I had been on the APA board of directors for 10 years, four of those as treasurer. It was my feeling, as I moved into the position, that my administrative experience and my APA experience would be useful, but that my training as a psychologist was the basic skill that I brought into the job. The organization was beset by financial and organizational problems, but it also faced serious morale problems. Its members were hurt, angry, and disaffected and its staff was in disarray. Recovery would involve listening to the members, leaders, and staff and rebuilding their trust and loyalty by giving them an organization they could respect and of which they could be proud.

The Initial Challenges

In my first year as CEO I focused on three major problems: finances, membership retention, and a permanent home for the APA. The first task was to stabilize the association's finances. The financial crisis in 1987 and 1988 had revealed that APA's financial management system was inadequate. Consultants were brought in to develop a new system. Drastic cutbacks, including salary and hiring freezes had resulted in a surplus for 1989 of $1.6 million, and demonstrated that the association was once again able to manage finance responsibly.

The second goal was to maintain the membership base. By 1987, disputes between academic and applied members of the association had erupted into open conflict. The failure of an effort, primarily led by academic members, to reorganize the association into a loose confederation had led to formation of a rival psychology organization, the American Psychological Society (APS). Their aim of attracting 20,000 members raised the specter that we might have two psychological organizations, one representing academicians, the other representing practitioners, and neither able to speak for psychology as a whole. Losing 20,000 members would mean the loss of three to $4 million in dues, a potentially crippling blow. But the loss of a unified voice for psychology would be even worse.

To prevent membership decline, we initiated an aggressive campaign to recruit and retain members. The campaign showed impressive results, and the membership of APA continued to increase. Most APA members who joined APS, retained their APA membership as well.

The third goal was to find a permanent home for APA. The sale of the buildings to cover *Psychology Today* debts had relegated APA to the status of a tenant in the buildings it had formerly owned. The District of Columbia government, not eager to lose a large employer, made it possible for APA to acquire a desirable site next to Union Station below market price, and also offered property tax abatements worth millions. A partnership was established with a nationally prominent real estate developer, and during 1989 the building program went into high gear.

The building was completed at the end of 1991, and was fully leased soon afterward. We were able to move in just as 1992, the Association's centennial year, began. The cash flow from our investment in the building, over $1 million a year, relieved the pressure to increase dues, thus helping us retain members. In 1997, we completed a second building to provide additional income and to provide space for future growth. The APA currently has assets valued at $50 million.

ROLE OF THE ASSOCIATION EXECUTIVE

The chief executive of a professional association is the principal link between the association's governance and its staff. An association executive is first of all a people manager who works actively with the membership, leadership, governance, staff, and the public. Psychological training and experience may be useful in each of these areas of responsibility. Some of the issues involved in working effectively with each of these elements are presented next.

Membership

Associations, if they are to survive, must be dedicated to meeting the needs of the members. The association ultimately belongs to the members, and their decisions, whether expressed directly or through elected representatives, set the policies and direction of the association. Typically, members are entitled to vote for the association's leadership and for major changes in the organization. Most importantly, they vote by their decision to join and to remain as members. Unlike charities, the recipients of whose services ordinarily have little or nothing to say about the structure and leadership of the organization, association members have full control of the association. If the members are dissatisfied, they can impact the organization by voting to change its structure or leadership, or they can simply leave.

Whether the members are measured in dozens or in thousands, the executive must establish a relationship with the membership. This is done principally by being aware of the needs of the members and communicating this understanding to them.

Because the CEO may never meet most of the members, especially in large associations, it is important to understand the networks that exist and to be sure that the contact is made, if not with each individual member, then at least with some of the leaders who may be more directly in touch with the membership. For example, since APA has divisions, chapters, and affiliate organizations, I try to keep in touch with the elected officers of those groups and to encourage them to let me know when there are problems.

When members see that the executive is accessible, understanding, and eager to communicate, they are likely to feel positively toward the organization. The executive is wise to remember that the organization belongs to the members. The executive's ideas, however good, are not worth much unless they are consistent with the needs of the members and are supported by them.

Keeping the lines of communication open to the members is an important part of the CEO's role. Information to members is often provided through newsletters and other association publications. The CEO should have some personal visibility (but not too much). One of the ways I have made myself familiar to the membership is to have a regular column in APA's newspaper, to make many of the information items to the membership, such as dues renewal notices, in the form of a letter from me, and to be actively involved in the annual convention and at other large gatherings of psychologists. I read and respond to every letter I receive from a member, and I include my address, telephone number, and e-mail address in every communication with members. That may sound like an invitation to be overwhelmed by correspondence, but in fact members rarely abuse the opportunity to communicate.

Leadership

All members are important to the organization, but in every association there is a subset of members who are more interested, who volunteer, and who assume positions of leadership. Leaders are vital to the association and to the executive in a number of ways.

First, leaders contribute many hours of work that the association would have difficulty affording if it had to be done by paid employees. Volunteers are a major resource to associations. Skillfully used, their work can greatly benefit the association.

Second, as people who represent the membership and who are also closely in touch with the capabilities and limitations of the association, they can help the association set realistic priorities and help communicate these to other members. When people with expertise in a particular area are selected for a committee to develop policy or products in that area, the association has the benefit of both their skills and their ability to reflect accurately the views of other members.

Committees are essential to the operation of a membership-driven association, but they can also place a burden on the staff. Bright, creative, and committed members can generate many new projects that require more work from the staff. Committee meetings, which may bring in members from around the country, often take place on week-ends, requiring staff to extend already full work weeks into six or even seven days. The CEO and the board of directors need to be careful to balance the need for member participation with the need to use staff time wisely.

The APA, with several hundred member-volunteers, reached the point where groups were meeting almost every weekend and staff members and managers were pushed to the limit to prepare for meetings, attend them, and still get their normal work done. As an experiment, I proposed one year to schedule all major boards and committees to meet on the same weekend in the fall and spring. This pattern, which came to be called consolidated meetings, relieved the pressure on staff and management and also improved the communication and cooperation among the committees. Some members initially objected to the change, but none would now want to go back to the old way of operating.

Governance

The principal governing body of a professional association is the senior policy-making body of the association—the group that makes the final decisions. When the body is large, a management committee may carry the day-to-day responsibilities, but final authority still rests with the senior policy-making body.

The principal governing body and the management committee are typically presided over by the chief elected officer of the association. The larger body may have representatives elected by the membership at large, or they may be elected by interest groups or geographically based chapters or affiliates. The chief executive may be a member of both the principal governing body and the management committee, but typically does not have a vote. Staff members do not ordinarily serve on either body. An executive who fails to develop a productive, mutually satisfying relationship with the governance has little chance of accomplishing his or her objectives or of surviving long as an executive.

Like the federal government, the governance of an association has a complex system of checks and balances that helps make the system operate fairly and democratically. Because of its complexity, many members of an association are not aware of how the parts of the structure operate together and exercise control over each other. Associations differ from each other in specifics, but the structure of APA is not atypical of professional membership associations.

First of all, APA is a corporation with a mission statement. The mission statement as expressed in the articles of incorporation and bylaws determines and limits the kind of activities in which APA can engage. Fortunately, the limits are broad, but they are binding. The law requires that an association honestly state its mission and that its operations be consistent with that mission statement. The mission of APA is to promote psychology as a science and profession in the public interest.

An association's bylaws take precedence over all other internal rules. Typically, they can only be amended by vote of the membership. APA's by-laws have remained fundamentally unchanged since they were ratified by the members a half-century ago. They establish the major structural units of APA: the council of representatives, which is the principal governing body, the board of directors, which serves as the management committee, the officers, the standing boards and committees, the chief executive officer, and the central office.

The Council of Representatives

Most larger professional associations have a representative body that is elected by the membership. This body (which may be called the governing council, council of representatives, house of delegates, etc.) may range in size from around 30 to more than 100 members. APA's major legislative and policy-setting body, the council of representatives, meets twice each year to deal with major financial and policy issues. The 125 members of the council are elected by the state and provincial associations (SPPAs) and by the 50 divisions that represent the substantive interests of the members.

The bylaws invest the council with extensive authority to determine the policies of the association. The council has "full power and authority over the affairs and funds of the Association . . . including the power to review, upon its own initiative, the actions of any board, committee, division, or affiliated group." Other groups within the governance have important functions, but only the council can set policy and appropriate funds.

As CEO, I serve as a nonvoting member of the council of representatives and participate actively in its annual meetings. The council often directs the CEO to gather information, make recommendations, or assign specific tasks to the staff. In the weeks before a council meeting, much of my time is spent working with staff to prepare agenda items and reports and developing recommendations to the council dealing with current issues. Between the fall and spring council meetings, I keep the council informed of major developments and respond to individual requests and questions.

The council receives and approves an annual budget of more than $64 million. Council members cannot be expected to examine all of the thousands of items that make up such a large budget, so it depends on the chief financial officer and the CEO to construct the budget, the finance committee to review it in detail, and the board of directors to oversee the budget process. But the council has the final authority on all expenditures and on all policy.

Like most legislative bodies, the council is a lively debating society in which the views of representatives are expressed with passion, conviction, and sometimes, eloquence.

The Board of Directors

As most professional associations have large boards of directors to ensure broad representation, most also have a management or executive committee to oversee the CEO and the central office. The APA executive committee, which is called the board of directors, is authorized by the bylaws to "exercise general supervision over the affairs of the Association." In any association, the board plays such a unique and central role that understanding how it operates requires a close-up examination.

The APA board of directors has twelve members, six of whom are the officers: the president, president-elect, past president, recording secretary, treasurer, and the chief executive officer (who serves without vote). The other six are members at large from the council of representatives. All but the three presidential officers, who are elected by the entire membership, are elected by the council. The president chairs both the council and the board of directors.

The APA's board of directors manages the affairs of the association, subject to the periodic approval of the council. In its corporate role, the board oversees the business of the association much like the board of any corporation. With the advice and assistance of the finance committee, which is elected by the council and the treasurer, the board presents an annual budget for the approval of council and monitors any major deviations from the budget during the year. The board has the authority to act for the council between its semiannual meetings.

Managing the affairs of a multimillion dollar corporation that is also a complex membership organization requires the board to make many decisions, but because the bylaws give the council final authority over the policies and finances of the association, most of these decisions require council approval. The ability of the board to exercise its administrative and supervisory responsibility thus rests not on the inherent power of the board but on its effectiveness in understanding the needs of the association, determining how those needs might best be met, and making decisions and recommendations acceptable to the council and the membership.

How does the board achieve these objectives? Understanding the needs of the association requires every board member to review an enormous amount of information. As the body to which virtually all governance groups, such as boards, committees, and task forces, report, the board receives, synthesizes, and mediates all information and recommendations from those groups, frequently referring the recommendation of one group to another for comments. Each board member takes particular responsibility for several of these groups and attends their meetings as a liaison of the board.

Another important function of the board is the evaluation of the CEO. Some associations are hesitant to evaluate the CEO, perhaps fearing that this would threaten the CEO or imply a lack of confidence. In fact, a regular evaluation and full feedback is very helpful to a CEO. If the board neglects this responsibility, the CEO may be confronted, too late, by dissatisfactions that board members have kept to themselves. A regular and thorough CEO evaluation helps to keep the lines of communication open between the CEO and the board. Each year, the APA recording secretary distributes copies of the CEO evaluation form to the council, the executive staff, and the board. The results are tabulated and mean scores for each group are obtained. This serves as the basis for a detailed discussion between the CEO and the board. If there are problems, this provides an opportunity to resolve them and to make plans to avoid them in the future.

Early in my tenure as CEO, the board made it clear as a part of their evaluation that they wanted me to provide them with much more detailed information between meetings. After I began sending them regular updates, first by memorandum and later by e-mail, they indicated by their ratings that they were satisfied with the information they were receiving.

At its bimonthly meetings, the board also receives the CEO's reports on central office operations and hears directly from many of the senior staff members. In addition, all board members have large networks, including the divisions, the state associations, council representatives, and individual members with whom they regularly communicate in order to reflect the views of various constituencies of the association.

Determining how the needs of the association may best be met requires the board to understand and balance the recommendations of all of the constituent groups in the context of the information they receive and the resources of the association. Debates within the board often consist of board members forcefully presenting the divergent views of the various constituent groups. The board then tries to craft its recommendations to the council in a way that respects the diversity of views, the existing policies of the association, the bylaws, and the available resources.

The relationship of the CEO to the board of directors is a particularly important one, as both have major responsibilities for keeping the association operating smoothly. According to the Board of Directors' handbook, the board "refrains from interfering with the CEO's management prerogatives, while the CEO defers to the Board in all policy matters." The board generates policy and recommends it to the council. The CEO is responsible for implementing the policy decisions. This arrangement frees the board and council from day-to-day personnel and management decisions and gives the CEO broad responsibility for operating APA according to the mandate of the members, the council, and the board.

Officers

All officers are important, but the CEO is likely to work particularly closely with the president and the treasurer. Presidents vary in the degree to which they involve themselves in policy development, management, and the politics of the organization. It is important for the executive to develop a positive, cooperative relationship with the president and it is the executive's responsibility to make sure that happens. Because the president and the executive are often the most publicly visible members of the association, it is important to avoid any appearance of a power struggle or a role conflict. The executive should defer to the president on all policy issues and facilitate the president's role as spokesperson for the association. It is important for the executive to spend some time with the president to define roles in a way that is mutually acceptable.

I have made a special effort to maintain close communication with each of the nine APA presidents with whom I have worked. Although we may already be well acquainted through APA work, I have found it useful also to have a long conversation with each new president about how we will work together. Presidents vary in their work styles. Some like to answer every letter, others like responses drafted for them. Some like to make public appearances, others do not. Some are able to spend a lot of time on association business and others have other responsibilities that limit their availability. It is usually not difficult to accommodate the different styles, but it is always important to know about them.

In some associations, including the APA, the treasurer plays an important role as a link between the CEO, the board, and the membership on financial issues. It is important for the treasurer to communicate with the leadership and with the membership, and the CEO should be sure that the proper information is provided. No secrets should be kept from the treasurer. Whether financial news is good or bad, it is essential that the treasurer be given ample notice and assisted in communicating the news to the membership. The treasurer, as a link to the leadership and the membership, can be a valuable ally.

Staff

The staff of a professional association can range from an executive and a few support persons to a staff of hundreds, but the goal is the same: to create a smoothly functioning team that works with the CEO to meet the needs of the association. With almost 500 employees, the APA central office provides staff for all the boards and committees, runs a large publishing and scientific database operation, invests in stocks, manages real estate, operates a computer center, publishes a monthly newspaper, and interacts with a great many private, state, and federal organizations and agencies.

It is important for each CEO to build a comfortable and congenial management structure. Some CEOs develop a horizontal structure in which many staff members report directly to the CEO; at the other end of the continuum, some CEOs prefer only one direct report, usually a deputy CEO. I prefer something between those two extremes.

Because the APA has a large staff, the administrative and supervisory responsibilities are spread among a large number of managers. The top managers, who report directly to the CEO, the executive management group (EMG), acts as a cabinet. In addition to operating their respective departments, they provide general advice and consultation on the operation of the central office as a whole. In addition to the CEO and the deputy CEO, the EMG includes the Executive Directors of each of the major functional areas and other key administrative staff. The major program areas of APA are divided into four directorates that focus on services to particular constituencies: education, practice, science, and public interest. There are also three offices that serve all of the membership: finance/administration, communications, and central programs. Other key staff members who serve on the EMG are the general counsel, the director of public communications, and the senior director for governance affairs. All other employees report to one or another of the members of the EMG.

Board members are involved in many aspects of the association's business so they have frequent contact with staff members. Because staff members report to the CEO, it is important that board members who need staff support request this from the CEO or someone designated by the CEO, such as a deputy, and not directly from the staff member. Similarly, governance members who are dissatisfied with the performance of a staff member should make this known to the CEO rather than confronting the staff member directly, as this would create confused lines of supervision. It is the responsibility of the CEO to ensure that the staff performs at a high level and it is to the CEO that governance members should look when there are problems with staff support.

The Public

Many associations receive special tax advantages because they provide services important to the general public. In turn, most associations include service to the public as part of their mission. Serving the public also benefits the profession. When public leaders and policy makers understand and appreciate the role of the profession, the profession benefits through favorable treatment in the laws and regulatory standards established for the profession, more funds for training programs, and greater use by citizens of the professional services of the members.

SOME REFLECTIONS ON BEING AN ASSOCIATION EXECUTIVE

Some association chief executives focus on internal management, others on working with leadership and governance, and still others on advocacy and relationships with external groups. None of these strategies, if pursued to the exclusion of the others, will result in a successful tenure as CEO. The association executive must focus on all three strategies and work continuously to achieve a balance among them.

Even associations that have few staff members need to have personnel policies that are clearly stated, communicated with the staff, and in compliance with relevant laws and regulations. Because association staff members often operate in the background and get little public recognition, it is important for the CEO and other managers to recognize their achievements and reward them accordingly. An effective staff helps to make an effective association.

There is no substitute for a well-qualified chief financial officer. Associations too small to afford a CFO may "rent" those services from an association management firm or use consultants, but the non-business-trained CEO who tries to be a chief financial officer may be doing the association a disservice.

Associations are governed by most of the laws and regulations that govern businesses and there are, in addition, special laws that apply to associations. Because it is almost impossible for a CEO to keep up with the legal complexities, it is important to have a general counsel who is well versed in business and association law. Larger organizations may have in-house counsel, but every association should have available to it legal counsel familiar with the association and its bylaws. Errors made in complying with financial, personnel, and tax issues can be ruinous to an association that lacks appropriate legal advice.

The favored tax status granted to many associations under the IRS regulations confers both advantages and limitations. Associations that have primarily scientific and educational purposes may be eligible for classification under the IRS code as 501(c)(3) organizations. This means that contributions to them are tax deductible (by the member), and they have the benefit of favorable postage rates. This also means that they are allowed to lobby but only to a limited degree, and they are precluded from any involvement in supporting or opposing candidates for election, directly or indirectly. Involvement in elections is the "third rail" for associations. A 501(c)(3) organization that assists or contributes to a candidate, however indirectly, can lose its tax-exempt status and be heavily fined. Associations classified under 501(c)(4)(5) or (6) have more political freedom but fewer tax advantages. Associations may seek a less restrictive tax category, but they must scrupulously comply with the rules that apply to their particular status.

The Relevance of Psychological Training

In what ways has my psychological training assisted me in managing the operations of APA? First, it may have helped me make a realistic appraisal of my limitations. Nothing in my training and experience prepared me to manage the finance office, the publications office, and the management information systems, or to oversee building over $100,000,000 in office buildings. I could not be a micromanager. It was essential to build a team of managers that I could totally trust and give them considerable independence and authority to run their departments. As trust was a major issue, I made the decision that the degree to which I could form a positive personal relationship with each manager was as important as the skills and abilities of the manager.

In selecting each member of the management team, I paid careful attention to evidence of competence, but I also attended carefully to evidence that the candidate's personal traits and characteristics would contribute to positive team building and not detract from the cooperative relationships among the other team members. I felt that years of interviewing, diagnosing, and counseling individuals with significant personality problems helped me be alert to evidence of traits that might interfere with the kind of team I wanted to build.

Despite the reputed unreliability of letters of reference, I found them a useful way to see how those who knew the candidate best reacted to the candidate, not just in terms of competence but in terms of personal characteristics as well. It is not surprising that most references rate the candidate in the top 10%; candidates rarely include among their references people who are not enthusiastic about them. I generally ignore the quantitative comments of that kind and instead read between the lines for more qualitative descriptions of behavior. A recommendation on one candidate said "A rope holder for me is the kind of person who, if you were hanging over a cliff, you would want to be holding your rope: this man is a rope holder." A recommendation on another candidate said "Absolutely brilliant; has no patience with people who don't think as fast." Since I knew what kind of team I wanted to build and the kind of relationships I wanted to foster among my managers, the decision was easy.

My management style was heavily influenced by my training in psychotherapy and particularly by the work of Carl Rogers. The idea of being a CEO who strikes terror into the hearts of staff or who goads staff into ever higher levels of performance has no appeal to me. I make every effort to select people who are self-starters and who are highly motivated to perform at a high level. If I had a manager who needed to be goaded or terrorized in order to perform, I would conclude that I had made a bad selection. Fortunately, that has not happened. I am much more likely to try to get managers to lighten up and take some time off than to spur them on to more work.

Listening is a skill that most psychologists learn and it is certainly one of the most important skills for an association executive. I listen carefully to my managers and try to be sure I understand what they are telling me. They have the direct face-to-face experiences in their respective areas that I need to understand if I am to make reasonable decisions. I seek every opportunity to recognize and express appreciation for the accomplishments of the executive staff; because they are competent and conscientious, the opportunities are easy to find. When a manager is having difficulties, I start out by determining the manager's perception of the situation and his or her plans for resolving them. I rarely suggest a course of action unless asked. I respect their judgment and believe they are more likely to solve problems in their own style than mine. It has rarely happened that a problem has not been amenable to this relatively nondirective approach.

CONCLUSION

Although associations are subject, as are all human systems, to occasional malfunctions, the general structure works pretty well to accomplish their purposes. The ultimate power resides, as it should, in the membership, and there are numerous levels of checks and balances to ensure that power is exercised responsibly. Winston Churchill, among others, has been quoted as saying that democracy is a terrible system of government unless you compare it with all of the others. The typical association structure may not be the simplest way of doing business, but it ensures a high level of fairness and shared responsibility.

The nonprofit sector is a strong and rapidly growing sector of this economy. As state and federal funds decline, many of society's problems will be addressed by volunteer work through nonprofit organizations. Professional associations employ hundreds of thousands of employees at all levels. Association management can be a challenging and rewarding career for a psychologist.

REFERENCES

de Tocqueville, A. (1835). *Democracy in America.* New York: J&HG Langley.
Ernstthal, H. L., & Jones, B. (1996). *Principles of association management* (3rd ed.). Washington, DC: American Society of Association Executives.

BIOGRAPHY

Raymond D. Fowler Raymond D. Fowler, Ph.D., is executive vice president and chief executive officer of the American Psychological Association (APA). He received his B.A. and M.A. from the University of Alabama and his Ph.D. in clinical psychology from Pennsylvania State University in 1957. As APA's CEO, he directs the operations of a central office staff of 500, serving a national and international membership of 155,000 members and affiliates. Dr. Fowler has been active in APA governance since 1965, serving as a member of the APA Board of Directors since 1979, as treasurer from 1983–1987, and as APA's 97th president in 1988. Dr. Fowler is active in international psychology and serves as treasurer of the International Association of Applied Psychology.

12

MANAGING A PSYCHOLOGY INTERNSHIP PROGRAM

ANTONETTE M. ZEISS

VA Palo Alto Health Care System, Psychology Service,
Palo Alto, California 94304

INTRODUCTION

I am the director of two training programs in a Department of Veterans' Affairs health facility. One is a psychology internship program, which also offers practicum training and a small number of postdoctoral training positions. The second is an interprofessional program (the Interprofessional Team Training and Development Program) which funds not only psychology interns but also trainees in pharmacy, social work, nursing, occupational therapy, audiology, and speech pathology. Because future healthcare will almost certainly be organized around interprofessional care (e.g., Pew Health Professions Commission, 1995; A. M. Zeiss, 1997; A. M. Zeiss & Steffen, 1996a), I will draw on experiences in both of these programs to describe the management role and skills needed for a psychologist in a training director position.

The first section of the chapter provides an overview on the specific responsibilities of an internship training director. This includes internal management activities and activities related to the Association of Psychology Postdoctoral and Internship Centers (APPIC) and to obtaining and maintaining training program accreditation from the American Psychological Association (APA) (1996a, 1996b).

The second section presents issues in creating, implementing, and maintaining an interprofessional training environment.

INTERNSHIP TRAINING DIRECTOR

The role of internship in the training of psychologists has been and continues to be a topic of controversy. To put current issues of importance to training directors in perspective, a brief overview of the original conceptualization of internship is presented in contrast to current themes in the operation of internship programs.

Original Conception of Internship Compared to Current Status

In the original development of the scientist–practitioner model ("Boulder model"; Raimy, 1950), the internship was proposed as the source of the majority of clinical training. In the decades immediately following the Boulder conference, many doctoral programs sent students on internship after the third year of training. Interns were expected to develop clinical skills and to develop a richer appreciation of research issues and hypotheses that were based on clinical experience. After internship, the student would return to his or her doctoral program to conduct dissertation research. It was expected that this research would be influenced by both didactic experiences in the doctoral program and clinical experiences at the internship site.

That model is now rare. Very few programs send out interns after three years of doctoral training, or before the dissertation is well under way. Doctoral programs have incorporated more and more clinical training into the preinternship doctoral program in the form of practicum and external placements. It is now typical for intern applicants to have at least 1500 hours of clinical training, and some have far more (I've seen applications reporting 5000 hours of supervised clinical training).

Despite these changes, the model of internship has continued to be predoctoral. That is, in almost all clinical and counseling programs, the doctoral degree is not conferred until internship (as well as all other requirements) has been completed. However, more recently, this remnant of the original conception of internship has been challenged. The Council of University Directors of Clinical Programs (CUDCP), for example, has passed a resolution stating that internship should become a postdoctoral experience (Routh, 1998). In this model, students would complete all course work and the dissertation before embarking on an internship. This model is often (but not always) paired with a call for a two-year postdissertation training experience and a relabeling of the experience from "internship" to "postdoctoral fellowship." In fact, many, if not most, interns do currently go on to a second year of training, usually postdoctoral, before going on the market for a first job and, in many states, before being eligible for licensure.

The original model of internship also called for students to seek internships broadly, based on clinical interests and training needs, rather than necessarily staying in the local area. This aspect of internship remains the same, although with variability across programs. Most internship programs receive applications from around the country, and sometimes from other countries, as well as from locally based doctoral training programs. Most doctoral programs have students who stay in the local area and other students who go thousands of miles away to do an internship.

Competition for internships has intensified. Originally, the assumption was that all intern applicants in accredited doctoral training programs would be able to go to an internship position in the year when their program expected the internship experience to be completed. It was expected that interns would receive adequate (though not rich) financial compensation during the internship year. In the last several years, these assumptions have not been met consistently. Currently, there are several hundred more applicants each year for paid internship slots than there are slots available (APPIC, 1997). As a result, many doctoral students each year face the difficult choice of either staying another year to accrue more clinical hours and publications, in order to be more competitive for a paid slot the following year, versus arranging an unpaid internship experience. Either of these options involves major costs and sacrifices to doctoral students. This change is not a result of a reduction in internship sites; the number of sites has grown, albeit slowly. Nor has the change occurred because of an increase in doctoral students in university-based, accredited programs of clinical or counseling psychology. Rather, the change has occurred because of a proliferation of doctoral students from professional schools, that is, free-standing, non-university based clinical training programs (APPIC, 1997).

These changes have led to concerns about the appropriateness of current internship policies and procedures. In addition to the call for a postdoctoral fellowship rather than a predoctoral internship, internships have been challenged to change their selection criteria and processes. There also has been a call (Kihlstrom, 1997) for doctoral training programs to develop their own locally based, funded internship experiences to ensure that all doctoral students have timely access to an internship experience.

In addition to these changes, which emphasize the timing and availability of internship, changes in the field of psychology dictate careful attention to the content of clinical internship. At one time "generalist" training meant obtaining assessment experience and intervention experience in both inpatient and outpatient mental health sites. This conception of generalist training has been challenged on several fronts, sometimes in contradictory ways. On the one hand, there is the recognition that generalist training now involves far more, while simultaneously there is increasing pressure for specialization at the internship level.

Generalist training is now understood to include, in addition to inpatient and outpatient mental health setting experience, experience in medically based settings with exposure to both primary care and specialty care programs. In addition, generalist training encompasses the following elements: 1) a broader life-span perspective, potentially including the whole spectrum from pediatric to geriatric settings; 2) experience in innovative programs that provide alternatives to traditional inpatient settings, such as partial hospitalization programs or dual diagnosis programs; and 3) experience in programs that involve interaction with the full range of healthcare professionals, not just other psychologists and physicians.

At the same time that expectations for generalist training are becoming more complex, pressure for specialty training is intensifying. This is particularly true for neuropsychology training. The requirements for Division 40, the Neuropsychology Division of the American Psychological Association, specify that half of the time during internship should be spent on neuropsychology training, and that one year of full-time neuropsychology training is required in addition for the intern to be eligible to apply for the board certification testing process in neuropsychology established by the American Board of Professional Psychology (Hannay *et al.*, 1997). Pressures for specialization are also growing in geropsychology, behavioral medicine, and rehabilitation psychology (and probably other areas by the time this chapter appears). The internship director needs to provide guidance for the program and for individual interns in dealing with the complexities of balancing the new model of generalist training with the emerging pressures for specialization.

Given these complex and shifting expectations about what an internship should entail and accomplish, the most important qualities an internship training director needs are a vision of the role of internship training and the ability to use available resources to support that vision. I do not mean to imply that the training director dictates to the staff in the training program what the goals must be and what they must do to support those goals. In fact, a training director who tried to operate in this way likely would fail. But the director must be able to articulate a vision of the purpose and philosophy of training; at best, this will represent a consensual view of the training staff as a whole.

A Checklist of Issues and Personal Qualities

In this section, I present issues that training directors need to see clearly so that they can provide leadership for their programs and personal qualities that are particularly functional in dealing with these issues. This is meant to orient training directors to the important issues and qualities they should nurture in themselves.

1. Leadership/Vision. I have already identified what I see as the most important issue for a training director, that is, the responsibility to provide a clear vision of what is most important in the training of psychologists and how to use local resources to support that training. Hand in hand with this go the responsibilities of developing this vision through collaboration with staff of the local program and guiding staff in developing and implementing that shared vision. Implicit in the responsibility of guiding a collaborative process is the need to provide balance in one's own management style as a training director. It is important not to use a micromanagement style, in which staff do not have the opportunity to develop their own ideas and their skills for implementing those ideas. At the same time, it is important not to be too hands off. The training director needs to be an effective and

involved leader, who emphasizes the core values of the program and ensures they are incorporated into training.

2. Flexibility/coping with change. Training directors also need to be good at coping with change, using flexible strategies to pursue goals. For example, as I write this, the VA system in which I work is going through a major change in the way funds for training of psychology interns (and all other associated health professionals) will be allocated across the country (Veterans Health Administration, 1997). A system that had been in place since the 1950s will be fundamentally altered. Training directors who can see the opportunities available in the new system and respond flexibly to the new demands will prosper. Other settings will face different specific changes, but every site will have changes in funding, programs available for training, responding to new APA accreditation requirements, and so on.

3. Interprofessional collaboration. Training directors increasingly need to be astute about interprofessional relationships. They need to be able to work effectively with other components of the healthcare system and to develop collaborative relationships with key leaders of the other professions in their healthcare system. They need to be able to advocate for psychology's role in team delivery of care and to support the roles and responsibilities of other disciplines as well.

4. Scientist–practitioner model. The training director is a visible model and exemplar of the training philosophy of the internship. As such, it is important for the training director to model scientist–practitioner function, not just espouse the ideal (Belar & Perry, 1991). The pressure of administrative responsibilities (usually combined with direct service and/or teaching responsibilities) can make it hard to pursue clinical research, but it is important for interns to see that the combination of clinical service with clinical science is integral to psychology's role and unique value in the healthcare system.

5. Advocacy/gatekeeping. Training directors need to be able to balance advocacy for interns in their program with willingness to be gatekeepers for the profession. Thus, they need to be able to guide tough decisions when interns are not succeeding. I have increasingly come to believe that one of the important functions of internship is to train psychologists for establishing professional roles and dealing effectively with conflict in the work setting. There are difficult people and difficult problems everywhere.

A Checklist of Activities: The "Yearly Round" of the Training Director

The issues just described and the personal qualities recommended for optimal function as a training director play out, to a large extent, in the context of a cycle of repeated activities that need to be carried out in timely fashion. At first, keeping up with the cycle seems effortful and requires continuous conscious thought and planning. Over time, most training directors develop strategies to allow them to go on "automatic pilot" to some extent in carrying out recurring tasks. The following section provides an overview of the flow of activities in our internship program. The details for specific timing of activities will obviously vary by program, but this set of activities will need to occur at some point during the training year for every program. To understand the context for the timing, some basic information on the internship I direct is necessary.

We have a training cycle that begins September 1 and ends August 31. Within that year, the interns have two half-time rotations in the first six months and then switch to two other half-time rotations for the last six months. Interns have a high degree of choice with regard to which rotations are assigned. We ask for mid-rotation evaluations and end of rotation evaluations; at each of these times, interns evaluate their experience with each supervisor and training setting; supervisors also evaluate each intern. They are asked to share their evaluations with each other, as well as turning them in to the training director. If any problems are reported, by either the intern or the supervisor, they are expected to develop a plan for improving the difficulty.

Some aspects of the "yearly round" are continuous throughout the year and require either constant attention or sporadic attention at unpredictable times. These include generating and maintaining funding for the internship, obtaining and maintaining APA accreditation for the program, working with APPIC on intern policies and recruitment procedures, and overseeing didactic training experiences such as seminars and special courses to provide training required for licensure eligibility.

Other activities are more time specific. At the conceptual level, I see the yearly round as guided by the following recurring internship activities: soliciting applications, reviewing applications, selecting interns, preparing new interns for arrival, orienting and socializing new interns, overseeing the rotation cycle (including evaluations), launching interns, and supporting the career development of former interns. Details of the timing of each of these activities, given our internship structure, appear in Table 1.

The most time-consuming activities in the yearly round are those involving intern selection. For our 17 funded internship slots, we receive well over 200 applications each year, or almost 12 applicants per slot; other programs experience similar ratios. All offers are made in accordance with APPIC procedures (Hall, Cantrell, & Boggs, 1997). In 1999, for the first time, these procedures will involve a computer match. The APPIC guidelines call for no early offers to be made and for no prospective interns to be asked for information about their relative ranking of programs to which they are applying. Thus, the selection process stretches from the earliest requests for brochures and application materials until the official "match" day, which traditionally has been the second Monday in February (that may change slightly with the new computer match system).

During this time period, programs must review applications and determine which applicants to consider. The training director must be able to help the program achieve consensus on the desired characteristics of interns and provide leadership on methods for attracting and identifying such applicants. We use the APPIC universal application form, which is available at the APPIC website, with some additional questions asking interns about their interest in specific aspects of our training program.

The APPIC form was developed by accumulating all of the information requested by participants in APPIC internship sites and organizing the information into a single format. It simplifies the lives of intern applicants, because most of the places where they will apply use this form; thus, they only need to fill out one form which can be submitted to multiple sites. However, the form is extremely lengthy and contains much information that is not relevant for most of the sites using it (though desired by another site or group of sites). Thus, we need to wade through a great deal of information to get to the items of interest to us. More importantly, this comprehensive format provides no information to the intern applicant about the specific interests and emphases of each site. An applicant to our program, for example, might erroneously conclude that we will evaluate him or her based on experience in administering an extremely long list of assessment devices, most of which have very limited empirical justification (if any). We use it only because it simplifies the application process for interns, and it does include some information more directly useful to us.

We use a complex computer database system to record relevant information about the applicant's vita and APPIC application form, such as the applicant's dissertation status, publication record, hours of training and supervision, and so on. It takes at least 80 hours to enter all of the data for all applicants.

We interview about 80 to 90 of the 200 applicants. The decision to interview is based on a set of imperfect variables; the most important of these are the graduate program, productivity of the applicant, and the supervision-to-training ratio (i.e., we look for applicants who have had intensive supervision for their training experiences, not the total number of training hours). Letters of recommendation are not considered in inviting interviews, but are reviewed in a later part of the process. Letters of recommendation have, unfortunately, experienced "praise inflation," such that it is rare to get a letter that mentions any concerns about an applicant or that provides any but the most positive ranking of the applicant relative to others the writer has trained. Grade point averages are similarly not useful, as most applicants have very high grade point averages.

Interviews to evaluate intern applicants are controversial. Critics correctly point out that no data support the validity of the interview process to select among highly qualified intern applicants. On the other hand, no alternative criteria have been suggested by which to select among a set of highly qualified candidates, in a system characterized by a lack of candid, accurate information about candidates' strengths and weaknesses from those in their graduate programs who know them best.

We, like many internship programs, use the interview to provide more detailed information about our program to the applicants. We also attend to behavioral cues that might suggest problems—defensiveness, articulating a strongly held theoretical point of view greatly at variance with that of our program, inability to respond to straightforward questions (e.g., about the candidate's dissertation research), and so on. We also look for information that would set some candidates ahead of others in positive ways. For example, I am very interested in hearing candidates dis-

TABLE I   Yearly Round

September
New intern orientation and final processing (see Orientation Planning checklist)
Mail brochures
Intern seminar starts (continues until end of July)
Mail final evaluations to former interns' graduate programs

October
Mail brochures
Handle phone calls and e-mails from prospective interns
APPIC sends material on computer match; review in relation to our needs

November
Send out mid-rotation evaluations in early Nov.; due end of Nov.
Set up intern applicant files and database
Mail brochures; respond to last minute phone and e-mail requests
Read files and enter applicant data in computer database
Meet with Selection Committee; set up dates for selection meetings

December
Complete data entry for intern applicants
Arrange and conduct intern interviews throughout month
Review APPIC match procedures with selection committee

January
Arrange and conduct intern interviews through designated end date
Send early rejection letters
Selection committee meets intensively

February
Selection/Match day
Receive intern acceptance confirmation
Distribute end of rotation evaluations early in month; due at end of month
Letters to schools for Memoranda of Affiliation

March
Intern rotation shift; distribute Tour of Duty forms
Update Welcome Book (sent to new interns)
Set up intern "buddies"; do mailing with names and general info
Send requests to staff for Intern Brochure updates

April
Send Welcome Book to incoming interns
Work on Intern Brochure updates

May
Finish Brochure updates
Start review/revisions of Training Manual
Send out mid-rotation evaluations
Review application format
Review end of year evaluation procedures
APPIC forms for Directory listing arrive; complete revisions

June
Brochure and application to printer
Call incoming interns to arrange rotations; prepare draft of assignments; circulate to supervisors
Send paperwork to incoming interns
Review current interns' leave usage to determine end dates

(continues)

TABLE I *(continued)*

July

    Send Brochures to universities

    End of Year letter to current interns (instructions for processing out of program)

    Complete rotation assignments for incoming interns

    Complete paperwork for incoming interns

    Prepare intern certificates

    "Launching day" for current interns (final seminar session; end-of-year party)

    Complete revisions of Training Manual

August

    Orientation planning/scheduling (separate check list)

    Complete processing details for new interns: keys, mail folders, offices assigned, pages requested, PIN numbers requested, final mailing, etc.

    Mail brochure/packets to new applicants

    Distribute and collect Exit Questionnaire

cuss their vision of the future of psychology, their awareness of problems or controversial issues within psychology (e.g., prescription privileges), and their emerging sense of how they might contribute to the development of the field (rather than simply perpetuating and using what they are taught). Does such information provide a valid basis for choosing among intern applicants? Clearly it is limited and there is no research evidence to support such procedures. We have not yet found a better alternative.

Another objection to interviewing applicants for internship is that the cost of arranging travel to multiple internship sites is a great hardship on interns financially, and it takes them away from their programs precisely at the time when they should be deeply engrossed in their dissertation research. These are valid concerns, and any training director needs to be flexible in balancing the need for information about applicants with the costs to applicants. When we invite interviews, we specify that these can either be face-to-face or by telephone, and that the mode of the interview has no direct impact on our decision-making process. We do make offers every year to interns we have interviewed by phone and to those who visited in person. We find that most applicants choose to come in person, despite our offer of an alternative. There seem to be two reasons for this. The first comes from the applicants' sense that internship year is an important time and therefore they need to have as much information about the program as possible; this is logical and reasonable. The second is that many applicants are convinced that they will only be considered if they visit in person. Sometimes these beliefs are reinforced by faculty in their graduate programs. Greater dialog between graduate programs and internship programs is needed to clear up misconceptions and to support each other in the difficult process of matching intern applicants to internship sites.

After intern selection, intern orientation is probably the next most time-consuming task. We have a detailed checklist for the many activities that must be planned and orchestrated for orientation of new interns. Conceptually, these activities fall into four categories: handling prearrival preparations for getting interns hired and on payroll, planning orientation activities, actual hiring of interns and putting them on payroll, and creating a welcoming environment. Our sequence is shown in Table 2 in some detail (I have tried to remove items that are too specific to our setting, but many still may not be relevant for all internships). Some of these preparations are handled by the training director, others by an orientation committee, and still others by secretarial support staff; how these responsibilities are distributed depends on local resources.

To understand some items on this orientation checklist, it may be helpful to know that all interns spend four days to a week together as a group to be oriented to our internship, the local VA healthcare system, the national VA system, and the local area. We emphasize interns getting to know each other and as many staff as possible, and we try to establish a welcoming environment that will promote cooperation and bonding among interns and across interns and staff. Interns are introduced to each other and various training staff in the course of a variety of activities designed to acquaint them with a new environment. They go on scavenger hunts to learn how to find things in our very spread-out hospital and clinic environment, have lunch with staff, explore the surrounding community, go through training on the local computer system, and so on. They go through an exercise de-

TABLE 2 Intern Orientation Planning: Preparation Checklist

Activity	When
1. Send mailing re. orientation schedule	July
2. Begin intern start-up paperwork	July
3. Work out planned rotations	end of July
4. Order keys	August
5. Determine offices	August
6. Order PIN #s for phone access	August
7. Arrange access codes for DHCP/e-mail	August
8. Arrange pagers	August
9. Set up orientation week schedule	August
10. Schedule rooms for orientation	August
11. Arrange materials for orientation	August
12. Arrange support staff for orientation	August
13. Distribute flyer & e-mail message to staff for intern welcoming party	August
14. Monitor completion of paperwork; plan time in orientation week schedule for any completions	August
15. Schedule photographer for first day of orientation	August
16. Arrange hospital orientation coverage	August
17. Order first day lunch	August
18. Get food, coffee for first day AM	September
19. During orientation week, schedule picture badge photos	September

signed to elicit their hopes and fears about the internship year, in an enjoyable context without pressure for revealing more than they feel safe to say. They also meet with interns from the previous year who are still in the area (e.g., doing post-docs). Traditionally, no staff are present at that meeting.

At the end of the week, there is a party at the home of one of the training staff, attended by staff, new interns, and previous interns. The following week, interns start their clinical experiences, but they continue to meet as a group on Wednesday afternoons for a seminar and an optional, confidential group meeting to discuss the process of internship. That group is led by a psychologist who is not a VA employee or part of the training staff.

A Checklist of Activities: Important Noncyclical Activities for the Training Director

Not all responsibilities of the training director fall easily into the yearly round structure. Four major issues that training directors must be ready to handle whenever they arise are APA reviews for program accreditation, dealing with interns who are not successfully completing the internship, dealing with supervisors who are not functioning effectively with interns, and dealing with changes in the intern structure as a result of larger systems' issues (e.g., closing of programs, loss of staff).

Attention to APA credentialing reviews is crucial. Most years, an annual report will be due at the start of July for APA-approved programs. More thorough reviews occur at intervals determined by the outcome of the last APA review; the maximum interval between reviews is five years. Credentialing is handled through the APA Education Directorate by the Office of Program Consultation and Accreditation (APA, 1996a, 1996b). It is wise to work proactively and collaboratively with the staff of this office. They are helpful and knowledgeable, and they want to make sure you are treated fairly in the accreditation process.

Dealing with intern failure or unethical behavior is probably the most wrenching and difficult issue for any training director. Gatekeeping for the profession is one of the responsibilities of internship training programs. Not everyone is suited to become a professional psychologist. Some interns run into trouble because of an inability to develop adequate skills in professional activities. Others display unethical behavior or cannot behave responsibly because of their own problems, such as substance abuse or emotional difficulties. When an intern encounters difficulties, the training director can help to normalize the experience and guide the intern in working out effective strategies in the immediate situation.

The process of dealing with intern difficulties should be fair and follow a planned method of handling problems, and it should involve collaborative decision making with all those involved with the intern who is having problems. In responding to supervisors' concerns about interns, the opposite side of this, advocacy for interns, is equally important. Interns have little power and can be taken advantage of by supervisors, caught up in turf battles within or across programs, and so on. The training director is in an excellent position to support the intern and to offer helpful guidance in difficult situations. Ideally, the intern can be encouraged to see this as part of training by seeing how such strategies need to become part of his or her set of professional skills, to be called on throughout his or her career.

It is crucial that due process procedures for intern problem review be established and documented so that they can be utilized if they are needed. These due process procedures ideally should be reviewed by all the program staff and representatives of the intern group on a frequent basis. The procedures should ensure that arbitrary decisions cannot be made by any individual and that interns cannot be treated punitively. At the same time, these procedures need to allow staff to make painful decisions in a fair, responsible way.

Some resources for developing due process guidelines are available. APPIC has a review of issues to consider in developing guidelines and examples of due process cases at the professional level (unfortunately, both cases as of this writing concern medical students, not psychology interns). The guidelines are on the APPIC web site (*webmaster@appic.org*) or available through the APPIC office. A thoughtful review of due process issues is provided in Lamb, Cochran, and Jackson (1991). Finally, Dougher, Callaghan, and Follette (1998) discuss problems that can arise in handling potential intern deficiencies when multiple supervisors conflict in their messages to therapists in training. Although the authors' emphasis is not on due process per se, the issues they discuss are helpful in considering how an intern might be labeled as problematic by one supervisor and not by another, thus underscoring the need for thoughtful, collaborative, and fair decision making when one supervisor believes that an intern should fail the internship experience.

Dealing with an ineffective supervisor is in many ways parallel to dealing with a problematic intern, but not entirely. Just as with interns, some supervisors may be perceived as ineffective and even destructive by some interns, while receiving praise from other interns. In most settings, however, there is no parallel devastating consequence for the supervisor like that of failing the internship. It is the responsibility of the training director to review evaluations of supervisors at least yearly and to handle consistently reported problems in a direct fashion. Although it is not pleasant to raise this type of problem with one's colleagues, the training director can approach supervisors with data on how they are perceived and in a collegial spirit effectively work out ways to improve the situation. Supervisors who continue to receive poor ratings, even after constructive efforts, may need to be told that they will no longer have interns assigned to them. Supervisors who do not cooperate with important program elements (e.g., respecting time constraints of interns or submitting paperwork) will also need attention from the training director, even if their intern ratings are positive.

Finally, training directors are plagued by changes, no matter how effectively they organize and run their programs. Wonderful supervisors resign. Good programs get reorganized or cut because of broader system decisions. Criteria for obtaining funding change, resulting in the redesign of intern assignment options. State laws may change in ways that influence which staff are eligible to be supervisors (e.g., California law has declared that only training hours accrued with supervisors who have been licensed for at least three years count toward licensure). When these changes occur, the need for flexibility and creativity becomes immediately obvious. At such times, training directors need good support systems and the ability to focus energy immediately on the issue at hand. A sense of humor and a willingness to see change as opportunity (not only as hassle) are other useful attributes to have at such times.

Committee Structure and Internship Training

Training directors can not carry out by themselves all of the activities that have been described, and it would not be wise to try. Internships thrive when the entire staff feels committed to the program and participates in decision making and in whatever work is required. At our program, we use a committee structure to involve a large number of staff in the recurring tasks of internship. Membership on these committees is by invitation of the training director, with volunteers encouraged. Almost all committees have intern members as well as staff members.

There is one overarching Training Committee, which takes responsibility for overall planning and program direction. That committee has membership from all of the constituencies of the program. In our case, that means there are representatives from inpatient mental health, outpatient mental health, behavioral medicine, neuropsychology, geropsychology, rehabilitation psychology, and specialty programs in post traumatic stress disorder (PTSD), family therapy, and substance abuse. Representatives of clinical areas are also chosen to provide representation of different theoretical orientations and research areas. The Training Committee meets one or two times each month and members of the committee generally also serve on other committees with more specific foci: evaluation, seminars, program review, orientation, research, and intern selection. The more specific committees have intern members as well as staff members.

The evaluation committee develops procedures for continuous mutual evaluation by interns and their supervisors. They develop the forms to be used and help prepare interns for the process of honestly and openly evaluating their supervisors. This committee is also working to develop methods for evaluating Exit Competencies, as mandated by the APA. Internship programs (like doctoral programs) have been asked to become more specific in defining their outcome objectives and developing methods to assess behaviorally whether those objectives have been accomplished with each intern. This is a worthy goal, but a complex and difficult task. Training directors have been wrestling with this mandate, sharing strategies and seeking additional guidance from APA. Our committee has developed a model protocol for measurement of Exit Competencies in behavioral medicine. It is currently being piloted and will then be expanded to other settings when the data suggest it can be used reliably.

The seminar committee develops the conceptual framework for the intern seminar series, which runs throughout the training year, and helps the training director arrange speakers, evaluations, payment for outside speakers, and so on. The seminar is used to provide training experiences necessary for licensure. In California this includes training in child abuse reporting, sexuality, and substance abuse; these training experiences make up about two months of the seminar schedule.

The program review committee generally has a small role, that of helping with the annual APA report. In the years when the program undergoes its re-accreditation review, the role of this committee becomes much larger. Members take on responsibility for helping with the self-study required as the first step in the re-accreditation process; that work is generally due to the APA Education Directorate about six months before the site visit. Collecting the necessary data and writing a detailed program description can take up to several months. The program review committee also coordinates the site visit that follows the self-study review and works with the training director in responding to the official report from APA, once it is received.

The orientation committee is responsible for coordinating the multiple details of new intern orientation. This committee also needs to think continuously about the rationale for all elements of orientation and to generate creative ideas for new orientation experiences.

The research committee is not strictly an internship committee, but it is important to involve interns in its operations and to use the committee to think about research opportunities that could be made available to interns. The formal role of this committee in our structure is to review research proposals submitted by psychology staff members, interns, or postdoctoral fellows. This review is then passed on to the facility research committee for final approval. The committee also disseminates information about grant opportunities and helps staff or trainees develop proposals. Serving on this committee helps to acquaint interns with procedures for reviewing research proposals, including reviewing informed consent procedures in medically based settings.

The selection committee is made up of six staff, including the training director. The training director records intern data and makes initial decisions on who to invite for interview, consulting with other staff on the committee as needed. Committee members review the folders of all invited applicants and those of a group of applicants who were not invited but who fall above a threshold for being cut early from consideration. Each applicant's folder is read by at least three committee members, including the training director. The folders of top applicants are read by all or almost all of the committee members. At least three selection committee members are also on the schedule for the phone or face-to-face interviews of applicants who respond to our invitation for an interview. The committee meets at least four times—once in late October or early November to review procedures, once in December to review ratings on folders read thus far (we think of this as a recalibration meeting), and at least twice in January (sometimes three to five times, if decisions between applicants are difficult) to rank the final set of candidates in preparation for intern match day. Every year to date, this group also has met on "call day" to share responsibility for calling to make internship offers. We have also made calls to all interns who would not receive offers from us, after filling our slots. We felt that this was a courtesy due to applicants who may be waiting to hear from us before deciding about other offers. If the computer match proceeds as expected, the "call day" activities will no longer be necessary. However, it may be helpful, especially for larger intern programs, to have selection committee members available on the day the match results are sent, in order to call the "matched" interns to express enthusiasm about working with them and to see whether they have questions.

MANAGING INTERPROFESSIONAL TRAINING

As mentioned earlier, future healthcare will almost certainly be organized around interprofessional care models (e.g., Pew Health Professions Commission, 1995; A. M. Zeiss, 1997; A. M. Zeiss & Steffen, 1996a). Thus it is vitally important for training directors to evaluate how their internship programs relate to this model of care.

Interprofessional Team Principles

Interprofessional teams are composed of members from more than one discipline, making a breadth of resources available to patients. These teams work collaboratively, with individual team members sharing assessments to generate an overall conceptualization of the relationships among biological, psychological, and social aspects of the case. This model is used to generate shared team goals for overall outcomes and to guide professions in working together to provide patient care. On an interprofessional team, all team members are assumed to be colleagues, there is no hierarchical team organization, and the group shares responsibility for program effectiveness and team process functions. One member may be designated team coordinator, but this is understood to be an administrative role and does not imply that the team member has higher status, a stronger say in resolving conflict, or the ability to make unilateral decisions. Because interprofessional teamwork requires so much collaboration and consensus decision making, team members must have a high degree of interpersonal skills and a commitment to developing effective working strategies.

The term "multidisciplinary" often is used erroneously as a synonym for interprofessional; the two terms refer in fact to very different forms of team organization. A multidisciplinary team does have members from more than one discipline, but work is not done with the level of coordination and collaboration that characterizes interprofessional teamwork. In a multidisciplinary team, each discipline does its own assessment, generates its own treatment plan, implements the plan, evaluates progress, and refines the plan based on their own evaluation. Multidisciplinary teams usually are hierarchical; that is, there is a designated program chief whose responsibility is to oversee the program, lead meetings, resolve conflicts, allocate case load, and so on. Other team members feel responsible for the clinical work of their discipline, but do not share a sense of responsibility for program function and team effectiveness.

In the United States, the interprofessional team concept has grown in influence and adoption over the last 15 to 20 years. The distinctions among different types of team programs were developed in the late 1960s and early 1970s and subsequently have been expressed most clearly by Takamura and associates (Takamura, 1985; Takamura, Bermost, & Stringfellow, 1979). Currently, this team model is used to guide direct service and training in a variety of inpatient and outpatient settings (e.g., Veterans Health Administration, 1995, 1997; A. M. Zeiss & Steffen, 1996a, 1996b; R. A. Zeiss, 1998).

There has been a growing international awareness of the role of interprofessional care in a variety of settings. In Europe, concerns about the care of cancer patients led the Council of Europe in 1987 to create a Select Committee of experts to consider coordination of care for patients. The committee recommended "the provision of joint professional education as a means of improving teamwork in cancer care." The European Health Committee has funded a review of interprofessional training of healthcare staff in member states, and interprofessional training modules are available in countries throughout Europe. The World Health Organization has supported the development of a network for interprofessional education based in Linkoping, Sweden (Goble, 1994).

Incorporating Interprofessional Team Training into Psychology Internship Training

Given the growing predominance of the interprofessional team model, it is important for psychology training directors to evaluate how well interns are trained in this model, including didactic opportunities and opportunities for clinical experiences in interprofessional settings. Referrals of cases to a separate psychology department for care offered independently of other healthcare services will become increasingly rare. Instead, increasing numbers of psychologists will be members of teams in medically based and mental health based settings (e.g., Robinson, Wischman, & DelVento, 1996; Strosahl, 1996; A. M. Zeiss & Steffen, 1996b).

Training directors have at least four simultaneous responsibilities with regard to developing adequate interprofessional team training experiences for their interns. First, the program must ensure adequate skill development in psychology and develop interns' identity as professional psychologists. Second, the program must support professional development more broadly, for example, by helping trainees understand job market realities, use professional organizations that can support them, take further steps in the process of obtaining licensure or certification in the profession, and so on. Third, the program must provide opportunities to help each intern understand how psychology fits into the overall healthcare needs of the patients he or she serves and how different professions can effectively collaborate in planning, delivering, and evaluating care. Fourth, the program must provide training in the interpersonal skills necessary for effective interprofessional team work, such as the ability to communicate information about a patient that is understandable to all professions on the team, the ability to share responsibility for leadership in team meetings, and the ability to resolve differences of opinion among team members (about patient-related issues, such as the correct diagnosis, or about team-related issues, such as the best way to construct team treatment plans).

Specific activities that a training director needs to perform to accomplish these four tasks will vary greatly by setting. However, some principles are relevant in any setting. First, this training must occur in interprofessional settings, that is, with trainees from multiple professions, not just psychology interns. Second, supervisors must understand interprofessional principles and be prepared to supervise the intern's team interactions, as well as his or her work with patients. Third, expectations for skill development as an interprofessional team member must be included in the program's goals and measured as exit competencies, as are more specifically "psychological" skills (e.g., assessment and therapy).

Models for interprofessional training seminars are available (e.g., Heinemann, Brown, Waite, & Zeiss, 1998; A. M. Zeiss & Lovett, 1998). The psychology internship training director can take a lead role in pulling together the training directors of other professions. Together they can develop a training seminar model, share responsibility for conducting it, and determine which clinical settings provide optimal exposure to interprofessional clinical experiences. They can also take responsibility for offering training to other teams to improve their function and to supervisors to enhance their inclusion of interprofessional experience in supervision. This is not an exhaustive list of ways to promote interprofessional training experiences, but should suggest ideas that could be adapted to local resources and settings.

SUMMARY

The training director is responsible for the effective management of the psychology internship program. In addition, the training director must think about the relationship of the internship program to the broader healthcare context. The training director must develop and maintain collaborative training relationships with other professions, support clinical programs that offer interprofessional care, and contribute to the development and ongoing provision of interprofessional training experiences for all healthcare trainees. In doing so, the training director is enhancing collaborative care in the healthcare setting. Equally as important, he or she is enhancing training for psychology interns that will optimally prepare them for the healthcare system into which they will emerge at the end of internship.

REFERENCES

American Psychological Association (APA). (1996a). *Book 1: Guidelines and principles for accreditation of programs in professional psychology.* Washington, DC: Office of Program Consultation and Accreditation.

American Psychological Association (APA). (1996b). *Book 2: Accreditation operating procedures of the Committee on Accreditation.* Washington, DC: Office of Program Consultation and Accreditation.

Association of Psychology Postdoctoral and Internship Centers (APPIC). (1997). *Supply and Demand Conference.*

Belar, C. D., & Perry, N. W. (Eds.) (1991). *Proceedings: National conference on scientist-practitioner education and training for the professional practice of psychology.* Sarasota, FL: Professional Resources Press.

Dougher, M. K., Callaghan, G. M., & Follette, W. C. (1998). Multiple concurrent supervision and the potential confusion. *The Behavior Therapist, 21(2),* 20–22.

Goble, R. (1994). Multiprofessional education: European Network for Development of Multiprofessional Education in Health Sciences (EMPE). *Journal of Interprofessional Care, 8,* 85–92.

Hall, R. G., Cantrell, P. J., & Boggs, K. R. (Eds.) (1997). *Internship and post-doctoral programs in professional psychology.* Washington, DC: APPIC.

Hannay, H. J., Bieliauskas, L., Crosson, B. A., Hammeke, T. A., Hamsher, K. de S., and Koffler, S. (1997). Proceedings of the Houston Conference on Specialty Education and Training in Clinical Neuropsychology. *Archives of Clinical Neuropsychology, 13,* 157–249.

Heinemann, G., Brown, G., Waite, M., & Zeiss, A. (1998). *Interprofessional training in primary care.* Manuscript in review.

Kihlstrom, J. (1997). E-mail citation on SSCPNet.

Lamb, D. H., Cochran, D. J., & Jackson, V. R. (1991). Training and organizational issues associated with identifying and responding to intern impairment. *Professional Psychology, 22,* 291–296.

Pew Health Professions Commission. (1995). *Critical challenges: Revitalizing the health professions for the twenty-first century.* San Francisco: UCSF Center for the Health Professions.

Raimy, V. (Ed.) (1950). *Training in clinical psychology.* New York: Prentice-Hall.

Robinson, P., Wischman, C., & DelVento, A. (1996). *Treating depression in primary care.* Reno, NV: Context Press.

Routh, D. K. (1998). The internship crisis. *Clinical Psychologist, 51,* 1–2.

Strosahl, K. (1996). Confessions of a behavior therapist in primary care: The odyssey and the ecstasy. *Cognitive and Behavioral Practice, 3,* 1–28.

Takamura, J. (1985). Introduction - Health teams. In L. J. Campbell & S. Vivell (Eds.), *Interdisciplinary team training for primary care in geriatrics: An educational model for program development and evaluation* (pp. II· 64-II: 67). Washington, DC: U.S. Government Printing Office.

Takamura, J., Bermost, L., & Stringfellow, L. (1979). *Health team development.* Honolulu, HI: University of Hawaii, John A. Burns School of Medicine.

Veterans Health Administration. (1995). *The Interdisciplinary Team Training Program* [descriptive brochure]. Washington, DC: Department of Veterans Affairs.

Veterans Health Administration. (1997). *VA's commitment to health care through health professions education.* Washington, DC: Department of Veterans Affairs.

Zeiss, A. M. (1997). *Looking ahead: Health care for older adults as a model for the future.* Presidential Address, Association for Advancement of Behavior Therapy, Miami Beach, FL.

Zeiss, A. M., & Lovett, S. (1998). *Interprofessional team training and development program: Seminar description.* Unpublished manuscript (available from authors).

Zeiss, A. M., & Steffen, A. (1996a). Interdisciplinary health care teams: The basic unit of geriatric care. In L. L. Carstensen, B. A. Edelstein, & L. Dornbrand (Eds.), *The Handbook of Clinical Gerontology* (pp. 423–450). Thousand Oaks, CA: Sage Publishing.

Zeiss, A. M., & Steffen, A. (1996b). Treatment issues with older adults. *Cognitive and Behavioral Practice, 3,* 371–390.

Zeiss, R. A. (1998). Interdisciplinary treatment and training issues in the acute inpatient psychiatry unit. *Journal of Interprofessional Care, 11,* 279–286.

BIOGRAPHY

Antonette M. Zeiss   Antonette Zeiss is Clinical Coordinator and Director of Training in Psychology Service at the VA Palo Alto Health Care System. She is a Fellow of APA Division 12 and a Charter Fellow of APS. She is a former president of the Association for Advancement of Behavior Therapy (1996–1997) and president (1999) of Section II (Clinical Geropsychology), APA Division 12. Her research and scholarly interests include treatment of depression, psychotherapy with older adults, sexual dysfunction, and processes in interprofessional teamwork.

13

INFORMATION MANAGEMENT IN BEHAVIORAL HEALTHCARE

RICHARD KELLEY FREEMAN

Wilford Hall Medical Center, San Antonio, Texas 78229

INTRODUCTION
INDUSTRY TRENDS
THE NEW ROLE OF INFORMATION
THE TECHNOLOGY GAP
HOW TO MANAGE INFORMATION
CONCLUSION
REFERENCES
BIOGRAPHY

INTRODUCTION

We are in the midst of a technological revolution that is changing every aspect of public and private life. Computer networks connect individuals across the hall and across the globe, information is disseminated at a speed that would make Gutenberg dizzy, and powerful technology is becoming so affordable that instead of promising a "chicken in every pot," our president is aiming for "a computer in every American home" (President Bill Clinton, 1997).

Most of us have directly benefited from this revolution: proofing, editing, and rewriting a document in minutes; locating a reference in seconds; communicating anywhere on the planet in nominal time and cost; the list goes on and on. At the same time, however, the revolution has demanded things from us in return: we are expected to deliver information immediately, to know news in "real time," to make data-based decisions, and to be available and functional at all times and places.

This chapter begins with a look at related trends in the behavioral healthcare industry that will affect our lives well into the twenty-first century—trends that are changing the structure of care delivery systems, the content and process of clinical services, and the management of clinical organizations. Next is a discussion of how these developments have created a new role (and a new market) for information and information technology. The growing demand for information is juxtaposed to the technological status of today's behavioral healthcare providers. The balance of the chapter focuses on how to plan, implement, and protect information systems in clinical practice.

INDUSTRY TRENDS

Structural Changes

Managed Care

Traditionally, behavioral healthcare (a.k.a. mental health) was one of the most ambiguous and expensive line items of healthcare. Providers were reimbursed on a fee-for-service (indemnity) basis by insurance companies that maintained a hands off approach to clinical care. As recently as 1989, the average length of stay for psychiatric treatment was as high as 30 days (Condon, 1996). Prevailing assumptions in the industry were that one form of mental health treatment was as good as another, that intensive long-term therapy was usually necessary for recovery, and that the effects of treatment were often too subjective to measure. Psychological testing may have been used for diagnosis and treatment planning, but it was seldom used to assess the effects of treatment.

This state of affairs, and a handful of widely publicized abuses by psychiatric hospitals and providers, made mental health a prime target during the restructuring of healthcare. The first stage of restructuring focused on cost avoidance: mechanisms such as session limits, preauthorization of services, and primary care gatekeepers all drove down behavioral healthcare costs dramatically. After all, if one could not objectively measure treatment gains of a long-term treatment, one could not objectively measure lost value if the treatment were shortened. Managed care is now moving toward a second stage, focusing on value (clinical outcome and patient satisfaction) rather than cost containment. This movement was in part hastened by widespread outcry over arbitrary limits on treatment, and by a handful of widely publicized abuses by managed care organizations.

Regardless of the stage, it is clear that managed care—and accountability—are here to stay. Enrollment in managed care programs (health care contracts that include care limits or oversight) has increased 60% from 1992 to 1996, so that today 69% of the 181 million Americans with health insurance are enrolled in some type of specialty managed behavioral health program (Oss & Stair, 1996). Managed care initiatives are also underway in the public sector, including Medicaid and state-level programs; as many as 15 states have obtained waivers to transfer their Medicaid programs to private managed care organizations (Condon, 1996; Manderscheid & Henderson, 1996).

Shifting Risk to Providers

Managed care organizations often serve as intermediaries between payers and providers, saving the payer (and making their own profit) by limiting expenditures at the point of care. Many healthcare providers, feeling the economic pinch of this system, are banding together to form their own networks and establish capitated contracts directly with payers. Under these capitated contracts, provider organizations are paid a set monthly fee based on the number of lives they will cover. The provider organization must use any savings to provide additional services or reduce enrollee costs, and must absorb any losses. By cutting out the middleman providers can increase their income, but they also assume financial risk. An economic shortfall comes out of their own pockets. One of the fastest-growing arrangements within managed care, the number of patients enrolled in risk-based contracts has increased 101% from 1993 to 1996 (Oss and Stair, 1996).

Integrated Delivery Systems

Structural changes in healthcare are occurring on a number of fronts (group practices, insurance companies, hospitals), but they all seem to be heading toward integrated delivery systems (IDS). Integrated delivery systems cover the entire spectrum of healthcare, from medical/surgical treatment to behavioral healthcare. An IDS will perform all functions of the current insurance, inpatient, and ambulatory healthcare delivery systems (Maloney, 1996).

Insurance companies, seeking greater control over healthcare utilization and costs, are moving toward becoming IDSs by, sequentially, initiating utilization review, then establishing discounted rates for treatment, then purchasing practices, and finally adding specialty providers. Hospitals, seeking to maximize income by reducing costly inpatient treatment, are moving toward becoming IDSs by sequentially increasing their ambulatory services, then managing capitated contracts, then purchasing outpatient provider groups, and finally increasing their insurance and administrative capabilities. Group practices, seeking to maximize their income, evolve into IDSs by sequentially developing their administrative capabilities, aligning with managed care plans, developing the ability to manage capitated contracts, and finally affiliating with a hospital (Maloney, 1996).

Because behavioral healthcare is significantly different from medical healthcare, many payers have separated ("carved out") the behavioral health services from their healthcare plans and hired a behavioral health program to manage these benefits. However, the current trend toward integrated delivery systems has motivated some behavioral healthcare programs to carve back into the mainstream (Manderscheid & Henderson, 1996). This is creating new challenges for integrating the administrative and clinical activities of these traditionally different organizations.

Increasing Outpatient Focus

A report by the Sachs Group (1995) predicted that inpatient psychiatric days will drop as much as 50%—from 18.6 million days nationally in 1994 to 9.2 million days in 1999. Psychiatric hospitalizations will likewise decline by 59% from 1.7 million to 712,000, during the same period. These declines represent both the biggest percentage drop and the biggest absolute decline across all of healthcare. The Sachs Group predicts that opportunities will increase in outpatient facilities and primary care networks.

Legislative Developments

The historically high cost and relative ambiguity of behavioral healthcare prompted many payers to carve behavioral healthcare out of their benefits packages. If such services were offered, it was often by a "carve out" organization and with many more restrictions than medical care. However, recent legislation signed by President Clinton (Health Insurance Portability and Accountability Act of 1996) provides parity for behavioral health services in healthcare plans. Hailed as a significant victory by consumer groups and professional associations, this legislation was strongly opposed by payers, who worry about increased behavioral healthcare utilization and costs. One can expect even greater pressure from employers and payers to be informed of the measurable outcomes brought about by their expenditures for these services (Sleek, 1996).

Clinical Changes

Empirically Validated Treatments

A common assumption held for years was that the many varieties of psychotherapy were equally effective, and that the personal tastes of providers and patients should dictate what form of intervention was used. This assumption derived in part from the perceived subjectivity of psychotherapy and in part by the conclusions drawn by Smith and Glass (1977) in their meta-analysis of psychotherapies. Although Smith and Glass's conclusions have been challenged for years, it has only been recently that the behavioral healthcare industry has begun warming up to the idea that some interventions may be more effective than others. The most notable development on this front was initiated by Division 12 (Clinical Psychology) of the American Psychological Association. Division 12 recently appointed a task force to identify clinical interventions that were supported by controlled outcome studies (Task Force on Promotion and Dissemination of Psychological Procedures, 1995). Although this movement has received harsh criticism from some, it depicts the zeitgeist in which providers, payers, and patients want to know what they're getting out of behavioral healthcare, and why.

Practice Guidelines

A related movement is practice guidelines (or clinical pathways), which are "systematically developed statements to assist practitioner and patient decisions about appropriate health care for specific clinical conditions" (Agency for Health

Care Policy and Research [AHCPR], 1993, p. ii). Managed care organizations, pharmaceutical companies, psychological testing companies, government agencies, and professional associations are all rapidly developing practice guidelines. The most widely publicized guideline in behavioral healthcare has been AHCPR's depression guideline. The current status of the guideline movement has been described as "dominantly proprietary and fracture along disciplinary lines" (Hayes, 1996, p. 170). Still, the guideline movement is striking a chord with payers and managed care organizations that want to predict health care costs better, and by a public that expects more consistency across providers.

Scientist–Practitioner

The scientist–practitioner model of psychology has been around for decades (Raimy, 1950). For many practicing psychologists, this meant that they had completed training in experimental design and statistical analysis and, if put to the task, could conduct an empirical study. However, industry trends toward emphasizing accountability, shifting risk to providers, utilizing empirically validated treatments, and creating practice guidelines have all forced more practicing psychologists to integrate the scientist–practitioner model at a number of additional levels (Freeman, 1996): they must be (1) *competent consumers* of treatment outcome studies; (2) *informed developers* of treatment protocols and practice guidelines; (3) *expert clinicians* who can deliver (and train others to deliver) treatment protocols effectively; (4) *program evaluators* who can make data-based assessments of whether their treatments are effective and efficient; and (5) *idiographic scientists* who assess treatment progress with individual patients and make data-based decisions about their care.

Provider Proliferation

According to statistics from the U.S. Department of Health and Human Services (Peterson et al., 1996), psychologists make up only 14% of the clinically trained workforce in behavioral healthcare; psychiatrists make up 7%; and social workers, counselors, marriage and family therapists, psychiatric nurses, and psychosocial rehabilitators make up the remaining 69% of the workforce. Some of these professions are growing rapidly: The number of marriage and family therapists in the United States has grown from 1800 in 1966 to over 46,000 in 1995; the number of people involved in psychosocial rehabilitation has grown from 21,000 in 1988 to over 100,000 in 1996; counselors, numbering over 61,000 make up over 12% of the behavioral healthcare workforce. Managed care organizations are utilizing these nondoctoral providers because many of them have significant clinical experience and are less expensive to hire, not to mention that nonprofessional and professional psychotherapists often achieve similar outcomes (Christensen & Jacobsen, 1994). This trend ensures that behavioral healthcare will increasingly be provided by individuals with varied training, experience, and clinical orientations.

Stepped-Care Models

Under indemnity (fee-for-service) reimbursement, providers are rewarded for increasing services; there is no incentive to develop more efficient treatments. Capitation reverses these incentives, because provider organizations must care for a beneficiary population out of a predetermined budget. Their profit (or loss) depends on how they manage service utilization. Thus, capitation has increased interest in less intensive, more cost efficient treatments. In a stepped-care model, a patient might begin with less intensive intervention, such as structured group therapy (Kelleher, Talcott, Haddock, & Freeman, 1996), bibliotherapy (Jamison & Scogin, 1995; Sanchez-Craig, Davila, & Cooper, 1996), minimal therapist contact (Rowan & Andrasik, 1996), or even computer-assisted self-care (Ferguson, 1996). More intensive intervention would be reserved for more severe cases, or for patients who have learned fundamental skills that will be used later in intensive intervention (Freeman & Kelleher, 1996). Stepped care may also mean that a patient may receive treatment from one or more providers; for example, a moderately depressed patient focuses on cognitive skills, behavioral activation, and assertiveness in three consecutive structured group-treatment modalities, each with a different provider.

Managerial Changes

Continuous Quality Improvement

Continuous Quality Improvement (CQI) is a management philosophy that bears interesting parallels to the scientist–practitioner philosophy in clinical psychology. Like the scientist–practitioner model, CQI was articulated well before 1950, but it, too, did not begin affecting the management industry until the 1980s. CQI is the managerial equivalent of the scientist–practitioner model in that it focuses on objective, data-based decision making. It also emphasizes regularly identifying opportunities for improvement, obtaining information from all aspects of the organization, and establishing continuous, data-based feedback loops for key organizational processes. CQI has been so widely accepted in large healthcare organizations that basic CQI principles are now included in accreditation criteria (Joint Commission on Accreditation on Healthcare Organizations, 1997). The book you are currently reading is testament to the fact that, more and more, psychologists are finding themselves in managerial positions; their scientist–practitioner roots should prepare them well for CQI-based management.

Provider Profiling

Managing people is different in today's healthcare industry, whose providers are suffering the growing pains of the new reimbursement models (Goldsmith et al., 1995). Providers that used to run their own shops are now straining under a system that forces them to share risks with other providers, and to collaborate on the development of clinical pathways. As aversive as it may be, providing profiling is an inevitable managerial responsibility in this context. Provider profiling involves much closer scrutiny of individual providers' outcomes, efficiencies, caseloads, and decisions for the purpose of identifying both inefficient and exceptional performers.

Risk Management

The financial side of management has also changed. Under indemnity reimbursement, financial management (and economic success) primarily centered on billing and accounts receivable. If you could keep track of what you were owed, and collect it, you generally did okay. Under capitation reimbursement, however, financial management (and economic success) centers more on risk. You have the money, but you also have the liability of providing a broad range of behavioral healthcare services to a large number of people. You want to provide good care, but you also want to stay in business. You want to be efficient without being ineffective. You can see the past, but you are not certain whether the future will follow the same pattern. Set all of this in the context of a rapidly changing, intensely competitive business environment and you get a managerial challenge that is not for the faint of heart.

THE NEW ROLE OF INFORMATION

Under indemnity models, claims and accounting information were prominent. Given the current trends in the behavioral healthcare industry, however, it is information collected at the point of service that is the central focus (Dewey, Brill, & Graves, 1996; Pigott & Broskowski, 1995). The American Psychological Association (APA) has established a special task force on promotion and dissemination of psychological procedures (1995), industry associations are convening outcomes conferences, and several best-selling professional books are exclusively devoted to outcome measurement (e.g., Fischer and Corcoran's, 1994, two-volume compendium of over 280 behavioral health outcome measures). Treatment outcome is becoming a major issue as payers compare provider organizations, as provider organizations profile different individual providers, and as individual providers attempt to make effective and efficient decisions about their patients.

Marketing

Practices and providers need clinical information to market their services to third parties (insurance companies, managed care companies, referral sources). A practice or provider that provides aggregate outcome data on a particular procedure (e.g., bar charts of BDI scores for depression management programs) will have a competitive advantage over a practice that provides subjective data (e.g., "Dr. Smith is an expert in the field of anxiety," or "the majority of anxious patients we treat show marked improvement"). Furthermore, being able to provide patients with graphical, objective information about their progress may provide an additional individual marketing edge, as well as enhance collaboration in treatment.

Administrative Aspects

The increased use of multidisciplinary treatment teams, stepped-care models, and group treatment increases the opportunities for patients to fall through administrative "cracks." In this setting, information about treatment utilization, compliance, and attrition becomes necessary to ensure quality care. When multiple providers are involved in a patient's care, information from one provider needs to be quickly available to other providers in order to provide timely, cost-efficient care. Furthermore, the increase in at-risk contracts has made it essential that organizations manage information about patients' benefits.

Treatment

The widespread interest in empirically validated treatments, practice guidelines, and clinical pathways is challenging the assumption that all interventions produce similar outcome. In addition, the emphasis on cost savings has given rise to concerns about quality care. These trends have made it important for organizations to compare their programs' outcomes with the outcomes reported in the scientific literature and by similar organizations. Clinical information is also more important in individual treatment, as providers seek to maximize treatment effects within a limited number of sessions. The growth of outcome measurement companies bears witness to this growing need (Gingerich & Broskowski, 1996).

Research

One of the emerging concerns in the clinical outcome literature is that data derived from highly controlled outcome studies with carefully screened, homogeneous samples may not be applicable to more representative clinical populations, which may include patients with multiple diagnoses. There is a need—both academic and economic—to collect data on more heterogeneous subjects for comparison with more rigorously controlled published studies to test the generalizability of traditional scientific research (Persons & Bostrom, 1995). In fact, there is a growing (albeit still debated) appreciation for *effectiveness* studies that report outcome on the "real" patients that seek help in "real" clinics (Seligman, 1995).

THE TECHNOLOGY GAP

The demand for information has created a fast-growing market for information technology. In a study of the top 20 managed behavioral healthcare firms, the Work Group for the Computerization of Behavioral Health and Human Services, Inc.

(1995), determined that the country's largest mental health organizations allocate 6 to 10% of their annual budgets to computer technology. This percentage is further divided into 39% for hardware, 42% for software, and 19% for training. Extrapolating from market research (Oss & Stair, 1996), the annual technology expenditures by these organizations is probably between $46 million and $77 million for hardware, between $50 million and $83 million for software, and between $22 million and $37 million for training.

At smaller levels, however, technology is probably underutilized in behavioral healthcare. Rosen and Weil's (1996a) survey of 213 California psychologists indicated that although three out of four psychologists used a computer in their practice, "nearly all uses involved little more than word processing." Only 3% of the sample had ever billed an insurance company electronically, and only 11% had ever administered a psychological test by computer. Factors that predicted computer usage were technophobia (negative correlation), use of psychological assessments, age (negative correlation), and percentage of managed care patients. If a similar trend holds for the 336,085 behavioral healthcare providers in America (Peterson et al., 1996), there is a tremendous technology gap between the industry's information demands and providers' ability to deliver it.

HOW TO MANAGE INFORMATION

Given the intense and ever-growing demand for information, it seems certain that organizations (and providers) that can collect, manage, utilize, and deliver it will be the big winners in the new behavioral healthcare industry. However, in light of the technology gap that seems to pervade the industry, the majority of organizations and individuals have quite a journey ahead of them. This section provides some guideposts for the journey, discussing how to plan, implement use, and protect information in clinical practice.

Planning

Whom Do You Need?

The first question to answer is *who,* not *what,* Dorothy Leonard-Barton of Harvard and William Kraus of General Electric (1985) write:

> The higher the organizational level at which managers define a problem or a need, the greater the probability of successful implementation. At the same time, however, the closer the definition and solution of problems or needs are to end-users, the greater the probability of success. Implementation managers must draw up their internal marketing plans in light of this apparent paradox. (p. 108)

Information and the technology that collects, stores, and analyzes it are only valuable to the extent that they help *someone* to make a decision or perform a task. It is absolutely critical to identify who these "someones" are, to find out what they need, and to engage them as much as possible in planning. Taking the time for participative planning enhances motivation to change, increases tolerance during implementation, demystifies the technology, increases system use, and helps to ensure the reliability of the system's data. It also makes for a better product, because end users know best what they need and what technology works for them.

The critical people to include at this stage are *feeders, readers,* and *leaders.*

Feeders

Feeders are the people who will enter data into the system. These can include scheduling personnel, intake clerks, providers, even patients. They are critical because they know what interface makes their input tasks easier. If the system interface does not adequately meet their needs and make their jobs easier, they are less likely to use it and more likely to make mistakes when they do (Baroudi, Olson, & Ives, 1986).

Readers

Readers are anyone who will use the data stored in the system. These can include managers who want to track trends in demand for services, payers who want to know the efficiency of a treatment program, inspectors who want to measure administrative accuracy, providers who want to assess symptom severity, researchers who want to know the comparative efficacy of different interventions, and patients who want to know their progress in treatment. Knowing specifically what these people need lets you know what data to collect and how to present it. Failing to address readers' needs may lead you to impressive technology and mountains of data that are utterly irrelevant.

Leaders

Leaders are anyone who controls resource allocation or strategic planning. These can include owners, chief executive, COOs, CFOs, directors, operating, and financial officers, and so on. They define where the organization is going, and they prioritize expenditures of time and money. Leaders look to the bottom line, not because they are insensitive to patient care, but because the very existence of patient care is predicated on the viability of the organization.

What Do They Want?

Another rule of thumb in planning information management systems is to *begin in the present.* That is, how can technology make employees' *current* jobs easier? System usage depends heavily on end-user satisfaction (Baroudi et al., 1986); without direct benefits for end users, system implementation can be derailed by employee resistance.

Feeders want *efficiency.* In paper-based offices, or offices that use separate computer programs for different tasks, feeders spend a lot of their time entering, validating, and editing the same data on different forms or in different systems. These monotonous, redundant tasks can adversely affect employee morale and data reliability. Feeders are most happy with integrated systems that require one-time data entry. Feeders want *simplicity.* They want easy-to-read screens with a similar point-and-click interface. Feeders want *accuracy.* Input screens that remind them of missing or inaccurate information make the job go faster.

Readers want *speed.* By the time they ask for information, they need it now and they want it to be current. Readers want *specificity.* Their decisions are more reliable if they are based on data that directly match their questions. Readers want *intelligibility.* Tables of numbers are not as easy to read as charts and graphs. Readers also want *power.* They want to have direct access to the data and user-friendly tools for analyzing it.

Leaders want a *return* on their investment. What financial benefits will accrue if information technology saves money or increases revenue? Leaders want *longevity.* They want today's solutions to work tomorrow, when the organization may be bigger, more spread out, and more comprehensive.

What Do You Have?

It is also important to determine what scope of information your organization wants to manage. Clinical organizations typically have three basic levels of information: *static, captured,* and *collected.*

Static

The first level of information is static information. Static information is information that will not change but is used often. Examples of static information are demographic information about patients, providers, or employees; clinical procedures; referral sources; and billing information. If a management information system is well designed, static information need be entered only once. Because static information is used repeatedly and is entered only once, it is important to ensure it is entered early and accurately. For example, an organization may allow optional entry of a patient's social security number, but it may mandate entry of their date of birth. In a well-designed system, static information is "cheap," that is, it requires time to create, but costs nothing to replicate for other purposes.

Captured

The second level of information is captured information. The term captured indicates that these data are recorded in the flow of operations while people go about their routine jobs. Captured information usually results from combining static information. Electronic patient records are an example: when a provider writes a clinical note (a routine, flow-of-operations task), information about the patient contact is recorded by the system. This new information combines the date of the contact with the static information about the patient, the provider, and the procedure. In a well-designed system, captured information is "free," that is, it does not cost the organization additional time or money to create.

Collected

The third level of information is collected information. Collected information changes over time and is not created in the flow of operations. It includes things such as customer needs (e.g., treatment goals), patient functional status, provider-based assessments, treatment outcome, patient satisfaction, and follow-up data. Collected information is "costly," that is, it requires expenditure of additional energy to collect.

Because collected information is costly, it is important to be thoughtful about what to collect. Remember that, in the real world, patients, providers, and technicians are not primarily research subjects. It would be easy to overwhelm them with data collection, but it is important to begin with collecting information that is directly relevant to their jobs or to their care. Collected information can be any one of a number of types.

Market Needs.   It is worth measuring what the market wants, because doing so will help to narrow down what other collected information you may need. For example, because in our clinic we assess customer needs with the Treatment Goals Checklist (Kelleher, Klepac, & McGaughey, 1987), we know that the top three reasons patients come to clinics like ours are depression, anxiety, and relationship difficulties (Kelleher, Freeman, Tims, & Klepac, 1995). This means that we will want to put more effort into identifying good outcome measures for these problems than we will for things like trichotillomania. This knowledge also helps us plan our program development, hiring, and training.

Quality of Life/Functional Status.   Patients do not seek behavioral health services just because of their symptoms, they seek services because of the impact those symptoms have on their quality of life. For example, treatment success with depression means more than decreasing neurovegetative signs, it means that the patient perceives that his or her life is better because of these changes. Especially with the trend toward integrating behavioral healthcare with medical care, these measures provide a common denominator to represent the relative value of behavioral healthcare to the larger healthcare community. The SF-36 Health Survey (Ware, 1992) is a good example of a measure that can assess the effects of treatment on a patient's overall quality of life.

Global Measures.   Global measures are currently the most widely used outcome measures by managed behavioral healthcare. They are less useful in guiding specific treatment decisions and are primarily used to document the pre–post effectiveness of treatments. Still, because they are widely used and recognized by nonclinical healthcare administrators, global measures provide a common language between providers and payers. Examples of global measures include the Symptom Checklist-90-Revised (Derogatis, 1983), the Brief Symptom Inventory (Derogatis & Melisaratos, 1983), and the Outcome Questionnaire (Lambert, Lunnen, Umphres, Hansen, & Burlingame, 1994). Ogles, Lambert, and Masters (1996) provide an excellent review of global outcome measures.

Nomothetic Measures. Nomothetic measures assess an individual's performance against a reference group. As such, they are useful for comparisons. Examples of nomothetic measures include the Beck Depression Inventory (Bec, Steer, & Garbin, 1988), the Dyadic Adjustment Scale (Spanier, 1976), and the Penn State Worry Questionnaire (Meyer, Miller, Metzger, & Borkovec, 1990). Fischer and Corcoran's *Measures for Clinical Practice* (1994) is an excellent source of nomothetic outcome measures for adults, families, and couples.

Idiographic Measures. Ideographic measures are not normed against a population; rather, they assess an individual's progress relative to where she or he was at the start of treatment. These measures track the more person-specific goals that patients bring into treatment, for example, frequency of arguments with a spouse, time spent engaged in pleasurable activities, and so on. Barlow, Hayes, and Nelson (1984; in press) provide guidance on measuring idiographic goals; "goal attainment scaling" (Kiresuk & Sherman, 1968) is another widely used method of standardizing idiographic measurement.

Patient Satisfaction. There are a number of initiatives underway to develop "scorecards" to facilitate comparisons between health care plans (e.g., National Committee For Quality Assurance, 1997). While they have their differences, these scorecards have the commonality of measuring patient satisfaction. Patient satisfaction does not equate to clinical efficacy, and its measurement is not without problems. Nonetheless, it is a common denominator that facilitates global comparisons between and within organizations, and it has become one of the industry's gold standards. Some organizations use published measures like the CSQ-8 (Larson, Attkisson, Hargreaves, & Nguyen, 1979); other organizations develop their own in-house measures.

Broad Guidelines. Nguyen and Olsen (1996) outline several key characteristics of a sound outcomes measurement system. *Practicality:* the measures are not so long or complex that they interrupt the flow of care; *psychometrics:* the measures have good reliability and validity; *benchmarks:* the measures have standards against which the organization can compare its performance; *confidentiality:* the process of collecting data respects and protects both staff and patient privacy; and *positive:* the process of collecting data is to facilitate continuous improvement rather than to penalize outliers.

Implementing

Where Do You Start?

Given the broad range of information management needs, it is easy to become overwhelmed and disorganized when it finally comes down to implementing an information management strategy. It is extremely important, however, to avoid the shotgun approach of upgrading every facet of the organization simultaneously. Change takes time and energy, and change is painful. Even though information systems are automated, the people working with them are not. Rushing or meandering during implementation will jeopardize the integrity of the system (McLean & Kapkin, 1983; Rosen & Weil, 1996a).

There is an endless number of data to collect, and an endless number of exciting analyses to perform on those data. It is best, however, to begin implementation by addressing the more mundane flow-of-operations needs (Currie, 1996). That is, what do people *currently* do that can be automated? There are several reasons for this recommendation. First, organizations develop according to their own hierarchy of needs: what they are currently doing is more important to survival than what they are not currently doing. Meeting these basic needs (current tasks) more efficiently will naturally free up resources to meet higher-order needs (additional system development). Second, people are more resistant to change if they do not stand to benefit personally from the change. Making their current jobs easier frees them up to participate in future developments; it also helps to allay their fears and win their support. Third, people know best what they currently do. By beginning implementations with flow-of-operations needs, the organization can capitalize on these internal "expert consultants," better ensuring a quality system.

Practice Management

Many organizations begin implementing information management by automating accounting functions. Automating accounts receivable can increase collections, and billing electronically can improve cash flow by reducing errors and speeding claims adjudication. These benefits make for an immediate and measurable payoff from the system, and the financial management capability can support future organizational growth.

In addition, these business functions are more easily automated, and a number of well-proven applications already exist. Many of these existing practice management applications are designed for a generic medical practice, and do not have the attractive look and intuitive interface of newer graphics based programs. Still, they are reliable and are backed by companies with years of experience. The price of these systems can run from several thousand dollars to tens of thousands of dollars, depending on the number of users and the breadth of the application.

Practice management software should collect and store static data about patients, payers, procedures, prices, and so on. This information should not have to be entered more than once into the system, and should be immediately available for a variety of uses like scheduling appointments, billing electronically, reporting to payers, adjudicating claims, and obtaining authorizations. More advanced features include benefits management (i.e., tracking patient benefits expended and remaining under different insurance plans) and capitation management (i.e., setting internal limits on benefits). Even though smaller organizations may not handle these functions in-house, it is wise to have a system that can grow with the organization should these needs arise.

In my military outpatient clinic, we started managing information by automating our biometric functions (the military equivalent of billing). Formerly, providers would complete bubble-sheets for each appointment, penciling in patient demographics and whether the patient attended the appointment. If and when the providers remembered to complete them, the sheets went to a central office. There, a clerk visually inspected them to ensure bubbles were properly filled and hand-fed them through a scanner. Still, 10% of the scanned records had errors, which the clerk resolved by making his best guess. We created a practice management application that eliminated redundant entry of static data and allowed providers to enter biometric data on-line. Immediately after implementation, we noted that more appointments were recorded, and the error rate dropped to zero (Freeman, 1995).

Clinical Record

It is also wise to ensure that practice management systems can interface with clinical management systems. Clinical management systems are typically built around an electronic patient record. In its simplest form, an electronic patient record enables providers to write their notes on-line and store them on a central computer. More advanced forms of electronic patient records enable providers to create standard note-writing templates for different procedures, initiate and track referrals to other providers, and score or track a variety of outcome measures (i.e., collected information).

If a good practice management system is in place, the electronic patient record should not require personnel to reenter static information about patients, providers, and procedures. Patient appointments scheduled with practice management applications should automatically create records for providers to write in clinical notes or to indicate that the patient did not attend the appointment. Likewise, electronic patient record systems should feed information back to the practice management applications. For example, a provider engages in a billable phone contact with a patient. When he or she writes the note, the procedure is automatically recorded in the billing system.

An electronic patient record that is integrated with practice management applications enables an organization to capture data in the normal flow of operations which can be used for a wide range of activities. Typical benefits include ensuring the legibility and completeness of clinical records by eliminating handwritten entries and by providing clinicians with cues when there is missing information, thus reducing time required for quality assurance (Campbell et al., 1988); profiling providers according to effectiveness and efficiency; and providing "real time" patient status so that at any point in time, anyone involved in a patient's care can monitor treatment utilization and compliance, without having to wait for or locate a chart.

One of the initial problems we addressed with our electronic patient record had to do with the timely termination of patient charts. We are a rotation at an internship site, and turn over three to four psychology interns every four months. Inactive cases that had not been closed bogged the clinic down at every rotation transition, when they could have been terminated more consistently throughout the rotation.

By analyzing information captured by our electronic patient record, we determined that more than 250 cases were terminated during this "crunch time." As we implemented various solutions to the problem, we were able to track our progress objectively and modify our solutions. When we could see, objectively, that terminations leveled out from month to month, we knew we had solved a major problem and had significantly improved our flow of operations (Freeman, 1995).

Decision Support

The most advanced level of information management involves applications that assist clinical decisions. This typically involves analyzing static, captured, and collected data to use with predefined rules that recommend a certain course of action. Decision support can range from simple to complex.

Administrative.   Administrative tasks can be facilitated by user-defined rules that establish reminders for personnel to complete certain tasks. The organization may determine, for example, that providers should be reminded if, after two days, they have not written a clinical note for a patient contact; if, after a chart has been inactive for a certain period of time, the provider is prompted to update the status of the case; or if, after a certain number of cancellations, a patient is contacted to determine intent to continue or obstacles to treatment. With the trend toward new models of care delivery, these types of automated reminders become extremely important to ensure continuity and quality of care.

Diagnosis.   Diagnostic decisions can be facilitated by decision tree applications that help providers rule out alternative diagnoses and consider additional medical conditions. For example, if a patient presents with neurovegetative signs of depression, has hypothyroidism been considered as a contributing factor?

Screening.   In a stepped-care model, screening patients for entry into certain programs can also be facilitated by automated decision support. For instance, an organization may decide, based on a predetermined combination of BDI scores, demographic factors, and prior psychiatric history, whether certain patients would be appropriate for a structured group treatment program.

Treatment Outcome.   Decision support can also assist providers in conceptualizing how to assess treatment outcome for a particular patient. There is a large number of nomothetic outcome measures (e.g., Fischer & Corcoran, 1994) and a virtually unlimited number of idiographic outcome measures. Decision support applications that allow a provider to select outcome measures based on a patient's diagnosis or treatment goals can overcome a major obstacle to assessing outcome in clinical practice.

Treatment. The most advanced possibility for decision support applications involves the use of "expert systems" that guide treatment. Expert systems are "computer programs that process information by making use of decision support tools to arrive at decisions comparable to those made by human experts provided with the same information" (Brown & Kornmayer, 1996). Although there have been some successful demonstrations of such systems in medicine (Buchanan & Shortliffe, 1984) and behavioral healthcare (Beutler & Williams, 1995), widespread use of this type of decision support system is still a long way off. Confidence in diagnostic reliability and consensus on which treatment is best for whom must come first.

Guidelines for Ensuring Reliability of Data

Perhaps the most common saying in information management is GI-GO, or "Garbage In, Garbage Out." This means that regardless of how many beautiful graphs you print, everything is absolutely worthless if the information in the system is not reliable. Information management systems can make garbage pretty, but they cannot make it useful. Several guidelines are critical to avoid the GI-GO trap.

Get as Close to the Source as Possible

Getting close to the source means that data entry should occur at the *event*. The further from an event data is entered, the more likely it will become corrupted (like my clinic experienced with its biometric accounting). For example, in a well-designed information system, providers and scheduling clerks have networked PCs in their offices or have easy access to them. This puts data collection as close as possible to the *event* of a clinical appointment. Front-desk personnel (or providers) schedule an appointment with a patient, which creates the initial billing information needed by the back office. As providers write their clinical notes, information is captured to verify which procedure was administered and whether the patient attended, canceled, or no-showed for the appointment. This information is immediately available to the back office, which can complete the billing process. No duplicated entry, no paper reports handed from providers to the back office, fewer opportunities for error, and timely completion of clinical notes (because provider reimbursement depends upon it).

Not only may data become corrupted further from the event, it is less likely to be entered at all. This is especially true with collected data, which require additional time and energy to collect. During a busy day, it is hard to find the time to manually enter a patient's outcome data into the information system. The "technophiles" may do it religiously, but the resulting data set will not be representative of the organization. One way to remove obstacles to obtaining collected data is to have a system that automatically scores and interprets the outcome measures. Scanners can move the collection process closer yet by automating the inputting of raw data into the system. Systems that allow patients to complete the measures on-line, however, are the closest to the source. This configuration minimizes the time involved in collecting the information and the chances of error, while maximizing providers' use of outcome measures (Flowers, Booraem, & Schwartz, 1993).

Mandate System Use

Electronic patient records can easily capture a tremendous amount of clinical information for a variety of valuable uses. To ensure that the data are representative of the entire organization, however, use of the system must be *mandatory* for all providers. Allowing employees not to use the system means that data will be primarily captured from the personnel who are most comfortable with technology. In addition, personnel less comfortable with technology will be slower to learn the system, if they do at all.

Mandates are most effective when they are supported by naturally occurring contingencies. For example, an integrated system may originate billing only when a patient's appointment is scheduled in the system, and may also reimburse a provider for the session only when he or she has completed a clinical note in the system. This arrangement pairs the desired behavior (using the system) with a naturally occurring reinforcement (payment). This will help to ensure that the captured data represent the organization as a whole, and will speed learning for all users.

One-Stop Shopping

One-stop shopping means that the reliability of data increases as the number of systems decreases. Many organizations implement information management systems in stages. Problems can occur, however, when different applications are implemented for different organizational functions. The systems may not exchange data with one another; this may necessitate duplicate entry and maintenance of static data (e.g., if different systems are used for accounting and patient records, two sets of patient data must be maintained). Users have to master more interfaces, which adds training time and increases the rate of human error. Many systems can be modified (at additional expense) to exchange data with other systems, but the patchwork system may be more subject to problems than a seamless system.

Practice management and patient record systems originally developed independently of each other, but more software companies are moving toward seamless systems. Some of these products may be purchased in modules that allow organizations to computerize at their own pace. Even with a modular implementation strategy, however, it is extremely important to assess a system across its entire range of modules. This will help you avoid the patchworking problem that can lower reliability and frustrate users.

Training

There are a lot of decisions to be made about hardware and software, but it is extremely important not to lose sight of the user in the process. As mentioned earlier, user training accounts for as much as 19% of the behavioral healthcare information technology market (Work Group, 1995). Inadequate training can increase the number of user problems, which can make users feel much *worse* off than before the system was implemented. Users can lose confidence in their ability and in the system's reliability, making subsequent implementations even more difficult.

When possible, it is preferable to train and implement with a test group before fully implementing the system. Problems that arise at this smaller scale are more easily corrected, and they will allow you to preempt problems later when you implement the system organization-wide. Although technophiles will jump at the chance to be in the test group, you will get more useful information if the test group has people with a range of abilities and job types.

Rosen and Weil (1996a) outline 13 key issues that are excellent guides to structuring the training.

1. *Time.* Sessions should be short and focused, with hands-on practice.
2. *Content.* Sessions should cover a single concept at a time and be practical and immediately useful.
3. *Hands-on.* Hands on practice should be introduced early and often. It builds early success, motivation, and confidence.
4. *Hardware.* Teach on the same equipment that is to be used to foster transfer of learning more effectively.
5. *Help.* Show all sources of help (manual, on-line, help desk) early in the process.
6. *Match.* Match training to pretested levels of skills, knowledge, and psychological style (Eager Adopter, Hesitant Prove-It, or Resister).
7. *Learning style.* Vary the teaching modality. Some people learn best through visual presentation, others through auditory channels, and still others through tactile (touch) lessons.
8. *Predict problems.* Computers have problems and may crash for no apparent reason. Prescribe this to the trainees and discuss the meaning and cure. It is amazing how many people feel that turning off the computer is not an option.
9. *Assumptions.* Do not assume any preknowledge. Ask!
10. *Modeling.* Research has shown that modeling is an excellent training method. Have someone demonstrate first, and then have the trainee perform the task with the trainer close by for assistance.
11. *Assist.* If a problem arises, the trainer should tell the trainee what to do and let the trainee do it him or herself. Pressing keys for someone is no help at all.

12. *Guided exercise.* Guided exercises (with pictures of the computer screen mixed in with the text) work well with novices.
13. *Summary.* Summarize information frequently to solidify learning.[1]

Even after formal training is complete, it is helpful to maintain an open forum for all users to fine-tune their system skills and coordination. In a networked system, the actions of one user impact the actions of other users, and personal proficiency does not guarantee organizational proficiency. For example, on extremely busy days in my clinic we initially allowed providers to put off their charting until the next morning. Thanks to our user group, however, we discovered that this practice prevented our front desk personnel from accomplishing important same-day reporting mandated by the medical center. We adjusted our policy to require that providers at least mark patient attendance on the day of the appointment.

Because user satisfaction can affect system use (Baroudi et al., 1986), the open forum should also make user satisfaction a regular focus. Doll and Torkzadeh (1988) identified five components of user satisfaction that provide a helpful template for this discussion. *Content:* does the system contain the precise information and detail that users need? *Accuracy:* does the system provide accurate information and analyses? *Format:* are system outputs presented in a useful, intelligible manner? *Ease of use:* is the system user-friendly? *Timeliness:* can the system quickly provide users with the information they need, and is the information up to date?

Using

Use Continuous Quality Improvement

Information by itself is inert, and the most important issue is how the *people* in an organization use the information they collect. Though computers are extremely fast, using their information takes time. Though computers can effortlessly analyze information, acting on the analyses requires human effort to adapt to organizational change. Continuous Quality Improvement (CQI) recognizes that the *context* in which information is put to use is more important than the information itself. As mentioned earlier, CQI means regularly identifying opportunities for improvement, obtaining information from all aspects of the organization, and establishing continuous, data-based feedback loops for key organizational processes.

Everyone in our clinic participates in at least one performance improvement group (PIG). Each group consists of at least one representative from each organizational level (provider, intern, administrative, and technician). The PIGs are mission-driven and data-fueled. That is, the PIGs do *not* focus on What can we do with all of this information? Rather, they focus on issues that relate to current opera-

---

[1]From "Easing the Transition from Paper to Computer-Based Systems," by L. D. Rosen and M. M. Weil, 1996, In T. Trabin (ed.), *The Computerization of Behavioral Healthcare: How to Enhance Clinical Practice, Management, and Communications.* Copyright 1996 by CentraLink and Jossey-Bass Inc., Publishers. Reprinted with permission.

tions or our strategic plan (How are we doing now? How can we improve?). The data from our information system aids them in answering these questions and in assessing the results of their improvements. The progress of the PIGs is shared regularly and publicly with the rest of the clinic; this promotes the data-based organizational culture that maximizes the value of our information system.

Begin with the Basics

As with system planning, it is important to begin with the basics. Use information from the system to improve existing processes before adding new ones. For example, in a system that integrates practice management and clinical records, one of the most important functions is patient scheduling, because billing and clinical notes are both based on the *who did what to whom and when* information that is embedded in the scheduled appointment.

Like many providers, we were used to creating and maintaining our own schedules, and initially did not remember or bother to enter scheduled appointments into the system. As this omission could have jeopardized the integrity of the system, we first used our data to print a daily report of patients that had no appointments scheduled in the future. Although at first it was frightening to see the pages of unscheduled patients morning after morning, the report continually became shorter until it was usually just a few lines long. Today, we can be much more certain that our patients are receiving timely care, that our charts are up to date, and that other analyses we conduct will be based on current information (Freeman, 1995)

Success with basic processes frees up resources and increases the confidence of personnel to tackle more advanced processes. For instance, we currently utilize our information system to track and act on such things as individual patient progress, group outcome, attrition, utilization, patient satisfaction, and provider note writing. We have captured the information we need for a number of other activities (e.g., enhanced prevention, automated follow-up) that we will initiate when our personal resources can service them.

Benchmark Your Data

As valuable as controlled outcome studies are, there is a growing awareness that something else is missing. Many, if not most, "real life" patients who walk through our doors are not as neatly defined, and treatments (even structured with clinical pathways) aren't as narrowly focused or controlled; what's more, economic factors affect real-world care. Seligman (1995), although acknowledging the value of traditional *efficacy* studies, emphasizes the need for *effectiveness* studies. Ultimately we need to know what works *in practice:* Do our services meet the needs of (and earn the satisfaction of) our patients within the constraints of our payers, and do we stay in business?

Benchmarking refers to the process of measuring what happens in practice. This information can be used to evaluate new programs and patterns within the organization, or to compare existing programs and patterns with other organizations. In my clinic, we look at group and individual outcome following the completion of a structured protocol. We are careful not to overgeneralize from one sample, but the process has gotten us in the habit of talking about the data. Such discussions can give birth to more structured hypothesis-testing analyses.

Protecting Client Information

APA's *Ethical Principles* require that client information should be accurately recorded and carefully guarded (APA, 1992). This mandate applies regardless of whether the information is stored on paper or on disk, but even greater caution should be taken with electronically stored information. Although paper-based systems are also subject to breach or failure, the cost of one breach or failure is *immeasurably* greater with an electronic patient record. For example, one breach of a paper-based system means someone walks off with as many pages as a person can carry; one breach of an electronic system means someone walks off with as many floppy disks as a person can carry, and each disk can contain *hundreds* of pages of information. The Work Group on Confidentiality, Privacy and Security (1996) has enumerated key issues related to information security of electronic patient records: authorization, authentication, integrity, disaster prevention and recovery, data storage, and audit trails.

Authorization

At the same time, there is an increasing number of people who want or need access to the sort of information an electronic patient record can provide. Providers, payers, utilization reviewers, researchers, policy makers, managers—each of whom could cogently argue that continued quality care depends on having access to "real time" information. An effective information system takes these information needs into account while providing *authorization* that ensures different levels of access to data; for example, the primary provider may have total access to all of a patient's information, a researcher may have access to anonymous demographic and utilization information, a scheduling or billing clerk may have access to procedures and billing codes, and so on. Authorization may also permit different users to perform different activities with the data (e.g., to create, edit, or delete information).

Authentication

Authorization will be different for different individuals, which makes authentication another critical issue in safeguarding information. Authentication means that the system has mechanisms in place to ensure that a user is who she says she is. Given that healthcare decisions will be based on the information, individual users must be identified and held accountable for what they enter, edit, or delete. The simplest form of authentication is having users log on to the system with unique user names and passwords; more advanced systems use fingerprints or retinal scans for even greater accuracy. "Timing out" features also help to ensure authentication by logging the user off if he or she has not used the system for a specified period of time.

Integrity

A significant advantage of electronic records is that they are much easier to create and edit than paper records. This advantage, however, also poses a security threat, as some information should *not* be changed after entry. System integrity addresses this threat by imposing restrictions on the manner in which information is changed. Authentication and authorization help to ensure integrity by allowing only a select few people to modify information. More advanced systems also track the time and date of the modification, and the user who performed it.

Disaster Prevention/Recovery

Many of us have had the unfortunate experience of losing valuable information due to a computer malfunction, and have learned the hard way to continually back up our work. With a clinic-wide information management system, disaster prevention/recovery is even more important. When a computer malfunctions, thousands of pages of vital clinical information can be lost just as quickly as a simple letter, with devastating results to patient care and organizational viability. Information systems should have built-in backup features, or the organization should implement its own policies to routinely back up the information. Backed-up information should be stored separately in case of fire or theft, and procedures should be in place to restore the information in the event of loss.

Data Storage

Authentication, authorization, and integrity guard the way that information is created and accessed *internally* (within the system). Data storage guards against *external* threats. System information is typically stored on a central computer, or "server." Ideally, physical access to this computer should be as carefully guarded as electronic access to its data: locks on the room and even the keyboard are good ideas. That is, even though authorization may restrict what a user can access within the program, the data files themselves may still be read with other, external programs. For this reason, information should be stored in *encrypted* data files that only the management information system can read.

Audit Trails

Larger organizations may find it necessary to ensure that their management information systems provide *audit trails,* which record all system activity and are useful to locate unauthorized activity, tampering, or other breaches. An audit trail will identify the user performing the activity, the machine the activity was performed on, the time and date of the activity, and what the user did (e.g., view, print, copy, edit, or create information).

CONCLUSION

We are all being carried into the next century by a technological revolution that will touch every aspect of our lives. This revolution is forging the tools for us to better realize the scientist–practitioner ideals articulated almost half a century ago: objective measurement of treatment outcome, decision support, immediate access to empirical literature, connectivity with other providers. This revolution also challenges us to learn new skills and adapt to change at a similarly rapid pace: as clinicians, as researchers, as managers. Failing to do so will certainly jeopardize our professional survival.

As daunting as this challenge may seem to some of us, we have the raw materials to face it. After all, daily we challenge our patients to face their fears, to believe in themselves, to be patient and observant, and continually to take small steps toward their goals. Behavioral healthcare will always be about people, not technology. Remembering this core value, while embracing the technological tools that serve it, offers us the potential to enrich our patients and ourselves.

REFERENCES

Agency for Health Care Policy and Research (AHCPR). (1993). *Depression in primary care: Vol. 1. Detection and diagnosis.* Rockville, MD: Author.

American Psychological Association (APA). (1992). *Ethical principles of psychologist and code of conduct.* Washington, DC: Author.

Barlow, D. H., Hayes, S. C., & Nelson, R. O. (1984). *The scientist-practitioner: Research and accountability in clinical and educational settings.* New York: Pergamon.

Barlow, D. H., Hayes, S. C., & Nelson, R. O. (in press).

Baroudi, J. J., Olson, M. H., & Ives, B. (1986). An empirical study of the impact of user involvement on system usage and information satisfaction. *Communications of the ACM, 29,* 232–238.

Beck, A. T., Steer, R. A., & Garbin, M. G. (1988). Psychometric properties of the Beck Depression Inventory: Twenty-five years of evaluation. *Clinical Psychology Review, 8,* 77–100.

Beutler, L. E., & Williams, O. B. (1995). Computer applications for the selection of optimal psychosocial therapeutic interventions. *Behavioral Healthcare Tomorrow, 4,* 66–68.

Brown, G. S., & Kornmayer, K. (1996). Expert systems restructure managed care practice: Implementation and ethics. *Behavioral Healthcare Tomorrow, 5,* 31–34.

Buchanan, B. G., & Shortliffe, E. H. (1984). *Rule-based expert systems: The MYCIN experiments of the Stanford Heuristic Project* (p. 86). Reading, MA: Addison-Wesley.

Campbell, J. R., Givner, N., Seelig, C. B., Patil, K., Wigton, R. S., & Tape, T. G. (1988). Clinic function and computerized ambulatory records: A concurrent study with conventional records. *Proceedings of the Symposium on Computer Applications in Medical Care,* pp. 745–748.

Christensen, A., & Jacobsen, N. S. (1994). Who (or what) can do psychotherapy: The status and challenge of nonprofessional therapies. *Psychological Science, 5,* 8–14.

Condon, B. (1996, September 23). No pain, no gain. *Forbes,* pp. 148–149.

Derogatis, L. R. (1983). *SCL-90: Administration, Scoring, and Procedures Manual for the Revised Version*. Baltimore, MD: Clinical Psychometric Research.

Derogatis, L. R., & Melisaratos, N. (1983). The Brief Symptom Inventory: An introductory report. *Psychological Medicine, 13*, 595–605.

Dewey, J., Brill, P., & Graves, S. A. (1996). Outcomes tracking: Why bother? *InfoConsult News, 1*, 1–4.

Doll, W. J., & Torkzadeh, G. (1988, June). The measurement of end-user computing satisfaction. *MIS Quarterly*, pp. 259–274.

Ferguson, T. (1996). Consumer health informatics: Turning the treatment pyramid upside down. *Behavioral Healthcare Tomorrow, 5*, 35–37.

Fischer, J., & Corcoran, K. (1994). *Measurements for clinical practice* (Vols. 1–2). New York: Free Press.

Flowers, J. V., Booraem, C. D., & Schwartz, B. (1993). Impact of computerized rapid assessment instruments on counselors and client outcome. *Computers in Human Services, 10*, 9–19.

Freeman, R. K. (1995, August). *COMIS: Information technology and clinical outcome for a new model of mental health care delivery*. Paper presented at the meeting of the Practice Directorate at the 1995 annual convention of the American Psychological Association, New York.

Freeman, R. K. (1996, April). *Managing information: Creating a data-based, data-generating clinic*. Paper presented at the meeting of the 1996 conference on Promoting Empirically-Supported Psychological Treatments, San Antonio, TX.

Freeman, R. K., & Kelleher, W. J. (1996, April). *An empirically-based approach to the design and management of an outpatient service*. Paper presented at the meeting of the 1996 conference on Promoting Empirically-Supported Psychological Treatments, San Antonio, TX.

Gingerich, W. J., & Broskowski, A. (1996). Clinical decision support systems. In T. Trabin & M. A. Freeman (Eds.), *The computerization of behavioral healthcare* (pp. 11–38). San Francisco: Jossey-Bass.

Hayes, S. C. (1996). AABT and AAAPP Sponsor National Planning Conference on Practice Guidelines. *Behavior Therapist, 19*, 170.

Health Insurance Portability and Accountability Act of 1996, Pub. L. No. 104-191 (1996).

Jamison, C., & Scogin, F. (1995). The outcome of cognitive bibliotherapy with depressed adults. *J. Cell. Comp. Physiol. 63*, 644–650.

Joint Commission on Accreditation of Healthcare Organizations. (1997). *1997–98 Comprehensive Accreditation Manual for Behavioral Health Care*. Oakbrook Terrace, IL: Author.

Kelleher, W. J., Freeman, R. K., Tims, M. R., & Klepac, R. (1995, August). *Psychology life skills: A new model of mental health care*. Symposium conducted at the meeting of the 1995 annual convention of the American Psychological Association, New York.

Kelleher, W. J., Klepac, R. K., & McGaughey, M. (1987, May). *What patients seek and what professionals offer in Air Force Mental Health Clinics*. Paper presented at the meeting of the USAF Biennial Behavioral Sciences Symposium: Operational Problems in the Behavioral Problems, Sheppard AFB, TX.

Kelleher, W. J., Talcott, G. W., Haddock, C. K., & Freeman, R. K. (1996). Military psychology in the age of managed care: The Wilford Hall model. *Journal of Applied and Preventive Psychology*.

Kiresuk, T. J., & Sherman, R. E. (1968). Goal attainment scaling: A general method for evaluating comprehensive community mental health programs. *Community Mental Health Journal, 4*, 443–452.

Lambert, M. J., Lunnen, K., Umphres, V., Hansen, N. B., & Burlingame, G. (1994). *Administration and Scoring Manual for the Outcome Questionnaire* (OQ-45.1). Salt Lake City, UT: IHC Center for Behavioral Healthcare Efficacy.

Larson, D. L., Attkisson, C. C., Hargreaves, W. A., & Nguyen, T. D. (1979). Assessment of client/patient satisfaction: Development of a general scale. *Evaluation and Program Planning, 2*, 197–207.

Leonard-Barton, D., & Kraus, W. A. (1985). Implementing new technology. *Harvard Business Review, 63*, 100–112.

Maloney, W. A. (1996). How information systems are opening the way for integrated healthcare. *Behavioral Therapist*, pp. 74–76.

Manderscheid, R. W., & Henderson, M. J. (1996). The growth and direction of managed care. In R. W. Manderscheid & M. A. Sonnenschein (Eds.), *Mental health, United States, 1996* (pp. 17–26). Rockville, MD: U.S. Department of Health and Human Services.

McLean, J. D., & Kapkin, I. A. (1983). Negative impact of computerized record keeping in a psychiatric department. *Canadian Journal of Psychiatry, 28,* 114–116.

Meyer, T. J., Miller, M. L., Metzger, R. L., & Borkovec, T. D. (1990). Development and validation of the Penn State Worry Questionnaire. *Behavioral Research and Therapy, 28,* 487–495.

National Committee for Quality Assurance. (1997). *Health plan employer data and information set.* Washington, DC: Author.

Nguyen, T. D., & Olsen, G. (1996). Computerization in county and community mental health centers. *The computerization of behavioral healthcare.* San Francisco: Jossey-Bass.

Ogles, B. M., Lambert, K. S., & Masters, K. S. (1996). *Assessing outcome in clinical practice.* Needham Heights, MA: Allyn & Bacon.

Oss, M. E., & Stair, T. (1996). *Managed behavioral health market share in the United States, 1996–1997.* Gettysburg, PA: Behavioral Health Industry News.

Persons, J. P., & Bostrom, A. (1995). *Clinically significant change in patients treated with cognitive-therapy for depression in a private practice setting.* Paper presented at the 1995 meeting of the Society of Psychotherapy Research, Vancouver, BC.

Peterson, B. D., et al. (1996). An update on human resources in mental health. The growth and direction of managed care. In R. W. Manderscheid & M. A. Sonnenschein (Eds.), *Mental health, United States, 1996* (pp. 168–204). Rockville, MD: U.S. Department of Health and Human Services.

Pigott, H. E., & Broskowski, A. (1995, August). Is outcomes analysis worth the effort? *OPEN MINDS Practice Advisor,* pp. 3–5.

Raimy, V. D. (Ed.). (1950). *Training in clinical psychology (Boulder Conference).* New York: Prentice-Hall.

Redick, R. W., Witkin, M. J., Atay, J. E., & Manderscheid, R. W. (1996). Highlights of organized mental health services in 1992 and major national and state trends. The growth and direction of managed care. In R. W. Manderscheid & M. A. Sonnenschein (Eds.), *Mental health, United States, 1996* (pp. 90–137). Rockville, MD: U.S. Department of Health and Human Services.

Rosen, L. D., & Weil, M. M. (1996a). Adult and teenage consumer users of technology: Potholes on the information superhighway? *Journal of Consumer Affairs, 29,* 55–84.

Rosen, L. D., & Weil, M. M. (1996b). Easing the transition from paper to computer-based systems. In T. Trabin (Ed.), *The computerization of behavioral healthcare* (pp. 87–107). San Francisco: Jossey-Bass.

Rowan, A. B., & Andrasik, F. (1996). Efficacy and cost-effectiveness of minimal therapist contact treatments of chronic headaches: A review. *Behavior Therapy, 2,* 207–234.

Sachs Group. (1995). *Health care 1999: A national bellwether.* Evanston, IL: Sachs Group.

Sanchez-Craig, M., Davila, R., & Cooper, G. (1996). A self-help approach for high-risk drinking: Effect of an initial assessment. *J. Cell. Comp. Physiol. 64,* 694–700.

Seligman, M. E. P. (1995). The effectiveness of psychotherapy: The *Consumer Reports* Study. *American Psychologist, 50,* 965–974.

Sleek, S. (1996). APA's efforts key to securing parity for mental health. *APA Monitor, 27,* 7.

Smith, M. L., & Glass, G. V. (1977). Meta-analysis of psychotherapy outcome studies. *American Psychologist, 32,* 752–760.

Spanier, G. B. (1976). Measuring dyadic adjustment: New scales for assessing the quality of marriage and similar dyads. *Journal of Marriage and the Family, 38,* 15–28.

Task Force on Promotion and Dissemination of Psychological Procedures. (1995). Training in and dissemination of empirically-validated psychological procedures: Reports and recommendations. *Clinical Psychologist, 48,* 3–23.

U.S. Department of Health and Human Services. (1993). *Depression in primary care: Vol. 1. Detection and diagnosis:* Part II (AHCPR Publication No. 93-0550). Rockville, MD: Author.

Ware, J. E. (1992). *SF-36 health survey.* Boston: Medical Outcomes Trust.

Work Group for the Computerization of Behavioral Health and Human Services, Inc. (1995). *The state of computerization among managed behavioral healthcare companies: A national survey.* Rockville, MD: U.S. Department of Health and Human Services.

Work Group on Confidentiality, Privacy, and Security. (1996). *Security features for computer-based patient record systems.* Computer-based Patient Record Institute.

BIOGRAPHY

Richard Kelley Freeman   Dr. Freeman earned his BBA in Finance from Baylor University in 1985, then received his doctorate in clinical psychology from Fuller Theological Seminary in 1993. From 1993 to 1997 he was on the faculty at Wilford Hall Medical Center in San Antonio, where he reengineered outpatient services around clinical technologies and treatment protocols and where he eventually served as Director of Outpatient Mental Health. In 1997, Dr. Freeman became the President/CEO of Psyquel, Inc., a practice management company located in San Antonio.

AUTHOR INDEX

SUBJECT INDEX